The Elementary School

VIRGIL E. HERRICK
University of Wisconsin

JOHN I. GOODLAD
University of Chicago

FRANK J. ESTVAN
University of Wisconsin

PAUL W. EBERMAN
University of Wisconsin

The

Elementary School

Englewood Cliffs, N.J.

PRENTICE-HALL, INC.

LIBRARY OF CONGRESS
CATALOG CARD NO.: 56-9212

First printing . . . . *May, 1956*
Second printing . . . . . . *June, 1956*
Third printing . . . *September, 1956*
Fourth printing . . . . . . *July, 1958*
Fifth printing . . . . *May, 1959*

PRINTED IN THE UNITED STATES OF AMERICA

25957

To the many thoughtful and conscientious teachers and administrators who have shared their educational experiences and hopes with us.

PREFACE

The modern elementary school is a complex social institution created by the people for the purpose of educating their children. Although few people disagree on the importance of education for the children, themselves, and for the society in which they live, many have strong convictions about what is important in that education and about how to accomplish it. Most people agree on the essential responsibility of the modern elementary school. Fewer agree on the breadth and range of practice through which this responsibility should be met.

This two-fold concept is important in understanding the present-day elementary school. A student of the elementary school should be interested in more than present practice or recommended programs. He should try to glimpse the historical past as well as the constructive future. He should see beyond practices, to their foundations in our society and in our understanding and appreciation of children. Especially, he should understand the purposes and philosophical considerations which underlie elementary school programs.

This book has five major purposes: (1) to help the reader appreciate the historical breadth and continuity of elementary school development in America and to perceive pertinent European influences; (2) to present the reader with the concept of the elementary school as a responsible, dynamic agency, educating children in a demanding and complex American society; (3) to reveal the nature and use of the important bases upon which decisions in education are made; (4) to examine and critically analyze present elementary school practices as they now exist in the different kinds of school programs and in the many important curriculum areas; and (5) to consider as honestly and constructively as possible what this analysis means for the future.

From nationwide educational experience and professional work, the authors bring to the readers vivid illustrations of practices in real schools, with real children, teachers, and administrators struggling with actual educational problems. And since the authors are closely connected with undergraduate and graduate programs in elementary education, they are in a position to correlate important educational ideas with classroom practices. Controversial positions and issues in education are not ignored, but neither are they permitted to waste time in burning straw men or in overclaiming a mystic and all-saving golden key to the solution of all educational difficulties. The author group primarily advocates research as a way of understanding and improving our elementary schools. Imaginative constructive thinking on the basis of social and educational values and goals is emphasized. All teachers, parents, and communities must consider the importance and value of the elementary school, and they must dream a bit of what they believe such schools can be in the future.

V.E.H.

CONTENTS

The school: part of the community · The school as a community institution · The school as a social institution · The roles of the school in its community · The community school · The school as community center · The community council · The school program and the community · Camping education · The extended school program · The school and community action · The challenge to educational leadership · The key ideas

Objectives of elementary education · Problems of over-all statements of objectives · Statements of objectives in educational programs having a basic social orientation · Statements of objectives in programs basically oriented to the individual · Developmental tasks as objectives · The functions of objectives · The elementary school and its purposes · The understandings of good citizenship · The abilities of good citizenship · The attitudes of good citizenship · In retrospect

Part Two

CHILDREN AND THE CURRICULUM OF THE ELEMENTARY SCHOOL

The responsibility of teachers and school staffs · What is meant by the words growth, development, learning *· The developmental characteristics of children · Children of two to five · Six to nine year olds · The nine to twelve year olds · Nature of development over the elementary school years · We can expect variation or differentiation in the ways children grow up · We can expect continuity in the development of children · We can expect interrelationships and consistency in development · We can expect that development in itself will create new needs · The nature of the conditions for learning · General conception of learning · The center of attention · Continuity of learning · Qualities of good organizing centers · Illustrative organizing centers · Multiple and interrelated causes · Centers of attention serve as activators of behavior · Common problems of learning and development · What about this problem of repetitions? · Can you teach all of the important facts? · Pacing · Mastery · How is adequacy determined? · Motivation · Competition as a means of motivation · Transfer of training · Multiple learnings · The role of frustration in learning · Problem solving · Role of the child · Role of the teacher · Summary*

Part Three

CURRICULUM AREAS IN THE ELEMENTARY SCHOOL

Part Four

DIRECTING, ORGANIZING, AND EVALUATING THE
TOTAL SCHOOL PROGRAM

PART ONE

OUR
AMERICAN
HERITAGE
AND THE
ELEMENTARY
SCHOOL

THE
ELEMENTARY
SCHOOL
TODAY

1

ELEMENTARY SCHOOLS ARE SOCIAL INSTITUTIONS BE-
cause they are created by men to meet an important social need—the education of children. Men,
communities, and states differ, however, in the
way in which they define "good education" and
in their willingness and ability to support programs of education. It is only natural, therefore,
that we can expect to find both uniformity and
variation in the practices of elementary schools.
To expect anything different would be to fail to
recognize the role that the elementary school has
played in American life and the responsibility
that the people of individual communities have
had for defining the kind of educational program they want for their children.

Elementary School Children

The number of children attending elementary schools forms the largest group of individuals attending schools of any kind. Caswell[1] in 1942 pointed out that out of each 100 students in educational institutions, roughly 75 are in elementary school, 24 are in high school, and 1 is in college. In 1952, 74 were in elementary schools, only 19 were in high schools, and 7 were in college. Proportionately, the losses in secondary school populations, due to the decreased birth rate of the depression years, have been more than matched by the gains made at the college level following World War II.

Enrollment of children in elementary schools of all kinds reached its highest point, 21.3 million, in 1929-1930, then declined to 17.7 million in 1944-1945, and moved upward to a new high of 24.5 million in 1951-1952. The United States Office of Education predicts that the impact of the record number of births on the elementary school will reach its peak in 1957, with an all-time high of 25.5 million children in public elementary schools. The enrollment in public secondary schools will climb to a peak of 7.2 million in 1960. The total enrollment in public elementary and secondary schools will reach a high level of 32,151,000 individuals in 1958, an increase of 28 per cent over the year 1950.

The range of ages and distribution of children attending the elementary school can be seen as follows:[2]

Grade	Age (Fall)	Enrollment	Per cent of change 1940-1950
Kindergarten	4-5	1,034,000	73.8
First grade	6	3,170,000	5.0
Second grade	7	2,645,000	13.4
Third grade	8	2,396,000	2.7
Fourth grade	9	2,254,000	2.9
Fifth grade	10	2,651,000	4.3
Sixth grade	11	2,056,000	5.5
Seventh grade	12	1,947,000	7.6
Eighth grade	13	1,752,000	3.0

During the period between 1940-1950, as indicated above, the elementary school population gained 3 per cent while the high school population lost 13.6 per cent. The low birth-rate years were 1932-1934, and children born in these years reached high school in 1950.

[1] Hollis L. Caswell, *Education in the Elementary School* (New York: American Book Company, 1942), p. 28.

[2] Federal Security Agency, *Statistics of State School Systems, 1949-1950; Biennial Survey of Education in the United States* (Washington, D.C.: Office of Education, 1952), Table III, p. 15.

In the above list of figures, the upsurge of numbers of children had reached the third grade. The years ahead will see this wave of school children move progressively through high school into college.

Examination of these data will reveal that one of the significant aspects of education in the past decade has been the dual extension of school populations downward into kindergarten and nursery school years, and the extension upward into the college period.

The Census Bureau[3] reported that in October 1950 there were 2,816,000 children of age five in the total population. Of these, 872,-000 were enrolled in kindergartens. There were also 59,000 children of age six enrolled in kindergartens. In addition there were 585,000 children of age five enrolled in the elementary grades. Thus 51.74 per cent of all five-year-old children in the country were enrolled in public or private kindergartens or elementary grades. In contrast, 70 per cent of all six-year-olds, and 98 per cent of all children between seven and thirteen, were in school. The kindergarten, while accepted in theory as a necessary part of educational programs for young children, is still far from being accepted in general practice. And further, there is a great overlapping of ages at all points. Some elementary programs may have children as young as four (rural); or kindergartens may have children as young as four or as old as six and seven. The greatest amount of controversy over institutional responsibility centers on age four. Both nursery school and the kindergarten claim this age as their special responsibility.

Plan of Organization of the Elementary School

No single statement can be made regarding the number of grades or years included in the elementary school. The pattern of grades or ages included varies in the different regions, states, and communities of the United States. Although the traditional pattern was eight grades, nine-grade elementary schools can be found in New England, seven grades in the southern states, and six grades in most cities. Most rural schools still follow the traditional pattern of eight grades.

The eight-grade plan of organization came into general practice during the last half of the nineteenth century. Since 1890 and the report of the famous Committee of Ten, the six-grade elementary school has been the recommended plan. In the past fifty years, the six-grade elementary school has gradually gained in popularity. In a recent

3 U. S. Department of Commerce, Bureau of the Census, *School Enrollment of the Civilian Population: October, 1950. Current Population Reports, Series P-20, No. 34* (Washington, D.C.: The Bureau, July 26, 1951), p. 12.

N.E.A. survey (1948), 68 per cent of the 1372 city school systems reporting had elementary schools organized on the basis of six grades. Twenty-three per cent had eight-grade elementary schools, and 9 per cent had other plans. These percentages are probably representative for most cities.

Little research data, and few convincing theoretical arguments, can be cited to show that the elementary school should be five, six, or seven years in length. A greater contribution to the common education of children and youth would perhaps be made if educators spent less time trying to chop the elementary school program into small segments, and more time concentrating on a continuous, organized developmental program over the thirteen years of the elementary and secondary school.

The six-year elementary school, with a kindergarten as an essential part of the program, is an effective organizational context within which to build adequate educational programs for children. Variations within this plan are usually made on the basis of the community's ability to support multiple units, enriching facilities, special teachers and resources, and programs of supervision and administration.

Elementary Schools in Rural Communities

Caswell[4] has effectively pointed out that the most important differentiating factor among elementary schools is whether they serve urban or rural areas. In rural areas, most teachers teach more than one grade, distances make supervision difficult, qualified teachers tend to migrate from rural to urban communities, and school buildings, supplies, and instructional resources are usually worn out, meager, or lacking altogether.

On the other hand, a rural teacher dealing with a small group of children throughout a school day has a demanding but unusual opportunity for effective teaching. The rural teacher is able to cut across grade lines and organize instructional activities around problems and persistent concerns of children, develop a cooperative and stimulating social and intellectual environment, use community resources, and make the total school program an integrated educational enterprise. Rural teachers are more likely to take advantage of these opportunities, however, if their training and supervisory resources provide them with the needed help and encouragement. The board members

4 Hollis L. Caswell and A. Wellesley Foshay, *Education in the Elementary School,* 2nd ed. (New York: American Book Company, 1950), pp. 36-41.

of the individual school districts are usually not able to provide this support and leadership, but look to the teacher and county superintendent for help.

In the past forty years, consolidation has considerably reduced the number of one-teacher schools. The decrease has been from approximately 200,000 in 1916, to 133,000 in 1936, to 60,000 in 1949-1950. The rate of decrease has been accelerating, and it is likely that the one-room rural school will soon become a rarity on the educational scene.

In 1949-1950 the average enrollment for one-teacher schools was 17.3; for two-teacher schools 50.2; and 88.7 for three-teacher schools.

In a survey[5] of 50,000 basic administration units out of a total of some 83,000 for the country as a whole, 10,000 (20 per cent) reported no teaching positions (children transported to other districts); 20,000 (40 per cent) reported one teacher; and about 10,000 (20 per cent) reported at least two teachers. Apparently, therefore, some 80 per cent of the basic administrative units of the nation have fewer than 10 teachers. The larger proportion of the children, however, are educated in the cities and consolidated areas which support the remaining 20 per cent of the nation's basic administrative units.

But the problems of educating children must be attacked on a wider basis than drawing a distinction between urban and rural communities. Cities could not live without the boys and girls of rural communities to replenish or swell their population; and the problems of living on the soil demand people whose education has been as broadly conceived and as adequately supported as that of city children.

Both rural and urban schools need adequate facilities and resources, well-trained teachers, effective leadership, and more comprehensive planning than just a one-room school. Our nation cannot permit wide discrepancies in educational opportunity to exist among states and among communities merely because of urban and rural distinctions and related factors.

Public Elementary and Secondary Education Is Big Business

About 51 per cent or more of the local tax paid by individuals of a community goes to support the public schools of that community. In 1949-1950, public school property was worth approximately $11.4 billion; and the school expenditure for that year exceeded $5.8 bil-

[5] *Biennial Survey of Education, 1948-1950,* pp. 7-8.

lion. There is a tendency for the percentage of financial support from the local community to decrease and the percentage of support received from county and state sources (39.8 per cent at present) to increase. Federal support of public education, while small at present, will probably increase in the future. The increase in county, state, and federal support of educational programs at the local level has stemmed from efforts to equalize educational opportunity and to improve educational standards.

The average expenditure per pupil (both elementary and secondary) in average daily attendance in 1949-1950 was $209, an increase of $30 per pupil over 1947-1948. Differences among communities and states are great, the range being from approximately $80 to $295, as contrasted with a range of approximately $32 to $138 in 1929-1930.

A survey of instructional costs per pupil in city school systems by the Federal Security Agency in 1950-1951 showed that the average cost per pupil in elementary schools ($160) was much lower than the cost per pupil in secondary schools ($242). The costs per pupil in elementary schools usually run from $80 to $100 lower than similar costs for secondary school pupils. Costs for educating individual children in rural communities, usually run higher than similar costs in urban communities, because of the small number of children per teacher and per school unit.

These data indicate that the cost of public education per pupil is increasing, that the unit costs for elementary school children are less than those for secondary, and that unit costs for children in rural communities usually run higher than those in city schools.

Along with the increasing consolidation of school districts comes the increasing need to transport children. Twenty years ago, practically all physically able children walked or provided their own transportation to school; now, 6.9 million pupils, or 27.7 per cent of all pupils enrolled, are transported at public expense. This additional service costs $31 per pupil transported for the nation as a whole. We can expect that more, rather than fewer, pupils will be transported in the future, because of the continuing trend toward consolidation and toward more flexible use of school facilities over the school district as a whole.

Larger sums for capital outlay, and for teacher salaries, are the major items which account for increased public total costs in recent years. This increase in costs partially accounts for the increased concern of the community about public education, and about whether there is a corresponding increase in the quality of the educational program. There is ample evidence that a new school building or an increased salary, per se, does not necessarily insure an improved educational program. Corresponding attention must be paid to teacher education and improvement, and to planning and developing the educational program and its instructional resources. Frequently, in the crisis of meeting first-things-first, such educational planning and development are neglected.

The Elementary School Teacher

Out of approximately one million public elementary and secondary school teachers, 600,000, or two-thirds, are elementary school teachers, and of these almost two out of three are women. For the past fifty years, the number of women far exceeded the number of men in elementary schools. This predominance of women teachers in the elementary schools still holds true, although an increasing number of men are teaching at the upper levels, providing special services, and becoming principals. There is real need for better balance of the sexes in the staffs of elementary schools. Young children and pre-adolescent youths need to work on their many developmental tasks in an educational environment which provides mature, emotionally well-balanced men *and* women teachers. At present, the typical elementary school teacher is a woman 42 years of age, usually married, and, if she teaches in a rural community, has less than four years training beyond high school.

During the past ten years very rapid progress has been made toward a single salary scale for elementary and secondary teachers, and also, in city school systems, for men and women. Increasingly, too, this has been true for Negro and white teachers in communities where they teach in the same school system.

The minimum beginning salary for inexperienced degree teachers has moved up toward $3200; the average salary for experienced teachers in the United States ranges between $3800 to $4200. In many cities, teachers at the top of their salary scales may earn from $5500 to $7500 for the school year. Many regions tend to pay less than these figures, rural communities characteristically so; and many metropolitan areas pay more.

The average elementary school teacher has had fifteen years of teaching experience, and although she did not go to summer school last summer, is definitely planning to go next summer or the summer after. She is trying either to meet the requirements for a degree at a nearby Teachers' College or University or to win additional increments on the salary scale. The car she now owns is either a Chevrolet or a Ford, and is 3½ years old. The car is a heavy financial burden, although for rural teachers it is a necessity.

Most teachers look forward to teaching in urban centers, to becoming special teachers, teachers in laboratory schools, supervisors, or principals. With some, the hope is to teach in the higher grades or high school; although this hope is less prevalent now, when elementary school teachers earn as much as high school teachers for equal training. One of the real problems of morale and motivation of the experienced teacher is to find important personal and professional goals which will give direction and significance to his work and life.

Public Elementary Education for Negroes

The decision of the U. S. Supreme Court in 1954 legally ended the practice of having separate schools for white and Negro pupils, which was the case in 17 states, and in the District of Columbia, prior to the decision. Fifteen to twenty years ago there were great differences in salaries of teachers, in instructional equipment, in age of school buildings, in the training of teachers, in breadth of programs, and in the average length of the school term between the educational programs for white and Negro children. By 1954, however, many states had made great strides in providing equal programs for Negro children. While the problem of segregated educational opportunities for Negro children will not be solved merely by the Supreme Court decision, great gains will be made in the next few years in providing more adequate programs for both Negro and white children in areas where they have been segregated. The Negro teacher, frequently excellently trained and qualified, will bear the major brunt of this change from segregated to non-segregated schools.

MAJOR GENERALIZATIONS ABOUT THE ELEMENTARY SCHOOL

It is wise to keep the following ideas in mind in any attempt to differentiate and organize one's thinking and understanding about the elementary school.

The Elementary School Has a Past, a Present, and a Future

The American elementary school has been in existence over two hundred years, and needs to be understood in terms of its history, as well as in relation to today's educational needs. A perspective of two hundred years makes one less inclined to think in terms of sharp black and white distinctions between the "old and good" and the "new and progressive" aspects of our present classroom activities.

A knowledge of the way our present schools for young children have developed will make us realize that many of the good schools of the early 1800's are very much like our good schools today in their general outline and breadth of purpose. Similarly, our poor schools today are very much like the poor schools of a hundred years ago. The future of elementary education will depend upon the degree to which we can continue to develop and extend the concepts and practices that history has again and again shown to be valuable.

The Elementary School Reflects the Nature of the Community It Serves

In our Constitution, education was reserved as a function of the state. The state passes on to the local community the state's duty to provide education. In this sense, the community is acting as an agent of the state and must be guided by its directives. At the same time, the school community has great freedom within the limits of these directives in determining the nature of its own program and in providing the kind of school building, equipment, teacher, materials, school day, and school year it wants.

The people living in a rural district which supports a one-, two-, or three-room rural school, however, represent a different kind of social community from the one which supports a state graded school, a consolidated school, or the schools of a county unit. Similarly, a village supporting its elementary school with six or eight grades is a different kind of educational and social community from a city of a million people supporting hundreds of different kinds of schools. Differences in use of common trading and service agencies, in ways of earning a living, in religion, and in cultural and ethnic backgrounds are all factors which determine the nature of a community's ability to formulate common educational goals, and its capacity to act as a coordinated social and legal unit in developing educational programs for children. Because our elementary schools are developed and supported in the main by such varying kinds of communities, we should expect their likenesses and differences to be reflected in the nature of the educational programs and school facilities they develop. The following chapters will document the different ways in which this is true.

The Elementary School Has Always Been Close to People

From the beginning of our educational history, the elementary school in its various forms has always been responsive to what the people want it to be. The close, significant relationship the elementary school has to the community it serves gives rise to the following expectations:

1. Parents and adults of a given community are going to be concerned about what happens to their children in school. We can expect, too, that at times honest differences in conception of what constitutes "good education" will create conflict between people and groups of individuals. Schools can expect to assume the responsibility for helping people resolve their differences and agree on what the common educational program for all of the children of the community should be.

2. We can expect that elementary school parents will visit schools more often than secondary school parents. Parent-Teacher Associations organized around elementary schools are more likely to be active and concerned than those organized around the high school. One of the reasons for this is that a young child's starting in elementary school is a significant event, frequently more threatening to his parents' egos and hopes than a child's going on to the different grades or sections of the common school.

3. Parents can be expected to urge that schools be built near their homes, and to build their homes near schools.

4. The adults of the community who do not have children, but who own property which accounts for a substantial portion of the taxes of the community, can be expected to have different feelings about school taxes from those of the parents who are sending children to school.

The Elementary School Deals with All of the Children

Few people today realize that the "free public elementary school" as we now know it had its beginnings in the first half of the nineteenth century. Prior to that time, "free schools" were for the poor and were supported by private voluntary donations, subscriptions, and endowments, rather than by government funds. At the beginning of the nineteenth century, people came to realize that if elementary education were to be genuinely free for everyone, and not be just for the poor and the upper classes, it would have to become a common school—a school for all—under government control, rather than be run under private, charitable, or religious control.

This concept of one public school offering "free" elementary education to all of the children of a given community is an important concept in our educational history, and is not one which came easily or was accepted with the same grace by all groups of people. In the minds of our forefathers, the elementary school served as a melting pot in the community for the many diverse groups within it.

To talk about the obligation of the elementary school to all children of a community is much easier than to put the obligation into practice. Teachers and administrators who think at all seriously about the responsibilities of a free common elementary school consider it natural and appropriate that:

1. Children coming from different portions of the same community will differ in the kinds of homes in which they live, the source of their family's income, the level of regard and respect in which their families are held, and the ways in which their families think about religion, politics, education, and the "good and bad" people of the world. These children, will also have different kinds of backgrounds, wear different quality clothes, and experience different opportunities to travel, and to own books, magazines, workshops, and sports equipment. These social and material differences will be accompanied by differences in height, weight, shape, appearance, in boyness and girlness, and in ability to please the teacher and do school work.

2. The educational program of the elementary school has to attempt to meet the needs of these children. The elementary school in this sense cannot be selective about children, nor build its program on the basis of special interest. A tough community mindedness will characterize its curriculum development, and a deep sense of educational obligation to all children will permeate its practices.

This concept of the common responsibility of a free public school to all of the children of a community is one of the fundamental principles upon which public education in America is built.

The Elementary School Cooperates with Other Institutions in the Community to Educate Children

In the minds of many, the elementary school is held responsible for making sure that the child is properly respectful to his elders, obeys his parents, worships his God, has his teeth fixed, is immunized against diphtheria and smallpox, and has better language skills and knows more about the world than his parents and other adults of his neighborhood. Yet the elementary school should not be considered the only educational institution of the community; it joins with other agencies of the community in providing our children with a well-rounded and adequate educational experience.

In America the responsibilities that parents have for the well-being and proper social and educational development of their children is well known and documented on both legal and moral grounds. The place of the church in the religious and moral education of the child has never been questioned in America, and the student of the history of education knows the important role that religion and religious institutions have played in the initial development of educational programs for young children in America. The importance of the home, the school, and the church in American life, and in the proper education of young children, has been a dominant theme in our educational thinking for the past 150 years.

It is natural, when more than one agency is involved in the education of the children of a community, that confusion will exist about the nature and extent of their mutual responsibilities for common educational functions. It is important that the present day elementary school identify its place and function in the cooperative enterprise of providing the children of a given community with an adequately conceived education.

The Elementary School Serves with the High School as the Common School for the Youth of a Community

In 1870-1871, 61.5 per cent of the total number of children aged 5-17 were enrolled in full time public elementary and secondary schools. The year 1939-1940 represents the highest point in the per cent of the children and youth of this age being in school—85.3 per cent. Since this time, there has been a decline to 81.6 per cent in 1949-1950.[6] It should be remembered, however, that these figures represent the proportion of children of this age going to elementary and secondary schools for the nation as a whole, and that these figures are restricted to public schools only. When all types of schools are considered, most communities can say that close to 100 per cent of all of the children of ages 5-17 are in schools of some kind, or are so handicapped that there are adequate reasons for their not being in school. Naturally these figures vary from agricultural communities employing itinerant laborers to residential communities in metropolitan areas.

The important fact made apparent in the above statistics is that *most, if not all,* of the children of a given community go on to high school after leaving elementary school. The common school for the children of a community has therefore changed from an elementary school to one which includes the secondary school, also.

[6] *Biennial Survey of Education 1948-1950*, p. 6.

The integration of the high school with the elementary school as the common school of a community for its children presents a number of problems. The mere fact that the same children go on to high school in a given community does not necessarily mean that the two programs are a part of one continuous program of general education. Historically, the elementary school has always served the needs of all the people; but the secondary school grew out of schools whose main purpose was to prepare a selected group of youths for college. These two quite different educational purposes and historical backgrounds have led to differing conceptions of educational responsibility on the part of the high school and elementary school. These differences of conception still exist in most communities and their reconciliation represents a major problem of educational planning and coordination.

Many of the Elementary Schools Are Not Public Schools

In 1951-1952, 3.7 million, or 12 per cent, of all the 30.5 million children and youths in elementary and secondary schools of all kinds were in private and parochial schools. Ten per cent of all children in elementary and secondary schools were in Catholic parochial schools, roughly 90 per cent of all non-public school children. In some communities there are more children in parochial schools staffed and controlled by religious groups, than there are in the public school staffed and controlled by the community and state. The same community may thus have two independent school systems serving the youth of that community, one, supported by the tax funds of the whole community, which educates less than half of the children, and the other, supported by the parents of a religious organization, which educates more than half of the children.

The old idea of the public elementary school being the common school for all of the children of a community, regardless of religion, race, or wealth, is becoming no longer true. Another old principle is gaining support: that while the parent does not have the right to determine whether or not his children are to be educated, he does have the right to choose the kind of school he wants, providing he is willing to pay extra for this privilege, and providing also that the school meets state requirements. This privilege of being able to choose a school makes some parents pay double, as they support both the public and the private or parochial educational programs of a community; and some feel that this is an unnecessary burden. Other parents feel that the presence of an independent elementary school system serving only a special group divides and disrupts the cohesive and coordinating influences of a community and of our democratic society.

Whatever position the reader takes on this important and critical issue, his understanding of the function of the public elementary school in a given community will be improved if he recognizes the growing importance of private and parochial elementary and secondary schools, and the effect this factor has on the moral and financial support given by his community to programs of public elementary and secondary school education.

The Elementary School Is Characterized by Both Uniformity and Variation

If a person were to visit elementary schools in Fond du Lac, Wisconsin; Harlingen, Texas; Bellingham, Washington; Jacksonville, Florida; or Skowhegan, Maine, his impression of the schools and of their educational programs would be a composite of many great similarities and differences. A closer look at the elementary schools of any one of these cities, however, would reveal almost as great a degree of likenesses and differences in the different schools of that city as in the schools of different communities. And further, in the same school differences can be observed when the kindergarten is compared with the upper grades, and when practices in homemaking and physical education are compared with those in arithmetic and spelling.

No simple rule, no general stereotype, and no broad set of generalizations can adequately explain the American elementary schools. Schools are complex social institutions, just as the Johns, Marys, and Nancys who attend them are complex social beings. Attempts to understand the elementary school must be based on the important ideas which underlie its development, upon the breadth and variation of its practices, on its common, persisting organizational problems, and on the realities of children, teachers, and parents, who by their hopes and efforts make these educational programs possible and significant.

BIBLIOGRAPHY

Caswell, Hollis L. and A. Wellesley Foshay, *Education in the Elementary School,* 2nd ed. New York: American Book Company, 1950.

Cook, Lloyd A. and Elaine F. Cook, *A Sociological Approach to Education.* New York: McGraw-Hill Book Company, Inc., 1950.

Federal Security Agency, *Statistics of State School Systems, 1949-50: Biennial Survey of Education in the United States.* Washington, D.C.: Office of Education, 1952.

Goodykoontz, Bess, Mary D. Davis, and Hazel F. Gabbard, "Recent History and Present Status of Education for Young Children," *Early Childhood Education*. Forty-sixth Yearbook, Part II, Chapter 4, National Society for Study of Education. Chicago: University of Chicago Press, 1947.

Kearney, Nolan C., *Elementary School Objectives: A Report prepared for the Mid-Century Committee on Outcomes in Elementary Education*. New York: Russell Sage Foundation, 1953.

Midcentury White House Conference on Children and Youth. *Children and Youth at the Midcentury. A Chart Book*. Raleigh, North Carolina: Health Publications Institute, 1951.

Olsen, Edward G., *School and Community Programs: A Casebook of Successful Practice from Kindergarten through College and Adult Education*. Englewood Cliffs, N.J.: Prentice-Hall, Inc., 1949.

Otto, Henry J., *Elementary School Organization and Administration*. New York: D. Appleton-Century Co., 1944.

Shane, Harold G., ed., *The American Elementary School*. New York: Harper & Brothers, 1953.

Willing, Matthew, John Guy Fowlkes, Edward A. Krug, Russell T. Gregg, Clifford S. Liddle, *Schools and Our Democratic Society*. New York: Harper & Brothers, 1951.

EVOLUTION
OF THE
ELEMENTARY
SCHOOL

2

THE EVOLUTION OF THE ELEMENTARY SCHOOL, ONE
important strand in the development of public
education, is in a very real sense the history of the
American people. This chapter will describe various elementary schools of the past, and some of
the factors responsible for their development.
Against this historical background, the changes
which have taken place in certain aspects of elementary education will be traced.

ELEMENTARY SCHOOLS OF THE PAST

One way to demonstrate the marked change
that has come about in elementary schools is to
take a backward glance at intervals of one hun-

dred years. Rather than describe the "norm" for each period, attention will be focused on what was a "modern" elementary school for that time.

One Century Ago

To determine what the "modern" elementary school was like, a citizen of Boston would have visited the new Quincy Grammar School, which had been opened in 1848.[1] This building was four stories high. Most school buildings of this period were only two stories high, the writing school being on the first floor and the reading school on the second. Each school was a separate institution, and children attended them alternately in the morning and afternoon. A three-story building indicated that a primary school, also a separate institution, was housed below the writing and reading schools.

The new Quincy Grammar School, however, was not made up of separate schools. Each of the first three floors was divided into four smaller rooms which seated 55 pupils in charge of one teacher. Every pupil had his own desk and chair; a cloakroom was attached to each classroom; there was even a central office for the principal. Teachers no longer had all the classes represented in their respective rooms, for pupils were sorted out into "grades" of like attainments. In order to maintain this similarity, standards had been set up for each grade, and pupils either "passed" or "failed" at the end of the year.

The fourth floor of the Quincy Grammar School was not partitioned off, but was used as a large assembly hall, accommodating the entire student body on long benches. The assembly room resembled the reading and writing schools, which had one large room or hall seating 180 to 200 pupils at long benches; usually three teachers supervised recitations simultaneously. The similarity went no further, however, because Quincy was the first *unified,* as well as *graded,* grammar school, and its principal was in charge of the entire building or school.

No change had been made in the subjects being taught at the new school. Reading, spelling, writing, arithmetic, music, geography, grammar, composition, United States history, declamation, and general history were included as before. The children at Quincy, it was contended, were getting more drill, and learning more subject mat-

[1] Ellwood P. Cubberley, *Public Education in the United States,* rev. ed. (Boston: Houghton Mifflin Company, 1934), pp. 311-12.

ter than before, because everything was being run "systematically."
Witness the daily schedule:

        9:00-9:05   Physical inspection of hands, hair, etc.
        9:05-9:20   Service Period (Patriotism and Citizenship)
        9:20-9:35   Spelling
        9:35-9:45   Penmanship
        9:45-10:00 Oral or Written Composition
       10:00-10:10 Recess . . .[2]

And so the day was scheduled with time allotted for every subject,
and bells to insure that everything was properly timed.

Carried away by their enthusiasm, certain public-spirited citizens
of Boston prophesied that this new departure in school organization
and architecture would set the pattern for the next fifty years. Little
did they realize that many of these innovations would be all too
familiar to school patrons one hundred years later.

Two Centuries Ago

The "district" school came into existence when the Indian menace
had subsided, and towns began to spread out. As distances to the
central town school increased to two miles or more, with little corresponding improvement in transportation, residents of outlying
sections began to follow the example set at the town meeting of Mid-
dleton in 1754, when the West End submitted the following petition:

We, the subscribers, living very remote from the town center where is located
the Latin-grammar school, do humbly petition that the town would vote us off
as a district and grant that the money which we pay towards maintaining a school
in this town may be laid out for schooling in the said district as near the center
as may be convenient.[3]

Prior to this resolution, a number of plans had been tried elsewhere. In 1725, Harwich had tried moving the school from district to
district, from west to east. School was kept from four months to over
eight in each section. To complete the circuit of six "removes" took
approximately three and one-half years.[4] Andover, in 1729, engaged

[2] Harold Rugg, *Foundations for American Education* (Yonkers-on-Hudson: World
Book Company, 1947), p. 520.
[3] Taken after a petition quoted in Benjamin Read, *History of Swanzey, New Hampshire* (Salem, Massachusetts: A. Smithson and Company, 1892), pp. 62-64.
[4] Warren Burton, *The District School As It Was* (Boston: Lee and Shepard, 1897),
pp. 112-14.

the services of Philomen Robbins, who covered the entire town in one year.

He began his school in the south end of the town and continued there three months and then went behind the pond on the first day of December and continued there until the last of January and then was sent and continued in the middle of the town into the last of February next and then was sent behind the pond in the third day of March, and continued there fourteen nights and then the 16th of March was returned to the middle of the town and continued there nine weeks.[5]

The shortness of the school term in these plans was held undesirable by the New England townspeople. Although the majority of inhabitants lived in the original community and preferred a stationary grammar school in the center of town, they could not overlook the needs of the growing minority of inhabitants living on the outskirts of town. The plan of designating "squadrons" or "precincts" for school purposes, named according to the four points of the compass, became the accepted means of making public education available to all the people of the town.

Control and support of these school districts was hotly argued. In some towns, the school term was proportionate to the amount of tax collected in the district. In others, the number of families and children to be served determined how long school would be kept. In a few cases, tax moneys were divided equally among the respective districts. As might be expected, the town selectmen maintained their control over the district teachers and schoolhouses. In time, however, opposition arose to such centralized administration, and it became customary to vote that "each squadron shall have the sole power of managing their own schoolhouse and lands, by leasing out the same, and employing schoolmasters as it shall be most agreeable to them."[6]

What was this district school like? It was a one-teacher school, generally maintained in a rude building located in the center of the district. A handful to more than a hundred pupils attended; their ages ran from beginners learning their A-B-C's to grown boys and girls brushing up for a short while during the winter season. Whatever books were available at home, or whatever books parents would consent to purchase, became the course of study. Learning was largely

[5] Sarah L. Bailey, *Historical Sketches of Andover* (Boston: Houghton Mifflin Company, 1880), p. 318.

[6] Edward Eggleston, *The Transit of Civilization* (New York: D. Appleton and Company, 1901), p. 89.

the process of memorizing what was in these books "by heart." It was a lone quest, assisted by only fleeting periods of personal attention from the teacher. The nature of the instruction and the physical conditions of the school invited disorder. The supreme test of a teacher's competence lay in his ability to maintain discipline. His main reliance was upon the rod.[7] This was the little red schoolhouse that overran most of northern and western United States, and provided an education "close to the people."

Three Centuries Ago

Today had Joseph to Dame Willoughby's school, his cousin Ellen accompanying him. Carried his hornbook.[8]

This diary entry was a sign of the times. In spite of their belief in personal salvation through an understanding of the Bible, many parents were too pressed with the immediate concerns of getting on in a new world to teach their children how to read. Few could afford to hire a private tutor. Without some rudimentary knowledge of the letters and reading, however, children would be denied entrance to the town-supported Latin grammar school. To meet this need, it became quite common after 1651 for some woman in the neighborhood to take over the instruction of several other children, as she taught her own children at home. Usually she was in need of extra money, and having been found by the Reverend to be "a person of sober life and conversation and . . . well-qualified to keep school and to teach reading and sewing,"[9] parents were willing to pay her threepence a week for this good work. While girls were not permitted to enter the town grammar school, they did attend the Dame School. For most of them, this was the only "formal" education they received. Some of the children were as young as three; the older girls might be ten years of age. Boys destined for the town grammar school usually left when they were seven or eight.

The kitchen, living room, attic, or barn became the schoolroom. As best she could, the Dame taught children how to read and spell, and something about the catechism. Girls were also introduced to the arts of knitting and sewing, and to household duties. Good manners and proper behavior were stressed for all. In view of the scarcity

7 Edward H. Reisner, *The Evolution of the Common School* (New York: The Macmillan Company, 1930), pp. 311-12.

8 Taken after Judge Samuel Sewell, *Diary and Memories* (Boston: Houghton Mifflin Company, 1893), p. 69.

9 William H. Small, *Early New England Schools* (Boston: Ginn and Company, 1914), pp. 178-79.

of paper and the necessity for constantly sharpening quill pens, writing was usually not taught. Exercises in counting were given occasionally, but never arithmetic, largely because of the Dame's own lack of knowledge.

More a governess than a teacher, the Dame had a watchful eye for her charges, and kept them busy in the manner she saw fit. The very young spent most of their time observing others recite, or getting into mischief and being punished. Older children might receive as much as twenty minutes of instruction each half day, since teaching was strictly on an individual basis. As a consequence, hours were wasted in simply sitting still, or playing and whispering. Little wonder that the older girls, especially, preferred doing the household chores.

Instruction in the letters and reading invariably began with the hornbook. The English alphabet and Lord's Prayer, printed by hand on parchment or paper, was glued to a thin piece of wood having a handle. Covered with a thin sheet of transparent horn for protection, it made a durable "book." Children who stayed on, most of whom were girls, then went to the catechism, next the Psalter, and finally the Bible. In most cases, however, only the barest rudiments of reading were learned.

The Dame School was destined to become the primary school of colonial New England. Communities began to assist in the maintenance of these schools by guaranteeing the Dame a certain income, or by helping parents defray the cost of the school. By the eighteenth century this semi-public institution was as common in New England as the town church and the cemetery.

HOW OUR PRESENT-DAY ELEMENTARY SCHOOLS BECAME WHAT THEY ARE

These brief glimpses of "modern" elementary schools of days gone by suggest the remarkable changes that have taken place in elementary education during the comparatively brief period of three centuries. These changes were inextricably bound up with the changing social structure of our country, as well as with movements in education as a whole.

The Colonial Period

Many motives prompted the early settlers to sever their ties with the Old World. Some came to America to gain riches or seek adventure; others to avoid religious persecution, find political refuge, or escape from personal involvements. Basic in all of these reasons was "a keen desire to found quiet and comfortable homes under easier conditions than Europe could offer."[10]

These immigrants brought their ideas and traditions with them. Most of them accepted the institutions and class structure of the society from which they came. Some were beginning to question the theory of absolutism in church and state, but no group migrated to establish a democratic social order in the New World.

The Southern Colonies. The Cavaliers, Royalists, and aristocrats of England, who settled the southern colonies, came for gain. Tobacco became king; debtors, criminals, children from English poorhouses, and Negroes took care of it. In time, two social classes emerged: the moderately wealthy, land-owning class, which included a few clergy and professionals; and the working class.

An aristocratic concept of life was reflected in the English *laissez faire* attitude toward schools. Education was deemed a private or church affair. Wealthier families engaged tutors or conducted a family school until their sons were ready for college in England, or the North, or—after 1692—in Virginia's own William and Mary College. In more populous areas, small, private, and select tuition schools were established to serve those who could afford them. Many churches established parish tuition schools, in which the clergy taught reading and the catechism. Private efforts of poorer families took the form of a community or "old field" school, which was built on a plot of abandoned or waste land, and "kept," on occasion, by an itinerant teacher.

The education of children coming from families who could not pay was generally considered a charitable function. Some churches maintained charity schools. Following English custom, endowments were created by philanthropically minded persons for the support of pauper schools, or for the maintenance of poor children in tuition schools. As the number of donations increased, attempts were made to control these funds and even augment them with contributions from the public purse, but the idea that public schools should be free and open to all was never contemplated. State concern in education was largely directed toward apprenticeship legislation for orphans and children of the poor. A two-class society was not conducive

---

[10] H. G. Good, *A History of Western Education* (New York: The Macmillan Company, 1947), p. 373.

to the establishment of a common school, and as a consequence, many children received little or no schooling.

The Middle Colonies. The Dutch, English, Swedes, French, Scandinavians, Scotch, Irish, Swiss, and Germans—the persecuted and economically oppressed from every North European country—found a haven in the Middle Colonies. This mixture of nationalities and languages represented a great variety of religious beliefs.

Church services and schools were conducted in the languages of the different groups; conflicts between cultures were frequent. Early efforts at public education, therefore, were short-lived. Throughout the colonial period, consequently, each church took upon itself to teach its own congregation, and a parish or parochial school was established wherever there were sufficient members to support it.

Where there were too few of one sect, a neighborhood school was established through the voluntary action of the people of the locality who desired it. While it was religious in tone, it was of necessity free from denominational teaching.

New England Colonies. In one of the greatest migrations in history, the Puritans established their "Godly Commonwealth" in Massachusetts. These skilled and semi-skilled laborers constituted the dominant middle class. They were a relatively homogeneous group, and the town was the center of their political life. Power was concentrated in the hands of the clergy, who ruled the church-state with a firm hand.

Hardly had the Puritans cleared their new land, when they erected their Old World institutions. A Latin grammar school was established in Boston in 1635, presumably to furnish scholars for Harvard College, which was established in Cambridge the following year for the purpose of training ministers. The Massachusetts laws of 1642 and 1647 departed from English tradition. The first gave parents and the masters of apprentices the responsibility of instructing their charges in reading and religion. Known as the "Deluder Satan Law," the second required communities of 50 householders to maintain a reading and writing school, and those of 100 householders to provide a Latin grammar school under penalty of a fine if they refused to do so.[11] Compulsory education was the policy for all the New England colonies except Rhode Island by 1671; compulsory schools by 1693.

With the eighteenth century came a decline in religious fervor, which lessened public interest in education. By the time of the Revo-

11 Cubberley, *op. cit.,* pp. 17-18.

lutionary War, support for the church's educational program had
given way to the needs of frontier life and a rising economic interest.
The number of Latin grammar schools had dwindled. The reading
and writing schools, which sometimes also taught arithmetic, had
never been very popular. They admitted children who had already
mastered the rudiments of reading. By and large, the private or semi-
public Dame schools assumed the major burden of elementary education during the colonial period.

Early National Period

The period from the Revolutionary War to the Civil War marked
the emergence of the democratic concept in every aspect of living.
Small farmers, shopkeepers, and prosperous artisans gained in political stature, which had a leveling effect on the colonial aristocracy
with its official position and wealth. A corresponding shift occurred
in the conception of government; the focus changed from protecting
property rights to promoting the "general welfare." Advances in scientific thought were preparing the way for the Industrial Revolution; life in general became more secularized. The election of Andrew Jackson in 1828 marked the triumph of democratic forces over
the aristocratic tendencies of the founding fathers.

Philanthropic Movements. The indispensability of popular education to the new government intensified philanthropic efforts to provide instruction in reading and writing for the poor.

Two of these movements were imported from abroad. The *Sunday
School,* which first appeared in Virginia in 1786, spread rapidly.
After 1824, however, control of these schools gradually passed from
organized societies to the churches, whereupon instruction was
changed from a day of secular work to a short period of religious instruction. The *Infant School,* organized in Boston in 1818, virtually
replaced the Dame School in New England, and had been trans-
formed into the primary grades of the common school in practically
all the Eastern cities by the time of the Civil War.

City *school societies* represented the greatest achievement of the
philanthropic movement. In addition to yearly subscriptions from
philanthropically minded citizens, these school societies were supported by aid from both city and state governments, and in some
cases were granted a tax of as much as one-half mill. The extent of
their influence is indicated by the most famous of these charitable institutions, the "New York Free School Society," founded in 1805.

When this society turned over its work to the public school system in 1853, "it had spent more than $3,500,000 and had provided instruction for children whose total attendance aggregated almost five hundred thousand pupil-years."[12]

The most spectacular innovation of the early nineteenth century for the purpose of extending educational opportunities, was the *monitorial school.* The plan developed by Lancaster enabled one master to supervise the instruction of as many as one thousand pupils in one large schoolroom. Besides being inexpensive, it gave the appearance of complete organization.

The very essence of the system was the monitor. When a child was admitted, a monitor assigned him his class; while he remained, a monitor taught him (with nine other pupils); when he was absent, one monitor ascertained the fact, and another found out the reason; a monitor examined him periodically, and when he made progress, a monitor promoted him; a monitor ruled the writing paper; a monitor made or mended the pens; a monitor had charge of the slates and books; and a monitor general looked after all the other monitors.[13]

Hailed as the most important discovery for the advancement of knowledge since the invention of the alphabet itself, this system became the basis for elementary education in most of the British Empire and Europe; it was extremely popular in the United States until the defects of the plan led to its general abandonment after 1840.

Common School Revival. By 1828 it was becoming increasingly clear that existing educational facilities were inadequate. Their improvement became the goal of an inspired minority. Associations such as the Western Literary Institute and the American Lyceum were organized to raise funds, improve education, and encourage public legislation. Educational journals were founded, primarily to help teachers, but also to interest the public at large in the cause of public education. Reports of European practices, such as those of Victor Cousin and Leland Stowe, were widely circulated and carefully studied for their solutions to the problems of school organization and support, as well as of teaching techniques. This was the age of educational statesmen: Thaddeus Stevens, James G. Carter, Horace Mann, Henry Barnard, Calvin Wiley, and Caleb Mills.

12 Newton Edwards and Herman G. Richey, *The School in American Social Order* (Boston: Houghton Mifflin Company, 1947), p. 262.
13 John Franklin Reigart, *The Lancasterian System of Instruction in The Schools of New York City,* Contributions to Education, No. 81 (New York: Teachers College, Columbia University, 1916), pp. 9-10.

Under these influences, there was a "common school revival." From the mildest form of permissive legislation in the case of those districts which consented to be taxed, there developed laws making mandatory a general tax for school purposes. The rate bill, a supplementary source of school revenue levied on the basis of the number of children in the family, was well on its way out in the North by the time of the Civil War. Despite considerable opposition, progress toward free, public, tax-supported schools was being made everywhere.

Public support led to public control. For this, improved administrative machinery became essential. By 1861 there was a state school officer in 28 of the 34 states; ten states had created the office of County Superintendent of Schools; and there were 26 City Superintendents of Schools.[14] There was a corresponding decline in religious influence over education. "Even in Massachusetts, churches did not receive state support after 1833."[15] Attempts made after 1840 to divide school funds among public and denominational schools were unsuccessful everywhere, and led to the erection of constitutional safeguards for public-school funds.

Improved administrative machinery also led to the development of the unitary system and grading in the larger cities. Instead of having independent primary schools, reading schools, and writing schools, as well as unrelated high schools, the separate school units were consolidated into the divisions of an extended period of public schooling. Variously known as primary, intermediate, grammar, and high, these divisions were subdivided into grades, each taught by a separate teacher.

Industrial Period

The Civil War was a second American revolution, marking the triumph of industrial forces in our culture. Spurred on by an abundance of natural resources, and an influx of immigrants at the rate of one million per year by 1900, the United States emerged as the foremost manufacturing nation of the world. This advance produced the highest standard of living in the world. It also created big cities. By 1930, urban dwellers were in the majority, facing acute problems of housing, sanitation, recreation, transportation, education, and government brought about by the exceedingly rapid growth of the cities they lived in.

14 Cubberley, *op. cit.,* p. 216.
15 Edwards and Richey, *op. cit.,* p. 379.

Popularization of Education. The Civil War temporarily checked educational progress, but by 1890 the expansion of education was in full swing. Compulsory school-attendance legislation which had been enacted by all the states by 1918, led to steadily increasing enrollments in elementary schools. From approximately 10 million children in 1880, the number jumped to nearly 24 million in 1930.

Early Childhood Education. The expansion of public education also took the form of extensions beyond the traditional elementary-high school levels. Froebel's kindergarten in Germany (1837) provided the model for a kind of education which stressed the values of play and self-activity for the very young. The first kindergarten in this country was established in Watertown, Wisconsin, in 1855, in the home of Mrs. Carl Schurtz. Credit for the first permanent public kindergarten goes to St. Louis (1873). In 1892, the International Kindergarten Union, now the Association for Childhood Education, was formed. Five years later, a National Congress of Mothers was called by kindergarten leaders, out of which emerged the National Congress of Parents and Teachers.

The Association of Day Nurseries of New York City was organized in 1897, but it was not until 1919 that the first public nursery school was started. Pre-elementary education was greatly stimulated during the Depression era under W.P.A. sponsorship. "By 1939, some 300,-000 children had been enrolled in 1,500 emergency nursery schools, most of which were housed in public school buildings."[16] When the federal government withdrew its support, in February, 1946, some of the program was taken over by local and state agencies although the number of public nursery schools remains small.

Reorganization of School Units. The great increase in enrollments, and the tendency for youth to attend school for a longer period of years led to a factory-like educational system.

By the turn of the new century the process had become complete and you could write the table of educational denominate numbers: eight years make one elementary education; fifteen Carnegie units make one secondary education; one hundred twenty semester hours or thirty-six majors make one college education.[17]

President Charles W. Eliot of Harvard University and President Harper of the University of Chicago led the attack on this form of

[16] R. Freeman Butts, *A Cultural History of Education* (New York: McGraw-Hill Book Company, Inc., 1947), p. 629.

[17] Henry C. Morrison, *The Evolving Common School* (Cambridge: Harvard University Press, 1933), p. 10.

organization of public education. They questioned the necessity of spending eight years on the common fundamentals when there were so many personal and social needs to be met, and they emphasized the relationship of a flexible school organization to the meeting of individual needs and the consequent retention of pupils. With the establishment of Joliet (Illinois) Junior College in 1902, and junior high schools in Berkeley (California) and Columbus (Ohio) in 1909, reorganization ceased to be an academic question. "By 1930 there were approximately four thousand junior high schools in the United States, enrolling over a million and a quarter pupils. In the same year, there were 171 public and 279 private junior colleges."[18]

Professionalization of Teaching. The expansion of public education and the systematic study of its problems were accompanied by the professionalization of teaching. The National Teacher's Association, which later became the National Education Association, was organized in 1857. Its membership of 2,500 at the turn of the century had grown to 50,000 by 1920, and has spurted above the half-million mark since World War II. A Department of Education, now the United States Office of Education, was created in 1867. A professorship in pedagogy was established at the University of Michigan in 1879, and the first Teachers College was founded at Columbia University in 1888.

To meet the demand for elementary school teachers, publicly supported "normal" schools expanded rapidly, and became a recognized part of the American school system. Attended almost wholly by women, they were like the earlier American academy, and practically never offered more than two years of education beyond the usual high school course. Concern for the improvement of teacher education at the beginning of the century led to the conversion of normal schools into four-year state teachers colleges, offering degrees in pedagogy and the arts. Once begun, this movement spread rapidly.

Thus, in 1920 immediately after the first World War there were in the United States 46 teachers colleges and 137 normal schools. Only eight years later on the eve of economic depression the proportion had almost reversed itself, there being 137 teachers colleges and 69 normal schools.[19]

Professionalization of teaching was also achieved by raising certification requirements. To attract more desirable students to the field

[18] Cubberley, *op. cit.*, pp. 555-57.
[19] John S. Brubacher, *A History of the Problems of Education* (New York: McGraw-Hill Book Company, Inc., 1947), p. 515.

and to retain those who had chosen teaching as a career, state-wide retirement systems and tenure laws came into being with the 1900's.

Scientific Movement in Education. The rapid expansion of education produced a host of problems which called urgently for systematic study. National committees were formed to bring about some order and standardization at all levels of education. The Committee of Ten on Secondary School Studies (1893), the Committee of Fifteen on Elementary Education (1895), and the Committee on College Entrance Requirements (1899) had profound influence on the structure and content of American education. A scientific approach to the improvement of educational practices was inaugurated with the work of the Committee on the Economy of Time (1911). School surveys became numerous after 1911, when Professor Paul H. Hanus of Harvard University made a brief and general report of the conditions and needs of the schools of Montclair, New Jersey.[20]

Education was becoming "scientific." G. Stanley Hall's *Adolescence*, published in 1904, stimulated further child study research and indicated the importance of psychology to education. Edward L. Thorndike's doctoral dissertation on animal intelligence, published in 1898, was the first of a long series of studies to determine the nature of intelligence, and to systematize the so-called "Laws of Learning." The standardized testing movement began with Rice's spelling test published in 1897, and was followed by Stone's test in arithmetic in 1908 and Thorndike's scale for handwriting in 1910. In response to the urgencies of World War I, the Binet-Simon individual intelligence test, published in 1905, was adapted for group testing, and was widely used in the public schools.

By 1920 the scientific movement was culminating in numerous new studies, more scientific procedures in the school surveys, new school textbooks embodying the new results and the indicated new procedures, and the rise of research departments in connection with city school systems.[21]

Development of the Educational Program and Organization of the Elementary School

Growth of Curricular Offerings. The elementary school curriculum has expanded from a limited offering of reading, writing, and certain elements of ciphering, to include a great variety of "subjects." Most of the new additions to the curriculum derived from two sources: the

---

[20] Edgar W. Knight, *Education in the United States,* rev. ed. (Boston: Ginn and Company, 1951), p. 546.
[21] Cubberley, *op. cit ,* p. 545.

expansion of the original three R's; and the inclusion in the elementary grades of a number of areas which had been previously taught in the academies or early high schools.

Of the three R's, communication, or literacy, received the first and greatest emphasis. Out of the general area of reading came such new "subjects" as English grammar, composition, declamation or rhetoric, and, at the end of the nineteenth century, literature. Writing became so fashionable that "penmanship" ranked second only to reading in importance. As a corollary, spelling became a subject in its own right. In the early part of the nineteenth century, arithmetic, too, branched out to include "mental" arithmetic.

New areas were also incorporated in the elementary curriculum in response to social developments. The rise of commercialism and nationalism led to the introduction of geography and history as separate subjects before the middle of the nineteenth century. In addition, the teaching of history provided opportunities for instruction in civil government, out of which grew the subject of civics. Reflecting economic interests, bookkeeping was introduced in some elementary schools near the beginning of the nineteenth century, although it was generally left in the province of the academies. As the importance of science to the expanding economy became apparent in the late nineteenth century, nature study was added to the curriculum.

The so-called "special subjects" became part of the elementary curriculum in response to a variety of influences. Drawing was added because of the practical need for mechanical drawing, as well as in recognition of the Pestalozzian requirements for the development of manual skills. Music, primarily singing, became popular during the first half of the nineteenth century. Physical education, as "exercise" or calisthenics, was slower to win approval. At the end of the nineteenth century sewing and cooking and manual training were made a part of the elementary program; these subjects were added as much for pedagogical reasons as for their vocational value.

Instructional Practices. As the preceding pages have hinted, the teaching-learning processes used in elementary schools have undergone considerable change. Until rather recently, the pupil's role was to memorize and recite, while that of the teacher was to explain and hear lessons. To measure the effectiveness of the combined procedures, tests were given at the end of the school year; the public, oral examination was replaced by a private, written "final" in the middle of the nineteenth century. Left to their own devices for so much of the day, some pupils developed a high degree of initiative and independence; others acquired a set of very questionable attitudes and behaviors. In order to maintain a semblance of order, teachers were generally authoritarian in their methods, and discipline was harsh.

The effect of all the factors surrounding the graded school of the generation following the Civil War was to develop a school machine. In contrast with the school conditions of a generation preceding there was a great deal more material included in the graded course of instruction, but the quality of teaching and learning was improved hardly at all. From the lowest grade to the highest the pupils followed an endless succession of book assignments which they learned out of hand to reproduce on call. The chief end of pupils was to master skills and learn facts as directed by a teacher who in turn was under the automatic control of a printed course of study, a set of textbooks, and the necessity of preparing her class to pass certain examinations on the contents of a specific number of printed pages. From the standpoint of discipline the physical cruelties of the earlier day had to a large degree disappeared, but the control exercised over the pupils was at least negative. The business of the school being what it was, any movement, any conversation, any communication were out of order. The spirit of control was military and repressive, not constructive and cooperative. Long rows of seats, military evolutions of classes, stated appearances for recitations, with the rest of the school time devoted to narrow prescribed exercises, had for their moral equivalent being quiet, industrious at assigned tasks, and submissive to the rule of the drill-sergeant in skirts who unflinchingly governed her little kingdom of learn-by-heart-and-recite-by-rote.[22]

In sharp contrast to these classroom practices stood the ideas of educational theorists from abroad. Comenius (1592-1670) demonstrated the value of sense realism in his book, the *Orbis Pictus*. Expressing a kind of faith in the inherent goodness of children, Rousseau (1712-1778) preached his doctrine of interest. Pestalozzi (1746-1827) devised his method of object instruction calling for pupil activity and first-hand experiences, including field trips and shop work. Promoted by the Normal School in Oswego, New York, his method became a vogue in this country for several decades after the Civil War. The theory of apperception, of learning the new in terms of the old, was Herbart's (1776-1841) contribution to an understanding of the learning process. His five steps, constituting a general method applicable to all subjects, included: (1) preparation or recall of familiar concepts; (2) presentation of new material; (3) association or comparison of steps one and two; (4) systematization or generalization; and (5) application or assignment. Slow to come to this country, the Herbartian method reached its peak of popularity at the end of the nineteenth

22 Edward H. Reisner, *The Evolution of the Common School* (New York: The Macmillan Company, 1930), pp. 427-428.

century. To Froebel (1782-1852), the function of method was to facilitate self-development through self-expression. To this end, he placed a premium on self-activity, play, freedom, and social relationships. His ideas were introduced with the appearance of kindergartens and nursery schools in this country, and were extended to other levels of elementary education through the "Progressive Movement" of the twentieth century.

Various techniques and methods of teaching were devised by American educators in the first three decades of the present century as an antidote to the formalism and rigidity of most elementary instruction of the previous century. The *problem approach* was based on problem-solving procedures, or steps in critical thinking, and involved: (1) awareness of a difficulty; (2) identification of the problem; (3) formulating hypotheses for the solution of the problem; (4) examining or analyzing hypotheses; and (5) testing one's conclusions. The *project method* was borrowed from the practical arts, and was characterized by purposefulness, life-like qualities of learning experiences, the solution of practical problems, and the direct involvement of pupils in the solution of these problems. Another widely accepted method was the *unit of work*, which attempted to bring related activities into some kind of focus, provided for comprehensiveness and continuity in learning, and facilitated group procedures and socialization. Other approaches to improved methodology included the *socialized recitation*, which involved both informal group discussions and highly organized class structures, such as student government; *individualized instruction*, which was usually applied to the skill subjects; and *supervised study*, which replaced the ineffectual arrangements and habits of study so often made in the name of "homework."

Curriculum Organization. As we have seen, during the greater part of the history of elementary education, schooling was practically synonymous with "book learning." The textbook determined what was taught, and the order of teaching. Whatever book the child brought with him to school, or whatever book the parent could be persuaded to purchase, constituted the curriculum for a particular child. Early textbooks, therefore, had a profound influence on the elementary curriculum.

During the Colonial Period, hornbooks and primers, the psalm book, and the Bible were commonly imported from England. Most famous of these early books was *The New England Primer,* which appeared about 1690 and was used for more than a century. After the Revolutionary War, textbooks by American authors appeared in increasing numbers. Noah Webster's blue-backed speller, published in 1783 as *The First Part of a Grammatical Institute of the English Language,* was the most popular book of the century, selling over a million copies annually before the Civil War. Lindley Murray, the "Father of English Grammar," published his *English Grammar* in 1795, and McGuffey's famous six readers, which appeared after the 1830's, constituted the subject of reading for fully half the children attending elementary school during the remainder of the century. In 1788, Nicholas Pike published a massive, encyclopedic text in arithmetic which stimulated the publication of a hundred or more such books in the next fifty years, among them Warren Colburn's *First Lessons in Arithmetic on the Plan of Pestalozzi,* published in 1821. Geography was represented first by Jedidiah Morse's text, published in 1784, followed by a number of competing texts, including Goodrich's ("Peter Parley") 1829 volume, *Method of Telling about Geography to Children* which used rhymes to make geography more palatable to young minds. History texts appeared comparatively late on the elementary horizon; Goodrich's ("Peter Parley") *History of the United States,* 1828, and Noah Webster's *History of the United States,* 1832, are most noteworthy.[23]

The trend toward the addition of new subjects (and new textbooks) to the elementary curriculum, as well as the invention of new methods to teach these areas more effectively, did not satisfy all the critics of elementary education. From the latter part of the nineteenth century to World War II, much fundamental thinking has been done about curriculum organization.

First to be scrutinized was the traditional subject organization of the curriculum. Studies of adult needs helped in the selection of *what* to teach, and determination of difficulty level aided in the grade placement of topics and subjects. This "scientific" approach to systematizing the subjects in elementary schools was hailed as the twentieth century's great contribution to educational progress.

Coincidentally with these efforts to prescribe the content and placement of various subjects, the number of discrete subjects constituting the elementary curriculum were being reduced and related to each other. From attempts to teach the history of a region before dealing with it geographically, the idea came of correlation, *i.e.,* teaching the history and geography of a region at the same time, although in different and separate classes. This principle of fusion or integration

[23] For a more detailed account, see Knight, *op. cit.,* pp. 423-428.

resulted in the combination of related subjects into broad content fields. History, geography, civics, anthropology, economics, and social psychology formed the social studies. Composition, declamation, and grammar were fused into English, which, combined with reading, writing, and spelling, constituted the field of language arts. Nature study, physical geography, and other science subjects were amalgamated into general science. In similar fashion, the broad fields of mathematics, physical education, and the arts came into being. The basic orientation of this approach was similar to that of the subject curriculum; but its adherents were particularly enthusiastic about the possibilities of integrating materials in the same broad area, and the flexibility provided when courses of study were organized in terms of principles or generalizations rather than specific topics.

Differing from the above two plans in being organized psychologically, rather than in terms of the logical structure of a subject field, was a plan of curriculum organization which culminated after World War I in the "Activity Movement" or "Progressive Education."

This child-centered approach was first put into operation in the Practice School of Cook County Normal School in Chicago, which was headed by Colonel Francis Parker from 1883 to 1901. As Director of the Laboratory School at the University of Chicago from 1896 to 1904, John Dewey put his similar theories of psychology and philosophy to the test. Published a dozen years later, his *Democracy and Education* became the guide for the new education. By World War I, a score of schools using this plan had been established under private auspices; a dozen more by the end of the war. They were child-centered schools, emphasizing the development of the "whole child." Children's interests and needs were met through an "emerging" or "experience" curriculum, as opposed to preplanned or prescribed curricula, which gave high priority to purposeful activity, critical thinking, and self expression. In 1918 the Progressive Education Association was formed; its peak membership was slightly under 10,000. In 1944, its name was changed to the American Education Fellowship[24] and is at present defunct.

Stimulated by the Depression, another group of educators advocated a social orientation for the curriculum. The utilitarian concept of social efficiency which underlay the activity and job-analysis approaches developed by Charters and Bobbitt in the twenties, provided a basis for identifying common areas of living or social functions.

[24] Rugg, *op. cit.*, pp. 536-60.

Stated differently by different writers, these generally included such areas as: conservation of human and natural resources; the production, distribution, and consumption of goods and services; basic institutions like the home, school, church, and government; and leisure-time pursuits, including aesthetics. To this basic social framework, certain features of the activity curriculum were added, which stressed the pupil's immediate concerns, problem-solving techniques, and group participation. Unlike the child-centered curriculum, which remained largely a private-school venture, the problems-of-living or areas-of-living curriculum organization was adopted by some public school systems. In 1937, Virginia published the first elementary curriculum guide based on this approach. Several years later, the teachers of Santa Barbara County, California, published voluminous accounts of their experiences with this kind of curriculum organization. A number of other cities and states have made similar attempts to use it after these pioneering ventures demonstrated how to put it into effect.

Organization and Administration

Reorganization of School Units. The past three hundred years have witnessed marked changes in the types of school units attempting to meet the educational needs of young people, in the relationships that these units bear to one another, and in the number of years over which they serve their pupils.

As indicated in Figure 1, other organizational patterns have emerged in response to the extension of public education, as well as to pedagogical considerations.

Grouping and Promotion. Elementary schools functioned for almost two centuries before children came to be taught in "classes," and before they were either "passed" or "failed" at the end of the school year. Instruction and learning were a private affair between tutor and pupil; progress was not so much judged, as accepted. Not until after the Civil War, with the rise of urbanization, did the classification of pupils into grades become accepted practice. Then, in the effort to keep classes as homogeneous as possible, grading and promotional policies became so rigid that the educational structure began to resemble the mass-production methods of the assembly line. Plans for introducing flexibility into the program appeared shortly before the turn of the century. Semi-annual and quarterly promotional plans were being tried in St. Louis, Missouri, and Quincy, Massachusetts before 1890, on the assumption that more flexible grading of pupils

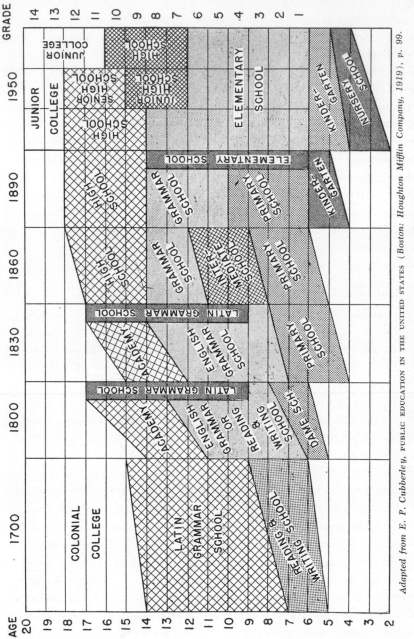

Adapted from E. P. Cubberley, PUBLIC EDUCATION IN THE UNITED STATES *(Boston: Houghton Mifflin Company, 1919), p. 99.*

Figure 1. EVOLUTION OF THE ORGANIZATIONAL UNITS OF THE AMERICAN PUBLIC SCHOOL SYSTEM

would lessen the amount of non-promotion. In the Pueblo (Colorado) Plan, introduced in 1888, rate of progress through the course of study was an individual matter, there being no such thing as non-promotion. The plan of having an assistant teacher coach slow learners, widely known as the "Batavia Plan," appeared in 1898. Its theory was that the coaching would enable all the children to cover the same ground, so that all could be promoted at the same time.

Parallel courses of study were organized in Cambridge, Massachusetts, in 1893. The same curriculum was offered as an eight-year program for the average pupil, and as a six-year program for the gifted. Differentiated courses of study were introduced in Santa Barbara, California, and in Baltimore, Maryland in 1898. Children were divided into slow, average, and gifted groups. While the rate of progress from grade to grade was kept constant, the amount of ground to be covered in each course varied. Confidence in psychological testing after World War I led to plans for homogeneous grouping. X-Y-Z ability grouping, which appeared in Detroit in 1919, was not so much an administrative arrangement as an attempt to adjust different courses of study and methods of teaching to children with varying capacities.

Thoroughgoing attempts to facilitate individualization of instruction through school organization also appeared. The platoon school was developed by W. A. Wirt in 1900. Known as the work-study-play school, it provided for the division of all pupils into two groups, called platoons. While one platoon studied the fundamental subjects in home rooms, the other engaged in activity subjects in special rooms. At midmorning and midafternoon, the platoons exchanged places, thus insuring economical use of all school facilities. In Winnetka, Illinois, a plan was instituted in 1919 which devoted one-half of each morning and afternoon session to the common essentials, and the other half to group or creative activities. Pupils worked strictly on an individual basis in learning the fundamentals, each mastering the successive units at his own pace. The Dalton (Massachusetts) Plan, also dating from 1919, distinguished between academic subjects, taught on the basis of individual progress, and physical, social, and emotional subjects, taught as "classes." Individualization was accomplished through "contracts," a series of related tasks undertaken at the pupil's own rate, in a room or laboratory specially equipped for each field.

Attempts to recognize individual differences through school organization also include the creation of "opportunity," or ungraded, rooms for children of various ages or capacities who did not fit into their regular classes. This idea finally led to the establishment of special classes and special schools to minister to the needs of atypical children. Such provisions were made in increasing numbers after World War I for pupils handicapped visually, aurally, orally, mentally, or physically, as well as for gifted children. Smaller classes, special equipment, flexible standards, and specially trained personnel made possible a higher degree of individualization of educational effort.

SUMMARY

We have noted the rather spectacular changes that have taken place in elementary education during the past three centuries. The religious motive for education, which characterized the colonial period, was augmented by the civic motive of the early national era, and the socio-economic emphasis of the present industrial age. These various motivations for public education reflect developments in our society. Rooted in European antecedents and traditions, the motivations are, nevertheless, products of American culture. As the culture changes, so do the schools. Education is not an isolated institution, but a social institution reflecting the general society in which it functions.

Progress has been the keynote of the story of elementary schools. Change, we have seen, has its small beginnings, and new ideas are generally resisted at first by professional and layman alike. While the advance has not been an even one, the ideal of universal education is closer to realization. The education of all the children of all the people has led increasingly to differentiated education in terms of function, methods, and materials. This expansion of function has resulted in an extension of public education, and in increasing need for integrating the work of the elementary schools with other educational units. The day is past when elementary educators can chart their course without reference to other school units.

Providing equal and adequate educational opportunities for an ever-growing number of children is a mid-century challenge of great moment. What happens to boys and girls in elementary schools will make a difference to them in terms of the personal satisfactions they can find in life, and to each of us who participate with them in our national culture, as well as to the world brotherhood which has been so tightly and explosively knit these past few years. History has shown us that each age requires a better elementary school than the one handed down by the preceding generations. We have also seen that "improvements in education do not, of their own nature and by their own power, spread and conquer the earth."[25] People must work for them—all kinds of people.

BIBLIOGRAPHY

Brubacher, John S., *A History of the Problems of Education*. New York: McGraw-Hill Book Company, Inc., 1947.

Butts, R. Freeman, *A Cultural History of Education*. New York: McGraw-Hill Book Company, Inc., 1947.

Cubberley, Ellwood P., *Public Education in the United States*. Boston: Houghton Mifflin Company, 1934.

Eby, Frederick, *The Development of Modern Education*. Englewood Cliffs, N.J.: Prentice-Hall, Inc., 1952.

Edwards, Newton and Herman G. Richey, *The School in the American Social Order*. Boston: Houghton Mifflin Company, 1947.

Good, H. G., *A History of Western Education*. New York: The Macmillan Company, 1947.

Knight, Edgar W., *Education in the United States,* rev. Boston: Ginn and Company, 1951.

Meyer, Adolph E., *The Development of Education in the Twentieth Century*. Englewood Cliffs, N.J.: Prentice-Hall, Inc., 1949.

Morrison, Henry C., *The Evolving Common School*. Cambridge: Harvard University Press, 1933.

Reisner, Edward H., *The Evolution of the Common School*. New York: The Macmillan Company, 1930.

Rugg, Harold, *Foundations for American Education*. Yonkers-on-Hudson: World Book Company, 1947.

25 H. G. Good, *op. cit.,* p. 538.

THE ELEMENTARY

SCHOOL

IN ITS

COMMUNITY

3

TODAY'S ELEMENTARY SCHOOL, A SOCIAL INSTITU-
tion, must seek both an ear and a voice in the affairs of men. The school that would study life,
and in so doing, live, is the concern of this chapter.

THE SCHOOL: PART OF THE COMMUNITY

Much of what has been written about school-
community relationships conveys the impression
that two separate and somewhat parallel institutions, the school and the community, have to be
brought into close relationship. Nothing could
be further from the truth. The school is part of
the organism communal; arbitrary separation of
the school from its community for purposes of

discussion is a convenience that must not be confused with reality.

Much writing suggests also that the school is a social instrument of the community with clear-cut functions to fulfill. Such an impression is misleading. Function, revealed historically, is found to be directly related to the nature of authority. Where authority is fully invested in a group with agreed-upon goals, and where the group in power recognizes the value of education as means, the school's function will be relatively clear. It follows, then, that we cannot expect schools to have a clear-cut role in a society where various groups are contending for dominance.

> . . . consider such situations as may come to mind wherein the policies and programs of a given school have been subjected to public discussion. Invariably, the discussions take on the character of a pitched battle wherein diverse groups struggle not for the common good of the school and community but for private, or private group dominance, the school being by no means a disinterested, or unattached, party to the fray. Such situations make it perfectly obvious that schools, no matter how socially detached they may appear at a casual glance, are actually socially involved. That involvement, however, is in terms of some segment of the society rather than in terms of the society as a whole.[1]

To the degree that the common beliefs and ideals which constitute the core of a culture are clear, that governing bodies truly represent their culture, and that schools keep tuned to community sentiment, we may expect the school to have relatively clear-cut functions. But, given these conditions, school people still have the professional responsibility of translating functions into programs which fulfill them. Since not all of these conditions are present to the optimum degree in modern America, school people must turn again and again to the community for its help in planning the educational program.[2]

THE SCHOOL AS A COMMUNITY INSTITUTION

The word *community* never has been used with exactness, and it becomes increasingly difficult to define it. Olsen warns against the danger of defining the term too narrowly. If our concept of community is to be realistic and of practical value to children and to the education of children, he says, then large spatial areas must be recognized in our thinking.[3] He bases his thesis upon the interdependence of

[1] Milosh Muntyan, "Community-School Concepts: A Critical Analysis," *The Community School,* Fifty-second Yearbook of the National Society for the Study of Education, Part 2 (Chicago: The University of Chicago Press, 1953), p. 39.

[2] *Ibid.,* p. 44.

[3] Edward G. Olsen *et al., School and Community,* 2nd ed. (Englewood Cliffs, N.J.: Prentice-Hall, Inc., 1954), p. 19.

city and village, county and state, nation and world. In line with this thesis, he defined four major comunity areas—local, regional, national, and international. The first of these he considers the service area of the school.[4]

PARENTS ARE A PART OF THE SCHOOL PROGRAM

Cook and Cook recognize the importance of such a view. "People, who are in communication, come to hold things in common, and because of this 'belief pattern' they form a community."[5] However, they add, the usefulness of such a definition is limited by its scope. By it, "Any group or institution, any kind of human association, any two friends, is a 'community.' "[6] Their definition illustrates the difficulty of making a single precise statement. It is, in reality, a summary of basic community characteristics:

From a sociological standpoint, a community is a configuration of land, people, and culture, a structured pattern of human relations within a geographic area. In a technical sense, this concept has seven fundamental characteristics.

1. A population aggregate
2. Inhabiting a delimitable, contiguous area

4 *Loc. cit.*
5 Lloyd A. Cook and Elaine F. Cook, *A Sociological Approach to Education* (New York: McGraw-Hill Book Co., Inc., 1950), p. 48.
6 *Ibid.*, p. 48.

3. Sharing a historical heritage
4. Possessing a set of basic service institutions
5. Participating in a common mode of life
6. Conscious of its unity
7. Able to act in a corporate way.[7]

Subsequent discussion of school and community relationships is carried on within the framework of this more exact definition.

It must be kept clearly in mind that the small, familistic society, characterized by intimate interaction, is rapidly disappearing from the American scene. At the opposite extreme, increasingly the American prototype, is the large urban center with its impersonal interaction. Beers' description of it is worth quoting at length. It is characterized by

. . . contractual, impersonal, indirect, and casual interaction; complex and elaborate division into groups and classes. Its regulation is more improvised, rational, and legal. It has a highly developed exchange economy, using money in a world market. Its emerging norms are those of efficiency. Its social solidarity is based mainly on the interdependence of specialized parts. Its social change is rapid and of broad coverage. It is sometimes characterized as an integrated society because of the ramifications of interdependence among its parts, but actually its need for further social integration seems more conspicuous than any present integration of its character. In this society the personality of each member is moored now here, now there, now nowhere. This is the kind of society in which most of us live today. It is the society of the metropolis. . . .[8]

Any picture of the American community is complicated by the fact that many people divide their time among two or more communities. Automobiles parked adjacent to the tracks of the Long Island Railroad reveal clearly that thousands who work on Manhattan Island live in the Borough of Queens. The scene is duplicated on Lake Street in suburban Chicago, Peachtree in Atlanta, and Main Street, U.S.A. Some people even maintain a home in Los Angeles, an apartment in Manhattan, and a permanent hotel suite in London. Atlantic City's population count is dependent upon what convention happens to be in town, or the season of the year. And families that once spent four seasons on the farm now frequently spend the winter in Florida or California. Can the school, then, ever hope to define for itself a meaningful role? Can it both serve and express its "community?"

[7] *Ibid.*, pp. 48-49.
[8] Howard W. Beers, "American Communities," *The Community School*, Fifty-second Yearbook of the National Society for the Study of Education, Part 2 (Chicago: The University of Chicago Press, 1953), p. 17.

THE SCHOOL AS A SOCIAL INSTITUTION

Within a society one finds patterns of social organization and behavior designed to accomplish certain objectives which are assumed to be desirable and even essential to the welfare of the group. These systems of social behavior are called *institutions*.[9]

Human experience, as expressed in any culture, results largely from the attempts of human beings to satisfy their needs. The fulfillment of needs is purposeful activity. A culture establishes institutions to assist in the satisfaction of these needs. The family, perhaps the oldest institution, guarantees the perpetuation of mankind. Economic institutions provide the basic necessities of food, clothing, and shelter. Government provides for the welfare and protection of the social group and its members. Schools provide not only for the transmission and interpretation of a culture's basic elements, but also for the preparation of worthy citizens for society. The function of this last institution warrants further examination here.

The Roles of the School in Its Community

The major functions of schools are to serve as agencies of society to conserve and transmit the cultural values to succeeding generations; to develop in the youth an understanding of, and an appreciation for, his social order; and to insure social progress, in so far as any institution can assure progress.[10]

The above brief statement of school functions allows for a wide range of interpretation in practice. Casual observation of a dozen elementary schools selected at random from several sections of the country probably would reveal several virtually withdrawn from community affairs, and others playing a role of aggressive leadership. Individual school perception of role in the fulfillment of function depends upon both a philosophical analysis of what seems desirable, and a psychological concept of how best to carry out what appears desirable. At the risk of over-simplification, three levels of school-community interaction may be defined describing the varying roles played by elementary schools in the fulfillment of their function in society.

1. *Isolation of the School from Its Community.* Obviously, complete isolation is an impossibility, since children and teachers carry with them the broader culture. But in a school "isolated" from its community, interaction with other institutions is at a minimum.

---

[9] Marion B. Smith, "The School as a Social Institution," *Sociological Foundations of Education,* ed. Joseph S. Roucek (New York: Thomas Y. Crowell Co., 1942), p. 31.
[10] *Ibid.,* pp. 33-34.

Children and teachers enter the building in the morning, and, in a very real sense, are cut off from the larger community until they leave it in the afternoon. In such a school, all learning may be centered in textbooks and whatever may be carried into the building. But such is not necessarily the case. This kind of school may sponsor Junior Red Cross or Clothes for the Needy drives from time to time, at the instigation of a community group; it may hold meetings with parents to interpret its work; speakers may be brought in, and, occasionally, children may go out on field trips. Essentially, however, there is no real interaction with the community as a whole. The involvement of children in affairs about them, and the interpretation of that involvement, are not seen as necessary to the fulfillment of the functions quoted above. There are many such elementary schools in modern America.

2. *Learning and Living in the School Oriented toward the Realities of Community Living and Societal Affairs.* In this kind of elementary school, fulfillment of function is seen as using the community both as a laboratory and a resource. Problems of city government become lessons in the social studies; family finance becomes classroom arithmetic; zoo, dairy, and power plant become the content of oral and written expression. Children explore the community. What they find, they bring back into the classroom. The theory is "do it" and "see it," as well as "read it." A large percentage of America's schools fulfill functions by performing such a role.

3. *The School as an Active Agent for Community Betterment.* Schools seeking to insure social progress by becoming agents in community improvement frequently play one or both of the following roles:

a. That of taking the initiative in stimulating community betterment. School personnel frequently take the lead in projects designed to beautify the community, improve public health, increase recreational facilities, and so on. The account of one such school's leadership is reported later in this chapter.

b. That of cooperating with several other agencies or institutions in well-organized community improvement activities. The story of one of these schools is told later.

Outstanding illustrations of elementary schools seeking actively to improve their communities are becoming more plentiful, but they are still so rare that accounts of most of them at one time or another find their way into print.

It must be clear that the three classifications above are very arbitrary. Few schools fit neatly into one or the other of them. Virtually all that fit into the third category, also fit into the second. Some schools fit into all three when classrooms are analyzed individually. The point of presenting such classifications here is to emphasize that elementary schools play no single, distinct role in American society. It has been pointed out that school personnel in modern times have received no clear assignment of function agreed upon by all the people. Such functions as have been inherited, or newly perceived, are not easily translated into practice. It naturally follows, then, that elementary schools in widely separated and differentiated communities, with differences in personnel, perceive and carry out a wide range of roles in the fulfillment of their functions.

THE COMMUNITY SCHOOL

It has been pointed out that the school is an integral part of its community. It follows, then, that all schools are community schools, differing from one another only in the degree of their involvement in community affairs. But there is a considerable body of opinion to the effect that the community school is a different kind of school.[11] Hanna and Naslund, representing this position, are quoted here at some length:

A community school is a school which has concerns beyond the training of literate, "right minded," and economically efficient citizens who reflect the values and processes of a particular social, economic, or political setting. In addition to these basic educational tasks, it is *directly concerned with improving all aspects of living in the community* in all the broad meaning of that concept in the local, state, regional, national, or international community. To attain that end, the community school is *consciously used* by the people of the community. Its curriculum reflects planning to meet the discovered needs of the community with changes in emphasis as circumstances indicate. Its buildings and physical facilities are at once a center for both youth and adults who together are actively engaged in analyzing problems suggested by the needs of the community and in formulating and exploring possible solutions to those problems. Finally, the community school is concerned that the people put solutions into operation to the end that living is improved and enriched for the individual and the community.[12]

Basic to this definition is the concept of purposeful interaction—the school consciously seeks to improve the community, and the

11 Paul R. Hanna and Robert A. Naslund, "The Community School Defined," *The Community School*, Fifty-second Yearbook of the National Society for the Study of Education, Part 2 (Chicago: The University of Chicago Press, 1953), p. 52.

12 *Loc. cit.*

community seeks to use school facilities and influence the school curriculum. It is descriptive of the third level of school-community interaction outlined earlier. Such a concept does not remove the problem of degree. While it might be possible to place individual schools on a five-point scale ranging from limited to extensive community interaction, the continuum is such that it becomes virtually impossible to say, "This is a community school, but that one is not." The authors therefore prefer to use the concept so well expressed by Hanna and Naslund to describe what is ultimately desirable in the community school's development.

The chances of a school's becoming an effective community agent are enhanced when the following conditions exist:

1. There is a clearly-defined service area. This is usually the case when a small town is served by one elementary school; when a small school draws its enrollment from a rural, farming area; when the service area is mapped out by some natural geographic feature such as a river; and so on.[13]

2. Enrollment is low enough to permit close association of principal, teachers, and pupils, in an atmosphere free from the regimentation common to large schools. Six hundred pupils is sometimes taken as the optimum maximum size for elementary schools.

3. Children live within walking distance of the school building. This is not to suggest that the consolidated school is eliminated from effective participation in community affairs. Such a school must simply build bridges of communication with the communities from which children are transported.

4. School, church, welfare, public health, and other agencies of a local service area work together for the welfare of young people in that area.

5. The program is designed with the children of the community in mind.

6. The program is concerned with the economic, social, and political problems of the community.

7. The school recognizes the family as the basic unit in American life, and affords training and experience conducive to improved family relationships.[14]

[13] The 108,000 schools of one, two, and three teachers (1950) in the United States probably have distinct service areas. See Association for Supervision and Curriculum Development, *Instructional Leadership in Small Schools* (Washington: The Association, 1951), p. 3.

[14] Southern States Work-Conference on Educational Problems, *Developing Administrative Leadership for Our Schools* (Tallahassee, Florida: State Department of Education, 1952), p. 2.

8. The school uses the community as a laboratory for observation and experimentation.

9. The building and equipment are designed for use by community groups.

10. Children, teachers, and parents participate in school planning.

11. Parents help determine the job of the school.

12. Teachers participate in community affairs.

Conditions such as these are brought about by forward-looking, democratic leadership, the kind of leadership that values human resources and that brings people together for cooperative planning and working.

The School as Community Center

The American school, generally speaking, is in use only six or seven hours per day.[15] For another six or seven hours of usable time, classroom, gymnasium, auditorium, and library go unused. Meanwhile, the patrons of the school—parents and children alike—often carry on meetings, recreation, and even formal education in dilapidated, poorly heated, poorly lighted, makeshift buildings built and maintained by their own direct contributions. The school buildings, which these same people build and maintain through taxation, stand unoccupied.

There are some difficulties involved in using the school as a community center. Increased wear and tear means shortened life of school property. Distinguishing the relative amounts of depreciation caused by regular school use, by other community activities, and by the passage of time is virtually impossible. Administrators are well aware of the headaches and heartaches brought about by divided control of public property. School principals are keenly sensitive to the tremendous responsibility for life and property entrusted to them, and do not readily open school doors to community activities which they cannot personally supervise. And one cannot expect school principals to return to their buildings each evening after having worked since early morning. This whole question of responsibility for public property is going unanswered—and, as a result, schools as community centers remain largely a hope rather than a reality.

Many of our schools are not too well equipped for their present function, let alone for this broader concept of function. Desks fre-

---

15 For an intriguing description of America, 1984, that includes a 15-hour school-use day, see Harold Rugg, *The Teacher of Teachers* (New York: Harper & Bros., 1952), pp. 256-64.

quently are fastened to the floor, as though immobility and learning go well together. They are arranged in rows, facing the front of the room, as though all knowledge emanates from there. Space for work benches, for storing tools and lumber, for art work and equipment, for committee meetings, and so on, is lacking. These shortcomings make school buildings largely unsuitable for community use, and partially explain why various groups seek other quarters. However, if cooperative action focused upon supplying the necessary facilities, these groups would be taken care of, and the schools would be equipped to do the expanded job today's schools must do.

The solution to the above problems is increased understanding. One promising approach to increased understanding among community groups is the community council, as described below. But, before a community reaches the level of cooperation implied by this kind of council, the school itself can take the initiative in attacking some of these problems. In the attack the school principal and superintendent must play an important role.

The Community Council

The community is made up of many institutions seeking to better community life. The total contribution of these institutions seldom approaches what is potentially possible. Part of the explanation for this discrepancy lies in poor communication and needless duplication of effort, which could easily be remedied through coordination and joint planning. But diverse community influences present major blocks to understanding and consolidation of effort. Many childless taxpayers object to general public support for education, and fight bond issues necessary for school improvement. Movement to the suburbs by wealthy home owners, and congested living conditions in deteriorating sections of the city seriously curtail the basis for tax-supported education. Religious groups who want their own schools, or who object to the support of certain health services, represent special interests that must be reckoned with. It is essential that this wide array of interests and influences of any given community find a wholesome outlet for expression. Many communities are finding that the community council provides such an outlet, as well as a coordinating focal point.

A community council may be described as a medium or form of organization through which representatives of government, civic groups, religious groups, social groups, business groups, fraternal groups, and interested citizens join forces for the purpose of promoting good conditions and eliminating poor conditions affecting community life.[16]

Chamberlain and Kindred identify seven major objectives of community councils:

1. To provide means through which all community groups and interested persons may increase their awareness and understanding of community problems.

2. To provide a means through which community agencies and organized groups may co-ordinate their efforts and pool their resources for solving problems of community life.

3. To engage in careful, long-time planning, define current problems, and recommend courses of action to agencies and officials best equipped to handle these problems.

4. To encourage the undertaking of community projects that are too large or too difficult for a single group or agency to deal with.

5. To develop a spirit of civic mindedness on the part of everyone who lives in the community so that they may, through the medium of the council, create the conditions under which they wish to live.

6. To serve as a clearing house for organizations and agencies, thereby enabling them to work together on problems of common concern without duplicating or wasting effort.

7. To help improve the quality of existing community services.[17]

There are many ways of organizing for community betterment. One excellent illustration is the Stephenson (Michigan) Community Coordinating Council, the essential features of which are summarized below.[18]

THE STEPHENSON COMMUNITY COORDINATING COUNCIL

The initiative for the Stephenson project came from the state superintendent of public instruction, who offered state assistance to any community seriously concerned with self-improvement. Local leadership came from the board of education, which sounded out community feeling by calling together small representative groups. This initial exploration was followed by a mass meeting representing fifty-two social, economic, civic, and religious agencies, and the organization of a temporary steering committee. The superintendent of schools was appointed executive secretary.

After identifying purposes, the Stephenson Community Coordinating Council organized seven problem-study committees: Education, Healthful Living, Community Services, Trade and Industry, Religious Life, Farm and Land Use, and Home and Family Living. When each had studied a problem and felt ready for

16 Leo H. Chamberlain and Leslie W. Kindred, *The Teacher and School Organization*, 2nd ed. (Englewood Cliffs, N.J.: Prentice-Hall, Inc., 1949), pp. 567-568.

17 *Ibid.*, p. 569.

18 Adapted from Joseph B. Gucky and Herbert Corey, "A Community Organizes to Help Itself," *Educational Leadership*, VII (March, 1950), 388-92.

action, it appointed an action committee of from three to five persons. Each of these committees remained intact only long enough to carry the problem to a satisfactory solution.

In slightly more than three years of operation, the program brought concentrated action to bear on approximately fifty projects of minor or major concern. To illustrate the kinds of problems tackled, two projects carried through by each committee are listed below.

1. Educational Committee
   a. Organized a core curriculum for junior high school students
   b. Established an outdoor education camp for elementary and secondary school pupils
2. Home and Family Living Committee
   a. Assisted the school in organizing a unit of study on "Preparation for Family Living" with specific reference to marriage problems and sex instruction
   b. Conducted a course in "Home and Landscaping"
3. Recreation Committee
   a. Organized a summer recreation program with a full-time director
   b. Constructed a new swimming pool
4. Community Services Committee
   a. Sponsored institutes for elective officials
   b. Cooperated with the village to construct a new bridge over the river
5. Religious Life Committee
   a. Organized a community choir for persons of all religious denominations
   b. Promoted a campaign to reserve Wednesday evenings for home or religious activities
6. Farm and Land Use Committee
   a. Assisted in organizing a pre-school teachers' conference on soil conservation
   b. Organized a Soil Conservation Field Day for the Upper Peninsula
7. Health Committee
   a. Initiated a plan for blood-typing all community residents on a voluntary basis
   b. Promoted educational campaigns for TB X-rays.

Programs such as this in Stephenson, Michigan, do not occur by chance. Leadership must detect needs, stimulate and challenge interest, make and carry out plans, and evaluate progress. School people are in a strategic position to provide such leadership.

THE SCHOOL PROGRAM AND THE COMMUNITY

The school cannot live apart from its community. The elementary school that is doing an effective educational job makes constant use of community resources. It carries out its program smoothly when cooperative working relationships have been established among community institutions. The success of various attempts to extend the tax-supported school program into the summer months has depended largely upon the kind of school-community cooperation already established. This section deals with camping and extended school programs, only two of many forward-looking educational ventures which bring the school into the community, and which depend upon rapport with the community for their continued existence.

Camping Education

School camping programs are no new fad, enjoying a brief and tenuous existence apart from the main stream of American education. They are well established from Washington to Florida, Texas to Connecticut, and Maryland to California. From 1946 through 1949, more than 12,000 pupils attended San Diego (California) County's Camp Cuyamaca, operated throughout the school year. Schools of Battle Creek and Calhoun County, Michigan, cooperate in the use of a camp owned by the W. K. Kellogg Foundation. North Idaho College of Education at Lewiston operates Black Pine Camp for its laboratory school children and teachers-in-training. In Florida, children are brought in buses to Myakka and Hillsborough State Parks for all-day study of natural life. Provo, Utah, maintains camp property and a year-round camping director. These are only a few of the dozens of illustrations which might be cited.[19]

There are two questions—simple to phrase, but far from simple to answer—that must be asked about school camping, just as they must be asked about any educational activity. First, does it lead to the attainment of worthwhile ends? Critics are quick to say that school camping is just refuse tossed up in the muddy backwash of Progressive Education. Schools are unjustified, they say, in using public funds to usurp the prerogative of the home and family. Too often, the defense offered to this criticism is apologetic and ill-founded. For instance, statistics are frequently prepared to show the number of problems involving arithmetic encountered and solved during two weeks of camping. Such statistics are interesting, but they do not justify the activity. It is like trying to justify the maintenance of a herd of dairy cattle on the basis of beef products sold. Activities must be justified on accomplishment of basic ends sought, and bootlegging arithmetic into a camping project designed to improve human relationships may actually corrupt the entire enterprise. Another lame defense is, "No,

19 For additional information about these or about nation-wide developments, write Life Camps, Inc., 369 Lexington Ave., New York 17, N.Y.

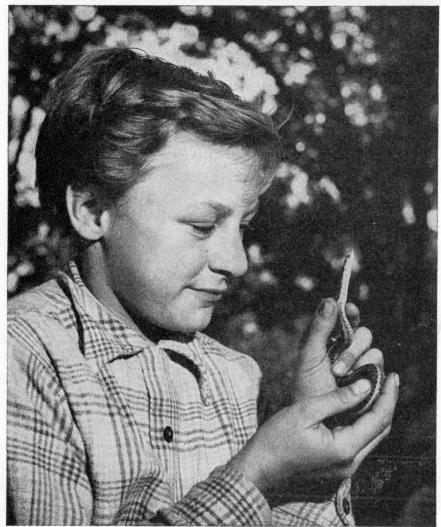

THE MILWAUKEE JOURNAL

SHE WAS AFRAID OF SNAKES BEFORE SHE CAME TO CAMP

it doesn't contribute much to the fundamentals, but it does develop the 'whole' child." Critics are unlikely to be satisfied with answers that appear to sidestep the issues at stake.

The second question about school camping is, to what degree does it accomplish given ends? School camping probably contributes to— or has the potential for contributing to—every educational goal ever formulated. The real issue is whether camping contributes to certain ends to a greater degree than do other activities. Absolute answers to such a question are not easily available. Perhaps the best criterion is whether youngsters are afforded frequent opportunity to practice the desired behavior which camping activities are designed to develop. The real test, of course, is the degree to which this behavior persists after the group returns from camp.

Enumerated below are several specific suggestions and principles for conducting school camping programs. These suggestions are not limited to camping, but may be applied to the consideration of almost any educational project. They are based on the experiences of teachers and schools now or previously engaged in such activities.

1. School faculties contemplating programs in camping education should begin with a thorough discussion of all that is likely to be involved. Moving out into the community with children is quite a different proposition from remaining within the comparative sanctuary of school walls. Are the teachers themselves ready for such an enterprise—for living twenty-four hours a day with children, for departing from school routine and traditions? Are there educational experiences to be obtained that cannot be obtained within the classroom?

2. Children and parents should be brought into the discussions before any specific planning is done. One of the main purposes of such meetings should be to interpret the school camp to parents as an educational, rather than a recreational, project.

3. Effort should be made to secure a director qualified for this work through special training and experience. A non-teaching director is able to make use of teachers' experience with children in a learning environment structured quite differently from the school's regular program.

4. Parents, children, and teachers must be directly involved together in planning, executing, and evaluating.[20]

5. Activities should be selected for their appropriateness for living outdoors.[21] Parents must be helped to see—and frequently this will be far from easy—that camping education is not an "extra" or a "frill," but simply the most expeditious way of accomplishing certain valid educational aims.

6. Camping education can be an experiment in cooperative group living. Consequently, camp life excludes competitive motivations imposed by adults.

[20] American Association for Health, Physical Education, and Recreation, "Report of the Committee on Camping in Education for the Year, 1948-49" (Mimeographed).
[21] Marion Jordan, "Adventures in School Camping," National Elementary Principal, XXXII (April, 1953), 20-21, 37.

7. Evaluation must be appropriate to the activity itself. Therefore, youngsters will not be tested on what they did and saw. What could be more inappropriate than to prepare a paper-and-pencil test asking pupils to fill in the names of trees seen, birds heard, and so on! In 1947, the Board of Education of New York City conducted an experiment to find out what fifth and seventh graders learned at camp.[22] While many formal school learnings were evaluated, the process was not allowed to interfere with the structure and selection of activities in the camp itself. Significant evidence of the development of democratic attitudes was found.

The Extended School Program

The term *extended school program* is used here to mean summer offerings, non-remedial in nature, sponsored by the school in addition to the number of days the school is required by state law to be in session. Summer schools designed to assist slow-progress pupils in keeping up with their grade-level are arbitrarily excluded for purposes of this discussion. Rochester, Minnesota, illustrates a twelve-month plan. Children attend school 180 days in the traditional portion of the year. Teachers then elect in rotation a pupil-service activity, participation in a system workshop, leadership in school recreation, travel, or summer school attendance.[23] Buildings are kept in use throughout the year. Usually such extended school programs are designed to offer something not extensively included in the regular program, and usually they involve close community cooperation.

Such a program as that shown in Table 1 does not come into being accidentally. Years of planning among school people and the preparation of a legal document preceded specific preparations for what was done in the summer of 1952.

THE SCHOOL AND COMMUNITY ACTION

It was stated above that elementary schools play a variety of roles in American communities. For purposes of clarifying many points stressed earlier, two actual cases exemplifying, first, the school's role as an instigator of community improvement, and, second, the school's role as a cooperating agency, are offered here. It will be noted that both schools illustrate both roles; but, in each case, one role pre-

[22] Reported in *Extending Education Through Camping*, available from Life Camps, Inc., 369 Lexington Avenue, New York 17, N.Y.

[23] For a detailed account, see Helen L. Klein, "When a Twelve-Month Plan is Carried Out," *Childhood Education*, XXVIII (February, 1952), 262-64.

The Extended School Program in Georgia

TABLE 1

ACTIVITIES IN GEORGIA'S EXTENDED SCHOOL PROGRAM, 1952 [24]

Activity	Pupil hours
Physical activities	
Swimming, games, sports, trips, first aid, driver education	4,092,598
Arts and crafts	
Painting, clay modeling, puppetry, papier-mâché, weaving, basketry, carving, sculpture, metal craft, simple construction, refinishing furniture	1,547,132
Music	
Choral singing, rhythms, instrumental music, voice instruction, music appreciation, folk games	1,447,877
Language experiences	
Reading for fun, reading for information, story telling, puppet shows, dramatization, choral reading	1,335,964
Vocational activities	
Vocational agriculture, homemaking, typing, home nursing	669,592
Science and nature study	
Field trips, collecting, experimentation	523,699
Camping	
Day camps, overnight camps, one week camp experiences	299,892
	9,916,754

dominates which is peculiarly appropriate to the particular school in its setting. Any other role would have been less in keeping with local conditions, and, consequently, less effective.

The first, Norristown, typical of many small villages in rural America, is located somewhat south and east of Georgia's geographic center. The other, Lithonia, also typical of many American towns, is only twenty miles from the heart of Atlanta. These two have been selected because they are geographically close, they operate within one state's educational framework, educational leadership was being exerted in both, and data for the same years were available.

THE NORRISTOWN COMMUNITY[25]

This is the story of Norristown and one of its most eventful years—1950 to 1951. It is the story, too, of the three-classroom Norristown School, a significant part of the Norristown community. The story begins in the school—and with educational

[24] From *Education in Georgia Moves Forward: Extended School Program* (Atlanta: State Department of Education, 1952).

[25] From material provided by Joan B. White, "Planning, Developing, and Evaluating a Program of Resource-Use Education in the Norristown School," a project in applied education submitted to the College of Education, University of Georgia, June, 1951.

leadership—but it spreads out into the farms, into the forty-four homes repre-sented in the school, into many other homes, into the churches. We conclude it here with early summer, 1951. But before this account is brought to conclusion, it tells a story of community betterment that affected virtually every phase of Norristown life.

The Community

Four stores, a "week-end only" movie house, and a church make up Norristown center in southeastern Emanuel County, Georgia. The school and another church are a mile north. Farming is the chief occupation in the community, cotton and corn being the main crops. Turpentine, pulpwood, and lumber from the pine forests supplement many farm incomes.

The School

The school itself must be described twice—before and after—because 1950 to 1951 was a face-lifting year. Three rooms are for classrooms, one for storage, and another for principal's office, library, and supply purposes. There is a small auditorium, and, in an adjacent crude wooden building, a lunchroom. Outdoor toilets grace the back campus.

If you had looked inside in September, 1950, you would have seen two-tone classrooms—dark brown and dingy gray—and worn, cracked blackboards. The sight outside was bleak. Gullies cut across the bare, cracked grounds.

Seventy-three pupils, two new teachers, and a left-over teacher from the previ-ous year made up the school family in 1950. They had little to work with. Few books, one set of maps, and a few pictures and charts were about all besides the usual textbooks.

The supervisor summed up her observations of school and community in September, 1950, as follows:

1. The school curriculum was concerned largely with teaching subject matter outlined in textbooks.
2. There was a need for changes in instruction, including the use of more teacher-pupil planning and problem-solving techniques.
3. The school campus was eroded; natural light inside the building was re-duced by dark colored paint on the walls.
4. There was a need for becoming familiar with, and for greater utilization of, resource people and agencies in the school and community.
5. Increased community participation in the school program was desirable.
6. Further development of resources within the school and community was needed.

Procedures

Plans to attack these problems began with supervisor-principal planning, but, as one activity developed, other problems seemed to be natural outgrowths of the first. As new problems were recognized, the process of planning for new ac-tivities began. Supervisor-principal planning moved into faculty planning and then into teacher-pupil planning. Planning with resource people and agencies as a rule preceded planning with community people. After a rather thorough job of planning had been done, the groups cooperatively participated in the execution of plans. Let us follow through one project in some detail to see this process in action.

Controlling Soil Erosion on the Campus

During a conference with the principal in the fall, the supervisor remarked on the badly eroded campus. She pointed out that a farmer might fill in the gullies and plough the campus. Resource agencies whose services were available to schools upon request were mentioned. The principal's reaction was that the faculty be given an opportunity to discuss such a project.

Faculty planning probed into the whole question of resource-use education, and then focused on the erosion problem. It was pointed out that parents would learn much about erosion control that could be applied at home by working on the problem at school with proper guidance.

Faculty planning moved naturally into the classroom, where it was discovered that pupils were discontented with the playground conditions that hampered their play. They had noticed similar problems on farms and cited examples. Printed materials, charts, and pictures supplemented texts in a study of erosion. Contacting the Soil Conservation Office resulted in a survey of the campus. It was decided that with the help of lay people in the community, the erosion problem could be solved. It was hoped that the effectiveness of a given type of terrace could be demonstrated on the school campus and its use on farms in the community encouraged.

Out of this problem of soil erosion grew smaller related problems. The planning group pointed up the need for establishing a permanent lawn in addition to terracing. These two activities led to recognition of the need for repairing the schoolyard fence. Then came suggestions for a new flagpole and paved walks.

Community awareness was aroused through informal contacts and through discussions in community meetings. Soon the community was ready to become a part of the planning group. Laymen participated through meetings of the existing community organizations—Farm Bureau, Home Demonstration Club, and Parent-Teacher Association. The Farm Bureau decided to sponsor the campus improvement project. Other groups and individuals were asked to cooperate.

Committees secured tools and equipment. Teachers and pupils planned for their role, and, finally, a school day was selected for work on the campus. Because of the careful pre-planning, the day's activities proceeded smoothly. At the close of the afternoon, the campus had been ploughed, fertilized, terraced, and Bermuda grass roots harrowed under. The fence had been repaired. A space had been designated beside the fence for a wildlife border. Trees had been pruned, and some underbrush removed from the wooded area. The committee charged with the responsibility of sowing rye grass completed its task the following week.

Before this project was completed, a plan to improve the physical appearance of the building was under way. The Parent-Teacher Association and the County Board of Education were active participating agencies. Then came a landscaping project with three community groups participating. Once again the P.-T.A. took the initiative, this time in improving facilities and equipment. Later projects were the planting of a school forest, and the establishment of a wildlife border in cooperation with the County Soil Conservation Service.

Norristown School, September, 1950, and Norristown School, June, 1951, were two quite different places.

Outcomes

The supervisor's summary of outcomes tells the rest of the story:

1. School plant and grounds are improved.

2. School-community interest is increased. Records of the Parent-Teacher Association secretary showed an increase in enrollment from twelve to sixty-six paid members from the 1949-1950 to the 1950-1951 school year. The County Agent stated that the attendance at Farm Bureau meetings had tripled since the beginning of the 1950-1951 school term. A two-way trend developed in school and community meetings. Teachers and pupils became participants in community organizations, and parents became participants in school planning groups.

3. Pupil interest in school is strengthened. Teacher observations indicated increased interest for school work on the part of pupils. Increased pride in school housekeeping was exhibited.

4. Instruction is improved. Observations of the supervisor, guided by *The Ohio Teaching Record,* showed improvement in instruction. Teachers increased supplementary materials. Use of field trips increased. With the development of a school forest, a long-range study of forestry was begun. Teachers and pupils improved in teacher-pupil planning. Planned work experiences were added to classroom activities.

5. Community environment is improved. Results of a questionnaire and observations of teachers and lay people indicated that the program of resource-use education had encouraged farmers to make some improvement in soil conservation practices.

The supervisor's conclusions bring into focus school benefits that result when a school identifies itself positively within community structure:

1. The program of resource-use education in the Norristown School resulted in progress in the development of problem-solving techniques in teachers and pupils.

2. Resource-use education resulted in increased teacher skill in:

    a. Utilizing community resources.

    b. Pupil-teacher planning.

    c. Democratic group processes.

3. Resource-use education promoted professional growth of the teachers involved.

4. This program of resource-use education helped teachers adapt the curriculum to the needs of the pupils and the community.

Analysis of the Norristown Study

Let us now look back over the Norristown story and relate it to the preceding general discussions of school and community. Several significant observations are warranted:

1. Throughout the entire project the school operated *within,* not *apart from,* its community.

2. Although initial leadership came from a single person, the proc-

ess of planning moved through groups of teachers, pupils, and lay people, with new leadership being exercised as the need arose. Resulting action was cooperative, and moved smoothly to completion because of common objectives, common knowledge of specific jobs to be done, and individual assumption of appropriate responsibility.

3. A school-initiated project focused on school improvement needs. It was seen, however, that self-improvement by one agency of the community, supported by the community as a whole, inadvertently leads to total community improvement.

4. Throughout the entire project, opportunities for carry-over into the larger community were utilized to the utmost.

5. The school kept its own objectives clearly in mind and never lost sight of its instructional obligations.

6. General community improvement resulted from the following elements evident in the process:

a. Community resources were involved in ways appropriate to their potential contributions.

b. Appropriate lines of communication were identified, kept open, and used.

c. Identifiable carry-over values were clearly related to improving the quality of community living.

An illustration of the role a school may play in the life of another community is found in the following report on the Lithonia community in Georgia.

THE LITHONIA COMMUNITY

The main business of the Lithonia community, population 1,500, is centered in its granite quarries, which furnish employment for 400 families. A few residents commute daily to Atlanta. The school, embracing elementary and secondary levels, with its surrounding park and recreational facilities, constitutes the focal point for recreational activity and the forum for civic affairs.

Things just seem to happen in Lithonia. No single person—the superintendent of schools in DeKalb County, in which Lithonia is located, the school principal, the mayor, the president of the Exchange Club, or the editor of the Lithonia Journal—seems able to tell the whole story. The principal, a key figure in much that has occurred in recent years, speaks casually of a meeting with all church groups as though it happened every day in every American community. If you ask him how Lithonia got that way, he'll ask you to come and see for yourself, or will invite you to an Exchange Club barbecue scheduled for the following Friday night. This account suffers because you can't describe Lithonia. You can feel it and appreciate it, but describing it is like talking about, instead of playing, Chopin's *Polonaise*. In all that has occurred, the school has played a part— sometimes leading, sometimes following, always cooperating in whatever the faculty deemed worthwhile and worthy of support. Much has been written about the community school. Most of what has been said can be seen in Lithonia.

It is impossible to say that the school did this, the churches that, and the community council something else. Mostly, everybody did everything. And yet there always was a beginning and, usually, at the heart of it, a single person. Sometimes he was joined by several individuals, sometimes by a group or several groups. Often, he was leader in one activity and follower in several others all going on at the same time and in some way related to one another.

Here are some of the things that just seem to have happened in Lithonia:

1. The school grounds and surrounding wooded area have been turned into a park and community recreational center.

   a. A gala Field Day was sponsored by the P.-T.A. to draw attention to the need for improved playgrounds and to speed up action.

   b. The entire community cooperated in the erection of a stadium on the school site. Some funds were provided by the County Board of Education, but these were more than matched in cash and labor through local initiative.

   c. A gay white and blue swimming pool was constructed nearby, and is used not only by the school but also by the whole community.

   d. Picnic area, barbecue pits, tables, bandstand, running water, and lights were added to the park. A lake is included in the plans for developing the 76-acre park area.

2. The Exchange Club sponsored a dinner to stimulate interest in Boy Scout activities.

3. A Lithonia Elementary Rhythm Band was organized, most of the instruments being made by parents.

4. Agricultural activities have been stimulated through the DeKalb Chapter, Georgia Farm Bureau Federation, the Farmers' Mutual Exchange, and the Veterans' Agricultural Class.

5. Exchange Club, Lithonia Women's Club, P.-T.A., Masons, Order of the Eastern Star, and the churches joined hands in an informal community council.

6. A School Safety Patrol was organized to work with the Police Departments of DeKalb County and Lithonia.

7. Members of the elementary school faculty prepared a handbook for parents of pre-school children. It contained many suggestions for helping children prepare for school. The P.-T.A. arranged for printing and distributing the books.

8. The Lithonia Journal dedicated its American Education Week issue to the schools, and included thorough coverage of school personnel, organizations, special features, and an analysis of school-community relationships.

9. The football schedule for the season was printed on a card, the reverse side listing some interesting facts about the Lithonia school.

10. School and community raised funds and contributed labor for a complete renovation of the cafeteria. More than $5,000 worth of modern equipment was installed.

11. A Health Council was organized with representation from every civic organization in Lithonia.

12. Some years ago, the city purchased a home near the school for a teacherage in order to relieve the difficulty of finding satisfactory housing for the teachers. One year, it was occupied by twelve of the schoolteachers.

13. The community and the school worked hand-in-hand for school beautification. Three and one-half acres were graded and sodded. Parking area and cement walks were built, and grass was planted in front of the school.

14. For four years, school and community worked closely for educational betterment that resulted in accreditation (1952) by the Southern Association of Colleges and Secondary Schools.

15. The summer before extensive development of Georgia's Extended School Program (described earlier), Lithonia was selected as a "pilot school" for experimentation with a summer program.[26]

One could go on and on listing achievements and accomplishments of the Lithonia Community. Each new project suggests another. Overall plans are long-term and well coordinated, but they do not prevent the utilization of new ideas in their fulfillment. It might be said that Lithonia has a philosophy of community living. That philosophy, better than any detailed analysis of why things happened, explains Lithonia. Nowhere has that philosophy been fully captured in writing, but perhaps the school principal, speaking only for the school, has come closest to putting it into words:

One of the most important questions facing our schools today is, "Is our school doing what it should for the community?" . . . We believe that American schools exist only to help improve the quality of the people's living and to help each person achieve the happiest and most useful life of which he is capable. Each school must plan and direct its course of action to achieve these ends. . . .

We believe, too, that our school should help its people to recognize those things that need to be done to improve the quality of their own living and should equip them with ways of solving their problems, whenever and wherever they may arise. These may be problems of health, of learning a skill, of getting and keeping a job, or others brought about by changing conditions and needs.

We believe that the school's responsibility for improving the "quality of living" in the community requires it to help people to improve their homes, to spend their leisure time in worthwhile activities, to work together cooperatively on community life.[27]

THE CHALLENGE TO EDUCATIONAL LEADERSHIP[28]

The illustrations cited in this chapter show clearly that action for community improvement is no accident. It is the result of careful planning, of resource identification, of shared effort, and of shared

[26] See W. L. Colombo, "We Experimented With an Extended School Program," *Georgia Education Journal*, XLV (February, 1952), 10-11.

[27] W. L. Colombo, "What We Believe Is the Job of Our School," *The Lithonia Journal* (November 16, 1951).

[28] Only the general need for educational leadership is presented here. The specifics of that leadership are discussed later (see Chapter 13) and, to avoid duplication, are not developed at this point.

responsibility. It has also been shown clearly that leadership is a crucial factor. Leadership of an unusual sort is both the prime catalyst and the major coordinating influence—the kind of leadership that creates new leadership at every turn and step of the way. The illustrations cited reveal school personnel assuming this kind of leadership. Such has been the case in every section of America.

Instead of condemning our schools because they could not in a few years compensate our children for the many deficiencies of modern society, whether urban or rural, we should be proud of the amazing job most of our public schools have done in the face of these extraordinary social transformations. If I am now passionately and wholly devoted to improving and expanding public education, it is because I saw during the chaos of the war effort, that our public schools are the one and only institution we possess that can become the focus of a new, more integrated, more joyous community life. Wherever the over-crowded war centers achieved a semblance of order and ethical control, wherever the war worker's children received adequate protection, they were brought about through the devotion, intelligence, and organizing genius of the public school administrators.[29]

But much remains to be done. Education must be a unifying, not a leveling, force. Through the classrooms of the American public school pass persons of all races, colors, and creeds. All of these pupils possess prejudices of one kind or another when they enter the classroom. Most, if not all, possess these or other prejudices when they leave. Prejudice is learned. It is learned very early in life from others —from the peer group, from parents, from other adults. It is learned, too, from repeated frustration. Young people face almost constant frustration as they struggle with their developmental tasks, and as they come face to face with the conflicting expectations of home and school, church and peer group, the material and the spiritual. "These contradictions have resulted in unresolved tensions which all too frequently spill over in the form of hostility and aggression toward minority group members."[30] Misunderstanding, hostility, and prejudice produce boundary lines—between rich and poor, black and white, Jew and Gentile. Only the unification of culture can rub out the boundary lines. Only education *within a permissive framework* can bring about this unification.

If education is to be the great unifying influence, what must education do? How is misunderstanding to be changed to understanding,

[29] Agnes E. Meyer, "School-Community Relationships," *Phi Delta Kappan,* XXXIII (April, 1952), 380.

[30] George W. Denemark, "Schools versus Prejudice," *Educational Leadership,* VIII (December, 1950), 144.

hostility to friendliness, and prejudice to acceptance and respect, not merely to tolerance? Denemark suggests five major approaches to the problem:

1. The creation of a democratic atmosphere designed to reduce the personal insecurities and tensions of children.

2. The encouragement of broadening intergroup contacts in situations involving cooperation.

3. The provision of opportunities for enhanced emotional sensitization to other cultural groups.

4. The promotion of situations in which individuals may be exposed to the inconsistency or invalidity of some of their existing attitudes.

5. Strengthening the social supports of democratic behavior.[31]

THE KEY IDEAS

In conclusion, a few of the major ideas developed in this chapter are summarized here:

1. The American people have not expressed, in clear and forthright words, a uniform will for their elementary schools that may be translated into a unified program. Conflicting community beliefs, ideals, and groups mean that the school must not only keep its fingers on the many community pulsations, but also must interpret these pulsations in terms of curriculum and instruction.

2. The wide differences among communities, together with the increasing trend toward complex, impersonal, urban communities, make it exceedingly difficult for the elementary school to fulfil its dual function of serving and expressing its community.

3. To speak of the school's need to be a part of its community is to speak as though there were an alternative. The school is irrevocably a part of its community, whether it wishes to be or not. Likewise, to describe an American community apart from its elementary school is to present only a partial description of that community.

4. Three levels of school involvement in community affairs may be arbitrarily identified:

a. Comparative isolation.

b. Learnings oriented toward the realities of community living and societal affairs.

c. Deliberate participation as an agent for community betterment. Schools sometimes function at more than one of these levels. Many elementary schools operate in all three at various times and in different aspects of their programs.

31 Denemark, *op. cit.*, pp. 146-48.

5. In far too many communities, each agency operates as if it were alone, frequently duplicating services and facilities. An effective agency for coordinating the diverse activities of all is the community council.

6. The degree of success experienced in moving the school program out into the community—in camping education and summer services, for example—depends heavily upon the rapport already established with other agencies, as well as upon the effectiveness with which others are involved in planning, acting, and evaluating.

7. It is particularly important for the school to assume an active leadership role in instigating programs of community betterment where few other agencies exist, or when these other agencies are ill-equipped for the task.

8. It is particularly important for the elementary school to assume a shifting leading-following role of cooperation when a diverse array of forces is already working for community improvement.

9. Leadership is the common denominator wherever forward-looking action is taking place. School people are in strategic positions for providing needed leadership. Whether or not they provide it frequently makes the difference between static dislocated communities, and communities that are actively seeking to improve the quality of living for all their people.

BIBLIOGRAPHY

Association for Childhood Education International, "Working with Community Agencies," Childhood Education, XXVIII (March, 1952), 291-321.

_____, Partners in Education. Washington: The Association, 1950.

Association for Supervision and Curriculum Development, "Citizens Participate," Educational Leadership, IX (February, 1952), 274-315.

_____, "Educator: Teacher and Citizen," Educational Leadership, X (October, 1952), 2-42.

_____, School Camping. Washington: The Association, 1954.

Bernard, Jessie, American Community Behavior: An Analysis of Problems Confronting American Communities Today. New York: Dryden Press, 1949.

Campbell, Roald F. and John A. Ramseyer, The Dynamics of School-Community Relationships. New York: Allyn and Bacon, Inc., 1955.

Clarke, James Mitchell, Public School Camping. Stanford, California: Stanford University Press, 1951.

Cook, Lloyd Allen and Elaine Forsyth Cook, A Sociological Approach to Education. New York: McGraw-Hill Book Co., Inc., 1950.

Educational Policies Commission, Strengthening Community Life: Schools

Can Help. Washington: National Education Association and the American Association of School Administrators, 1954.

Hymes, James L., Jr., *Effective Home-School Relations.* Englewood Cliffs, N.J.: Prentice-Hall, Inc., 1953.

National Society for the Study of Education, *The Community School,* Fifty-second Yearbook, Part 2. Chicago: The University of Chicago Press, 1953.

Olsen, Edward G., ed., *School and Community Programs.* Englewood Cliffs, N.J.: Prentice-Hall, Inc., 1949.

——, ed., *School and Community,* 2nd ed. Englewood Cliffs, N.J.: Prentice-Hall, Inc., 1954.

Pierce, Truman M., Edward C. Merrill, L. Craig Wilson, and Ralph B. Kimbrough, *Community Leadership for Public Education.* Englewood Cliffs, N.J.: Prentice-Hall, Inc., 1955.

Sanders, Irwin T., *Making Good Communities Better.* Lexington, Kentucky: University of Kentucky Press, 1950.

Yeager, William A., *School-Community Relations.* New York: The Dryden Press, 1951.

THE OBJECTIVES
OF THE
ELEMENTARY
SCHOOL

4

ANY ATTEMPT TO USE EDUCATIONAL OBJECTIVES IN the improvement of educational programs for children presents two kinds of problems to teachers and school staffs. One problem is how to make more effective use of our present objectives to give more significant direction to the learning activities of children in school. The other, and perhaps more fundamental, problem is how to obtain better educational objectives than the ones we now have, to provide this direction. These problems go hand in hand and their solution is vitally important.

In this book the word *objective* is used as a convenient term for what is usually meant by the expressions *aims, ends, goals,* and *purposes.* Sometimes a distinction is made between *aims* or *ends* as the general objectives of education, and *goals* as the immediate objectives of the learner or class. Some have distinguished between teacher *objectives* and pupil *purposes.* Actually, the sense and instructional use are the same for all these terms. Here, therefore, all of these terms will be used interchangeably to mean the educational value to be achieved—with some preference being given to the word *objective.*

Objectives of Elementary Education

The basic responsibility of the elementary school, as conceived by the citizens of this country, is to help young children become more effective members of our American democracy. The watchword of the elementary school is good citizenship for young children, rather than preparation for college or for some particular vocation. An appreciation of this basic responsibility is necessary before some of the differences between the programs of secondary schools and elementary schools can be understood.

Statements of general objectives for elementary education are definitions of the essential qualities, or of the important areas of experience necessary to develop good citizenship in young children.

One of the early definitions of good citizenship, often quoted, was the statement of the Commission on the Reorganization of Secondary Education.[1] This statement emphasized the attitude that "good" education should make some significant difference in the lives of people in the present as well as in the future. Although directed toward *secondary* education, and the "educated adult," the Cardinal Principles of Secondary Education have affected the elementary school and its practices as much as, if not more than, those of the secondary school. The emphasis the Commission put on health, worthy home membership, vocational efficiency, worthy use of leisure, ethical character, and good citizenship was new in general education, and broadened the conception of the educational task of the common school.

Some of the weaknesses of the statement the Commission made are: 1) the areas of experience indicated are important in any social order, and thus do not adequately define what good citizenship should mean in a democracy; 2) it is plagued by overlapping concepts—"good citizenship," for example, includes all the others; 3) the use of the statement depends on how the value words "fundamental,"

[1] U. S. Bureau of Education, *Cardinal Principles of Secondary Education,* Bulletin No. 38, 1918.

"worthy," "good," and "ethical," are defined; and 4) regarding vocational efficiency as a major objective for elementary and secondary schools has no clear-cut relationship to the social and economic responsibilities of young children and adolescents. The Cardinal Principles of Secondary Education share their weaknesses with many other similar statements.

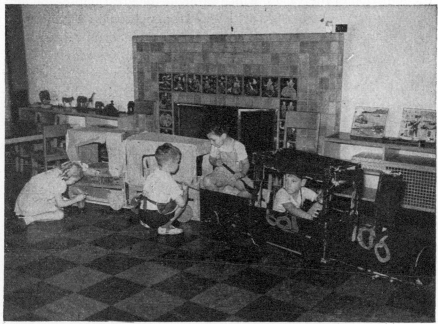

University of Wisconsin Summer Laboratory School

WE LEARN TO LIVE AND WORK TOGETHER

An important adaptation of the Cardinal Principles of Secondary Education was made by a Committee for Elementary Education working under the direction of the State Department of Education of New York. This adaptation has been used by many school systems over the country in addition to New York's, to define what they want their elementary schools to accomplish. This committee said that the function of the public elementary school is to help every child: 1) understand and practice desirable social relationships; 2) discover and develop his own desirable individual aptitudes; 3) cultivate the habit of critical thinking; 4) appreciate and desire worthwhile activities; 5) gain command of common integrated knowledge and skills; and 6) develop a sound body and normal mental attitudes.[2]

2 Committee for Elementary Education, *Cardinal Objectives in Elementary Education—A Third Report,* University of the State of New York Press, 1932, pp. 9-16.

This definition of characteristics important for good citizenship is useful for elementary schools because of its emphasis on the important abilities and processes of personal and social development, and because it pays less attention to worthy home membership and vocational efficiency. It shares with Seven Cardinal Principles many of the weaknesses indicated previously.

The period of the 1930's, which brought the great depression and the preparatory phases of World War II. also brought a realization that educational programs could not ignore their social responsibilities. Under the threat of autocracy and Fascism, the general objectives of the elementary and the secondary school were reconsidered to determine what good citizenship in a democracy should mean and the Educational Policies Commission was created by the National Education Association to help decide this question of the characteristics that an educated adult in a democracy ought to have. The Commission considered four aspects of an adult's citizenship: 1) the person himself; 2) his relationship to others in home and community; 3) the creation and use of material wealth; and 4) his socio-civic activities. The major categories under which specific objectives were listed were therefore: 1) self-realization; 2) human relationships; 3) economic efficiency; and 4) civic responsibility.

This attempt to describe the qualities of good citizenship in a democracy has several advantages over previous definitions: 1) it consistently focuses its attention on the "educated citizen" as an object of major attention in education; 2) it emphasizes important supplementary areas of development in good democratic citizenship; 3) it defines what these areas include, with some consistency of definition as to level and degree of inclusiveness; and 4) it accounts for, and points up, the reciprocals between the development of the individual and his social responsibilities. This statement shares with previous statements certain weaknesses: 1) it centers on the educated adult— the problem of how to help the young child develop to this point still remains; 2) many of the objectives are not appropriate for young children—e.g., "The educated person protects his own health and that of his dependents . . . is skilled in homemaking . . . succeeds in his chosen vocation," etc; 3) the objectives are not related to usual areas of instruction in the elementary school, and applications to programs of learning and instruction are not easily made. This last weakness, however, merely points up the general problem of how to use general statements of objectives to influence education programs.[3]

The most recent attempt to state the general objectives of the elementary school was made by the Mid-Century Committee on Outcomes in Elementary Education.[4] The purpose of this Committee was to formulate an authoritative list of objectives which would be so generally applicable that most, if not all, schools would accept the statement as their over-all definition of purpose. This would naturally, facilitate the development of appropriate means by which to evaluate the educational outcomes of such programs. After much discussion and advice, the Committee identified the following curriculum areas as important: 1) physical development, health, body care; 2) individual social and emotional development; 3) ethical behavior, standards, values; 4) social relations; 5) the social world; 6) the physical world; 7) esthetic development; 8) communication; and 9) quantitative relationships. Each of these areas is to be considered in relation to the a) knowledge and understanding; b) skills and competencies; c) attitudes and interests; and d) action patterns appropriate to children at the third, sixth, and ninth grade levels.

This Committee made a valiant effort to grasp the over-all relationship that general statements of objectives have to the entire elementary school program. It emphasized the importance of each of the nine curriculum areas at every grade or age level, and the continuity of the appropriate knowledges, skills, attitudes, and action patterns over the entire period of elementary education. Unfortunately, the Committee did not profit from the experience of previous committees struggling with this same problem. The list of nine curriculum areas lacks any unifying characteristic, and the items become mixed up with each other when any attempt is made to use them either as areas of the curriculum, or as defined objectives. The statement of goals indicates that important knowledges, skills, attitudes, and action patterns should be developed in the nine curriculum areas; but it still does not tell what they are, or why they are important. Emphasis on the individual in relation to the nature of the society in which he exists,

3 Educational Policies Commission, *The Purposes of Education in American Democracy*, (N.E.A., 1938).

4 This committee was initiated and sponsored by Russell Sage Foundation, Educational Testing Service, the United States Office of Education, and the Department of Elementary School Principals of the National Education Association. Their report is found in Nolan C. Kearney, *Elementary School Objectives*, (New York: Russell Sage Foundation, 1953), p. 189 ff.

MAKING THE SPIRITUAL COME TO LIFE

while present, is far less important than in previous statements, and thus the basic orientation is one which returns to the old subject fields.

Problems of Over-all Statements of Objectives

The statements of objectives just discussed are commonly used as definitions of the ultimate purpose of programs of elementary and secondary education *i.e.*, the development of good citizenship in a democracy. The basic referent for these definitions is the kind of person the educational program ought to try to produce—the educated citizen—and not the subject areas into which the educational programs of most schools are divided. These subject divisions are not derived from analyses of what a good citizen in a democracy needs to know and to be able to do; they are derived from what it is important to know and to be able to do in order to understand and use the subject matter of any given field of knowledge. Because of this difference in basic orientations, most teachers see very little relationship between what they do with children in teaching reading, science, and arithmetic, and the general statements of objectives of elementary education.

One important way of resolving this dilemma is to define the over-all objectives of an elementary school solely in terms of the important educational processes necessary in all subject fields, and in all learning experiences, irrespective of level.

Examples of the common process areas which may be used as statements for the whole program of general education, as well as for the elementary school, are: 1) the process objectives having to do with the use of the arts of language for the purpose of effective communication; 2) those having to do with techniques and procedures of effective thinking; 3) those having to do with developing effective human relations; and 4) those having to do with the effective selection and use of learning resources.

The La Grange, Illinois elementary schools developed their statements of objectives in this way. The curriculum of the school is organized around broad subject fields. The general statement of objectives for La Grange's total elementary program is as follows:

STATEMENT OF OBJECTIVES[5]

Our philosophy of education emphasizes a clear understanding of the interests, characteristics, abilities, and needs of the individual, the way he learns, and the kind of society in which he lives. The function of the school is to encourage and assist each child in developing his individual talents. The school should provide opportunities for each child to grow in social usefulness to the end that he will become a responsible, participating member of the society in which he lives.

The child moves toward this goal by living through experiences which provide for growth in:

I. *Mental and physical health.*

The following functions of the teacher serve to define this objective:
1. Fosters a feeling of *security* within the child through her complete acceptance of him.
2. Helps the child to gain a feeling of *adequacy* by helping him develop skills which will give him status with peers, status academically, status socially, and status physically.
3. Provides *freedom* for the child to work on developmental tasks and provides *guidance* when necessary.
4. Provides a safe and healthy physical *environment* for the child.
5. Aims to develop in the child *habits* and *attitudes,* and provides *information* for physical health and safety.
6. Provides for physical *activities* conducive to good health and good use of leisure time.
7. Works with the home and other agencies in the community to solve health and safety problems of the child.

5 La Grange Elementary Schools, "Objectives of the Elementary Schools of La Grange," Mimeographed statement, District No. 7 La Grange, Illinois, 1948.

II. *Proficiency in the use of the tools and resources of learning.*

The following functions of the teacher serve to define this objective:

1. Aims to insure continued growth in the *tools* of learning such as reading, computation, scientific method, etc.
2. Aims to develop in the child increasing *application of these tools* to problems which he faces.
3. Aims to help the child learn to use increasingly the *resources* of the school and community such as people, printed matter, audio-visual aids, community activities, etc., in solving his problems.

III. *Ability to do critical thinking.*

(Definition of critical thinking, developed by the staff: "Critical thinking is a process that involves the recognition of a problem, the acquisition and selection of data necessary to the solution of the problem, and development and application of a common set of criteria for evaluating the solution, for putting the solution into action, and for testing the solution.")[6]

The following functions of the teacher serve to define this objective:

1. Aims to provide a *climate* which is conducive to identifying and defining problems. This climate involves the quality of the leadership and the interpersonal relationships.
2. Aims to develop in the child skill in *selecting* problems which are significant. A problem is significant when the solution is a felt need of the learner and when the solution leads to achievement of school objectives.
3. Aims to develop in the child skill in *formulating hypotheses and gathering data* appropriate to the testing of these hypotheses.
4. Aims to develop in the child skill in *selecting criteria for evaluating* the adequacy of the solution.

IV. *Responsibility as a member of a democratic society.*

(Numbers 4 and 5 of the original statement combined.)

The following functions of the teacher serve to define this objective:

1. Makes himself *a part of the group* in spirit, easily *accessible* to all, accepting and working within its standards of achievements and code of behavior.
2. Cooperatively discusses and defines *goals* and *means* for achieving those goals, encouraging and even suggesting *alternative plans.*
3. Encourages individual and group *reactions, initiative, leadership,* and the relinquishing of individual freedoms to achieve group goals.
4. Insures that the group has before it a *perspective of the activity,* including an overview of the steps involved and a time perspective of the activity.
5. Insures freedom of group members to *choose* their own *groups* and leaders and choose their own *tasks* with the group plans, offering guidance when necessary.
6. Depends for his prestige upon the value of his *contributions* to the growth of the group and encourages action on the basis of *logic* or scientific evidence rather than on an authority of position or person.
7. *Shares responsibility for evaluation* of individual and group efforts with

[6] *Ibid.*

the persons concerned, and evaluates more frequently on the basis of plans and performance to *realize group goals* than on the basis of plans and performance to realize individual goals.

8. *Uses no person* as a means to attain ends not their own and *favors no person* more than others because of differences.

Similar definitions were made by the La Grange staff for the headings V. "Appreciation for aesthetic contributions toward the enrichment of life," VI. "Sensitivity to ethical and spiritual values," and VII. "Awareness of socio-economic relationships and responsibilities."

These process objectives have been defined in terms of what a teacher could do with children in order to accomplish them, rather than in terms of children's behavior, since teachers are the major educational agents and will use this statement to influence the educational experience of children.

More important, however, in determining the nature of the statement of general objectives for the elementary school, is the character of the basic orientation of the curriculum. As has been pointed out, one common referent has been the various subject fields into which man's knowledge can be categorized and organized. It is possible to consider two others: 1) the nature of the society and its implications for the child's learning and development; and 2) the nature of the child himself and his continuing experience.

Statements of Objectives in Educational Programs Having a Basic Social Orientation

The traditional division of the educational program of the elementary school into subject areas is not the only way to define statements of over-all objectives. It is possible to develop an educational program on the basis of social experience, rather than on subject fields. Instead of statements based on the characteristics of the educated adult, the over-all orientation is then in terms of "persistent problems of living" or "major functions of social life" or "basic areas of living." In these areas of social living, individual and social needs are meaningfully resolved, and are not considered as opposing and essentially conflicting demands. With this approach, too, a significant meaning can be given to democratic living as an essential part of all the learning experiences the child has in school, rather than something reserved for the assembly programs, halls and washrooms, and parent and teacher nights. Subject matters and intellectual skills are resources to be utilized in the solution of important social problems—important both in the social experience of the child and in the more general social experience of adults. Subject matters are not, however, used as a basis for organizing the learning activities of children, and traditional subject headings are not used to divide up the time schedule of the school day.

The Virginia state program represents one of the earliest attempts to develop a curriculum with this basically social orientation (1930); this program organized the educational experience of the school[7] around eleven major functions of social life. These functions are: 1) protection and conservation of life, property, and natural resources; 2) production of goods and services, and the distribution of the returns of production; 3) consumption of goods and services; 4) communication and transportation of goods and people; 5) recreation; 6) expression of aesthetic impulses; 7) expression of religious impulses; 8) education; 9) extension of freedom; 10) integration of the individual; 11) exploration.

The 1938 Georgia state program used "persistent problems of living" as its basis.[8] These persistent problems are similar to the above "functions of social living."

A more recent use of social functions to give a social perspective to educational programs is found in the Santa Barbara, California, statement.[9]

Stratemeyer and others, in the plan developed for the Horace Mann–Lincoln Institute of School Experimentation, used the concept of persistent life situations as one of the important referents for planning and developing an educational program. Stratemeyer and her associates identified three kinds of persistent life situations calling for: 1) growth in health, intellectual power, moral choice, aesthetic expression, and appreciation; 2) growth in social participation—person to person relationship, group membership, intergroup member-

7 The reader interested in studying the development of this program should read the *State of Virginia Courses of Study for the Elementary School* (Richmond: State Board of Education, 1934 and 1942).

8 The 1938 Georgia state course of study provides background material for understanding how these persistent problems were used to define the scope and continuity of an educational program over the period of the common school. A scope and sequence chart is helpful in giving this perspective. The new 1954 Bulletin returns to a subject matter orientation.

9 *Santa Barbara County Curriculum Guide for Teaching in Elementary Schools*, Vol. II (Santa Barbara: The Shauer Printing Studio, Inc., 1940), p. 20. Recent changes in the Santa Barbara schools redirected this development back into the traditional subject framework. This has been true of many attempts to improve educational programs in the past few years.

ship; and 3) growth in ability to deal with environmental factors and forces—natural phenomena, technological resources, economic-social-political structures and forces. These three kinds of persistent life situations appear in five major aspects of human life: 1) in the home—as a member of the family; 2) in the community—as a participant in civic and social activities; 3) in work—as a member of an occupational group; 4) in leisure time; and 5) in spiritual activities.[10]

A comparison of the Cardinal Principles of Elementary Education with these statements of social functions will show that the statements merely develop further the social emphasis in education which came to the fore at the turn of the century. The comparison will also point up the logical dilemma every staff finds itself in when it tries to reconcile statements of persistent life situations with present school programs organized on the basis of subject areas.

Any emphasis on the school's becoming an integral part of its community, as was pointed out in the previous chapter, will force the staff to consider 1) the personal-social problems of living in that community as possible organizing centers of its curriculum; 2) the democratization of social processes of living and working; 3) a broader selection and use of personal and physical educational resources; 4) the more effective leadership of the school, in the broader cooperative development of the educational program of the community; and 5) the participation and use of school staff and the physical resources of the school in community enterprises. This effort to become community centered, if it ever goes beyond allowing the community to use the physical plant in order to build good public relations, will push the school toward a more effective social orientation of its program, which should be reflected in appropriate statements of the social processes and areas of living which will serve as the basis for the development of the educational program of the school.

Statements of Objectives in Programs Basically Oriented to the Individual

The child and his needs have long been an important referent for selecting the learning activities of children in programs of elementary education, in nursery, kindergarten, and primary grades. The problem here is not one of either the child, the subject field, or aspects of social living being the most important consideration in developing

10 F. B. Stratemeyer, H. L. Forkner, M. G. McKim, *Developing a Curriculum for Modern Living* (New York: Bureau of Publications, Teachers College, Columbia University, 1947).

adequate programs of education for children; the question is which of the three will serve as the *initial* focus in a program. It makes a difference which you *start* with in terms of defining the objectives; but in all programs, the child, the nature of social living, and the importance of man's experience and knowledge will undoubtedly be considered at appropriate points.

When the child and his emerging needs are regarded as the important initial orientation of the program, no formal over-all statements of objectives are made. Instead, the staff of a school spend much time clarifying their understanding about the nature of desirable learning and desirable educational experiences. Attention is focused on what each child needs to help him identify, define, and deal with his personal-social problems on ascending levels of maturity and social participation. In staff discussion, time is spent exploring how the teacher and a group of children can identify and define their significant needs as a basis for planning and developing an adequately conceived pro-

Morgandale School, Milwaukee, Wisconsin

LEARNING IS NOT LIMITED TO THE FOUR WALLS OF THE CLASSROOM

gram of educational experiences. These felt needs of children become the basis for determining the learning experiences of children, and for identifying the understandings, abilities, and appreciations used in dealing with these needs in the present and in the future. In this sense, the instructional objectives of children emerge from an examination of their experience, and are defined in terms of the understandings, abilities, and attitudes necessary to deal with them adequately. The objectives are always being examined, tested, and reformulated on the basis of their effectiveness in dealing with the continuing experience of the child. For this reason, they have been frequently called *outcomes,* rather than aims or objectives.

Four important ideas underlie this approach to the definition of educational objectives: 1) the important understandings, abilities, and attitudes of an educational program cannot be predicted far in advance; instead they must emerge from the critical examination and evaluation of one's experience; 2) *basic* or *essential* understandings, abilities, and appreciations must, *by definition,* be found in ongoing experiences of children and youth; the only problem is to learn how to discover and use them; 3) the perceived concern or, "felt needs," *of the learner* are the only possible organizing forces which have meaning and significance for him, and from which important educational objectives can be derived; and 4) the perceived concerns of a group of children, if developed adequately, will necessarily cut across all the important problems and concerns of a society. What meaning does a social problem have apart from the social experiences of people? *Statements of Children's Needs.* The survey of the statements of needs of children seems to indicate:

1. In addition to basic physiological needs, all statements seem to emphasize the child's fundamental need for recognition and affection; or, in more familiar language, his need to be liked and to succeed. (Note the similarity to the first tenet of the democratic way of life— confidence in one's essential worth.)

2. A knowledge of the child's needs and their relative importance to him can never be gained from reading a list, but only from observation. The teacher or parent must observe a child to discover the nature of his needs and the kind of experiences necessary to insure his fullest satisfaction. The child himself, of course, is in the best position to be an active responsible agent in the meeting of his needs.

3. Schools have tended to emphasize the intellectual and physical needs of the child, and to ignore the emotional and social.

4. The determination of the child's needs and satisfactions is a

continuous process; to forget the interrelationship and interdependence of these needs with the child and his environment is to over-
emphasize one necessary element of experience at the expense of
the others.[11]

Developmental Tasks As Objectives

The recognition of the roles that a maturing physiological organism, a demanding social environment, and an emerging purposive
self play in determining the "needs" of a developing individual
caused Havighurst, Tryon, and others of the Chicago group to use
the term "developmental tasks" to describe the things the child has to
meet and solve in some way in order to grow up.[12] In this sense, these
"tasks" serve as definitions of things the elementary school must consider in its effort *to contribute* to the child's immediate and ultimate
well-being.

Many of the developmental tasks are common to more than one
period of the child's life; for instance, developing a concept of self,
learning sex roles, learning to get along with age mates, achieving
independence from parents and adults, developing bases for security,
developing intellectual skills and techniques of communication, and
broadening and deepening intellectual concepts. While the general
task remains relatively constant, the specific manifestations of these
general developmental tasks and the periods of their critical importance to the child vary widely during the different growth periods of
his life.

An examination of these developmental tasks of childhood and
youth reveals that they extend and emphasize previous lists of social
and integrative needs of human beings. Also, it is evident that these
developmental tasks do not begin to cover everything a young person

---

[11] A frequent distinction is made between individual and social needs. This distinction may sometimes be made in a discussion of the *origins* of needs; but in any consideration of their *nature,* it is obvious that all needs are both personal and social.
Thus, many authors use the term *personal-social needs.*

It is true also that "needs" can be considered as shortages or deficiencies. From this
point of view anything the school or teacher wants for children and which they do not
have to the degree desired is a need. In this sense, all objectives are needs. There is
some value, however, in restricting attention to the needs growing out of the tension
in the personal-social experiences of children, which can be resolved through the child's
being an active agent in their resolution.

[12] See for example, Robert Havighurst, *Developmental Tasks* (Chicago: University of
Chicago Press, 1949. Reprinted by Longmans, Green, and Co., 1950); Caroline Tryon,
Mental Hygiene and Education, (A.S.C.D. Yearbook, 1950); Stephen Corey and Virgil
Herrick, *The Developmental Tasks of Children and Young People in "Youth, Communi-
cation and Libraries,"* Frances Henne, Alice Brooks, Ruth Ersted, eds. (Chicago: Ameri-
can Library Association, 1949), pp. 3-13.

must learn. The lists can be useful in developing adequate programs of education in elementary schools, as they indicate situations which every boy and girl must be able to meet and handle in some way in order to grow up.[13]

The Functions of Objectives

Objectives do not solve all the problems of developing significant educational programs for children, but they do have some very definite jobs to perform.

Objectives Define the Direction of Educational Development. Objectives, as has been indicated, are important value statements about what the learner is trying to accomplish or what the educational program is trying to achieve. Their first important function, therefore, is to serve as a statement of the values which will distinguish good educational behavior from bad. Objectives, in this sense, define the nature of the educational maturities that children, teachers, parents, and society are striving to achieve, and differentiate between learning, *per se,* and learning which results in education. Learning which results in development related to, or moving toward, educational objectives constitutes education. Learning which results in development opposed to, or moving away from, educational objectives constitutes mis-education. Objectives therefore define direction; they are not ends in themselves. Objectives are not consumed in the process of learning but illuminate learning. Objectives are not facts to be mastered, but values whose characteristics can always be incorporated into the behavior of children to some degree. Objectives cannot become the specific learning tasks of the classroom, but emerge from classroom activities as valued learning products.

Objectives Help Select Desirable Learning Experiences. A second function of objectives is to serve as the premise upon which children and teachers select desirable learning experiences.

This is not to say that a child or a teacher always knows precisely the specific goals being achieved in any learning enterprise, or that all learning activities are selected on the basis of knowing these objectives in advance. At times, the teacher who has definite objectives in mind will select and limit the learning experiences accordingly. At other times, a trip to the firehouse may be examined carefully to see

13 The reader who wishes to see an application of the concept of developmental tasks to an educational program should read "Guides to Curriculum Building," Junior High School Level, Wisconsin Cooperative Educational Planning Program, Problems Approach Bulletin No. 2, Curriculum Bulletin No. 12, January, 1950, Chapter II.

what information, understanding, abilities, and attitudes ought to be derived from this experience in order to exploit its educational potential to the fullest and to help children to deal more effectively with similar situations in the future. What is important is first, that whether objectives are known in advance or are seen more clearly as a given learning experience develops, both children and teachers must come to some agreement about what is being accomplished; and second, that the relationship between the things children do and these purposes be clearly established in the children's minds.

While objectives are an extremely important tool for teachers and children to use in selecting things they must do to accomplish desired goals, it should be recognized that no one, especially not teachers and administrators working with elementary school children, should conceive of them as being the *only* basis for determining learning activities of a desirable educational program. Other, perhaps equally important bases for selecting learning activities are: 1) the plan for ordering or arranging the continuity or sequence of learning over a day, week, school year, or series of grades; 2) the children, their experiences, speeds of development, and ways of learning; and 3) the educational resources of the teacher, school, and community. The use of these screens for selecting learning activities will be discussed in the chapters on curriculum and the various instructional areas.

Using a list of objectives as one of the important definers of the necessary scope of an educational program or learning experience leads to a number of directives for teaching and evaluation in the elementary school.

First: a community, a staff of a school, or a teacher with children should always worry about whether an educational program includes all of the significant and essential elements of a good education. The statement of objectives is one specific answer to this problem at any particular time, and should be an honest, realistic definition of what that program or learning experience is actually trying to achieve.

Second: if a statement of objectives is a definition of the number of important aspects of a good learning experience or educational program, then any appraisal or evaluation of that program should consider *all* of these aspects when judging the adequacy of that program. Too often an elementary school is judged adequate or inadequate solely on the basis of its concern or lack of concern for phonics, spelling, or handwriting, without any consideration given to other and more important aspects of an adequate educational program.

Third: every teacher should capitalize on the fact that any learning experience developed with a group of children will always contribute to more than *one* objective. Efficiency in teaching often means exploiting to the fullest the objective-developing potential of a limited number of experiences. This has important implications for teaching and curriculum development.

Fourth: every teacher should recognize that the educational scope of any learning experience will include possibilities for the development of facts, concepts, or understandings (content); important skills and abilities (processes); and attitudes (values). She should exploit the experience to develop the potential of all three.

Fifth: every teacher should realize that while objectives are one important definition of scope, there are other significant definers of scope, too—the nature of the experience, problem, topic, or object being considered; and the capacity of a child to perceive and hold in some kind of relationship a number of different things.

Objectives Help Define the Emphasis to Be Made in an Educational Program. A statement of the objectives for an educational program may define the necessary components of an adequate educational program, but still not indicate the nature of the emphasis which will give proper balance and focus to the program of instruction. In general, the same basic objectives give direction to all levels of the educational program of the elementary school. Still, the kindergarten and primary grades emphasize the initial developments of languages, motor behavior, number concepts, and the pupil's understanding of himself and his immediate expanding social and physical environment more than do the middle and upper grades. Similarly, the work of the middle grades stresses the study and development of geographic and political areas and the experiences of people removed from the child's immediate existence in time, space, and culture. The authors feel that no listing of objectives can indicate adequately the nature of the emphasis of an educational program at a particular time. Further, it is likely that the nature of the proper emphasis in a list of objectives is not determined by studying the objectives, but by studying children and their emerging patterns of development in particular social settings.

Objectives Form One of the Major Bases for Evaluation. Without a knowledge of the objectives of an educational program, it is impossible to judge the program's adequacy. All evaluations of human behavior are defined in terms of what it is considered important to achieve. Objectives provide a definition, and thus constitute a major basis for the appraisal of the educational development of children.

Therefore, it is important for communities, teachers, and children to have available a statement of objectives which will give direction to any appraisal of the value of the educational experiences children have in school.

If objectives are to be effective in helping children and teachers evaluate learning experiences, the objective must be defined in terms of behavior that characterizes their achievement. Appropriate appraisal instruments, rating schemes, inventories, and so forth, may be developed from objectives behaviorially defined. Without well-defined objectives and appropriate measurements, programs can only be operated on expediency and on the basis of judgments whose educational bases are unknown.

The Elementary School and Its Purposes

We have examined various statements of educational purpose and considered briefly the functions objectives perform. We come now to a broad outline of the American elementary school.

Good Citizenship Is Our Major Responsibility. The elementary school is conceived as having a major obligation to help children become increasingly competent to meet and deal with the problems of growing up to be constructive, participating members of our society. The emphasis is on helping a child meet his obligations as a member of his home, peer group, community, school, church, state, nation, and world in so far as these obligations are meaningful and important for a six, seven, eight, nine, ten, eleven, twelve year old. The perspective includes both the immediate and the possible future; but there is no intention of trying to produce a miniature adult or to recreate the adult world for a seven year old. The educational program is planned so that seven year olds grow into eight year olds, and eight year olds into nine year olds on their own terms, and thus the foundations for meeting the problems of a ten year old are continually established. The idea is that when an individual is twenty-one years old, he will be able to meet his problems efficiently and adequately because of experience and education of the previous twenty years.

Definitions of Objectives Are Definitions of Good Citizenship. The statements of objectives of the elementary school have to be considered as defining the knowledge, abilities, and qualities of good citizens in the American democracy. We have seen that the "good citizen" was defined as the educated adult, in terms of abilities he must have to meet his responsibilities as a citizen adequately.

These statements are valuable; but to be educationally useful, they will have to be defined further in terms of what they mean for the behavior of children and youth attending the elementary schools of America. At present, how this should be done has not been satisfactorily resolved. Either the over-all definitions of good citizenship have to be revised to correspond more to the actual instructional program of the elementary school; or the instructional program should be reexamined and changed to correspond more to our stated objectives. It is the position of this book that the second alternative will lead to greater progress and to more significant educational programs.

The Understandings of Good Citizenship

The understandings of good citizenship are those which will aid the individual to understand himself, his human relationships, and his physical and biological world. Much effort has been spent trying to identify the areas of experience in which important understandings are found. Our subject fields represent one such an attempt to categorize and preserve the important generalizations man has made regarding his experience.

In this effort to deal with important understandings, the emphasis is on broad general ideas and concepts rather than on factual minutiae of day to day experience: *e.g.*, "man is interdependent" rather than "we can buy bread at the corner grocery store"; "air occupies space, has weight, and can exert force," rather than "the wind blew down Farmer Jones' barn"; "a number can be a statement of quantity or a statement of relationship," rather than "$2 + 3 = 5$, or $5 = 10/2$."

All concepts of "good citizenship," and similarly all concepts of a desirable program of education for elementary school children agree on the importance of "knowing." The major problem is, what should the pupil know, and how can his areas of understanding be selected and developed best?

At present, the various subject fields of the elementary school curriculum furnish the most widely used definition of these areas. Social-centered and individual-centered curricula however, assume that many of these understandings of the future are not *now* known, and that the learner should constantly study his personal-social problems in order to discover and develop generalizations useful for dealing with them now and in the future.

Regardless of how a school may select important understandings or teach them, all teachers and school programs should pay serious and continuous attention to their selection and adequate development.

The Abilities of Good Citizenship

Important as the understandings of "good citizenship" are, the abilities of "good citizenship" are perhaps even more significant. Abilities and skills carry the products of one educational experience over to the next, and are not restricted by problem or subject matter. An examination of various statements of objectives will reveal how important these common processes or abilities are in any educational program.

In general, most of these abilities important in "good citizenship" can be put under four headings:

1. The abilities important for effective communication. All programs of elementary education are concerned about the adequate, continuous development of the child's ability to read, write, speak, and listen.

2. The abilities important for effective thinking. Strange as it may seem, the emphasis many programs put on information *per se* has not always meant a corresponding emphasis on intellectual processes important in gathering, assessing, generalizing, and applying such information. The traditional conception of the young child as being unable to think is perhaps responsible; also the old belief that calling words, learning letters, forming syllables, and memorizing combinations had to be done before the child could use his skills in thinking and action. Much more useful and accurate is the idea that the child can understand, does think, and will use the products of his living and learning in situations that have meaning and significance to him in all areas and on all levels of the elementary school program.

The processes involved in clarifying understandings, generalizing on experience, and predicting future constructive actions are essential to any adequate program of elementary education.

3. The abilities important for living effectively with oneself and with other people. The abilities involved in a child's being able to see who he is and where he is going, both as an individual and as a member of his various groups, are important abilities to teach in a program of elementary education. How to get along with his peers and adults, how to work effectively with others, how to deal with the problems of human relations—these abilities lie close to the heart of "good citizenship," and are emphasized in all the major statements of objectives. Little conscious attention, however, is paid to this important process area in most elementary school programs. If it is important to pay direct attention to learning to read, is it not even more

important to pay direct and continuous attention to learning how to live more effectively with one's self and with other people?

4. The abilities and skills associated with identifying, selecting, and using effectively human and material resources for learning and development. It has been said that America is embarrassed by material

Beloit Public Schools, Beloit, Wisconsin

COMING TO UNDERSTAND THE MEANINGS OF THE HOLIDAYS

and personal wealth, and is impoverished by her inability to utilize her resources effectively. Most individuals, as well, lack skill in identifying and using available resources. Similarly, many children cannot "help themselves," cannot use their resources to deal with problems of living and learning.

The elementary school program should consider that developing abilities in this area is a necessary and continuing aspect of the education of children in the elementary school.

It is obvious that all four of these groups of abilities are a part of all teaching in all areas at all levels. They are the important common denominators of the educational experiences children have in school. The effectiveness of educational programs would be increased tremendously if serious general attention were paid to the achievement of these process objectives with all children.

The Attitudes of Good Citizenship

In addition to understandings and abilities, a good education must concern itself with the nature of the effect that education has on the individual, and with the way in which his values and attitudes are created and influenced. Attitudes are always mentioned in statements of objectives, and all programs of education for children claim to develop attitudes. This is true—any kind of an experience to which the learner consciously responds, develops and influences some kind of attitude. The problem is, what attitudes are most important and how can they be developed most effectively?

Examination of various statements of objectives indicates that the following attitudes are important in giving direction to programs of elementary education. Elementary school programs should help develop:

A disposition on the part of children and adults to accept people as essentially worthwhile, to expect differences of many kinds, and to consider them natural and enriching.

The development of confidence on the part of children that they can learn, that things can be improved, that ideas and abilities will make a significant difference in dealing with personal and social problems.

An appreciation of the importance and value of man's past experience for dealing with the present and the future.

A respect for the rules and values by which men live, and for the ways in which these rules and values can be changed and improved.

Faith in the future and in man's ability to improve his own welfare.

A disposition to see that the consequence of learning is more effective living and action.

Even this brief résumé of some of the attitudes to be developed in programs of elementary education indicates their importance in giving direction and meaning to the experiences children have in school.

IN RETROSPECT

The elementary schools of America are seen by the adults and parents of a community as instruments for the effective individual and social development of children in our society.

The general statements of educational objectives define what we want development to be.

Definitions of the nature of good citizenship for children may be made by emphasizing basic understandings, abilities, and attitudes; or by indicating persisting common social functions; or by revealing emergent needs or developmental tasks of children. The definition depends upon what is taken as the initial basic referent.

Objectives serve as bases for determining the direction of educational development, for selecting desirable learning experiences for children, for determining the scope of learning, and for the appraisal or evaluation of the effectiveness of educational development. Objectives are more likely to serve these ends if they are perceived clearly by children and teachers, defined appropriately, and used consistently.

Objectives for the elementary school indicate its task is to help children understand themselves and the physical and social world in which they live, to develop those abilities and skills which permit effective judgment and action, and to encourage the inculcation of those values and attitudes which promote the child's faith in himself, his fellow men, his future, and his God, so that he will be able to live effectively both within himself and with others.

BIBLIOGRAPHY

Beck, Robert T., Walter W. Cook, Nolan C. Kearney, *Curriculum in the Modern Elementary School.* Englewood Cliffs, N.J.: Prentice-Hall, Inc., 1953.

Caswell, Hollis L., and Doak S. Campbell, *Curriculum Development.* New York: American Book Company, 1935.

———, and A. Wellesley Foshay, *Education in the Elementary School.* New York: American Book Company, 1950.

Georgia Program for the Improvement of Instruction. Atlanta, Georgia: State Department of Education, 1937.

Lee and Lee, *The Child and His Curriculum.* New York: D. Appleton-Century, 1950.

Macomber, F. G., *Guiding Child Development in the Elementary School.* New York: American Book Company, 1941.

Miel, Alice, *Changing the Curriculum.* New York: D. Appleton-Century, 1940.

NEA Educational Policies Commission, *Education for All American Children*. Washington, D.C., 1948.

———, *Education for All American Youth*. Washington, D.C., 1944.

———, *The Education of Free Men in American Democracy*. Washington, D.C., 1941.

PART TWO

CHILDREN
AND THE
CURRICULUM
OF THE
ELEMENTARY
SCHOOL

CHILDREN: THEIR LEARNING AND DEVELOPMENTAL PROCESSES

5

A KNOWLEDGE OF THE DEVELOPMENTAL AND LEARN-
ing processes of elementary school children by the
teacher is not a magic wand that will automatically solve all educational problems; it is, however, valuable and necessary for helping the
teacher make his teaching more effective. This
chapter will indicate the nature of some of this
knowledge, and how it helps in teaching and
educational planning.

THE RESPONSIBILITY OF TEACHERS AND SCHOOL STAFFS

Whether educational programs for children
are conceived as child-centered or subject-centered, conservative or progressive, social or indi-

vidual, children are always taken into consideration at some point in the educational program. The following are characteristics of school programs where teachers are consciously trying to understand children and to put this knowledge into practice:

1. The staff of the school is expanding its grasp of the available scientific information about children.

2. The staff's understanding about children is neither so static that no new knowledge or point of view can creep in, nor so variable that no working agreements or generalizations about children can ever be reached.

3. There is some continuous attempt to identify the manner in which a knowledge of child development and learning can be used in the control and direction of the learning experiences of children.

4. Theoretical knowledge of children is never substituted for knowledge about specific and individual children. Knowledge of the general characteristics of children serves only as the framework within which the knowledge of individual children takes on perspective and significance.

It is probable that the staff of a school can never become thoroughly conversant with all known information about children. Any assumption that a teacher or anyone else can know *all* about a child is unrealistic. Any teacher who aims for this goal cannot live long enough to attain it; and he is under constant pressure to use any understanding he has in dealing with many children every day of the school year. Teachers, like parents (and like the child himself), are always acting upon incomplete knowledge.

It is necessary, therefore, for any teacher who professes to use his knowledge of children in guiding their educational experiences, to develop two related points of view. First, he should realize that he must always strive for a more adequate understanding of the child and his development and learning. And second, he should realize that he has to test generalizations about the nature of the child's development and learning in his own teaching, in order to be able to develop better ones.

Four broad ideas about what it is important for teachers to know underlie this chapter:

1. Teachers must know the developmental characteristics of the children they are teaching.

2. Teachers must know the nature of the learning processes through which effective development in school takes place.

3. Teachers must know what to expect from children on the basis of the above knowledge.

4. Teachers must know how to use this knowledge in selecting, organizing, and developing learning experiences with children.

University of Wisconsin Summer Laboratory School

CHILDREN PAINT THEIR IDEAS BEFORE THEY CAN WRITE

What Is Meant by the Words *Growth, Development, Learning*

Growth and *development* are frequently used interchangeably to indicate some kind of change in the direction of some defined goal or maturity. This change may be of many kinds—increase in size (growing taller); increase in function (becoming stronger); increase in complexity of adaptive patterns (improved coordination and skill).

Learning, too, is concerned with change or the modification of behavior in both quantitative or qualitative terms, and is affected by the total growth of the child. *Learning,* as far as the child in school is concerned, is a process of behavioral change, resulting from interaction between the child and his environment and moving in the direction of desired educational goals. This definition, while suffering from the defects of many educational definitions, does emphasize that learning for the child in school is active, complex, and purposeful, and places major importance upon educational goals as a determinant of the qualitative aspects of the learning.

Teachers, then, in dealing with the problems of development and learning will want: a) to be aware of the changes in the child and his behavior which are brought about purely by maturation, and which would have occurred whether the child was in school or not; b) to be aware of the limits placed on development and learning by the child's level of maturation at any given time; and c) to realize that learning and development are concerned fundamentally with progress *toward* goals, not with accomplishment or change *per se*.

This Heredity-Environment Problem. The way a teacher perceives the role heredity and environment play in the learning and development of children makes a great deal of difference in the way he accepts children and holds out hope for them.

There is little question that both heredity and environment (culture) are active forces in the development of children. At one time it was a popular indoor sport to attempt to indicate exactly the relative influences of environment and heredity. More recently, the complexity and interrelatedness of the causal factors behind any human behavior have been recognized, and the relative impossibility of tracing them back either to heredity or environment has been pretty well demonstrated. Certainly it is unrewarding for a teacher to spend much time doing this. Much more useful to him and to the children is the idea that a child is the product of the interaction of both these forces over a period of time. It is the responsibility of the teacher to concentrate on making sure that the learning and social environment of the child, so far as the school can influence it, makes its maximum contribution to his development, and not to worry about what the accidents of circumstance have produced.

THE DEVELOPMENTAL CHARACTERISTICS OF CHILDREN

The challenges and the richness of the experience of teaching are due to the fact that real human beings come to school and crowd into our classrooms, and no general rule or automatic procedure is ever sufficient to deal with them adequately. While we want to understand what some of the general characteristics of development are, we must always keep our eye on the specific child or group of children to which these broad generalizations will be applied. This point is well documented by teachers' conversations!

"Mary tries hard, but I guess she never will do as well as her sister. Perhaps we shouldn't expect too much from her. She is a sweet lovable little girl, though."

"Bill sure is a trouble maker. He seems to take delight in getting into mischief. I'm sure he's spoiled at home, and I have to put up with him at school."

"I just do not know what to do with this grade. I have five children who should have stayed in third grade, another five who should be in fifth, and the rest probably are fourth graders—but I don't see how I can get them ready for fifth grade by the end of this year. I'm only about halfway through the book."

Teachers may know all about reading, arithmetic, and science, or all about the information available on children in books, but still not be able to apply their knowledge to their practices with children.

Children of Two to Five

Not many children of two to five are in school, but these years profoundly influence what the child does when he gets there.

The first five years of life are the period of highest rate of growth; more so even than the more dramatized adolescence. The child proportionately does as much growing in the first five years of his life as he does in the next ten. The young child is proportioned differently from an adult. In relation to the rest of his body, his head and upper part of his trunk are larger than they will be when he grows up. His heart and lungs will increase thirteen to twenty times as he grows to maturity. The proportional relationship of his nervous system, on the other hand, will decrease to one-eighth of the infantile proportion, indicating that a high level of maturity of the nervous system is reached at an early age.

The young child is mainly concerned with himself and with the meeting of his primary needs. His socialization varies according to his place in his family group, the social class position of his family, and the nature and range of his opportunities to play and live with other children. His most important social tool is his growing ability to use language. He has an oral vocabulary of about 2500 words and most of the forms of speech by the time he enters first grade.

Most, if not all, of his motor skills have been established by this time, and while he will develop increased skill and coordination in the subsequent years, he runs, jumps, throws, and handles his body sufficiently well to meet most of the demands placed on him. Any problem of seeing, hearing, speaking, or physical movement by the end of this period is not fundamentally one of physical maturation, but more one of learning and development. His ears, eyes, and voice are ready to perform whatever he is able to learn.

During this time, the young child gradually learns to perceive his own identity as a physical unity and as a social entity called Mary or Johnny. Combined with this perception is his growing awareness of the realities of his physical and social worlds. An increasingly difficult task for him is handling his growing need to share his emotional world with other people. The way he works on this determines in many ways his readiness to go to kindergarten or to begin school. He has gradually grasped the nature of the value system within which he is living. He has learned that parents value certain behaviors and not others; that his playmates will encourage and respond to some ways of playing and will discourage other ways. He is beginning to sense his difficult task of learning how to live with people; and how to cope with some of the conflicting demands upon him.

Six to Nine Year Olds

Much has been made of the fact that six to nine year olds are in a stable stage of their general development. The relationship between mental age and chronological age is most constant, they grow physically at an even tempo, and most of their skill patterns are able to take care of their needs. Perhaps one of the major tasks of the six to nine year old is learning the social skills of living in groups of varying size and complexity. Six and seven year olds are not able to work effectively in large groups, to assume leadership of activities involving many children, or to deal with complex social organizations and behavior. They have, however, a growing awareness of the social, economic, and intellectual differences that exist among people. The important thing for a teacher to remember is that the way the child learns and values these differences will determine whether he comes to understand and appreciate them or whether he develops prejudices and maintains certain attitudes toward ethnic and minority groups.

During this period of a child's life he is learning the common language skills which enable him to read and write, speak and listen. He becomes increasingly skillful in using concepts of quantity and relationship, and in manipulating them through a number system. His parents and his teacher are very important people to him, and he trusts and depends on them.

The Nine to Twelve Year Olds

The child in middle childhood, while continuing the development of his earlier period, begins to change the role of parents, teacher, and other adults in his life; his playmates and own associates become more important. This change makes this age not as emotionally satisfying for teachers as younger children. It is therefore all important that teachers of middle grade children be able to give them security and a feeling of importance, while permitting or encouraging their growing initiative and independence.

Havighurst points out that children during these years are working very hard on:

1. Learning physical skills necessary for ordinary games.
2. Building wholesome attitudes toward themselves as a growing organism.
3. Learning to get along with age-mates.
4. Learning an appropriate sex role.
5. Developing fundamental skills in reading, writing, and calculating.
6. Developing concepts necessary for everyday living.
7. Developing a conscience, morality, and a scale of values.
8. Developing attitudes toward social groups and institutions.[1]

During this period many girls are moving into the adolescence growth spurt, while most of the boys are in a pre-adolescent period where they seem to stand still physically. The understanding teacher will help the girls to accept their rapidly changing bodies, and assure the boys that their time to change their voices, develop more pronounced muscles, and grow much taller is still ahead. It is natural, then, for teachers of this period to find boys and girls choosing their own sex more often than the other and for boy-girl relationships to be based more on pulling, tugging, and chasing than on friendship and mutual liking. Girls at this age are much more interested in boys as social objects of increasing excitement than boys are in them. Mature and understanding men and women teachers in the middle grades are valuable as standards against which both boys and girls may test and relate their growing perceptions of their own future sex roles. The teacher who uses competition between boys and girls as a way of motivating the spelling lesson is not very aware of the social and emotional development of children at this age level.

The teacher of middle grade children will want to be very sensitive to the many ways in which boys and girls of this period are trying to

1 Robert J. Havighurst, *Human Development and Education* (New York: Longmans, Green and Co., 1953), pp. 25-41.

grow up, and understand the tremendous importance their feeling of
self-respect and confidence has for them. He will need to sense how
much they want to be treated like "big" boys and girls, although
they are still so very unsure of themselves and their roles in their
world. Children at this age are very concerned with life and death and
the nature of the universe, with being fair, with themselves, and with
being right. Differences become very important, particularly visible
differences in size, shape, color, and the like, which set one child apart
from others of his own age.

Nature of Development over the Elementary School Years

Caroline Tryon and Jesse W. Lilienthal give us some sense of the
child's growing-up processes in their discussion of the specific phases
of the common developmental tasks through infancy, early childhood,
late childhood and early adolescence.[2] Only a few of these tasks will
be discussed here to show the nature of the child's progress in working on them.

I. *Achieving an Appropriate Dependence-Independence Pattern*
   Establishing one's self as a very dependent being. (Infancy.)
   Adjusting to less private attention: becoming independent physically while
      remaining strongly dependent emotionally. (Early childhood.)
   Freeing one's self from primary identification with adults. (Late childhood.)
   Establishing one's independence from adults in all areas of behavior. (Early
      adolescence.)

II. *Achieving an Appropriate Giving-Receiving Pattern of Affection*
   Developing a feeling for affection. (Infancy.)
   Developing the ability to give and share affection. (Early childhood.)
   Learning to give as much love as one receives: forming friendships with
      peers. (Late childhood.)
   Accepting one's self as a person really worthy of love. (Early adolescence.)

V. *Learning One's Psycho-Socio-Biological Sex Role*
   Learning to identify with male adult and female adult roles. (Early child-
      hood.)
   Beginning to identify with one's social contemporaries of the same sex. (Late
      childhood.)
   Strong identification with one's sex mates and beginning to learn one's role
      in heterosexual relationships. (Early adolescence.)

2 Jesse W. Lilienthal III and Caroline Tryon, "Fostering Mental Health in Our
Schools," Association for Supervision and Curriculum Development Yearbook (Washington, D.C.: National Education Association, 1950), pp. 90-124.

VII. *Managing a Changing Body and Learning New Motor Patterns*

Developing physiological equilibrium, eye-hand coordination, and satis-factory rhythms of rest and activity. (Infancy.)

Developing large muscle control and learning to coordinate large muscles and small muscles. (Early childhood.)

Refereeing and elaborating skill in use of small muscles. (Late childhood.)

Controlling and using a "new" body. (Early adolescence.)

IX. *Developing an Appropriate Symbol System and Conceptual Abilities*

Developing a preverbal and verbal communication based on rudimentary concept formation. (Infancy.)

Improving one's use of the symbol system based on an enormous elabora-tion of the concept system. (Early childhood.)

Learning to use language actually to exchange ideas and to influence one's hearers; beginning to understand real causal relations; and making finer conceptual distinctions and thinking reflectively. (Late childhood.)

Using language to express and to clarify more complex concepts and to move from the concrete to the abstract or applying general principles to the particular. (Early adolescence.)

These examples of the nature of the development of children in achieving selected developmental tasks, when related to our knowl-edge of children, allow us to make several major generalizations about the nature of children and their development. It is valuable for teachers who work with elementary school children to keep in mind that:

We Can Expect Variation or Differentiation in the Ways Children Grow Up

There is no method of grouping, teaching, or classifying children which will eliminate the individuality or variation that exists among and within children. Actually, to do so would destroy the richness and breadth of group experience and would prevent distinctive per-sonality development. Differentiation in development is a prized re-source to be conserved and exploited not something to be denied and destroyed.

We can expect that children will be both alike and different in many ways. All children, for example, are alike in the sense that they are working on the same tasks of growing up; they differ in the ways in which they work on them, in their speeds of development, and in their points of beginning and their final levels of maturation. The same child will vary with respect to the nature of the development of the different areas within his personal growth pattern. Oral language develops before written language, sexual development long after neural development, awareness of self before awareness of others. No teacher will expect the accomplishments of every child to be "at level" in all subject areas or his development to be at the same point in all phases of his developmental pattern. The reader will realize that this concept is very different from the concept of growth used by many teachers to appraise the accomplishments of both individuals and groups of children.

The teacher who recognizes the contribution of development will capitalize on it by organizing his teaching in and around topics and centers of interest which permit and encourage individual children to contribute and learn according to their varying capacities, speed of learning, and depth of insight and understanding. He will expect that adequate learning and encouragement will not eliminate these differences but will actually accentuate them.

We Can Expect Continuity in the Development of Children

As one looks at the ways in which children develop, and examines the growth that takes place year by year, he is struck with the essential continuity of this development. Children are growing today into children of tomorrow. Learning and development are not a series of unrelated jumps or new features; instead they occur as a slow extension and progression of the same developmental pattern. Observant teachers know that children's likenesses and differences organize themselves around developmental areas where one phase merges into the next.

This continuity in development and learning makes it important that teachers in one grade take an interest in what children have been doing in previous years as a basis for appraising the child's behavior. Teachers should expect also that children will continue to develop in the same areas over a long future period. The record of a child in the first grade makes an interesting comparison with the record of the same child at the sixth grade or in high school. Although growth and change have occurred, he is still recognizably the same child, facing many of the same problems.

We Can Expect Interrelationships and Consistency in Development

In looking at the development tasks of children and the ways in which children in infancy, early and late childhood, and adolescence work on them, a careful observer sees that children work on the same tasks at each age level and that progress in one area is important for progress in another. As the child develops into a more social being,

progress in language, in motor development, and in his conceptual-
ization of himself is necessary to his being able to join with other
children in their play, in conversation, and in friendships. Similarly,
his increased ability to work and live with people has positive influence on his other areas of development.

The area of the language arts illustrates the important interrelationships among the learning activities of children. The oral language
experience of children is the basis upon which his reading and writing
development is built. Development in one phase of language is related to (and often dependent upon) the nature of the growth in other
aspects of the child's developmental pattern. Many times a teacher is
impressed with the gains a child makes in reading when reading has
not been the object of specific attention. This is the reason why undue efforts to push ahead in one area of learning without considering
the nature of development in all areas is bound to be not very
rewarding.

Because of the interrelationships among areas of development, and
the consistency of these relationships over periods of time, it is possible to talk about "patterns" of behavior and development. Olson
in his work at Michigan has been able to illustrate this consistency in
the growth pattern of an individual child by graphing the various
aspects of growth in the same child over the period of the elementary
school, thus showing how his achievement is a function of the child
"as a whole."[3]

We Can Expect that Development in Itself Will Create New Needs

Learning and development have frequently been considered as a
process of resolving tensions, frustrations, and problems; an approach
which implies that after the particular tension or problem has been
resolved, equilibrium or adjustment remains for relatively long periods of time. Out of this notion came the idea of the importance of
"mastery" in the learning of the elementary school child. Perhaps a
more realistic concept of learning and development is the one which
states that effective learning and development by their very nature
force the child into new needs for *more* learning and development.
The more the child sees, the more information he is forced to re-
organize and relate to previous learning; the more he does this, the
more he perceives and desires to learn.

Development, by the very nature of its progression toward maturity, creates the need for more development. The teacher who under-

[3] Willard C. Olson, *Child Development* (Boston: D. C. Heath and Co., 1949), pp. 177-188

stands this aspect of development will recognize that learning in school is not a process of piling away valuable learning products. Effective learning in the sense of development is really the gaining of the understandings and skills which open and broaden horizons, and create a need for more learning and more effective teaching.

THE NATURE OF THE CONDITIONS FOR LEARNING

The previous section pointed up the nature and characteristics of the development of elementary school children during the time they spend in elementary school. Since so much of the time and effort of the elementary school teacher is spent in trying to influence the learning of the child within the limits of his inheritance and maturities, it is important to clarify the principles of learning and indicate how they can be applied to effective teaching and instruction.

General Conception of Learning

As has been pointed out, learning is concerned with the modification of behavior. Learning in school is concerned with the modification of behavior not in the sense of change for the sake of change, but for the purpose of achieving some *desirable educational purpose or goal.*

This concept of responsibility of the teacher for learning leads to the following axioms:

1. The child, as a total being, is the active agent in any elementary school program. It is impossible to ignore this important fact in any thinking the teacher may do about the nature of learning.

2. Learning in school should concentrate on the changes in behavior which can be influenced by the experiences children have.

3. Learning in school should be most concerned with changes in behavior which are directed toward desirable educational goals.

When viewed in this light learning is seen as a complex made up of children, educational purposes, and the conditions necessary for resolution and development. From this point of view, then, the learning behavior of children ought to:

1. Have some kind of psychological *unity.*[4]
2. Be unified around some *organizing center.*
3. Have some kind of *continuity.*
4. Have *multiple* and *interrelated* causes.
5. Be activated by the *reintroduction* of the goal for learning.

[4] See J. W. Tilton, *An Educational Psychology of Learning* (New York: The Macmillan Co., 1952).

Helping the Child to Perceive the Unity of His Learning

Learning in school is facilitated for a child if he can sense that it is related to himself and his goals, and what he sees himself doing to accomplish them. This perception of the "totality" by the learner constitutes the psychological unity of his learning.

The importance of this perception by the child in promoting efficient learning has been summarized in various ways:

A child's learning is both richer and easier if he shares in selecting and setting the goals of learning, in planning ways to gain them and in measuring his own progress toward them.[5]

Learning takes place more readily if the child accepts as useful and important to him the activities in which he is expected to engage.[6]

Whether the child participates in setting up the goal for learning, or whether the teacher determines it for him, the goal does not become a part of the unity of his learning activity unless the child perceives its importance and relationship to the things he is doing to accomplish it. The child's participation in its determination merely makes this *more likely* to happen.

The Center of Attention

It is difficult for anyone to have a very clear notion of the psychological unit of learning for another individual. This makes it necessary for the teacher to examine the nature of the centers of attention or interest around which he is attempting to organize the activities and behavior of children, and thus create some kind of unity of experience. Do these centers permit the child:

1. To relate his own sense of awareness and purpose to the center of attention being proposed?

2. To consider and evaluate the relationships which exist between him and the center of attention, educational goals, ideas, and procedures in effective learning?

3. To consider and evaluate the relationships which exist between one center and other foci of attention?

In any teaching situation the child is confronted by more than one thing to pay attention to; and each topic permits development in many different directions. Thus there is no need to talk about "concomitant," "incidental," or "indirect" learning as another and dif-

[5] Camilla M. Low, "Guidance in the Curriculum," A.S.C.D. Yearbook (Washington, D.C.: NEA, 1955), p. 52.

[6] *Loc. cit.*

ferent kind of learning. It is expected that any learning experience of sufficient comprehensiveness to include and hold the attention of a group of children will incorporate foci of attention on many different levels of importance both to the child and to the educational goals being achieved.

Many of the problems of transfer of learning from one situation to another derive from lack of recognition by the teacher and children that familiar ideas and facts can be related to many different centers of attention. Transfer of learning is therefore aided when teachers help children perceive the relationships which exist between one focus of attention and another.

The topic, questions, problems, and objects which serve as centers of attention, besides providing a means for unifying experience serve also as cues in learning. The past experience of the child is always the basis upon which he builds his future experience, and it tends to reduce the time and effort involved in making a response to a center of attention. In this sense, the words in a reading lesson can only serve as a cue to the meaning that the child's past experiences have developed for him. This is the reason that some authors have defined reading as "bringing meaning to the printed page."

Continuity of Learning

Learning, particularly the purposeful learning of greatest importance to the school, always has a future—some extension in time, in logic, and in use. The continuity of his experience as seen by the child himself may not correspond to the sequential development of that experience as desired by the teacher or as indicated by the text or by other children. The teacher, if he is to be effective in promoting the development (continuity) of the child's learning, must become aware of what the child perceives as the extensions of his learning experiences.

The centers of attention perceived by children are the points at which the extensions in their learning take place. The problem is not whether there *is* continuity, but how to capitalize on the continuities that always exist in the ongoing experience of the child.

The continuity of a child's learning is strengthened if:

1. The instructional activities are organized around centers of attention which have valid extensions in understanding and in educational use.

2. There is constant effort to reach agreement among teacher, child, and other children about what they are trying to accomplish, and

the relationships between that and other present and future activities to be developed.

3. The present planned sequences worked out in advance and provided to children—the next page, the next chapter, the simple to complex, the near to far, the immediate to the remote, the next topic to be covered, etc.—are tied into, and if possible grow out of, the actual perceived continuities in the child's learning experiences.

4. Skill programs, drill activities, etc., are developed in situations where applications are made and relationships are seen by the child as having some significance and educational perspective.

5. A constant, consistent effort is made to use the child's present and past experience as a basis for next steps, for moving to the next topic, for relating new centers of attention, and for evaluating the possible consequence of future plans.

Qualities of Good Organizing Centers

To be instructionally useful, organizing centers should have the following characteristics for teachers and children.[7]

1. *Qualities of Significance.* For teachers, this means that the organizing center holds promise for developing in children those behaviors which come from deepening and broadening certain understandings, skills, and value referents that underlie the curriculum. For children, this means that the center holds promise for activities that are of intrinsic interest, and which they recognize as worthwhile.

2. *Qualities of Accessibility.* More than geographic accessibility is implied here. Ideas, for example, must be made accessible to children in terms that they can understand. If the books expressing ideas which might be used as organizing centers even for young children are all written at the college level, then these ideas are lost as organizing centers. Accessibility in a physical sense means the proximity of nature trails, quarries, swamps, and other areas to serve as focal points for developing class activity.

3. *Qualities of Breadth and Scope.* If the entire class is to work as a single group, then the organizing center must lend itself to the demands of the many variations represented in that group. Similarly, the center must usually provide readily for moving several curricular elements along together, as well as a ready stimulant for writing, speaking, and speculating about significant life problems.

4. *Capacity for Organizing and Relating.* A likely organizing center

[7] Virgil E. Herrick, "Approaches to Helping Children Improve Their Instructional Practices," *School Review,* LXII (December, 1954), 533-34.

is one that lends itself easily to learnings that have gone before and that are likely to lie ahead. It encourages children's efforts to "tie things together," to perceive related wholes. Likewise, it facilitates the organization of group effort in such a way that individuals engage in worthwhile tasks with a minimum of time lost in getting started, accomplishing something, and moving ahead from task to task.

5. *Capacity for Development.* A good center encourages children to catch hold of it and then "to run with it." First explorations yield several alternatives for productive study. Action leads to new avenues that hold promise for further rich learning.

Illustrative Organizing Centers

The deceptive and yet enchanting thing about the whole concept of organizing centers is that, instead of qualities such as those outlined above being inherent in a given center, the center is itself described, defined, and created by the qualities. In effect, the qualities are in the mind and eye of the viewer. The milkman kicks a pebble at the doorstep in delivering milk and to him it is only a pebble. The geologist residing there picks it up and enchants his children nights in a row with stories of how it came to be. The girl in the match factory watches the clock and thinks of the week-end ahead, while box after box passes under her scrutiny on the production line. The woodsman picks up a single match and brings forth endless tales of woodland giants, raging fires, and reforestation. To the geologist and the woodsman, a stone and a match are organizing centers for learning and teaching. An organizing center is whatever a teacher and a class can get their hands on and their minds around to enrich the quality of classroom living. Visualizing in the center the qualities that make it worthwhile determines the usefulness of that organizing center.

Since what is an organizing center for one teacher and class is not recognizable as such to another, the process of identification becomes complicated. Nonetheless, an attempt is made below to indicate some types of organizing centers for learning and teaching:

1. *Ideas.* Big ideas have traditionally served as organizing centers for learning: ideas about time, space, the future, man and his identity, the source of truth, and so on. Ideas, carefully selected, readily satisfy the requisites for good organizing centers for elementary school instruction. Ideas satisfy the criterion of development especially well; a group can take them and move with them. Problems of living are similar effective centers of attention for organizing learning.

2. *Materials.* On the assumption that teachers are guided more in

setting up learning situations by the materials accessible to them than by any other single source of direction, most educators believe improvement of materials promises improvement of instruction. Teachers who depend heavily upon text materials, for example, are restricted by the suitability of these materials for the instructional goals they have in mind. If thinking about materials is extended to include encyclopedias, films, filmstrips, record players, and so on, it becomes obvious that materials hold much promise for classroom organization of instruction.

3. *Displays, Collections, Exhibits, etc.* To some, a science corner in the classroom is just a miscellaneous array of inanimate or even animate "stuff." To others, it is a source of stimulating thought and activity. Book and science collections, museums, stamp and coin collections, and so on, offer much to the teacher who is able to see their possibilities for leading children into further exploration.

4. *Places.* Use of places as organizing centers ranges from playground application to foreign travel. Classes in Atlanta make effective use of places when they visit the Cyclorama to see the Battle for Atlanta brought to life in vivid color and form; in Pittsburgh groups go to the exact site of Fort Duquesne to study the past; in Detroit pupils visit an automobile factory to study mass production; in San Francisco they visit a cruiser in the Bay to compare naval equipment of past and present.

5. *People.* Much effective learning can be tied around names such as Columbus, Galileo, Disraeli, Handel, Shakespeare, Whitman, Franklin, and Ford.

In each instance given here, the idea, material, exhibit, place, or person represents a beginning point; an opportunity to get a toehold in profitable learning.[8] The intent to learn, however, becomes truly muddled when the vantage point, the organizing center, becomes a thing of inflated inherent value. Great names are important, yes; but the teacher who sees their potential for involving children in significant learning processes has a perspective that is fundamental to good teaching.

Multiple and Interrelated Causes

A persistent effort has been made in educational psychology to identify the individual stimulus connected with a particular response,

8 For a discussion of setting up a classroom to provide centers around which rich living can be organized, see Peggy Brogan and Lorene K. Fox, *Helping Children Learn* (New York: World Book Co., 1955), pp. 336-42.

in order that children's learning could be controlled and predicted. This effort has been accompanied by a similar attempt to analyze and subdivide educational goals into their simplest smallest components, so that children might master each one at a time and the particular stimuli-response pattern be identified and used to assure efficient learning. Psychologists forget, however, that the reacting agent in this effort is a very complex organism—the child; and they also forget the breadth of experience each child brings to his learning in school, and the fact that he has a mind of his own. Who can determine the specific stimulus in the ordinary classroom situation which actuates the behavior of a particular child?

A teacher should not expect, then, that poor reading will be caused exclusively by poor vision; instead he will try to examine those inter-acting factors which, because of their relationship to each other, offer a better explanation and predictor of learning than any single factor taken alone.

Centers of Attention Serve as Activators of Behavior

One concept of how to promote desirable learning involves trying to develop relatively automatic connections between the proper educational stimuli and the correct response. Then the presentation of the stimuli will activate the response desired. Many of the drill and mastery programs in the elementary school have been built on this kind of thinking about learning.

The concept that the center of attention or core of concentration in a learning experience may activate behavior does not discard what else is known about different aspects of learning; it merely focuses attention on what is significant in educational learning—the goal and its role in the control and direction of learning. In dealing with the accomplishment of an educational goal—be it learning how much is 3 x 4, or how we get our food—experience brings a reduction and differentiation in the behavior of a child in his attempts to deal with these goals. His behavior becomes more purposeful in the sense that he has discriminated among and reduced the means necessary to accomplish what is desired. Future experience with these goals will allow the goal itself to activate behavior—not in the completely automatic sense—but in the sense of more thoughtful control and direction of behavior. This concept of learning is much more useful to the teacher than see-ing learning as a series of simple stimulus-response patterns.

COMMON PROBLEMS OF LEARNING AND DEVELOPMENT

There are many common problems of learning and development which face a teacher in his attempts to help children learn. The questions of how often to repeat, how fast to go, to what degree to accomplish, how to motivate, how many different things to consider at one time, and how much responsibility to place on the shoulders of children are important questions which confront every teacher and are the ones which have to be answered in some fashion in the day-to-day experiences of teaching. Generalizations about the nature and conditions for effective learning and development are *one* of the tools a teacher can use to deal with these questions effectively.

What About This Problem of Repetitions?

Every teacher realizes that unless a child has some chance to connect 6 x 7 with 42, or the printed symbol *ball* with its sound and meaning, not much learning in terms of these goals can take place. At the same time, the teacher realizes that he cannot go on presenting this combination and word to a child indefinitely.

There is no question that a child must experience 6 x 7 equals 42 if he is to learn it; but does it follow that efficient learning takes place by "repeating" it over and over? Thorndike has shown that repetition can take place an infinite number of times without learning, if there is no effect and no understanding on the part of the learner making the repetitions.

Efficient learning is not achieved, then, by maximizing the *repetitions*—but by maximizing the *satisfactions* and *understandings* the child gets out of his educational activities. To spend twice as much time drilling in the same old way, instead of achieving the desired goal twice as well, may actually produce no gains and may create emotional obstacles to future learning. Did you ever have to repeat the experience of sticking your tongue on a frosty pump handle or of putting your finger into a lighted match? When the effect and understandings are maximized, the repetitions are minimized. Major dependence upon repetition alone to produce efficient desired learning wastes both time and effort. Effort spent by the teacher to get as much satisfaction and understanding (purpose) into the learning activities as possible will pay great dividends in effective learning.

Satisfactions and understanding are maximized when the child can relate his activities and thinking to a known center of attention, when he can perceive the results of relating, and when the center of attention has some personal and educational significance for him. When the child can see that his activities and struggles to learn will make some desirable difference in what he is trying to do, he will learn efficiently.

Much of our difficulty with the problem of repetition grows out of what we mean by the word *repeat* in learning. From the point of view of this book, the repetition of any experience for a child is impossible. It is possible, however, to talk about the extent to which efforts are made to present similar cues, goals, conditions, etc. for the ongoing learning development of particular children. In these terms, the importance of the center of attention, the related elements in the learning situation, the continuity of the experience, the verification of the worthwhileness of the learning activities, carry much more significance than the ordinary meaning of the word "repeat."

Can You Teach All of the Important Facts?

It is impossible for a teacher to pay direct attention to all important facts and skills in the sense of making every learning specific a major focus of attention. No child or group of children would ever have time; and furthermore, it would be psychologically impossible for the children to grasp the number of available important facts. Pella, for example, found that the science texts for the primary grades presented some 3756 separate science concepts for children to learn. Most reading programs expect a child to be able to use a reading vocabulary of from 2000 to 3000 words by the third grade. The usual geography course in the sixth grade covers South America, England, Europe, Africa, Asia, and Australia. Attempts to pay specific attention to each possible fact in the above areas, while made by many teachers, are not based on adequate concepts of learning or of children.

No teacher can cover all of the important facts and skills at the *level* of the fact. However, this educational task can be attacked at the level of the relatively few important generalizations or concepts which subsume large numbers of supporting specific facts. Another approach to this problem uses the child's learning to deal with persisting life situations or with emerging educational and personal needs as the important center of attention and as a basis for the selection of the important facts and skills. The learning tasks of children in school become more reasonable and possible when activities are related to centers of attention which allow children to select, develop, and use the specific facts and skills in some meaningful relation to each other and to areas of use. Facts meaningfully related are much more manageable educationally than facts in isolation. The child depends upon his understanding and sense of purpose in the former; in the latter, the child must depend upon his capacity to memorize and recall large numbers of relatively isolated and discrete specifics. The first is possible, constructive, and developmental; the second is relatively hopeless and emphasizes out of context a skill not of critical importance to developing a responsible, resourceful, and constructive member of our democratic society. Perhaps worst of all, it is the poorest way of achieving what is desired—a fund of organized and useful knowledge.

Pacing

Have you ever watched a high school instructional film on the electron theory? You were able to keep up in the beginning; but as the film kept grinding away, and the voice of the commentator kept making sounds, your attention and understanding were still back on the little dots bouncing around in the frames you had just seen but could not follow. With repeated viewings you realized that you were able to follow each idea as it was presented, if the ideas did not come too rapidly. But if the film moved too fast, you broke down and just leaned back and watched the "pictures." This problem of pacing, or knowing how fast to go, is present in all learning, and it is one of the important constituents in the "difficulty" of learning in school. Things may not be hard in themselves; but they become difficult if they are presented too fast.

When the teacher offers large numbers of relatively isolated centers of attention for children to consider, the only control he has over the pacing (in addition to his dexterity in writing words on the board, shuffling the cards, or saying two-times-three-add-four-divide-by-two-times-ten-add-fifty-and-divide-by-twenty) is his observation of the behavior of children and their reaction to what is going on. Evidence of tenseness, anxiety, giving up, are all present when the pace of the learning activities runs beyond comfortable learning levels.

One way to handle the problem of pacing is to organize the educational activities of a group of children around cores of attention which permit more than one kind of pacing—the natural time extensions of the problem itself, the number of applications possible, the variety of activities necessary, the depth and level of insights and understanding gained, and the over-all movement of the learning process. The learner is the one who knows best how fast to go, and he must, therefore, partially determine the pace.

It is true, however, that pacing, in the sense of forcing the attention of the learner on the learning task, is frequently effective in promoting efficient learning. The danger is that this kind of pacing is frequently used before the child completely understands the goal to be accomplished or has the skills necessary to accomplish it. In this situation, increasing the tempo of the learning adds further external frustrations to an already frustrating learning situation. Speeding up the reading of a child in a reading situation where he has already gained some control of the process is very different from speeding it up in a situation where he is already floundering.

Mastery

Some form of the concept of mastery has always been present in the thinking about the learning of children in school. Usually, mastery means the child's ability to respond correctly to a given educational stimulus, or to understand a particular concept. Behind this concept of mastery is the belief that it is possible to divide the educational task into units which children can encompass and "master" as a basis for going on to additional units of learning. A unit is mastered when *receive* is spelled correctly, when 9 and 7 always equal 16, and when the capital of New York State is always Albany. These units of learning, when mastered, become the tools for additional learning in the sense that little or no attention has to be paid to them.

The problem of knowing the degree to which development should take place at any one time is always a persistent and difficult question in learning. If one sees the task of the educational program at the level of the combinations of addition, lists of words to be spelled, places to be located, items of information to be known, then it is possible to apply some concept of mastery. If, however, the educational program is perceived at the level of important concepts such as interdependence, in social studies; air has weight, occupies space, and exerts force, in science; or functional relationship, in mathematics, then the common concept of mastery cannot be applied. These are not concepts which are mastered at any one time in a complete sense —they are always susceptible to further interpretation. This is particularly true of language, of thinking, and of social action. When can one say that he has mastered the art of thinking?

A much better concept of learning is to see mastery as the problem of the degree of learning which is adequate for the learning task, the normative conditions, and the extent to which the child can profit from the experience at any given time.

How Is Adequacy Determined?

For most teachers adequacy of learning or development is determined by the learning task itself. If 3 x 4 is 12, learning is adequate. If the child puts periods and commas in all the correct places in the workbook exercise, then he is progressing satisfactorily.

The problem gets more difficult, however, when one wonders how many of these learning tasks a child ought to be able to do at a particular time. Here a teacher shifts to some arbitrary standard—what he thinks is all right or what he thinks children of this age should do, or what the average accomplishment of this group or similar groups is. These are the usual standards for determining adequacy.

If a teacher tries to use his understanding of children to solve this problem, he must start measuring the child's present accomplishment against where he started and his ability to learn. Some teachers fit one aspect of the child's learning in place in the child's pattern of general accomplishment, which, in the eyes of the authors, is the most promising approach to use.

What is important to realize when appraising the adequacy of a child's development is that many different norms are used by the child and by other people to judge the adequacy of the same behavior. Consequently, there will be many different judgments about how well the child is progressing. The most educationally constructive norm, however, is the child's own developmental pattern.

Motivation

Motivation means that the child wants to do something to such an extent that he is willing to modify his behavior in order to do it. The problem of motivation from the teacher's viewpoint is how to help modify and direct this *quality of wanting* so that the child will accomplish desirable educational goals.

In attempting to deal with the motivational problem of a child in school, it is important to know what he is trying to do. The purposes or goals which give direction to his learning, and the values which he has attached to or derived from these goals, are organized in some kind of value hierarchy within himself. The teacher can only infer the nature of this organization of motives from what he says and does. Many of these motives can not be verbalized or rationalized by the child, and can be inferred only by observing what themes occur persistently in his behavior over a period of time.

Interests of children frequently have been considered as symbols of previously valued experience; as such they are seen as a means to achieve educational goals. In this approach to motivation, it is hoped that the feelings of satisfaction associated previously with the center of interest will be transferred to the educational goal, and will reinforce the learning activities connected with its accomplishment. The problem is how to make sure that the interest will lead to the educational goal, that its dominance will not be greater than the goal itself, and that the association will be made in such a way that the educational goal (not the interest) becomes the motivating force for future behavior.

The authors of this book prefer to regard this use of interests as merely one way to use incentives in learning—other incentives, for example, are social approval, rewards, and the like. The fundamental problem of motivation from the point of view of the teacher is still how to develop and use goals and purposes which have value and significance to the learner. Educational goals and the perceived goals of the learner must become one at some point in the learning activities, if the "motives" of the learner are to become the dynamic driving force in his learning in school. Different procedures for achieving this fusion do not disagree on its importance—merely on the conditions and procedures for its accomplishment. The educational program which uses the "things the child is trying to do" as a basis for arriving at educational goals will maximize the role of the child in the identification, definition, and development of his goals. Teacher-pupil planning in this kind of program is one important way to incorporate the experience and purposes of a given group of children into their educational activities.

Competition as a Means of Motivation

Competition is frequently used to motivate learning goals. Competition is striving *against* another person to achieve a goal which cannot be shared; cooperation is striving *with*. Competition imbues the person against whom one is striving with many attendant personal aggressions. Since educational goals can be shared by all children to some degree, and since the intrinsic value of these goals should be sufficient incentive in themselves, competition is an artificial and sometimes antagonizing motivation for educational activities.

This same point of view is held in respect to all rewards and devices used to achieve educational goals. They are valuable only as they enhance the present and *long-term* development of desirable educational objectives. Rewards and devices should not become ends in themselves, to be more dominant in the learning situation than the desired educational goal. Much better motivations are the values inherent in the educational activities themselves. The important long term motivations in learning are those which come from the child's understanding of himself and his world and his increased feeling of competence to deal with it.

The motivation of educational activities is more desirable when:

1. It is an integral part of centers of attention which have some continuing educational significance.

2. The child is as free as possible to relate his behavior to the accomplishment of personal and educational goals in a situation which enhances the valuing of the means-ends usefulness of that behavior, and minimizes its relationship to his growing sense of personal worthwhileness.

3. The educational activities are organized around attention centers which permit the incorporation of many interests, the use of many avenues for learning, the valuing of different levels of contribution, and the testing of tentative judgments about the level at which the accomplishment should be pitched in order to keep it within reach of all children.

4. Positive constructive incentives are emphasized. Both rewards and punishments, successes and failures, rights and wrongs, must be related to the educational goals and evaluated accordingly.

5. Group goals are sufficiently comprehensive to include individual goals and the recognition of individual roles and contribution.

6. A child is helped to recognize and improve his motivational and value systems, thus giving control and perspective to his behavior. Conferences, group discussion, and individual and group evaluations help the child examine and interpret the role of goals and related motives in giving direction and significance to his behavior.

Transfer of Training

There is no disagreement as to whether transfer of training takes place—only about the degree, the way it occurs, and the means by which it can be enhanced. The authors feel that transfer is maximized when the center of attention of the experiences children have in school is related to the attention centers of their daily living. The development and continuity of these centers assure that present learning will be used to deal with future experience. The role of the learner in the definition of these centers of attention and in the application of his learning to their development is paramount in insuring transfer of training in this developmental sense.

Multiple Learnings

Any experience the child has in school is so complex that he is always learning multiple and interrelated things. It is impossible to conceive of a situation where *one* educational goal is accomplished exclusively. A lesson on a visit to the firehouse in "Our Community Helpers" includes objectives related to understanding the role of the fireman in our community life, development of a reading vocabulary, use of instructional materials, social processes important in working together as a class group, and many others, all involved in the adequate development of this experience and—what is more important— all related to each other. The fact that every learning experience always achieves multiple objectives also means, of course, that any given objective can be achieved by several ways.

The Role of Frustration in Learning

One theory about learning is that as learning progresses, the initial frustration diminishes to near zero and remains that way. This approach derives from the accomplishment of minute and isolated instructional goals. If, however, learning is conceived as dealing fundamentally with the development of significant centers of attention in an ongoing experience, then frustration is apparent on many levels and is an essential element in all learning. The problem is not how to eliminate it, but how to keep it essential to the resolution of educational goals, without relating it to people, procedures, and educational perspectives.

Additional understanding of a problem does not limit the perception of things to be considered, but instead broadens the number of possibilities and future developments. This continually expanding horizon of potential knowledge can itself be frustrating, unless the teacher helps children see that this vista is the enriching aspect of all true learning.

Problem Solving

From the authors' point of view, problem solving is not a particular kind of learning, but an aspect of all learning. It is impossible to have problem solving without previous learning. Problem solving skills are intimately related to what the individual does in dealing with the centers of attention within his experience. Analysis of how the person deals with these centers has lead to discussion of problem solving in such terms as "trial and error," "application of a principle," and solution by "insight." It is quite likely that any person will use all these techniques in dealing with his problems, either in multiple patterns or in some order or sequence. Actually, while problem solving has received much attention in the psychology of learning, little is known about this complex process.

A number of suggestions about problem solving may be of some value.

1. To have any significance, problem solving must be based on a felt need on the part of the learner. Many of the situations in most classrooms do not require problem solving in any fundamental sense, but have to do mainly with the materials and procedures of learning. Facts and skills become a part of problem solving when they are used as tools for the resolution of the problem. They are not problems in themselves.

2. Problem solving demands that a background of pertinent information be brought to bear on its solution. Implicit in this concept of problem solving is problem definition. Also, pertinent information must be identified and gathered (frequently new learning is necessary); information ordered and organized in relation to the problem situation; information tested and tentative hypotheses evolved; and an evaluation, re-examination, and prediction made on the basis of the results of the problem-solving process.

3. Problem solving demands action. Thinking is not done in a vacuum, but is a part of all purposeful learning. Thinking in problem solving resolves some perceived end when present available response patterns are not adequate to deal with it satisfactorily. Making them memorize rules of problem solving is not a useful way to teach children how to solve problems. As obvious as it may seem, children learn how to solve problems by having the opportunity to deal with many kinds of problems in many areas and on many levels.

4. Problem solving is facilitated when there is time for children to examine the problem area and define its sub-problems, to collect information about it, to test out tentative solutions, and to project and test probable future consequences. Temporary and fleeting problems of a limited nature are not useful centers of attention in teaching children to do this kind of thinking.

5. Problem solving, in the sense of goal seeking, is a part of the learning activities of all children. It is not an activity to be reserved either for the mature secondary school pupil or the intellectually bright. Differences of nature and of degree are to be expected in the problem solving of the same individual in different areas of his experience, or between two individuals in the same area.

It is obvious, in the light of the above five points, that many schools and teachers provide limited opportunities for children to carry on problem solving activities in the course of their school day.

Role of the Child

The child can learn only through his own activity. The child's responsibility in learning is to become increasingly able to control and direct his behavior. A growing capacity for self-direction is an important objective of elementary school programs, and should be an essential characteristic of a child's learning.

As has been pointed out, the individual who has greatest access to the essential data of the learning activity is the learner himself. To deny to the educational programs in school the important contribution of the learner is to restrict learning to the limited contribution of the teacher and his resources. The role of the child in the learning activity is fundamental; his increasing self-direction and responsibility in learning are important goals.

Role of the Teacher

The role of the teacher is to assist, encourage, support, free, and cooperate with the child in controlling and directing his learning development. Obviously, the role of the teacher is neither one of a merely interested observer of the child's struggles, nor a dictator of goals and how to accomplish them. The teacher is an active, dynamic, constructive force in learning. Helping the child to become increasingly directive and responsible is neither easy nor simple, it demands on the part of the teacher more maturity, rather than less; great patience and confidence, rather than pressure and intolerance; and consistency and breadth of perspective, rather than arbitrariness and inflexibility.

SUMMARY

Generalizations derived from our knowledge of the learning and development of children are important resources for teachers and workers in education. These principles deal primarily with increasing the efficiency and direction of the learning of children.

A knowledge of the principles of development will help a teacher expect variation in the growth patterns of children, continuity and relatedness in their progress, and the constant emergence of new needs and tensions as the result of increased development. Respect for the child and his level of maturity will make the teacher realize that much of the child's progress is due merely to maturation processes and not to learning, and that progress in learning must take place within this framework.

Both learning and development must be related to achievement of desirable educational goals. Important factors in promoting effective learning, therefore, are involved with the child's being able to relate his own behavior to desirable goals, to sense his progress, to feel confident of his ability, and to grasp the significance of what he is doing.

The nature and the level of development and learning are determined by the nature of the experiences children undergo, and their capacity to profit from them. The bases, therefore, for judging the adequacy of the degree of learning achieved by a child will necessarily be multiple—what the nature of the task demands, the teacher's or parent's expectation of what a child should do, and the average accomplishment of other children. The authors feel, however, that the most constructive and educational standard for judging adequacy of learning is the maturity of the developmental pattern of the child himself.

The important agents in learning and development in school are the child, his peer group, and his teacher. The primary agent, responsible for seeing his own goals and for relating his own behavior to them, is always the child himself.

BIBLIOGRAPHY

American Council on Education, *Helping Teachers Understand Children.* Washington, D.C.: American Council on Education, 1946.

Association for Supervision and Curriculum Development. 1955 Yearbook, *Guidance in the Curriculum.* Washington, D.C.: N.E.A.

Burton, William H., *The Guidance of Learning Activities.* New York: D. Appleton-Century Co., 1944.

Forest, Ilse, *Early Years at School.* New York: McGraw-Hill Book Company, Inc., 1949.

Havighurst, Robert J., *Human Development and Education.* Longmans, Green and Co., 1953.

Hildreth, Gertrude, *Child Growth Through Education*. New York: The Ronald Press Co., 1948.

Hurlock, Elizabeth B., *Child Development*, 2nd ed. New York: McGraw-Hill Book Company, Inc., 1950.

——, *Developmental Psychology*. New York: McGraw-Hill Book Company, Inc., 1953.

Lee, J. Murray and Dorris May Lee, *The Child and His Curriculum*. New York: Appleton-Century-Crofts, Inc., 1950.

Millard, Cecil V., *Child Growth and Development in the Elementary School Years*. Boston: D. C. Heath and Co., 1951.

National Society for the Study of Education. 49th Yearbook, *Learning and Instruction*. Chicago: University of Chicago Press, 1950.

Olson, Willard C., *Child Development*. Boston: D. C. Heath and Company, 1949.

Saucier, W. A., *Theory and Practice in the Elementary School*. New York: The Macmillan Co., 1951.

Stephens, J. M., *Educational Psychology*. Henry Holt and Company, 1951.

Tilton, J. W., *An Educational Psychology of Learning*. New York: The Macmillan Co., 1951.

Zubek, John P., *Human Development*. New York: McGraw-Hill Book Company, Inc., 1954.

NEA Educational Policies Commission, *The Purposes of Education in American Democracy*. Washington, D.C., 1938.

National Society for the Study of Education. 44th Yearbook, *American Education in the Postwar Period, Part I, Curriculum Reconstruction*. Chicago: University of Chicago Press, 1945.

Otto, Henry J., *Elementary School Organization and Administration*. New York: D. Appleton-Century, 1944.

Ragan, William B., *Modern Elementary Curriculum*. New York: The Dryden Press, Inc., 1953.

Smith, B. Othanel, William O. Stanley, J. Harlan Shores, *Fundamentals of Curriculum Development*. Yonkers-On-Hudson, New York: World Book Company, 1950.

Stratemeyer, Florence, *et al., Developing a Curriculum for Modern Living*. New York: Bureau of Publications, Teachers College, Columbia University, 1947.

PLANNING AND ORGANIZING THE CURRICULUM

6

THIS CHAPTER IS CONCERNED WITH HELPING THE reader examine and understand the instructional program of the elementary school—the kind of instructional program in which a group of children and their teacher try, through appropriate experiences, to achieve what they believe to be significant educational objectives.

Children, the Teacher, and the Situation— All Important Factors

In analyzing the experiences children have in school, it is very easy to concentrate on particular aspects of these experiences and consider them all-important. But school experiences involve more than a child or a teacher; they include children, teachers, the physical situation, various foci of attention, motivations for learning, ideas and processes, and instructional material and activities. We must observe the curriculum in all its facets, and in terms of the interrelationships which change as children work with other children and their teacher to achieve significant educational objectives.

An Actual Classroom Experience. The day-to-day experiences of children with their teacher in school are where all the high-sounding lists of objectives, beautifully illustrated textbooks, and curriculum planning come to some kind of educational realization. The following actual classroom record may help us get a feeling for the activities which actually occur in many of America's elementary schools.

A group of six and seven year olds were reading the book, *Stories about Sally* when the following incident took place. In the story, Sally was visiting her aunt and was being very helpful by making beds and doing other things.

TEACHER: Do you have any ways that you help at home?
BARBARA: I wash the dishes and dry them and put away the silverware.
JAMES: Silverware?
TOMMY: You know—that's knives and forks and what you eat with.
BILLY: I keep my room clean. I pack away my toys.
JAMES: I have to do that every night, too.
JEAN: I make my bed. Sometimes I put away the silver.
TEACHER: I know something else you do. How did you help make your birthday cake?
JEAN: I cut the dates for my birthday cake.
SANDRA: I take care of my brother and sister. And when they're in my mother's way, I take them in my bedroom and play with them.
SUSAN: I take care of my baby sister. Sometimes I give her her bottle. Sometimes I undress her, too. She pulls my hair when I get too close to her.
TOMMY: I wash mittens and help my brother get his clothes on for school.
KAREN: I cover my baby sister when she's uncovered.
GARY: I take the garbage out. And I clean my dresser drawers.
MICHAEL (*Just moved to Milwaukee from Indiana*): I helped move the furniture when we moved here. I shovel the sidewalks.
MICHELE: I go to the store for my mother.
JEANETTE: I answer the telephone when my mama's busy.
TEACHER: You're all such good helpers at home! It's no wonder you're such good helpers at school.

These same boys and girls planned together what room helpers are necessary to keep their room clean and attractive. They suggested the needs of watering the plants, cleaning the aquarium, feeding the fish, keeping the library table attractive, arranging books on the bookshelves, passing the wastepaper basket, passing straws and crackers, and numerous other jobs. They seemed to get pleasure and a feeling of belonging from sharing responsibility for the care of their school room.

Of course, episodes like this differ with the activities of children—it might involve problems of word-attack in a reading lesson, for instance. However, some of the common aspects of curriculum apparent in this incident are:

1. Teacher and children, and children and children (usually through the medium of language) share, point up, clarify, or extend information, understandings, and feelings, both about themselves and whatever is the center of attention at that moment.

2. There is always some center of attention in the experiences children have in school. The behavior of a child is more directed and focused if he feels he is a part of the center of attention to which he is reacting. A group of children find it difficult to share and contribute both to each other and to the center of interest, unless there is consensus as to what that center is.

3. There is always some movement of attention and thinking in learning and curriculum. Here the attention moved from *Stories about Sally* and how she made beds for her aunt, to Barbara's washing and drying the dishes at home, Gary's taking out the garbage, Michele's going to the store for her mother, and from there to the planning the whole group did for taking care of their own school room. There is more educational awareness in the thought and action of a group of children, if the center of attention has enough breadth to encompass the specific interests of a group of children and to move from a story book to the individual homes of each child, and then back again to their own schoolroom.

4. The perception *by children* of the objectives of instruction must grow out of their own experiences. In this episode, the objectives had to emerge from the specifics of the topic under discussion. Yet the point of the objectives of this episode seemed perfectly clear to children.

5. Examinations of this one record of classroom activity indicates something that is true about most classroom experiences—children gain ideas, share and work together, and apply their learning to their own schoolroom living and to their life at home. These important aspects of the child's learning do not take place in lessons especially devoted to each aspect; instead they were all tied in together around the center of interest being discussed. An important problem in plan-

ning and organizing a curriculum is how to provide this kind of integration in the children's learning experience.

Looking at a School Day. While it is not possible to present one school day which would show the breadth and complexity of the daily practices of thousands of elementary school teachers, it is likely that almost every teacher will find familiar items and time arrangements in the following schedules. These schedules, although a step removed from the blow-by-blow narration of a classroom record, nonetheless give the reader some idea of the scope and range of the educational program over the school day.

GENERAL SCHEDULE FOR GRADES 1, 2, 3 [1]

Approximate time	Activities
8:30 to 9:45	Health inspection and milk or supplementary breakfast if needed.
	Morning business (including functional use of mathematics as needed in collecting money, keeping records of attendance, lunch, etc.).
	Sharing and planning (use of oral and written language as needed).
	Science and/or social studies (including use of reading, speech, written language, arithmetic, and art as needed, and work in social groups).
9:45 to 10:15	Recess—toilet and drink, quick energy nourishment (such as fruit juice, crackers, cookies, or clear vegetable soup), and outdoor play.
10:15 to 11:15	Reading and language experiences (or science and/or social studies continued, if necessary). Development of skills in reading, speech, and writing including phonetics, handwriting, and spelling.
11:15 to 12:00	Lunch (preceded by washing hands, toilet and drink).
12:00 to 1:00	Rest, followed by toilet and drink.
1:00 to 1:30	Mathematics experiences, including work on skills. Corrective work on other skills as needed, or free activities.
1:30 to 2:00	Aesthetic and creative experiences—art, music, rhythms, folk dancing, dramatics, creative speech and writing, literature (including poetry), and supervised play.
2:00 to 2:30	Finishing incomplete work, and putting materials and workroom in order.
	Summarizing and evaluating day's activities.
	Anticipating and planning for the following day.
2:30	Calm and quiet dismissal (see that children use the toilet and get drink before leaving the building).

[1] *Handbook for Elementary School Teachers of the Public Schools of Hawaii,* Part I. Introduction and General Guide (Territory of Hawaii; Department of Public Instruction, December, 1946), p. 87.

Science and social studies may be treated separately each day or may be combined or alternated but an adequate and balanced program of experiences in each should be provided in course of each semester. (Science should include development of simple concepts in botany, zoology, physics, chemistry, and health; social studies should include simple concepts in social living, history, geography, citizenship, and economics.)

GENERALIZED PROGRAM FOR GRADES 5 AND 6 [2]

8:00 to 9:00	Coming into the room, putting away wraps, getting ready for the school day. In most schools the teacher is supposed to be in his room by 8:15.
	The time from 8:45 to 9:00 is usually spent in doing the household duties of feeding the fish, putting out food for the birds, sharpening pencils, chatting, or discussing the events of the day. In some schools, school business is handled at this time. In other schools the school day opens with a prayer or the reading of a short selection from the Bible.
9:00 to 9:15	Health inspection and instruction. School nurse. (Many schools do not have medical resources and the teacher is responsible for this.)
9:15 to 9:50	Oral and written language (use of language in telling stories, making reports, conducting meetings, writing letters, making notes, writing reports major theme with emphasis on grammar and usage).
9:50 to 10:00	Recess
10:00 to 10:20	Music (Usually taught by the room teacher although in many schools a music teacher may come to the room or the children may go to the music room for this activity.)
10:20 to 11:00	Arithmetic
11:00 to 12:00	Social Studies (Varies between school programs; in most schools, school studies have geography as its base, with history and civics added.)
12:00 to 1:00	Lunch (Village and city elementary schools where the children go home for lunch have from an hour and a quarter to an hour and a half for lunch. In schools where most of the children stay for lunch, the lunch period ranges from 30 minutes to one hour.)
1:00 to 1:15	Spelling
1:15 to 1:30	Penmanship
1:30 to 2:20	Art (three days per week) Science (two days per week)
2:20 to 2:30	Recess

[2] Developed by the authors from their study of teacher programs found in the public school systems surveyed by them in the eastern, southern, and middlewestern states. Again, this one program cannot represent the total range of practice, but most fifth and sixth grade teachers will find their own program at some point in this statement. Rural schools (one and two room) with all grades taught by one or two teachers have a very complex time schedule.

2:30 to 3:10   Reading, Library, Current Events
3:10 to 3:30   Physical Education, games, make-up work
3:30   Dismissal

These general time schedules are more valuable for giving the reader a picture of the range of activities over the school day than they are for revealing the way each of the indicated activities are developed with children. Of course, the time of scheduling and the extent of time given over to each activity varies widely between and within schools. The size of the school, whether or not the children are transported, the grade level, and the nature of classroom and teacher organization partially determine the nature of the daily and weekly time schedules and the part children have in planning it.

Looking at the Daily Subject Pattern. Another way of looking at the pattern of the elementary school curriculum is to examine the average amount of daily time spent on various subject areas over the different grade levels. Again, the specific 20 or 30 minutes allotted to each subject only suggests what the teaching schedules actually are; the following table, however, does indicate the amount of emphasis given to different subject fields over the grades of the elementary school.

APPROXIMATE AVERAGE TIMES SPENT ON VARIOUS SUBJECTS IN ELEMENTARY SCHOOLS
IN PASADENA, CALIFORNIA IN MINUTES PER DAY*

Subject areas	Grades				
	K	1	2	3	4, 5, 6
Reading	20	60	50	50	50
Language	15	20	20	20	20
Spelling		10	10	15	15
Handwriting		10	10	15	15
History, civics	20	25	30	30	35
Geography		20	20	20	25
Arithmetic	10	15	20	25	45
Music	25	20	20	20	20
Art	25	20	20	20	20
Physical education	20	20	20	20	20
Total	135	220	220	240	270

* Clyde M. Hill and Lloyd N. Morrisett, *Report of the Pasadena School Survey.* (Pasadena, California, Pasadena City Board of Education, 1951), p. 126.

What Daily Time Schedules Show about the Curriculum. A careful study of the forgoing time-schedules indicates some support for the following generalizations about the educational program of elementary schools:

1. The school day of the child in most elementary schools is bounded by the subject divisions into which the curriculum is di-

vided. Examination of the programs of thousands of teachers in all parts of the country indicates that it is the rare teacher who organizes his program on any other basis, or who experiments with large blocks of time within which he plans flexibly with children. Teachers are more likely to experiment with large blocks of time than they are to eliminate subject divisions.

This finding, which any parent or teacher can verify for himself, means: a) Few teachers and schools are trying to use the social or personal experiences of children as a basis for organizing the curriculum of the school. b) The last twenty years have not brought much experimentation in curriculum organization. Elementary schools today, as far as the divisions of the curriculum are concerned, are not much different from the schools of thirty years ago. The differences, if any, are in the nature and quality of the experiences children are having within the subject form of curriculum organization.

2. In terms of time and emphasis, the reading school of yesteryear is still the reading school of today. It is the common practice in primary grades to have two reading periods a day for most children; in the middle grades, a major amount of time is allotted to direct reading instruction. Combined with the related language activities of oral and written language, spelling, handwriting and literature, it means that a large portion of the school day at all levels is given over to the teaching of the language arts.

3. Science, home, and manual arts subject areas are conspicuous by their absence in the daily educational programs of many schools. This raises the serious question as to whether boys and girls can afford to grow up in a modern world of technology and science with as little experience in these important areas of general education as is indicated by the time schedules of most schools. The question becomes even more pressing when the 15 to 25 minute periods of time two to three times a week given to science are examined in the light of the opportunities they provide for children to learn something of the methods of thinking and experimenting important in science. Chapter 9 discusses this point more comprehensively.

4. With the exception of arithmetic, the proportional emphases of subject areas in the primary grades are about the same as similar emphases in the middle grades. In general, within the subject areas included in most programs, increased maturity is achieved by increase in levels of understanding and skill within the same subject fields. This points up the critical importance of securing and enhancing the con-

tinuity of the development of the child in these subject fields over the common school period.

5. The social studies program of the elementary school wavers between being organized on the basis of the broad field of social studies, or on the more limited areas of history, geography, and civics. In the primary grades, the broad field concept of social studies is used. In the middle grades, separate classes in history, geography, and civics, with geography as the basic orientation, is more characteristic than one common program of social studies. Unfortunately, the contributions anthropology, sociology, and economics may make to the understanding of human relationships and to social living are not often found in the social studies program of the elementary school. This problem is examined further in Chapter 8.

6. The teacher of the ordinary grade group at any level in the elementary school is confronted with the tremendous task of curriculum planning and organization. Note the statement in the time schedule for grades 1, 2, 3, on page 129: "Science should include development of simple concepts in botany, zoology, physics, chemistry, and health; social studies should include simple concepts in social living, history, geography, citizenship, and economics." How many elementary school teachers have this broad background in their own general education, or have the kind of training in curriculum planning and organization which would enable them to meet this tremendous responsibility?

Some Common Denominators in Curriculum Planning and Organization

An examination of the activities of children in school, and the scope and nature of the educational programs designed to contribute to their development, reveals certain common denominators which run through all instructional activities and curriculum programs.

The Commonness of Our Major Objectives. All different aspects of the elementary school program contribute to common over-all objectives. This common responsibility for promoting children's personal development and good citizenship is seen most clearly when attention is focused on the common process areas of the curriculum.

The Commonness of Our Major Object of Attention—the Child. All programs, all ways of organizing the curriculum, all ways of teaching and the use of instructional materials have as their ultimate purpose to make effective changes in the behavior of children. Children are one of the common centers of attention in an educational program, and they can serve, together with objectives, as important reference points in planning and organizing the curriculum of the school.

The Commonness of Both Content and Processes in All Learning Experiences. We can expect that the learning experiences children have in school will include both ideas and processes. Any adequate conception of education must always consider both.

The Commonness of Our Referents for Curriculum Decisions. There are three major referents for deriving objectives and for making curriculum decisions. These are our cultural heritage (man's knowledge), the society, and the individual. Approaches to curriculum always use all three.

The Commonness of Our Teaching Tasks. Certain common teaching responsibilities confront a teacher, regardless of how he teaches, the age level of his students, or his teaching field. Every teacher will have to handle the problems of determining the direction of learning, the selection of appropriate learning experiences, the way in which the activities of children should be organized, the nature of his evaluations, and the nature and extent of educational planning.

These common teaching tasks are stated in more detail in the following list. In considering these tasks, however, teachers and curriculum committees should realize that merely listing them does not automatically solve them properly.

Common Tasks of Teaching and Curriculum

I. *The identification, definition, and use of objectives* to provide direction, scope, and emphasis to the learning of children in school, and to provide the teacher with one of the important bases for the selection of desirable learning experiences and their adequate evaluation, and for curriculum planning.

The Key Tasks of Curriculum

II. The selection of learning experiences of some educational significance.

III. The organization and development of these experiences so that all of the essential educational elements are considered; the experiences are organized around foci which are sufficiently comprehensive to include children, ideas, materials, plans, activities, and evaluations; and the relationships among these elements are seen and used to predict and control future behavior. Proper organization and development of learning experiences of children are concerned with adequate breadth, useful perception of relationships, and effective continuity of learning.

IV. The evaluation of the products of learning so that their relationships to objectives are perceived, their adequacy of development at that time is determined, and their consequence for future improved behavior is examined.

V. The formulation and carrying out of plans which include the important people of the teaching-learning enterprise—children, teachers, staff, parents, and adults—at their proper points of responsibility and in relation to their performing their respective functions in insuring and developing effective and desirable educational programs for children.

In considering this list of common teaching responsibilities, it is valuable to keep the following ideas in mind: a) All five of the tasks are related and do not occur in the teaching-learning process in the order in which they are listed. b) *Tasks II and III are the key tasks* (selecting, and organizing and developing learning experiences) and are the ones to which all the others contribute. c) The tasks, while valuable for indicating what decisions must be made, and how the curriculum and instructional jobs are to be performed, do not provide any educational answers. Other curriculum frameworks and value systems will also have to be applied to these teaching-learning-action-points.

Different Approaches to Curriculum Planning and Organization

There are only three fundamental approaches to planning and organizing the elementary school curriculum. These three approaches either 1) consider man's cultural heritage as the basic referent; 2) consider man's social experiences and social organizations to be basic; or 3) consider the individual and his perceived needs as basic.

The Subject or Broad Field Approaches to Curriculum Organization. Both subject and broad field forms of curriculum organization are based on the same kind of curriculum thinking. Differences between these two subject-oriented approaches are determined on the extent to which broader areas of subject matter are considered. These differences may be seen more clearly in the following descriptions.

The Subject-Centered Curriculum. The concept of a subject as merely a place where man can store, arrange, and differentiate his accumulated knowledges and experiences has long since been replaced by a more adequate concept of subject instruction and organization. Each subject has three distinguishing characteristics: 1) A unique body of content; 2) its own intellectual discipline (the scientific method, historical method, mathematical thinking, etc.); and 3) its own pattern for organizing its content. Objectives are derived from important generalizations and intellectual processes of the subject field. The logical pattern of organization of the subject defines many of the teaching patterns and sequences. The breadth of the curriculum is determined by the number of subjects taught. There is real need in a subject-centered curriculum to look at the total program in order to secure some balance and adequate relationship among and within subject fields.

An important definition in the subject curriculum is the definition of the topics or subject matter to be covered, and the order in which this is to be done. There is some reason to believe that teachers find definitions of sequence much more useful in selecting learning experiences for children than definitions of objectives. Teachers can get their fingers into topics or areas to be studied; but objectives by their very nature are abstractions.

Common ways to arrange sequences in learning experiences are: from the simple to more complex; from the concrete to the more abstract; from the near to the more remote; from one period in time to another; from things of first importance to those next in importance; from the first step in a process through the order of the steps as they appear. Frequently, however, arrangements of topics, stories, chapters, and problems in courses of study and in text materials seem to have little rhyme or reason. It is helpful if children can see the sense of the way things develop, so that they can predict what is coming next. Much teaching would be improved if more adequate instructional sequences were developed.

Children are considered in good subject teaching in two ways. First, their educational backgrounds and intellectual maturity are examined to see if they are ready to go on to the next topic. Second, the experiences of the children are surveyed to identify any centers of interest which can be used to organize and motivate the activities necessary to achieve the desired subject matter objectives. If no appropriate interest centers can be found, new experiences must be developed.

The available instructional materials and resources serve as another screen for selecting desirable learning experiences for children. Text materials are thus an important determinant of what is taught in most schools. Teachers will use text materials and instructional resources more effectively if they realize that:

1. The textbook cannot assume the responsibility for generalizing about important ideas or for developing and using skills. These can only be done by children with the help of their teacher.

2. The textbook should not be given the sole responsibility for organizing and developing the major ideas and relationships in a subject field, or for relating this pattern of ideas to the problems and experiences of a particular group of children.

3. The textbook should not be given the sole responsibility for determining what children are taught. It is possible to bring the textbook as a resource to the children, as well as bringing the children to the textbook.

4. A textbook cannot determine the speed with which a child moves through his learning activities, or the speed with which they move past him. There is very little a textbook can do to help a child pace his learning according to his purposes and according to the nature of the content being studied. This is the responsibility of the teacher and children.

5. Learning, if it is to be valuable, must be evaluated and then applied to future learning and behavior. A textbook can do very little about this problem. Children and teacher must assume responsibility for this important aspect of all learning.

The above five points indicate that there are many important aspects of an educational program which demand the attention and efforts of a teacher. It is not likely that instructional materials or learning aids can ever substitute for effective teaching.

In the evaluation program of most schools, facts and information are appraised much more easily than understandings; understandings are evaluated more easily than abilities; and abilities are tested much more easily than attitudes. Thus it is natural that most of the evaluations of the learning of children tend to be limited to the level of facts and information. Good subject teaching emphasizes the importance of the evaluation of both understandings and intellectual processes, and especially the learner's perception of the logical structure of ideas within the subject as a basis for dealing with his problems of living. This last idea is not often a concern of most teachers, nor is it frequently considered in evaluation programs. The theory of the subject curriculum, however, considers it very important.

Planning is done mainly by the teachers and by the people who write the instructional materials or who plan the course of study. This planning has to do mainly with the definition of the important understandings and abilities to teach, topics or areas to be covered, instructional materials to be used, estimates of how rapidly to develop, the degree of accomplishment to expect, the teaching procedures to be used, and the evaluation devices to apply. Planning with children usually has to do with time, materials, specific interests to use, and personal arrangements. It is not often that plans are concerned with what should be learned, or with the major curriculum decisions.

Advantages and Disadvantages of the Subject Curriculum

Some of the advantages of the curriculum organized on the basis of subjects are: a) The pattern of subject organization is familiar to parents and teachers, has a long historical tradition, and has a great deal of instructional material already available for use. b) Sequence plans can be developed over the period of the elementary school which enable teachers and parents to see what the educational program is planning to do. c) Specific learnings can be identified and the learning activities of the classroom directed to their adequate "mastery." The child is always learning something.

Some of the criticisms of the subject curriculum are: a) The logical, rather than psychological, organization of the subject makes it necessary to teach a great deal of relatively meaningless material to children. This puts much emphasis on memory and drill as learning and teaching tools. b) Critics of the subject curriculum claim that life problems of any significance always demand subject matter and skills from more than one subject area; the child's day or an adult's day does not divide itself up into spelling, handwriting, arithmetic, physical education, history, etc.; and children and their problems are brought to books and subject matter, rather than books and subject matter being brought to children and their problems. c) Many critics of the subject curriculum challenge the assumption that textbook and course-of-study makers can predict ten to fifteen years in advance what the child will need to know and be able to do.

Subject specialists, on the other hand, claim that the important ideas and abilities to be taught to our young children cannot be fleeting and limited in nature, but must be basic and universal in character. They question the ability of the child and the teacher to judge adequately what these important ideas and skills are, and say that more confidence should be placed in the judgment of experts in the subject matter itself. The common response to this is usually that the subject curriculum is essentially autocratic, and provides little place for the skills of thinking, selecting, planning, action, evaluating, replanning, etc., which are important for a person who lives in a society in which there is no higher authority than the people.

Another criticism is that the division of the school day into nine to fifteen different subject areas violates what we know about the ability of any learner to keep a number of isolated elements in mind, and to perceive any of the relationships which may exist among them. And further, this fractionation of subjects also violates the very theory of subject organization itself. Many of the divisions, such as handwrit-

ing, spelling, physical education, reading, and the like, are not subjects in any basic sense at all, but are merely skill areas which have
been elevated to the level of subjects for teaching convenience. Each
lacks a body of distinguishable subject matter, a related intellectual
discipline, and an identifiable logical organization.

An examination of the arguments pro and con in respect to the
subject forms of curriculum organization reveals that behind these
claims and counter-claims lie definite convictions about the nature of
effective learning, about the nature of the child and his role in making the important decisions of curriculum, about the nature of our
society and the role of the elementary school in maintaining our basic
social beliefs, and about the nature of the teacher's role in effective
curriculum planning and development. Educational programs stem
directly from what people believe about these four areas. Before
changes in curriculum can be made on a long-term basis, changes
must be made in the value systems which underlie a given program.

Organization of the Curriculum Around Broad Fields

As more emphasis was placed on the importance of good citizenship, and the need of the curriculum of the elementary school to help
the child deal with his common and persistent problems of living, increasing attempts were made to bring together related subject fields
around a common area of knowledge. Naturally, social studies led the
way in this approach.

In the broad field of social studies, for example, curriculum workers attempted to identify the common social concepts and processes
found in all social fields which might be essential in explaining and
controlling the complexities of human relationships. Other attempts
at organization tried to identify common persisting problems of human living to which all of the social sciences could make their respective contributions. A third approach to the problem of finding a common organizational base was to attempt to identify regions of the
world which could be defined in terms of their characteristic people,
customs, resources, climate, and political and social organizations.
More recently, there has been some effort made to bring all three of
these concepts—common generalizations and social processes, persisting and general problems of human living, and characteristic regions
of the world—into one adequate framework for social studies.

Science is usually taught as a broad field in the elementary school
curriculum. In high school it is broken down into the characteristic
subject fields of botany, biology, physics, and chemistry. The organiz-

ing elements in a broad field approach to science have been the major concepts of science, the scientific method as a process of discovery and a way to test truth, and the classic topics of heat, light, magnetism, animals, plants, atoms, the universe, etc., pulled from all areas of science. Science is a relative newcomer to the elementary school curriculum, which may account for its present form of organization.

Other movements in the direction of the broad fields have been in language arts (reading, writing, spelling, oral and written composition, literature, grammar, and listening), the fine arts (music, painting, drawing, dramatics), health and physical education (games, rhythms, developmental activities, health instruction), and home and manual arts. Arithmetic is usually taught as a subject, with some attempts being made to develop programs of general mathematics in the upper grades and at junior high school level.

The basic idea which underlies the broad fields form of curriculum organization is the same as that which underlies the subject approach, and, consequently, each method of organization has most of the same advantages and disadvantages. The broad fields form of organization, however, has the advantage of dealing with broader areas of subject matter. This enables the teacher to organize his school day around five or six subject areas, rather than nine to fifteen, which permits the use of larger blocks of time. This form of organization also tends to cut down on the extreme compartmentalization of the strict subject organization, and enables the teacher to deal with the children's problems of personal and social living on a broader basis.

The effort to bring related fields of knowledge together as a means for organizing and relating subject matter fields more adequately to children's problems of living is tied to the long-time effort of teachers to relate and correlate (fuse, integrate)[3] appropriate subject fields and educational processes to the children. In the elementary school, activity programs, project teachings, and the development of various kinds of unit plans have characterized the attempt to focus the necessary and important aspects of the child's education around fewer and more meaningful organizing centers. At the secondary school level, the core curriculum plan of curriculum organization has received considerable attention.

As the reader might expect, strict subject specialists are not at all

3 All of these terms are concerned with the learner's organizing and relating important parts of his educational experience. In general, correlated, fused, and core curriculums have to do with the plans and educational arrangements made by the teacher and the curriculum organization to facilitate the learner "integrating" the products of his experiences in school.

happy with any attempt to destroy the distinctive quality of specific subject fields. On the other hand, people who are convinced of the importance of direct attention to the problems of the child's personal and social living are equally dissatisfied with the broad field form of curriculum organization. Teachers who have difficulty in obtaining textbooks organized for broad fields, who therefore have to concern themselves extensively with the problem of instructional organization, and who find it difficult to handle the many fields of knowledge necessary for teaching a broad field, are even less happy when confronted with the task of introducing this form of organization into their instructional planning and teaching. This merely indicates, however, that it is difficult to make any kind of educational change which demands readjustments and extension in the routines and responsibilities of teachers.

The Problems of Living Curriculum.[4] All of the major statements of objectives for education since 1918, and the work in curriculum done by Bobbitt and Charters in the 1920's, and by Caswell in the 1930's, have emphasized the importance of the social orientation of the school and of persistent problems of social living[5] as bases for organizing the curriculum of the elementary school.

In a sense, the problems or areas of living form of organization of the curriculum merely expands social studies to the point where it becomes the general background for the whole curriculum of the elementary school. This is why we find many of the ideas and organizing

[4]The reader will profit from studying the following references on the areas of living approach to curriculum organization.

Florence B. Stratemeyer *et al.*, *Developing a Curriculum for Modern Living* (New York: Bureau of Publications, Teachers College, Columbia University, 1947). The whole book is an elaboration of this point of view.

Hollis I. Caswell and Doak S. Campbell, *Curriculum Development* (New York: American Book Company, 1935), pp. 173-184. This book is out of print, but it is a very valuable reference on curriculum in general, and on the problems of living curriculum in particular.

B. Othanel Smith, William O. Stanley, Harlan J. Shores, *Fundamentals of Curriculum Development* (Yonkers-on-Hudson, New York: World Book Company, 1950), pp. 512-525. This difficult book will give the reader an excellent perspective of the social context in which education must take place.

State Department of Public Instruction, *Course of Study for the Elementary School* (Richmond: State of Virginia, 1934, 1938, 1942). A number of courses of study at the state and local level are valuable in providing understanding about this approach. These three Virginia editions will give the reader a picture of the changes that take place in a program of this kind as it passes through different phases of development.

[5] Various phrases have been used instead of problems of living—*areas of living, functions of living, persistent life situations,* etc. All of these phrases express the idea that within the affairs of man, we find common problems, areas of living, persisting situations, and social processes or functions with which all men have to deal in some fashion in order to get along with the business of living. If this concept is kept in mind, the different phrases used will not cause much trouble.

plans of this form of curriculum organization present in many social studies programs of the elementary school. Problems of social living are frequently used as the basic themes of study and as organizing centers which allow children and teacher to move from one geographic area, political division, or cultural region to another with perspective and continuity.

The way in which this kind of curriculum is planned in individual schools varies a good deal. The key idea is to use the identified areas of problems of living as a framework for planning and organizing. The planners make sure that all of the areas are considered during a school year, and that attention is paid to them at different levels of maturity as the child moves through the school. The divisions of time in a school day correspond to the units or projects being worked on and their need for attention at that time—not to the subject divisions. An important aspect of the work of the teacher is to help the children in their planning for problems, for activities, for personal relationships, for time, for methods of action, and for the necessary culminating and evaluatory activities.

The point of this form of curriculum organization is that persistent social problems extend into the lives of individual children and adults; therefore, important aspects of the social development of all people must and will be a part of the program of the elementary school. If these persistent problems of human living are examined closely enough and dealt with adequately at the child's level of understanding and degree of social responsibility, all of the important subjects and intellectual processes are identified and brought to bear on the social problems to be resolved. It is conceded that some of our present subject matter taught in the elementary school will be left out, and desirably so. On the other hand, much important subject matter dealing with health, personal guidance, housing, consumer education, diet, getting along with others, science, and the like, will be added. The claim is made that more, rather than less, subject matter is taught and that more educational resources—books, people, and libraries—are used in this approach to curriculum than in others.

Critics of this approach to curriculum feel that the basic skills of language—reading, writing, spelling, speaking, listening—and of arithmetic are either left out or left to the incidental attention of teachers and children. It is true that much of the material in arithmetic which lacks direct social application would not come to the attention of elementary school children in this plan. The same would be true about much of the material in the language arts. It is argued, however, that in this approach to curriculum organization the basic skills and functions of language or arithmetic, if they are truly basic, are bound to be included in the various areas of the child's social experience. Rather than less opportunity for their development, there would actually be more; and the teaching of these skills would always be related to their social function. Of course, this places more responsibility on the teacher and staff.

A further criticism of this framework for curriculum planning is that it does not provide for the systematic, continuous development of important ideas and educational abilities. Continuity in learning is important and its occurrence must be insured. In the areas of living approach, an important part of the curriculum planning is concerned with the problem of what should come next in view of the past experiences and the nature of the problems that have been studied. At the staff level, the framework of areas of living and related social processes is studied to see which plan would best enhance a continuous development at each age level over the period of the elementary school. Within this broad plan, teachers prepare for their work with children by the development of resource units. This advance planning frees the teacher to work intensively with children to fill in the details when these units are actually taught. Continuity is thus provided for in two ways: first, by the use of the framework of agreed upon areas of living and related social processes; and second, by the continuities inherent in the ongoing experiences of children themselves which are exploited by on-the-spot teacher-pupil-planning.

The implications of the problems of living approach for organizing the curriculum for the staff and teachers are:

1. The staff and individual teachers must develop the social framework of areas of living and related social processes within which the educational program of the school will take place. Special attention must be paid to the problem of developing effective continuities over a given school year and through the years of the elementary school. The usual definition of sequence is made in terms of the expanding social experience of the child from his home to the world about him.

2. Since most of the important curriculum decisions must be made by the staff with the children, teachers *will have to know what these decisions are* and how to make them in a way that is socially and educationally effective.

3. Since no one textbook is used, the problem of instructional materials will be both difficult and continual. This one point discourages many teachers from exploring the possibilities of this form of

curriculum organization in their present social studies program. A school using this curriculum organization must move to develop curriculum materials centers in each school where all kinds of instructional materials may be collected and files of materials developed for the use of children and teachers. The relation of the room library, school library, and community library must be studied and the necessary cooperation secured. The resources of the community have to be identified and used.

4. Records of the school must be expanded to include curriculum records of the work of particular children and groups over more than one year. The cumulative folders must contain information of greater educational significance than collections of work papers and test records.

5. Problems of working and planning with children must be studied and made a part of the working experience of the staff. Child study and community study progams will be important parts of the continuous study program of the school. Parent-teacher conferences will be valuable in planning for the education of the child. Each teacher must have staff resources to call on in the areas of child study and guidance, health, curriculum planning and development, materials, and the arts.

The Child-Centered Curriculum.[6] This approach has often been called the emerging curriculum, or the child-needs approach to curriculum organization. These phrases indicate the underlying concept of this kind of curriculum organization—that any meaningful, significant program of education for adults or children must emerge from their felt needs or concerns. His felt needs must serve as the focus of curriculum organization for the child, particularly, because his curriculum cannot exist outside of his experience and his perception of it. Contrary to what people usually believe about this plan, the child is not limited to one concern at any one time, nor does he remain at the level of his original perception of it. This approach places great stress on the teachers' and children's examining a number of felt needs and selecting those of greatest significance to them at that time. It is understood that some of these concerns may be discarded and others added as the emerging experience of the children dictates.

6 The reader interested in further study of the emerging needs approach to curriculum organization will find the following references profitable:

A. Thomas Hopkins, *Integration, Its Meaning and Application* (New York: D. Appleton-Century Company, 1937), pp. 253-275; L. Thomas Hopkins, *Interaction: The Democratic Process* (Boston: D. C. Heath and Company, 1941); William H. Kilpatrick, *Philosophy of Education* (New York: The Macmillan Co., 1951), pp. 312-329; and B. Othanel Smith, William O. Stanley, and Harlan B. Shores, *op. cit.*, pp. 412-463.

A major assumption is that if these felt needs are properly selected and worked on over sufficient time, they will include all the persistent problems of living, and will necessitate the development of all basic knowledges and skills. How else can a persistent problem of human living be identified, other than by watching to see if it happens again and again, and by determining the extent to which it provides an obstacle to more effective living? After all, basic skills are considered basic because they are a necessary and continuing part of the phenomena to which they are related; they are not basic because the course of study calls them so. The job of effective curriculum planning is to help the child to identify these persistent problems and to lead him to develop the skills necessary to deal with them effectively.

The future is best taken care of by the child's trying to do the best he can with the present, not on a hand-to-mouth basis, but by dealing with the present on such terms that the ability to meet and handle the future is always improved. The future can never be predicted; one can only speculate about it in the light of the best possible analysis of the present.

Since the curriculum of the child cannot be known in advance, it is not possible to make lists of needs, nor to develop an over-all framework for the curriculum. It is possible, however, to develop a philosophy of education within which the staff of a school may define the parts that the school, the teacher, and the community play in the education of children. There is a need for a philosophy which will help to determine how the experiences the child has in school may be made maximally educative. In formulating any such philosophy, the following questions ought to be considered: What is the nature of the child as a biological-social being? How can we help children to identify, select, organize, and develop important educational concerns and felt needs? How can we help the child evaluate and plan effectively? How can we plan effectively as a staff so that the emerging educational programs of these children have adequate significance, breadth, organization, and continuity?

In a curriculum organized on the basis of the felt needs of children, a particular group of children with their teacher may start off the school year with an attempt to identify what they need to work on. This planning does not take place in a vacuum; they must consider what is happening to them in the present, what they have been doing in the past, what the demands of their present situation are, and what they want to be able to accomplish in the future. Rather than worrying about what he can do to fill up the time, a teacher soon starts worrying about how to get done all that needs to be done, or how to select the most important things to do from the many important things that cry for attention. This is the kind of thinking and planning the child will have to do for the rest of his life.

The teacher helps to determine which of the list of things on the agenda are of the first-things-first nature. Then an attempt is made to identify those needs on the list which, if worked on, will take care of a number of others. These concerns are considered more important than others. Then this selected list of felt needs is examined to see if some of them may have to be worked on simultaneously for work to be effective. Or the list may be examined to determine if there is some implicit order, in the sense that work on one felt need leads to another. Finally there may be a question about whether some of the problems need to be worked on at all, or if some may be postponed.

This planning would not be carried through completely, nor would it be made on a level above the children's comprehension. Most attention is spent on getting started at what seems to be a good spot with the understanding that as the work progresses and experience is gained, more effective decisions will be made and other felt needs will be added to the working agenda.

All the criticisms and difficulties of the areas of living curriculum are accentuated in the emerging curriculum. Yet the reader should realize that the emerging curriculum form of organization is really the basis upon which he organizes his own life. If he works with adults outside the framework of the school, in community activities and in programs of adult education, he knows that this is the form of curriculum planning and organization which is most effective. Any elementary school principal or supervisor will be well advised to use this form of curriculum planning and organization with teachers, in planning and developing their programs of in-service education.

Most teachers use this form of curriculum organization in planning the out-of-class activities of the school day, school parties, programs with parents, recreational activities, and the like. Health, physical education, social studies, and the arts are the areas in school programs which are most accessible to this form of curriculum planning.

Suggested Ways to Improve the Organization of the Elementary School Curriculum

Any educational and social improvement is the result of hard work, long continued effort, and the synthesis of many different and sometimes conflicting ideas and points of view. The process of improvement, however, should include some general plan or framework within which more specific plans and action can be related and evaluated.

1. In curriculum planning and organization, the total scope of the curriculum, as well as its particular parts, must be considered and used in developing educational programs with children.

Ways of Considering the Problem of Comprehensiveness

a. Look at the *total* range of important objectives and try to have them *all* reflected in the educational program. If we state that certain objectives are significant and necessary, then we are obligated to incorporate them into the experiences children have in school.

b. Look at the total range of subject divisions considered important and see what is necessary to get an over-all adequate and balanced development. In many elementary schools, for example, science, economics, health, physical education, and the arts are areas of the curriculum emphasized least.

c. Look at the total range of abilities considered important for effective learning. More stress is frequently placed on the arts of language than on effective thinking and evaluating. More emphasis is commonly placed on promptness and neatness than on understanding and effective ways of living and working together. More attention is usually given to the use of a textbook and workbook than to the problem of seeking, selecting, and using wisely a broad range of learning resources.

d. Look at the definitions of comprehensiveness in teaching and the various curriculum fields. Many comprehensive teaching plans emphasize the importance of moving from the experiences of children to generalizations about these experiences, to the consideration of the relationship of new generalizations to old, and to the application of this framework of ideas to appropriate problems in the experience of children and adults. Many subject areas have definitions of characteristic regions, essential arithmetical processes, persistent problems of human living, etc., which are definitions of the total scope of things to be considered.

e. Look at plans for the total school day, week, month, and year. The consideration of the scope of things to be developed over time is a useful way of giving comprehensiveness to the planning and organization of the curriculum.

2. In curriculum planning and organization, the whole of an edu-

cational program should have some understandable relationship to its parts. There should be some over-all planning framework which has sufficient comprehensiveness to include all of the parts, and sufficient depth to promote and support the development of each part.

Ways of Considering the Problem of Relationship or Curriculum Design

a. Relationships exist among the persistent tasks of teaching. Objectives, evaluation, and planning are valuable in the selection, organization, and development of learning experiences.

b. The various approaches to curriculum organization are useful curriculum frameworks for relating the work of the children, teacher, and staff.

c. The teaching plan for any subject field is an over-all framework teachers can use. These plans usually include definitions of objectives, sequence, screens for selecting learning experiences, characteristics of proper organizing centers, teaching plans or cycles, evaluations, and resources. Frequently these plans are in the form of some kind of unit planning.

d. Statements of some theoretical framework help in perceiving relationships. One framework which the authors have found useful is as follows:

Foundation Areas	Objectives	Instructional Organization of School
Beliefs about learning and development.		Classification and grouping.
	Experiences of children must have significance, breadth, organization, continuity.	Evaluation and promoting.
Beliefs about nature of society and of man.		Teacher group or departmental or cycle plans.
Beliefs about function of school and children and teacher's role in it.		Time schedules.
		Instructional and physical resources.

Nature of organizing and developing centers.

Subject matter.	Persistent problems of living.	Felt needs of children.

3. In curriculum planning and organization, our beliefs about what is important and good in education are basic to our acceptance

and use of both the ends and means of education; therefore, they should be made explicit so that they can be examined and tested.

Ways of Considering the Problems of Educational Values

a. Many of our educational values become apparent when we evaluate children and their educational accomplishments. Our procedures for marking, promoting, grouping, and classifying children are good places to look for them.

b. The way in which the teacher deals with the intellectual, social, physical, and sexual differences in children and parents tends to reveal his value patterns.

c. Studies of teachers' and children's verbal value statements about themselves and their achievements, and about others and their accomplishments will reveal important aspiration levels.

d. An examination as to what the staff believes to be the nature of effective learning, effective development, or effective social behavior provides a working basis for the examination and improvement of instructional practices.

e. A consideration of the ways in which teachers help children determine the truth or goodness of what they do helps identify the nature of the standards or norms used for action and decision making.

All of the above are difficult to obtain and to examine. Yet these are the sort of value judgments which have tremendous consequences for children.

4. In curriculum planning and organization, we should broaden our consideration of the range and nature of proper educational resources.

Ways of Considering the Problem of Educational Resources

a. What is the range of instructional materials available for use with children? Is it limited to textbook and/or workbook, or does it extend to other materials, library, and community resources?

b. What is the range of instructional materials and resources available to teachers and staff? Are there teacher helps, instructional libraries, material centers, resources for development of instructional materials for children, and curriculum consultants?

c. What is the range of instructional materials and resources available on the local, state, regional, and national level? Are libraries, educational institutions of the region, and state and national resources identified and used?

d. What is the range of personnel resources for instruction and learning utilized within the group of children,[7] the staff of a school, the adult members of a community?

5. In curriculum planning and organization, we should consider more carefully the proper nature of organizing centers for effective learning. The centers we use for organizing and planning are probably more important in determining the actual learning activities of children than any other single curriculum decision made by the teacher.

Ways of Considering the Problem of Organizing Centers

Do the instructional centers developed with the children have:

a. some educational significance of their own?

b. adequate comprehensiveness—can they include ideas, processes, children, groups, a number of catch-hold points, a number of application possibilities, low and high ceilings of development?

c. organizing capacity—can the organizing centers tie children, ideas, materials, and activities together in some meaningful fashion? (Large ideas, problems, tasks, functions, etc., do this better than objects, people, geographic spots, and great documents.)

d. capacity for movement or extension. Does the center provide for:

intellectual movement—from facts to generalizations to applications?

social movement—from one person or culture to another?

geographic movement—from one location to another?

movement in time—from a past, to a present, to a future?

6. In curriculum planning and organization, the instructional organization of the school should be related to the educational program of the school.

Ways of Considering the Problem of Instructional Organization[8]

Are the following procedures consistent with the curriculum planning and organization of the school? Class and grade organization; classification, grouping, promotion practices, marking, reporting, evaluation procedures; presence and use of common resources and physical facilities; and the staff organization, role of principal, supervisors, and special services.

---

[7] This refers to children sharing their experiences with each other and to the contribution that they make to each other's development. It does not mean children teaching each other on a formal basis in the old concept of a pupil monitor, or of Nancy drilling Joe in the corner on his table of 3's.

[8] This problem is treated more fully in chapter 13.

7. In curriculum planning and organization, it is important to consider the roles of children, teachers, staff, and adult groups in planning and in making decisions.

Ways of Considering the Problem of Roles of People in Planning

a. What educational plans and decisions have to be made and who should make them?

b. At what levels in the planning and decision making are different individuals and groups involved?

c. What decisions need to be made in common with a number of people?

d. What degrees of responsibility for planning and decision making are to be held by different individuals or groups of people? What degrees of freedom do they have?

e. What is the focus for planning and decision making? Ultimately, the focus must be on the children and teacher, for they are involved with the real educational actions.

A Backward and Forward Look

The elementary school curriculum exists only in the lives of real children. In helping make the experiences these children have in school significant to them, and as important educationally as possible, teachers, the staff, and the adults of the community should participate in making plans and evolving forms of curriculum organization which they believe will accomplish these ends. Curriculum plans all involve children, desirable learnings, and important social applications; they differ, however, as to which of these referents is considered most important.

Most schools use the subject and broad fields forms of curriculum organization, both of which are based on the same kind of curriculum thinking. Persistent problems (or areas of human living), and the emerging needs of children are used by most teachers as organizing centers for some part of their instructional program. Few teachers, or schools, however, organize their entire school program on either of these bases.

Suggestions for improving curriculum planning and organization have to do mostly with the importance of planning and organizing in terms of some comprehensive framework against which educational values, children, facilities, teachers, ideas, processes, and the like are seen in some understandable relationship to each other. The nature of the organizing centers for learning, the range of resources available, and the adequate relating of instructional organization and responsibilities for decision making are important both to the educational program and for children and their effective learning.

Good curriculum planning helps bring breadth and significance to the experiences children have in school; it realizes the intelligence and imagination of teachers; and it helps marshal the resources of the school and community for effective learning. It is the one sure way of insuring good education for all of America's children.

BIBLIOGRAPHY

Beck, Robert H., Walter W. Cook, and Nolan C. Kearney, *Curriculum in the Modern Elementary School*. Englewood Cliffs, N.J.: Prentice-Hall, Inc., 1953.

Caswell, Hollis I. and A. Wellesley Foshay, *Education in the Elementary School*. New York: American Book Company, 1950.

Featherstone, William B., *A Functional Curriculum for Youth*. New York: American Book Company, 1950.

Gwynn, J. Minor, *Curriculum Principles and Social Trends*. New York: The Macmillan Company, 1950.

Herrick, Virgil E. and Ralph W. Tyler, *Toward Improved Curriculum Theory*. Supplementary Education Monograph, No. 71. Chicago: The University of Chicago Press, 1950.

Hopkins, L. Thomas, *Interaction: The Democratic Process*. Boston: D. C. Heath and Company, 1941.

Lee, J. Murray, and Dorris May Lee, *The Child and His Curriculum*. New York: Appleton-Century-Crofts, Inc., 1950.

Miel, Alice, *et al.*, *Cooperative Procedures in Learning*. New York: Bureau of Publications, Teachers College, Columbia University, 1952.

Ragan, William B., *Modern Elementary Curriculum*. New York: The Dryden Press, 1953.

Saucier, W. A., *Theory and Practice in the Elementary School*. New York: The Macmillan Company, 1951.

Smith, B. Othanel, William O. Stanley, and J. Harlan Shores, *Fundamentals of Curriculum Development*. Yonkers-on-Hudson, New York: World Book Company, 1950.

PART THREE

CURRICULUM

AREAS

IN THE

ELEMENTARY

SCHOOL

THE
LANGUAGE
ARTS
PROGRAM

7

BY LANGUAGE ARTS, WE MEAN COMMUNICATION through the medium of language, in contrast to other communication using color, sound, or bodily movement as media. All forms of communication involve two functions: *expressing* an idea or feeling, and *receiving* of messages. In language arts, expressing ideas to others is accomplished through speaking and writing; receiving ideas involves reading and listening. These processes are taught in elementary schools as oral and written expression, handwriting, spelling, grammar, reading, and listening.

LANGUAGE ARTS AS A COMMUNICATION PROCESS

The process of communicating by language can be regarded in a variety of ways. Inasmuch as the interaction between speaker and listener and writer and reader is the basis for communication, communication is essentially *social* in character.[1] Their social nature may be short-circuited as, for example, by the child who delights in repeating a nonsense syllable time and again, or by the adult who "talks to himself"; but the language arts are the most effective instruments available for regulating social relationships.

The language arts involve *intellectualizing*. Communication implies that something is being transmitted, usually an idea or feeling. The importance of "thinking out loud," "listening carefully," and "reading thoughtfully" has long been recognized. Language and thinking power develop together.

Transmitted ideas via the language arts evoke *emotional* responses. Words and ideas take on an emotional quality; they engender certain moods, feelings or attitudes. One does not react dispassionately to such words as "home" or "war."

The language arts are *creative*. Language is creative in the sense that ideas are put into use by the recipient. In reading, for example, the communication process is considered complete only when the reader has applied the ideas which he has read.

Language as a Vehicle of Communication

Language Is a Convention. It is a code using verbal symbols. The words we use—their spelling, pronunciation, and syllabication—as well as written forms, capitalization, and punctuation are simply matters of common agreement. We have, for example, agreed to designate a new product by the term "nylon." We have also agreed to spell it with a "y" instead of an "i"; to give "y" the long "i" sound instead of the short; and to accent the first syllable. We see that

. . . language is the result of evolution. A language which is current, which is used, cannot remain static. It is never fixed. Its grammar changes. New words are introduced. Old words are lost or change their meaning. Inevitably one is led to the conclusion that grammars and dictionaries are descriptive, rather than prescriptive. They describe what is, not what must be.[2]

[1] Walter Barnes, "Language as Social Behavior," *Educational Method*, XVI (March, 1937), 275-288.

[2] National Society for the Study of Education, *Teaching Language in the Elementary School*, Forty-third Yearbook, Part II (Chicago: University of Chicago Press, 1944), p. 40. Quoted by permission of the Society.

Words Have Many Meanings. In the development of the English language, several definitions often have been given to the same word. Note the meanings, some of them quite contradictory, which are associated with the word "strike":

> to *strike* a match or *strike* a flag
>
> to *strike* a balance or *strike* it rich
>
> to *strike* a person or *strike* up a friendship
>
> to *strike* gold or *strike* out.

These multiple uses of the same symbol interfere with ease of communication especially for the young child who, in learning one meaning of a term, thinks he "knows the word" and *attempts to apply it in all cases.*

Development in Language Arts

Growth in Language Arts is Continuous.[3] Language development begins with the birth cry and continues throughout life. The child's first sounds soon become attached to differentiated meanings, and by the age of six he has acquired a speaking vocabulary sufficiently extensive to engage in a wide variety of worthwhile experiences. The length of his sentences has increased to about five words, and he uses virtually every form of sentence structure. The beginnings of reading are evidenced at about eighteen months when the child points to identified pictures in a book, and at two years of age when he actually names pictures in a book. By six years of age, generally speaking, he has an experiential background which will enable him to understand printed symbols. Writing begins around the age of three-and-a-half years when the child enters the so-called scribbling stage. At six years of age, he prints most of the capital letters, often with several rever-

3 See the following:

Dorothea A. McCarthy, "Language Development in Children," *Manual of Child Psychology*, 2nd ed., Leonard Carmichael, ed. (New York: John Wiley and Sons, Inc., 1954), Chapter IX.

National Society for the Study of Education, *Child Development and the Curriculum*, Thirty-Eight Yearbook, Part I (Bloomington, Ill.: Public School Publishing Company, 1939), Chapters IX-XIII.

Arnold Gesell, *et al., The First Five Years of Life* (New York: Harper & Brothers, 1940), Chapter VIII.

A. F. Watts, *The Language and Mental Development of Children* (Boston: D. C. Heath and Company, 1944), Chapters II and III.

Virgil E. Herrick and Leland B. Jacobs, eds., *Children and the Language Arts* (Englewood Cliffs: Prentice-Hall, Inc., 1955), Chapter 4.

sals, can print both his first and last name, and can usually write numbers from one through twenty.

These are the beginnings upon which school programs base the further development, expansion, and refinement of communication skills.

Language Arts Development Is Related to Total Development. Growth in language power is affected by mental, physical, social, and emotional development. There is a high correlation between measures of language skill and mental ability. Poor motor coordination, hearing loss, and endocrine disturbances are some of the more common physical disabilities associated with inadequate language development. According to Piaget,[4] language development is an expression of socialization. The language of the self-centered child is egocentric; that of the socially-oriented person is socialized.

Many Factors Influence Language Arts Development. Socio-economic background, sex, and sibling relationships are some of the more important factors which are related to linguistic development. Children of upper and middle-class families are generally superior in their language activities to children of lower-class families who often display little appreciation for "good English." When boys are compared with girls in the usual measures of language development, they are consistently outstripped. Association with adults also appears to stimulate language power, for the only child excels both children from large families and twins, who have fewer opportunities to imitate adult speech patterns.

PRACTICES IN LANGUAGE ARTS INSTRUCTION

No widespread survey has been made of language arts programs which includes reading, writing, speaking, and listening. Comprehensive studies of "English" instruction in New York,[5] Wisconsin,[6] and California[7] reveal certain common tendencies, however, which may be generally representative of language arts instruction.

[4] J. Piaget, *Language and Thought of the Child* (New York: Harcourt, Brace & Company, Inc., 1926).

[5] From *Evaluating Instruction in English in the Elementary Schools of New York* by Dora V. Smith. Copyright, 1941, by The National Conference on Research in English. Published by Scott, Foresman and Company, and used with their permission.

[6] Robert C. Pooley and Robert D. Williams, *The Teaching of English in Wisconsin* (Madison, Wisconsin: The University of Wisconsin Press, 1948), p. 196.

[7] George F. Sensabaugh, "A State Survey of English Courses of Study," *English Journal*, XXXVII (May, 1948), 229-235.

Objectives of Language Arts Instruction

Objectives in language arts instruction are a mixture of the traditional stress on mechanics combined with the more recent tendency to regard language as one phase of total development. In the New York study, for example, major emphasis was given to the development of skills and abilities in the teaching of oral and written composition. Knowledges and skills received more attention than attitudes, appreciations, and habits combined, on the basis of the number of times they were mentioned as objectives for teaching literature.[8]

Some schools, instead of confining their aims to reading for understanding, critical interpretation, and evaluation; to expressing ideas and opinions clearly and effectively in speech and writing; and to observing correct usage and social amenities in communication, have moved toward a more balanced set of objectives which encompass more aspects of child growth. The aims set up by the Spokane teachers for oral and written expression illustrate this broader point of view:

To develop more adequate personalities in social relationships through improved facility and ease in oral expression.

To develop in children desirable habits and skills in speaking and listening that will foster worthwhile participation in social life, which is an essential attribute in a democratic society.

To develop ability for clear expression in everyday speech and writing.

To develop appreciation for effective usage as a means of improving expression.

To develop appreciation of a rich vocabulary because it makes possible more adequate expression.[9]

Emphases Given to Various Phases of Language Arts

The Wisconsin study disclosed that an average of three hours and fifty minutes per week, or forty-six minutes per day, was devoted specifically to English instruction. This varies from three hours per week for rural third grades, to three hours and forty-five minutes for sixth grade rural classes, to four hours and forty-five minutes for urban classrooms.[10] The study shows little agreement on the amount of time being given to each area of the language arts.

8 Dora V. Smith, *op. cit.*, pp. 50-54.
9 Spokane Public Schools, *A Course of Study in Language Arts for the Spokane Elementary Schools* (Spokane, Washington: Board of Education, 1946), p. 5.
10 Pooley and Williams, *op. cit.*, p. 31.

Of the 478 lessons specifically designated as English which were observed in the Wisconsin study, not quite one-third dealt with oral English; an equal number of lessons dealt with skills such as usage, grammar, spelling, and word study. Approximately one lesson in four was in composition, but only one in seven was devoted to literature.[11] Although the data are not strictly comparable, somewhat similar emphases were observed in the 221 classes in the New York study.

Organization of Instruction in Language Arts

The textbook determines very largely what is taught in language arts. Seventy per cent of the teachers included in the Wisconsin study depended on the textbook as the course of study. Half the teachers followed the textbook exclusively, while another fifth modified the course of study to fit the textbook. Only one-fourth of the teachers, 19 per cent of the rural and 30 per cent of the urban, followed a prepared course of study.[12] These data are borne out by the New York study. Of twenty-six communities visited, only two used no basic textbook, and another two depended upon drill books.[13]

The practice of keeping language arts instruction apart from other curriculum areas is clearly indicated in the Wisconsin study. Spelling was universally taught as a separate subject. Eighty per cent of all English teaching observed was done in separate periods. In English classes, somewhat less than half the teachers observed consciously made application to other fields of instruction, with one-third making no effort of any kind in this direction. In one classroom out of five, English was taught in the setting of other subjects, principally the social studies. This is twice as likely to occur at the kindergarten-primary level than at the intermediate level, although a somewhat greater tendency to integrate language arts with areas other than social studies is noted in the upper grades.

ORGANIZING THE LANGUAGE ARTS CURRICULUM

The different ways in which language arts programs are organized may be seen as attempts to account for the common elements involved in all language arts activities. These elements include: (1) the *mechanics* necessary to effective communication; (2) choice of language *medium* to be used as communication vehicle; (3) selection of *ideas* to

---

11 *Ibid.*, p. 63.
12 *Ibid.*, p. 29.
13 Smith, *op. cit.*, p. 65.

be communicated; and (4) the *social situation* or problem which creates the need for communication. These elements are interrelated in the process of communication as it actually takes place. Curriculum designs are simply different ways of dealing with these elements.

Concentrating on the Mechanics

Some schools and classrooms place primary emphasis in language arts instruction on the mechanics of language arts. In such an organization, the social situation is tantamount to: "learning to read more rapidly" or "learning to use *who* correctly." The content (what is to be read, or the principles of language usage) may come from subject fields outside the area of the language arts, as in reading, or constitute the subject matter of the area, as in grammar. In both instances, however, instructional materials are systematically organized in order to facilitate learning, which almost invariably demands that the language arts process in question be taught separately.

This approach appears to be clear cut. Yet, the questions of what to teach and in what order are not simple. This is dramatically illustrated in spelling. An analysis of seventeen spelling series revealed agreement on exactly one word: "long" is to be taught in the second grade.[14] Of the 8,645 words listed for grades two through eight, only 6.26 per cent were common to all seventeen spellers. A similar lack of agreement was noted in an analysis of eight textbook series with respect to grammar, correct usage, capitalization, and punctuation.[15]

Further clarification can be anticipated regarding the problem of "what to teach," because this question focuses attention on the *products* of learning. Decisions regarding products or outcomes are susceptible to "scientific" investigation through the determination of adult *usage* or *opinion* about what is most important for children to learn. "What is the best order of presentation?" places the focus on the *learning process*.

Emphasizing Language Arts Processes

Some plans attempt to develop the interrelationships among various language arts processes. Newark schools, for example, have organized their language arts program in terms of three broad areas: (1) reading and literature; (2) language, including oral and written expression, usage, and spelling; and (3) handwriting. "The interde-

14 Emmett A. Betts, *Spelling Vocabulary Study* (New York: American Book Company, 1940), p. 3.
15 Pooley and Williams, *op. cit.*, pp. 46-52.

pendence of these integral phases of the language arts is recognized, and reference is continually made to instructional interrelationships."[16] Much of this integration, however, is left up to the teacher. The Long Beach guide for language arts instruction combines oral expression, written expression, and work study skills; suggestions for reading, spelling, and handwriting are contained in other publications.[17]

In this kind of language arts instruction, the social situation is identified with a language arts process such as "learning how to dramatize stories," or "learning how to make reports." These are broader definitions of the social situation, and encompass several language arts skills. The content (the stories to be dramatized or reports to be given) comes from the same sources, however, as that in the organization based on mechanics; that is, principles of dramatization from the language arts field, and subject matter from other fields to report about. There can be little question about the reinforcement of learning inherent in this fusion of the various phases of language arts. Many schools are moving in this direction.

A Functional Approach

A functional approach to language arts programs places emphasis upon social situations to give meaning to language arts activities. These situations are selected from outside the field of language arts, such as a unit on "Life in the Cold Far North," or an excursion; this places the language arts in functional relationship to the rest of the school program. One way to bring language arts into this kind of relationship with other areas is to make language arts and social studies the core of the instructional program.

Media and mechanics in this approach are determined by the needs of the social situation. A fourth grade unit on "Life in the Cold Far North," for example, incorporated the following language arts experiences: vocabulary, reading, oral expression, written expression, creative writing, literature, and dramatization.[18]

TEACHING SPEAKING AND LISTENING

It is very difficult to think about the language arts program in the elementary school without narrowing one's attention to the nature of

16 Newark Public Schools, *Language Arts in Our Schools* (Newark, New Jersey: Board of Education, 1950), p. 5.
17 Long Beach Public Schools, *Guide to the Teaching of Language Arts in the Elementary School* (Long Beach, California: Board of Education, 1950), pp. 24-29.
18 *Ibid.*, pp. 138-143.

the specific language act being performed. It is common practice to consider the problems of instruction as they are related to teaching speaking, listening, reading, writing, handwriting, and spelling.

Basic Considerations

Teaching Speaking and Listening. In spite of the tremendous output of the printing press, communication is still primarily an oral process. Recent developments in radio, sound movies, and recordings have emphasized the importance of speaking and listening. Speech is also more important than writing because the child learns to talk long before he learns to read or write, and because errors in writing usually have their foundations in speech habits. In recognition of this, schools are placing greater emphasis on the development of speaking and listening habits.

Freeing the Child for Speaking and Listening. Listening is the forerunner of speaking, just as speaking precedes and is the basis for reading and writing. The first goal of language development in the home and, later, in the school, is to encourage and support the development of easy confident speech. Unless the child feels free to talk to others about the things he feels and wants to know, and the ideas and activities he wishes to explore, the child, teacher, and the school will lack the basis for all development in communication, language itself.

The Physical Setting Is Important. Most writers about the language arts stress the importance of the child's feeling comfortable, relaxed, and at home in his school environment as a prerequisite for effective learning and as a basis for speech and language development. Though not the essential factors, movable furniture, instructional equipment built for child use, a variety of adequate materials, acoustically treated ceilings, room for movement and work, and provisions for interest centers, all help in providing a physical environment where a child can find a place for interesting things to do and to talk about. Seating arrangements which permit teachers and children to see and respond to each other's faces are also important for effective speaking and listening.

The Child's Previous Experience in Language Should Be Considered. To speak and listen effectively, the child needs to be able to hear and to talk. In language development, the ear serves the same function for speaking and listening that the eye does for reading.

Besides the physiological equipment for speaking and listening, the child's background of experience in language is an important determinant of the conditions within which present development can take place. The nature of the child's home environment, his peer group experiences, the extent of his travel and cultural resources—all contribute to the conditions which may encourage or discourage his effective language development.

The Social-Emotional Setting for Language Is also Important. The development of wholesome, accepting, supporting personal relationships between teacher and children and between a child and other children provides the setting in which effective speaking and listening can occur. Within this context, the withdrawing child finds time and place for sticking out his language neck to see what will happen to it. Here, too, the child who is over-eager to talk can find realistic, constructive controls which will help him to find his place with others in a situation where language is a means for sharing and enjoying.

A Major Requisite for Language Development Is the Presence of Many and Continuing Interests. Speaking and listening become important to children when there are many interesting and significant things to talk about and listen to. Language activity becomes non-communicating, and thus destructive of itself, when it becomes its own reason for being. Language development cannot feed on itself, but must always grow out of the need of people to communicate things of importance. The spring from which effective language development flows is continued and enriching experience in living and learning.

Talking Must Be an Approved Form of Behavior. Although many teachers believe to the contrary, studies have shown that many teachers spend a large percentage of the school day in talking to children. An effective language arts program would legalize talking for children and would actively stimulate and encourage its place in the learning activities for children. Effective control and direction of talking come with its use and evaluation, not with its prevention.

The Social Forms Involving Speaking and Listening

Listening is a natural and appropriate part of speaking and belongs in all situations where oral language is used. There is no need to have one special program for teaching listening, and another for teaching speaking; the same learning situation provides the opportunity for effective instruction in these two related language functions. In many ways they are better taught together than apart.

Conversation. Conversation, like talking, grows out of an intimate, face-to-face, informal social situation. The talking may range from spontaneous, unorganized chatter about everything to the serious, directed imparting of information. The important thing to remember is that much of our social life is made up of talking and conversation accompanied by a proper mixture of intelligent and responsive listening. The two go hand in hand.

Telephoning is a mechanical aid to conversation. In telephoning, however, the situation is not a face-to-face one, and greater demands

University of Wisconsin Summer Laboratory School

REPORTING ON THE NEWS OF THE WORLD

are placed on the listener to interpret and respond to slight changes in tone and manner of speaking. Effective telephoning involves the proper use of social conventions, appropriate skill in the use of the mechanical equipment, and the purposeful selection of the speech forms and grammatical constructions useful in achieving the reason for telephoning.

Planning, Discussing Explaining, Evaluating. All of these activities involving speaking and listening ultimately result in some clarification of meaning, either for the speaker or for the listener, and they usually imply a need for an active response. Planning, discussing, explaining, and evaluating are done more effectively when the educational purposes to be achieved through language are clear, when things can be looked at and examined repeatedly, where groups are small, and where the consequences of these activities can be acted upon by children.

Reports, Directions, Announcements. In these activities the child moves from a personal speaking situation to one in which he presents or shares his purpose and information to more than one person at a time. Usually, the time and arrangements for speaking are more formalized. This all suggests the importance of helping children achieve clarity of purpose in speaking, advance preparation of material for presentation, skill in dealing with an audience situation, and the development of evaluations after some lapse in time. Corresponding skills in listening to reports, directions, and announcements need to be stressed as a natural part of this kind of language experience.

The Telling and Reading of Stories. Storytelling, or story reading, by the teacher and by the children provides a situation in which speaking and listening are combined with the enjoyment of a story. In this activity, attention is not difficult to get, interest usually runs high, and the telling and listening functions are natural means to enjoyment and satisfaction. Children's literature is a valuable and important part of their language experiences.

Poetry and Choric Speaking. Poetry and choric speaking provide an opportunity for children to use speaking and listening as a means for creative expression and enjoyment. Poetry makes greater demands than prose on the listener because of its form and its condensation of ideas. Both poetry and choric speaking offer the enjoyment of rhythms and pleasing sound patterns. In each, too, there is an opportunity for audience presentation. Choric speaking provides the shy withdrawn child with group support for expression. Similarly, the over-expressive child will meet the experience of having to join with others in a controlled expression of ideas and feelings.

Programs and Assemblies. Although assemblies and programs in which all the children of a school participate are frequently beyond the interest and understanding of kindergarten and first grade children, informal brief programs within their own room, or in small parts of all-school projects, are valuable experiences in language and social development. All levels of the elementary school can profit from the opportunity to develop programs and assemblies as a part of their language arts program.

Radio, Recordings, Transcriptions, Television, Sound Films. All of these media offer opportunities for valuable listening experiences both in and out of school. The alert teacher can capitalize on them for diagnosis and treatment of speech through recordings, the dramatic experiences of television and radio, and the availability of many recorded speech and listening situations valuable for effective language development.

Growth in Listening and Speaking

Children at any grade level vary greatly in their ability to use language. Speaking and listening present no exception. While the teacher will observe all his children pass through discernible stages of development, different children will develop at different times and in different ways. Ruth Strickland presents the following sequence of listening development as a valuable clue to degree of maturity:

Little conscious listening: distracted by people and things in the environment

Half listening: holding fast to own ideas and waiting to insert them at the first opportunity

Listening passively: apparent absorption but little or no reaction

Listening: responding with items from own experience as result of associations brought to mind

Listening: some reactions through questions or comments

Listening: some genuine emotional and mental participation

Listening: meeting of minds[19]

In speech, the teacher will observe and try to help the child develop clarity of expression through accurate articulation of sounds, and clear enunciation. With the development in speech production comes a growing maturity in the child's use of grammatical and social conventions of speech and in the use of language which expresses his meanings clearly and imaginatively. The teacher will expect to see the child move to higher levels in his use of speech forms as he passes through the elementary school.

READING INSTRUCTION IN THE ELEMENTARY SCHOOL

Reading is becoming more important in our culture. This is true in spite of an increasing use of other media of communication. Today, jobs depend on the ability to read want ads, applications for employ-

19 Ruth G. Strickland, *English is Our Language: Guide for Teaching Grades I and II* (Boston: D. C. Heath and Company, 1950), pp. 42-43.

ment, directions, and social security forms. Modern warfare finds the illiterate soldier a menace to himself and to his country. As the world becomes more complex, and as other activities crowd out time formerly spent in reading, it becomes necessary to read more in less time with greater efficiency, in order to live intelligently and happily. Although the traditional reading school has gone, reading is still one of the most important single areas in the school curriculum.

Instructional Practices[20]

Changing Purposes in Reading. The former emphasis on *learning to read* has shifted to *reading to learn.* Most comprehensive is the goal of *growth in and through reading.*

Reading and Child Development. One way to develop effective reading instruction is through a child study program which enables the teacher to know the pupil in school, at home, and in the community. In this approach, reading is considered a tool for accomplishing the child's purposes, not something that is done in isolation and at a certain period of the day. In this sense, reading integrates pupils' experiences in and out of school, and an experiential background is built up which gives meaning to word symbols; in turn, reading skills developed in basic reading instruction are utilized in functional situations. Modern reading programs enable children to live and grow better.

Reading and the Language Arts. Growth in reading is dependent on, and influences development in, other phases of language facility. Reading readiness programs for young children are in reality language programs emphasizing speech rather than perception of visual symbols. In reading instruction, great stress is placed on discussion and writing activities. This fusion of reading with speaking, listening, and writing activities has resulted in a better balance among reading and the other language arts. No longer are our schools merely reading schools; neither is reading being lost sight of in the modern curriculum.

Reading and Instructional Materials. Reading is no longer taught solely from printed materials. Important for the development of meaningful experiences are the innumerable auditory and visual aids

[20] For an extended discussion of this topic, the reader is referred to: Gertrude Hildreth, *Learning the Three R's,* 2nd ed. (Minneapolis: Educational Publishers, Inc., 1947), Chapter VII; National Society for the Study of Education, *Reading in the Elementary School,* Forty-Eighth Yearbook, Part II, Chapter III. (Chicago: University of Chicago Press, 1949); David H. Russell, *Children Learn to Read* (Boston: Ginn and Company, 1949), Chapter V.

used to stimulate interest in reading, to help explain word meanings, to test the pupil's ability to interpret what is read, and *for other important purposes*. Maps, diagrams, models, exhibits, study prints, stereoscopic slides, projected slides, film strips, motion pictures, sound movies, phonograph records, and the radio are finding their way in-

STORIES COME ALIVE THROUGH CREATIVE DRAMATICS

creasingly into reading programs. Materials are being published which combine text and filmstrip[21] or movie to provide a concrete basis for verbal symbols and experiences with signs and symbols which do not involve words.

Broad Reading Programs. The reading program at all levels is broadly conceived to include basic instruction, extensional reading, and recreational reading. Definite instruction in basic reading skills, rather than occasional check exercises, are given to all pupils. Extensive reading in the content fields and literature involves the use of a great variety of materials such as periodicals, textbooks, supplementary books, reference books, etc. Recreational reading of the individual should include an abundance of materials read for sheer enjoy-

[21] Glenn McCracken, "Better Reading Through Filmstrips—Part I," *See and Hear*, VI, Issue 2 (October, 1950), 16-17; "Better Reading Through Filmstrips—Part II," *See and Hear*, VI, Issue 3 (December, 1950), 10-12.

ment or for the satisfaction of personal needs not met in other activities. The importance of the library in such a comprehensive reading program is self-evident.

Continuous Reading Guidance. In order to meet interests and needs at all stages of development, reading must be planned specifically throughout the public school program. It cannot be assumed that fundamentals in reading can be mastered once and for all at the lower school levels or that, once mastered, they automatically transfer to new situations. For guidance purposes, cumulative records are being kept of the reading experiences of children. As new materials and resources are made available for the solution of increasingly complex problems, specific guidance is being provided. Oral reading, for example, is no longer merely the beginning stage in reading, but is of concern throughout the entire range of public education now that mechanical recorders, radio, and television have become part of our culture.

Individualized Reading Instruction. Individualized instruction has been found extremely helpful in teaching reading. It is recognized that no one *system* of teaching methods will be effective with all children, and that many approaches must be employed in the classroom. This necessitates grouping in the classroom, and the use of a wide range of materials. Instruction limited to a single basic reading series and one system of teaching cannot meet the many needs represented in the usual class, and is therefore likely to produce many failures.

Remedial Reading. Modern reading programs provide remedial assistance for those failing to make satisfactory progress. Rather than permit pupils to fail for a number of years, the emphasis is on earlier identification, diagnosis, and remediation of difficulties. More effort is being given to the search for causes,[22] especially the physical and emotional. Although specialization in reading has developed to a high degree, there is a tendency for remedial reading specialists and clinics to work through and with the regular teacher in classroom situations. In many instances, diagnostic and corrective teaching has been incorporated in the developmental program of the classroom.

Improving Reading Programs. Reading programs are being improved through the continuous evaluation and modification of existing practices. Systematic use is made of a wide variety of appraisal techniques, which include standardized and informal tests, observation, anecdotal records, check lists, reading inventories, interviews,

22 Helen M. Robinson, *Why Pupils Fail in Reading* (Chicago: University of Chicago Press, 1946).

etc. Teachers, pupils, parents, and other school personnel participate in the appraisals.

INSTRUCTION IN WRITING

Oral expression is considerably developed and reading has already been introduced before the child begins to concern himself with written activities. Even more than in reading, there is a lag between what he would like to communicate and his expressive skills: written composition, handwriting, and spelling. While deficiencies in reading may be compensated for or even camouflaged, the products of written expression are often accepted as a measure of one's education, or of the effectiveness of an educational program.

Written Expression

Objectives. Clear and effective communication has always been the aim of written expression. Traditionally this has been associated with a knowledge of the forms and techniques required in language activities such as writing letters, preparing reports, taking notes, and so forth. Correct usage, capitalization and punctuation, sentence sense, and paragraphing have been much emphasized in order to enhance clarity and organization. Attention, too, has been given to the social amenities involved in language activities, including the courtesy implied in proofreading. To these has been added an interest in the creative possibilities of written expression for boys and girls. More recently, emphasis has been placed on the natural, free-style conversational writing,[23] informal and casual, rather than on the formal literary style which once made written expression such an artificial experience for boys and girls.

Current Practices. Recognition is being given to the fact that children must have a *reason for writing* and *something to write about.* In the kindergarten and first grade, an awareness of need for, and interest in, written expression is cultivated through situations which have meaning to the child—such as writing his name on his own possessions, noticing signs, and recording children's stories or group experiences. In grades one and two, simple group compositions are developed cooperatively and written by the teacher on the blackboard or on oak tag. These cooperative efforts stem from the children's need for writing in their everyday living, and may include letters to sick classmates, invitations, thank-you notes, signs, announcements, and original stories or poems. When writing becomes sufficiently ad-

[23] Rudolf Flesch, *The Art of Plain Talk* (New York: Harper & Brothers, 1946).

vanced, children may copy these group efforts, either to take home to parents, or to record in their personal notebooks. As the technical aspects of written expression are mastered through writing group compositions, with the assistance of oral preparation or discussion, the child begins to compose and write independently under the teacher's guidance. In grades four through six the more refined forms and skills necessary to engage in written language activities are developed as needed.

Programs of written expression are becoming *more comprehensive.* Instead of devoting most instruction to drill on items of correct usage

Kathleen Moon and Fulton County (Georgia) Schools

CHILDHOOD IDEAS TAKE FORM THROUGH PUPPETS

and form, the social and thinking aspects of writing are given increased attention. Instruction in letter writing, for example, emphasizes: selecting content, writing clearly, writing correctly, and observing social amenities.[24]

The *mechanics of writing*—correct usage, vocabulary, capitalization, punctuation, sentence sense, and paragraphing—should be taught functionally. The use of a comma after the salutation of a letter, for example, is taught in connection with the writing of a friendly letter, rather than as part of a unit of work on the comma as such. With this approach grammar becomes a source of standards for speaking and writing, instead of subject matter to be memorized, and is developed inductively in connection with the pupil's immediate writing needs.

Although there is a trend away from emphasis on form or mechanics to word functionalism, there is some question about *creativity in written expression*.[25] Some believe that originality is possessed only by a few highly talented individuals; others that creativity does not make its appearance until after the elementary school period. *In a sense, everyone can create.* In functional language, the purpose is practical and primarily concerned with communication. Creative writing is personal, and very often is an outlet for self-expression. Stimulation of thought and emotional response, as well as sensitivity to "verbal magic," is not to be set aside for a special school period wherein the "finer" things in life may be pursued. Opportunities arise in everyday classroom activities for the development of self-expression. The use of one such opportunity for creative expression is illustrated by the following episode. Here teacher and pupils responded to sounds and rewrote their central story to make it sound "pretty—like a poem."

A FIRST GRADE STORY OF "OUR TRIP TO THE DAIRY" [26]

Here's the Text of the Story:	*And Here's How It Developed:*
John was awake all night.	This was an under-privileged group to
He heard the rain come.	whom trips were something special, so

---

[24] Paul McKee, "The Nature and Scope of the Language Arts Program," *Language Arts in the Elementary School,* Department of Elementary School Principals, Twentieth Yearbook (Washington: National Education Association, 1941), pp. 248-49.

[25] Hughes Mearns, *Creative Youth* (Garden City, New York: Doubleday, Doran and Company, Inc., 1925).

Gertrude Hartman and Ann Shumaker, eds., *Creative Expression,* 2nd ed. (Milwaukee: E. M. Hale and Company, 1939).

[26] District of Columbia Public Schools, *Language Arts Curriculum Bulletin* (Washington, D.C.: Board of Education, 1950), pp. 14-15.

It was soft rain.
It said sss-sss.
"Stop, rain!" said John, "so we can go on our trip!"

When we came to school there was a shower, but it stopped just in time—so we went to the dairy.

We went walking together, softly, quietly. In the puddles our feet went splash, splash!

On the bus we dropped our dimes, ding, ding, ding, in the fare box—but not on the floor.

At the dairy, Mr. Ballard showed us the cans sliding on the track. Some went up, bumpety, bump—

—And some came down, clickety clack.

Then we saw the cold room. Cold, cold, cold, room. We shivered.

Then came the best part—looking down at the milk bottles—sshh—sshh—sshh—sshh.

Then in the cases—clink, clink, clink. The milk was cold, as cold as ice.

The dairy was so clean, the floor was wet. June almost slipped. It had a clean smell. The machines made a busy noise.

the anticipation was high. John reflected his feeling about the trip in his story and also in the picture he made of himself in bed, thinking of the day's trip. (Red rain drops dot the surface of the picture.)

Accompanying this text is a happy picture with a gay umbrella, showing children going to school.

"How did it feel, walking in the rain?" asked the teacher. "How did it sound?"

"What happened next?" the teacher asked as the children proceeded from one event to another. (The child's natural accent on *sound effects* is revealed again here. The picture, too, shows those "dinging dimes.")

Too bad, not to be able to show the picture here! There is a row of cans and under it a spiralling line, which shows, even without words, that the cans are moving along.

"And how did they sound coming down?" asked the teacher, and the children recalled the clickety-clack sound.

"How did we feel in that cold room?" asked the teacher. (The picture, with dark background and very white milk bottles, feels cold, too!)

"How did the milk sound, going into the bottles?" the teacher asked.
(The picture shows a row of children looking down at the milk going into the bottles.)

Here are some words that recall *sounds* and *feelings*.

How does one record in pictures a busy noise? This child made dots and dashes above the machines that actually *make a busy noise* as you look at the picture!

Then we had a happy surprise—chocolate milk! Yummy, yum, yum. We drank it all. It certainly was good and cold.

What greater climax to a trip—or a story—than chocolate milk?

Handwriting

At one time handwriting was the mark of an "educated person." It was a kind of class distinction. Today we accept handwriting as a matter of course. Everyone writes! Writing is a basic tool for communication—a means to the end of recording ideas for personal or social reasons.

The increasing use of typewriters, speed writing, and secretaries has raised the question of how much writing, and what kind of writing, should be taught in our public schools. There are some who argue that handwriting is one of the most poorly taught of all school subjects.

Objectives. The penmanship era which stressed highly elaborate and stylized writing forms is long since past. Modern schools are more intent on developing legible writing which is produced comfortably and automatically. Also important are adequate speed, versatility in the use of media and writing forms, care in the use of writing materials, and the arrangement of writing on paper and printed forms. Fundamental to the success of the entire program is the development of a desire to write well so that others may read easily.

Current Practices.[27] Handwriting has become more meaningful. Instruction is based on the premise that, in and of itself, handwriting has no intrinsic value to children. It is important to a pupil only if it helps him do something he considers worthwhile. For this reason, situations which require writing become the focus for instruction in penmanship. Handwriting is not taught in isolation from other phases of the language arts or other experiences of the school day, but is commonly emphasized throughout the school day.

More attention is being given to *writing readiness* than formerly. Although more than 90 per cent of the schools begin teaching handwriting in grade one, there is a growing tendency to postpone formal instruction until children understand what handwriting is about, and develop a real desire to acquire this skill. Emotional, mental, and muscular maturity are taken into consideration by teachers, as well as

---

[27] Hildreth, *op. cit.,* pp. 600-604; Ada R. Polkinghorne, "Current Practices in Teaching Handwriting," *Elementary School Journal,* XLVII (December, 1946), 218-224.

G. Arnold, P. W. Eberman, T. L. Harris, and V. E. Herrick, *Handwriting in Wisconsin* (Madison: University of Wisconsin, 1951).

the visual ability to discriminate between small differences in letters.

Handwriting *instruction* is being streamlined. Simpler letter forms, both in manuscript and cursive writing, are favored over more elaborate styles. "Systems" of handwriting are becoming less important than the cultivation of a natural, comfortable, personalized style of handwriting. The unbreakable rule of free arm movement is giving way to a combination of hand and finger movement which is more adaptable to the conditions under which much writing is done. Mechanical devices are being discarded in favor of the direct practice of actual writing. Mass practice is being supplanted by individual exercises governed by a diagnosis of handwriting deficiencies and tied to the individual's handwriting needs. In three-fourths of the schools, handwriting instruction is provided for on a planned basis.

A wider *variety of materials* is now being used in penmanship instruction. The blackboard is used somewhat extensively throughout the grades, but most particularly in first and second grades. Crayons are widely used in beginning writing activities. Other instruments used include pencils for beginners in grades one and two, ordinary pencils in third and fourth, and pen and ink in grades four, five, and six. Fountain pens for writing "with ink" are replacing the old pen and nib. Unruled paper is used most frequently in grade one, although it appears to some extent in all grades. Inch ruled paper is used most widely in grades one and two; five-eighths inch ruling in grades three through six. In short, children are asked to begin by writing large letters, and gradually to decrease the size of their handwriting.

There is a growing tendency for children to learn *several kinds of writing*. Approximately seven-eighths of the elementary schools begin with manuscript writing. Of these, one-eighth continue with manuscript writing throughout the grades; the remainder make the transfer to cursive writing in grade two or three.[28] The typewriter, furthermore, has been introduced in the lower grades to make it possible for children to compose before they have acquired adequate motor control for handwriting. In the intermediate and upper grades, typing is becoming a definite skill to be learned as a common writing need. Some schools are beginning to use the term "recording" to include manuscript writing, cursive writing, and typewriting.

[28] Frank N. Freeman, "Survey of Manuscript Writing in the Public Schools," *Elementary School Journal*, XLVI (March, 1946), 375-380.

Spelling

Spelling is a tool in writing. Its only function is to make written communication understandable. Because of many non-phonetic words, useless silent letters, homonyms, and variable pronunciations, spelling in the English language is a very complicated process. Despite this fact, our society does not condone poor spelling. Inability to spell is often associated with lack of education.

Instruction in spelling is focused on the acquisition of a basic spelling vocabulary which can be utilized automatically in written expression. To help the individual learn how to spell words beyond this basic list, instruction in spelling is also concerned with the development of independent study habits. The accomplishment of these objectives depends on the individual's recognition of the need and the development of a desire for correct spelling. Teachers, therefore, are concerned with helping the child develop an editorial sense and a spelling conscience which will make him sensitive to incorrect spelling, and a willingness to use the tools and take the time necessary to correct faulty spelling.

Current Practices.[29] Perhaps more than any of the other language arts, spelling instruction is highly systematized. Regular periods for spelling are scheduled in the daily program, the series of activities for the week are generally specifically indicated, and periodic reviews are carefully planned. Almost universally, a study outline or method of learning to spell is the basis for these programs. In the lower grades, it is customary to find more group teaching of spelling, whereas in the upper grades more time is allotted for individual study. Of late, spelling has become of increasing concern in secondary schools.

Spelling *readiness*[30] is becoming as important as reading readiness. Along with writing readiness, it depends on such factors as visual and auditory discrimination, the acquisition of basic speaking and reading vocabularies, recognition of writing needs (including an interest in words), and adequate muscular coordination. For these reasons, formal spelling is generally introduced in the second grade; at all levels, word meaning should be developed prior to learning to spell particular words.

Spelling instruction is becoming more *functional*. Fewer words are

29 Edward W. Dolch, *Better Spelling* (Champaign, Illinois: Garrard Press, 1942).
Hildreth, *op. cit.*, Chapters XV-XVIII.
30 Alta McIntire and H. L. Hampton, "Spelling Readiness: A Challenge," *Elementary English Review* (January, 1944), 24-25.

being taught, but their selection is generally based on studies of adult and/or children's usage.[31] It is probable that very few words are used mainly either by adults or by children; most words are probably important to both age groups. Many spelling words peculiar to childhood activities can be learned as the need arises. Words unique to adult activities will be learned as the pupils develop a spelling conscience and independent study habits. Spelling programs should move from learning how to spell specific words to skill in word selection and adequate use.

Although spelling *instruction* still emphasizes visual impressions, auditory and kinesthetic experiences are also included in present methods of teaching. More emphasis is placed on written spelling than on oral.

Greater concern is being shown for the *individualization* of instruction in all spelling programs.[32] Adjustments are often made in methods used, difficulty level of words to be mastered, number of words to be learned, and/or the amount of time spent on spelling. Good spellers, for example, are excused from spelling lessons, or are encouraged to engage in enriching supplementary activities involving the use of the spelling words for the week.

The use of phonics in an unphonetic language, and the use of *rules* in an illogical language, are no longer the golden keys to effective spelling. They do, however, have a place in learning to spell. The problem is to determine when and to what degree such aids should be used.

EVALUATION IN LANGUAGE ARTS

Elementary schools have traditionally devoted a great deal of effort to the evaluation of language arts development. These attempts have produced an astonishing array of instruments and techniques for appraising various language skills, abilities, attitudes, and interests. The

[31] T. G. Foran, *The Psychology and Teaching of Spelling* (Washington: Catholic Education Press, 1934).

Ernest Horn, *A Basic Writing Vocabulary—10,000 Words Most Commonly Used in Writing*, University of Iowa Monographs in Education, First Series, No. 4 (Iowa City: State University of Iowa, 1926).

Paul McKee, *Language in the Elementary School*, rev. ed. (Boston: Houghton Mifflin Company, 1939), pp. 335-336.

Henry D. Rinsland, *A Basic Vocabulary of Elementary School Children* (New York: The Macmillan Company, 1945).

[32] Grace Fernald, *Remedial Methods in the Basic Subjects* (New York: McGraw-Hill Book Company, Inc., 1943).

A. I. Gates and D. H. Russell, *Diagnostic and Remedial Spelling Manual* (New York: Bureau of Publications, Teachers College, Columbia University, 1937).

advent of standardized testing in the field of spelling released a flood of "objective" tests for reading, spelling, and language usage, as well as scales for evaluating handwriting and composition. The clinical approach, using diagnostic and case-study techniques for educational evaluation, was greatly stimulated by the concern for improving reading instruction. Recent developments in the field of mass communication have brought sound recorders into use in attempts to appraise growth in oral expression.

A number of different standards must be applied in order to determine the learner's progress. Achievement may be described in terms of:

.. (a) the purpose of the learner, (b) the completion of language tasks—forming the loop in the letter *h,* spelling *c-a-t,* writing the salutation in a letter correctly, (c) comparison with other children of the group, (d) comparison with other groups of children, (e) comparison with adults, and (f) comparison of the progress the child is making in language.[33]

Because growth in the various phases of the language arts is unique for each individual, interrelated, and influenced by total development, no uniform standard of adequacy can be applied to all pupils. The most realistic approach is to regard the individual as the basic referent.

IN RETROSPECT

The language arts constitute a form of communication essential for personal integration and effective participation in a democracy. Growth in language power is continuous, and is only one phase of the total development of the individual. Elementary school programs in language arts exhibit much variance in their objectives, in time they allot to specific language activities, in the ways in which they are organized, and in their methods of instruction.

There is a growing conviction that language arts instruction must be made more meaningful; that it should both grow out of and nourish child experience. This point of view implies that: (a) the language arts are tools to be utilized in all areas of instruction; (b) the language arts instruction should center in realistic social situations which provide reasons for, and opportunities to grow in, the arts and skills of communication; and (c) mechanics of language arts should be intro-

[33] Virgil E. Herrick, "Children's Growth and Development in Relation to Language," *Children and the Language Arts,* Virgil E. Herrick and Leland B. Jacobs, eds. (Englewood Cliffs, N.J.: Prentice-Hall, Inc., 1955), p. 98.

duced when and as they are needed to facilitate the transmission of ideas.

Instruction devoted to the development of language abilities must be on a more individual basis than at present. Programs should be flexible, present many avenues to learning, and utilize many and varied resources. Guidance must be based on continuous evaluation of pupil growth in language by the learner, teachers, and school patrons. Better personal and social living depends, among other things, upon better communication.

BIBLIOGRAPHY

Burrows, Alvina T., *et al., They All Want to Write*. Englewood Cliffs, N.J.: Prentice-Hall, Inc., 1952.

Dawson, Mildred A., *Language Teaching in the Grades*. Yonkers-on-Hudson: World Book Company, 1949.

Department of Elementary School Principals, *Language Arts in the Elementary School*, Twentieth Yearbook. Washington: The Department, N.E.A., 1941.

Hartman, Gertrude and Ann Shumaker, eds., *Creative Expression*, 2nd ed., Milwaukee: E. M. Hale and Company, 1939.

Herrick, Virgil E. and Leland B. Jacobs, eds., *Children and the Language Arts*. Englewood Cliffs, N.J.: Prentice-Hall, Inc., 1955.

Hildreth, Gertrude, *Learning the Three R's*, 2nd. ed., Minneapolis: Educational Publishers, Inc., 1947.

McKee, Paul, *Language in the Elementary School*, rev. ed., Boston: Houghton Mifflin Company, 1939.

National Council of Teachers of English, *An Experience Curriculum in English*. Chicago: The Council, 1939.

———, *The English Language Arts*. New York: Appleton-Century-Crofts, Inc., 1952.

———, *Language Arts for Today's Children*. New York: Appleton-Century-Crofts, Inc., 1954.

National Society for the Study of Education, *Reading in the Elementary School*, Forty-Eighth Yearbook, Part II. Chicago: University of Chicago Press, 1949.

———, *Teaching Language Arts in the Elementary School*, Forty-Third Yearbook, Part II. Chicago: University of Chicago Press, 1944.

Russell, David H., *Children Learn to Read*. Boston: Ginn and Company, 1949.

Strickland, Ruth G., *The Language Arts in the Elementary School*. Boston: D. C. Heath and Company, 1951.

Watts, A. F., *The Language and Mental Development of Children*. Boston: D. C. Heath and Company, 1944.

THE
SOCIAL
STUDIES
PROGRAM

8

WESLEY CLAIMS USE OF THE TERM "SOCIAL STUDIES" as early as 1905 to include economics, sociology, and civics.[1] In 1916, a committee of the National Education Association gave the term official recognition; and in 1921, teachers in the social subjects set up a new organization under the name, National Council for the Social Studies.[2] Many teachers will recall encountering the term at a much more recent date and associating with it a variety of meanings. However different the

[1] Edgar B. Wesley, *Teaching the Social Studies* (New York: D. C. Heath and Company, 1937), p. 5.
[2] Edgar B. Wesley and Mary A. Adams, *Teaching Social Studies in Elementary Schools*, rev. ed. (Boston: D. C. Heath and Company, 1952), pp. 17-23.

many definitions may be in detail, all appear to emphasize two basic ideas. The first is that the content of the social studies has been drawn primarily from the social sciences and adapted for instructional purposes. The second is that this content, however organized, is to be used in increasing understanding of, and skill in, human relationships.

THE NATURE OF THE SOCIAL STUDIES

Preston stresses the fact that the term implies no particular scheme of subject organization. He argues that it may be used, for example, to denote history and geography taught as two separate subjects or combined and merged.[3] It is difficult to conceive of satisfying the fundamental purpose of the social studies, however, through content limited to history or geography alone. No one body of content suffices in dealing with problems of human relationships. Present writers are in agreement with Preston that the social studies imply no *particular type* of fusion, synthesis, or integration of subject matter. Michaelis so well expresses the point of view underlying this chapter that he is quoted here at some length:

The social studies are concerned with people and their interaction with their social and physical environment; they deal with human relationships. In the social studies, attention is given to ways of living and working together, use of the environment to meet basic human needs, customs, institutions, values, and life situations—the cultural heritage and its dynamic on-going characteristics. The social studies in the elementary school embrace material related to human relationships drawn from history, geography, political science, economics, anthropology, sociology, science, and the arts. They include content and activities that may be used to develop insight into human relationships in such a way that children build competence in basic social processes and skills essential in democratic living. The social studies make rich contributions to the growth and development of children because the central function of the social studies is identical with the central purpose of education—the development of democratic citizenship.[4]

Thus, certain basic concepts must be kept in mind for the remainder of this chapter to be understood properly:

1. The content of the social studies is material drawn from a number of special disciplines. These special disciplines are mainly, but not necessarily, the social sciences.

[3] Ralph C. Preston, *Teaching Social Studies in the Elementary School* (New York: Rinehart and Co., 1950), p. 4.

[4] John U. Michaelis, *Social Studies for Children in a Democracy*, 2nd ed. (Englewood Cliffs, N.J.: Prentice-Hall, Inc., 1956), pp. 2-3.

2. The material used always represents some combination of content extracted from several fields. This is necessitated by the breadth and depth of the problems of human relationships with which the social studies deal.

3. The organization of content extracted for instructional purposes need not take any particular form or pattern. But it is obvious that the structural organization of any one of the specific subject fields, such as history, geography, or civics, is not adequate in itself to provide for a program of social studies to cover the needs of elementary school children.

4. The separate disciplines of social studies, as well as the basic orientation of this field—human relationships—demand the recognition that intellectual and social processes of language, making judgments, using the tools of the social studies, and living and working effectively with people are fundamental to all teaching and learning in the social studies. These intellectual and social processes are the "carrier agents" of social living, and are thus common and persistent objectives for all experiences in social studies.

5. The key word in "social studies" is *social.* No body of content is barred from use. If it satisfies the social criterion, it may at some time be included in the content of the social studies as it contributes to the solution of human relationships problems.

PURPOSES OF THE SOCIAL STUDIES

There is general agreement about the major purposes of the social studies. Michaelis, from an analysis of 44 courses of study, reports the following:

The major purposes of the social studies are to help each child to:

1. Become a democratic person whose behavior is guided by democratic values, who is loyal to the American way of life, and who appreciates the sacrifices and contributions made to promote democratic living here and throughout the world.

2. Develop modes of behavior consistent with democratic values, such as responsibility, concern for others, open-mindedness, creativeness and cooperation, and to use them in relationships with others.

3. Develop group-action skills and social competency in inter-group relations, recognizing the value of group decision making; showing respect for differences of opinion, and exhibiting high regard for rights of minorities yet abiding by majority decisions.

4. Develop the ability to think critically and creatively and use problem-solving skills in situations involving human relationships; use dependable sources of information; locate, evaluate, select, organize, and present information effectively; and base action on sound conclusions.

5. Appreciate and respect other persons, cultural similarities and differences among peoples, and the contributions of others to our ways of living, realizing that human dignity and personality are of first importance in human relationships regardless of race, color, or class.

6. Acquire and use functional information, concepts, and understandings of: basic social functions of human living such as production of goods and services,

University of Wisconsin Summer Laboratory School

CHILDREN WORK AS A GROUP FOR THEIR PETS

transportation and communication, conservation of resources, esthetic and religious expression, education, recreation, and government; the impact of scientific advance and education upon ways of living; the effect of moral and spiritual values upon human behavior; ways to improve family life, community living, and national-international welfare; and the increasing interdependence characteristic of modern living.

7. Become responsive to needs and problems of others and act courageously and with integrity to bring about changes consistent with democratic ideals and processes.[5]

[5] *Ibid.*, p. 12.

University of Wisconsin Summer Laboratory School

WE LEARN ABOUT OUR STATE

CURRENT PRACTICE IN THE SOCIAL STUDIES

Subject-Oriented Practice

There are a number of different types of subject-approach, all of which may exist together in a given school. Single subjects, correlation of several subjects, and *fusion* of subjects into large organizational units (such as in the case of the *broad fields*) are variations of subject-oriented practice.[6]

Single-Subject Orientation. The trend for the past several years has been away from the single-subject type of organization. An interesting illustration of this trend is to be found in the first and second editions of a text in elementary education, published years apart. Analysis of some daily programs listed in the first edition shows that history, geography, and citizenship, subjects normally included in the

---

[6] It will be noticed that an integrated approach is not listed here as a variety of subject-oriented practice; nor is it included elsewhere in this chapter. Integration is something that occurs within the child. The term "correlation" refers to the process of relating like materials or like elements of subject matter, and adequately describes what is involved. For further discussion see Hollis L. Caswell and A. Wellesley Foshay, *Education in the Elementary School*, 2nd ed. (New York: American Book Co., 1950), pp. 229-31.

social studies, were provided for separately in the time schedule.[7] Examination of the later edition shows only the classification of social studies.[8] In the single-subject orientation, it is common practice to find either history or geography taught in the morning, and the other in the afternoon. When single-subject organization and textbook teaching come hand-in-hand, as is frequently the case, the immediate needs and problems of children may be neglected.[9]

Correlated Subject Orientation. In correlation, like elements of the social studies are brought together in order to provide increased insight into large wholes. It is an attempt to establish connections and relationships.[10] According to Wesley, this attempt may be quite incidental, or it may involve systematic curriculum planning.[11] In the first case, the teacher usually seeks to relate the material of several subjects. For example, the effect of a severe winter climate along the Labrador coast (geography) might be considered in discussing the failure of early attempts at settlement (history).

Systematic correlation, on the other hand, involves some sort of recognized and planned-for inter-subject relationship. It may be something as simple as teaching the history and geography of Brazil during the same weeks (even if at different times of the day). Or, it may involve a detailed outline of natural relationships, together with cross references and suggestions for bringing together like elements from as many subjects as possible. No matter what correlations are attempted, however, basic orientation is still to the subject.

Whether the correlation is systematic or unsystematic, the problem of "what to correlate to what" remains a perplexing and frustrating instructional problem for most teachers and curriculum committees. For example, should persistent social problems and processes like food, shelter, clothing, transportation, communication, governing, etc., be used as referents to relate people, ideas, geographic regions, and political divisions of the world? Or, as school practice most commonly illustrates, should the geographic area being studied be used to bring together people, ideas, climate, social problems and processes, topography and time, and cultural perspectives? Whether we like it or not,

[7] James H. Dougherty, Frank H. Gorman, and Claude A. Phillips, *Elementary School Organization and Management* (New York: The Macmillan Co., 1937), pp. 66-69, 72-74.
[8] Dougherty, Gorman, and Phillips, *Elementary School Organization and Management,* rev. ed. (New York: The Macmillan Co., 1950).
[9] Michaelis, *op. cit.,* pp. 32-33.
[10] Edgar B. Wesley and Mary A. Adams, *op. cit.,* p. 215.
[11] Wesley, *op. cit.,* pp. 241-244.

all approaches to social studies instruction must deal with this problem in some fashion.

Fused Subject Orientation. To many, the term "social studies" implies the *fusion* of several social sciences for teaching purposes. The point of view expressed earlier in this chapter clearly implies disagreement with this automatic linking of a term and an idea. The literature reveals considerable confusion among such terms as *correlation, integration, unification, fusion,* and so on.[12] The position taken here is that fusion goes a step farther in removing the unnatural barriers between single subjects and in promoting natural relationships. The result is the disappearance of lines of demarcation among those subjects fused. Fusion in the social studies involves molding together those subjects or aspects of subjects which must be understood as a whole if insight is to be gained into the social aspects of living.

Fusion results in the identification, or at least designation, of major study topics or units that cut across subject lines. An analysis of courses of studies reveals units such as Communication, Our City, Community Living, Life in Other Lands, Colonial Living, and so on. Material from a number of subjects, not necessarily the social sciences, is involved in the study of such units. It has been said, too, that fusion results in confusion, since the end product is another subject that is much more complex and difficult than any going into the making of it.[13]

There is increasing tendency in most fusion programs of social studies to see the important persistent social problems and processes as themes to which people, geographic and political regions, the specifics and generalities of human living everywhere, and the appropriate areas of the social studies and the school curriculum can be meaningfully related.

Experience-Oriented Practice

In general, the second major type of curriculum organization is that which is oriented to the ongoing experiences of children. A social studies program organized around the experiences of children uses the children's interests, problems, and questions in directing learning

---

12 For varying definitions of terms, including *fusion,* pertaining to organization of the social studies curriculum, see the following:

Edgar B. Wesley, *op. cit.,* pp. 239-254; Wesley and Adams, *op. cit.,* pp. 216-217; W. A. Saucier, *Theory and Practice in the Elementary School* (New York: The Macmillan Co., 1941), pp. 311-316; Preston, *op. cit.,* pp. 62-69; and Michaelis, *op. cit.,* pp. 31-35.

13 Wesley, *op. cit.,* p. 246.

activities. The need for such a program is suggested by Jersild and Tasch in their findings on children's attitudes toward the school program. They found that above the first three grades, children who complained far outnumbered children who spoke well of learnings classified under the social studies.[14] But this finding is in contrast to the finding that these same children expressed interest in many topics under this heading.[15] This discrepancy led Jersild and Tasch to conclude: "In view of findings regarding the personal flavor of children's wishes and interests, it is likely that their reactions to the social studies might be different if these were approached more by way of issues that touch upon children's own feelings and that have a bearing on emotional currents in their own lives."[16]

Knowing the interests likely to be held by children of various ages[17] makes it easier for the teacher to relate classroom instruction to existing motivational forces. Reference to the out-of-school activities of eleven-year-olds, for example, establishes an immediate psychological bond between teacher and youngsters.[18] A knowledge of children's heroes and ideals is an asset in teaching aspects of the social studies.[19] The intercultural efforts of one school were aided, in one instance, by common interests held by the pupils.[20] The work of Jersild and Tasch shows the teacher that there is one area of outside interest and activity of which he always can be certain. "At all age levels the most popular things outside school are those falling in the category which includes sports, games, play and the like."[21] For teachers of the social studies, it is of particular importance to know that the popularity of social activities and of matters of vocational preparation increases with age.[22]

One of the commonly-stated aims of the social studies concerns the improvement of human relations. Research indicates that children are more concerned about other people in the community than about

[14] Arthur T. Jersild and Ruth J. Tasch, *Children's Interests and What They Suggest for Education* (New York: Teachers College, Columbia University, 1949), p. 28.

[15] *Ibid.*, p. 28.

[16] *Ibid.*

[17] See, for example, A. M. Holmes, "Interests of Kindergarten Children," *American School Board Journal*, CXI (August, 1945), 52.

[18] Eleanor Volberding, "Out-of-School Behavior of Eleven-Year-Olds," *Elementary School Journal*, XLVIII (April, 1948), 432-441.

[19] M. L. Stoughton and A. M. Ray, "Study of Children's Heroes and Ideals," *Journal of Experimental Education*, XV (December, 1946), 156-160.

[20] A. M. Jones, "Pupils' Common Interests Help School's Intercultural Efforts," *Clearing House*, XX (April, 1946), 493-494.

[21] Jersild and Tasch, *op. cit.*, p. 47.

[22] *Ibid.*, p. 48.

other elements of community living.[23] It follows, then, that currents of feeling in the lives of children hold more promise for instructional success than do topics of more remote concern.

Orientation Around Children in Particular. It is impossible to discuss all the varieties of teaching situations in which teachers find themselves. It is equally impossible to take each general type of situation and discuss every way of moving toward an instructional program oriented around the experiences of particular groups of children. It is possible, however, to take one teacher in one situation and show how she moved with a group of children in planning a social studies program related to their concerns. The next few pages constitute a description of such an attempt.

SOCIAL STUDIES AT MOULTRIE, GEORGIA[24]

The social studies program of the Moultrie (Georgia) elementary schools has a purpose. Worked out by the teachers, it is stated as follows: "The study of social problems should enable boys and girls to live, work, and play with each other in such a way as to realize their own greatest growth and make worthwhile contributions to the group. In short, the function of the social studies is to enable each child to live more effectively in a democratic society."

Jane Comer's social studies program that year grew out of this stated purpose, a permissive framework, and the daily concerns of her seventh graders. Usually, the school day began with a sharing period planned by the children. The intent was to talk about things that would interest others and promote understanding of one another. It was suggested, one day, that they discuss home jobs and responsibilities. Contributions came quickly and soon discussion shifted to jobs away from home. Sue suggested that home responsibilities and the various types of jobs be listed. Work at home included washing the family car, cleaning the yard, bringing in wood, washing dishes, caring for pets, and so on. Jobs away from home included helping in stores, working on farms, delivering papers, etc. It was computed that twenty per cent of the group were "salaried," ninety-seven per cent had home responsibilities, and only three per cent were "unemployed."

"But why should we have chores to do at home?" someone asked. Group discussion introduced the idea that all have responsibilities in a working world and must be depended upon to do a proportionate share. "This means, then," someone else proposed, "that parents, too, have responsibilities." Discussion shifted. The children came to realize that they knew very little of their own parents' jobs and so, for the next several days, they raised questions at home. Soon they were able to list a wide range of occupations and considerable information about each. It was observed that the list was representative of occupations in Moultrie.

---

23 *Ibid.*, p. 56.
24 Through the courtesy of the late Mrs. L. G. Cox, Supervising Principal of the Moultrie elementary schools. Material used here has been adapted from a report of Jane Q. Comer, seventh grade teacher.

One youngster pointed out the relationship to occupations given in the geography book and suggested a re-classification. This was the result in their own words:

OUR PARENTS' WORK IN MOULTRIE

1. Lumbering and forestry 3
2. Own or operate farms 6
3. Work in travel, transportation, or communication 4
4. Merchants 4
5. Construction or building 3
6. Service jobs 9
7. Manufacturing 6
8. Housewives .... All mothers
9. Recreation 1

Then, the group took upon itself the task of getting real insight into these activities. Ways of getting and sharing information were listed. Up until then, the class had worked as a large group. But several weeks later (a total of ten or more working hours), individual and small group projects were selected. Frequent evaluation periods provided for selection of materials, ways of working, and choosing work partners. Time was utilized in checking on progress made—the availability and use of information, how well information was being prepared for sharing and was being reported on, what should be done next. Standards for writing reports were set by the class and suggestions for good English usage were placed on a chart. Drawings were checked for application of color, depiction of ideas, and attractiveness in the arrangement of ideas.

By the time the study was completed and reports had been made, rich understanding of their town had been derived. Comparisons of Moultrie with the surrounding Colquitt County had been made. These seventh graders learned that more people worked in agricultural jobs than in any other. Further discussion revealed the significance of agriculture as a national industry. The group decided unanimously to study this industry and to start with Colquitt County, extending the study over the nation and to possessions and territories. "Let's get to work," they said.

But planning came first. Six major questions were listed. Then came "sources of information" and "ways of sharing." Committees were set up to collect, to work, to write. Some groups went out into the community. They interviewed many people, visited farms, checked out books from the city library, and found maps, charts, and booklets at the Chamber of Commerce, County Agent's Office, and the A.A.A.

The study moved just as easily into Georgia, the southeastern states, the western states and so on. Each phase was brought to a formal, satisfying conclusion, but in an open-ended way. Thus, the conclusion of one study opened the way to the next. Through evaluation, planning procedures improved. Boys and girls became more expert in finding information and their knowledge of sources expanded. More interesting ways of reporting and summarizing were explored.

Many persons reading this account know of situations very similar to this one. Some will conclude that this group proceeded very much as does their own. While the description is largely self-explanatory, certain elements of the situation and its setting warrant emphasis.

1. This class, like others in the system, had a guide or course of study which gave not only a purpose for the social studies, but also a theme for the grade, and which suggested topics for study.

2. The group operated within an organizing framework that provided opportunities for sharing individual experience. Through this sharing, the teacher was able to gain insight into the real concerns and interests of the children.

3. The class activities in the social studies grew easily out of a normal group situation. It was not necessary for the teacher to provide external motivation. Her basic understanding of purpose, and of elements which gave promise of achieving purpose, made it possible for her to guide the spontaneous contributions of children into meaningful learnings.

4. The primary focus was upon the real concerns of children. Subject matter was introduced as a vehicle for problem solving.

5. Activities proceeded in a sequence that was both logical and psychological. The sequence was psychological because it began with, and proceeded in keeping with, the present experience and felt concern of boys and girls. It was logical because it moved from the simple and immediate to places more remote and concepts more complex.

6. The material from a number of fields was correlated naturally. No scheming on the part of the teacher to introduce art, music, and so on, was necessary. Material was drawn together whenever the process improved understanding.

7. Children were "in on" the learning process at all stages. They helped initiate the ideas, they assisted in the formulation of plans, and they carried these plans out under the teacher's guidance. Even the standards for judging the "goodness" of their learning were of their own devising.

8. The teacher participated as a member of the group. She was a guiding member, not a spectator.

9. Groups did not work together just for the sheer joy of doing so. Central in all group activities were meaningful problems to be solved.

10. The problems studied were real social studies problems—problems involving human relationships.

SOCIAL STUDIES THROUGH THE GRADES

Concepts and understandings, skills, values, and attitudes are not learned in the abstract. The teacher may insist that he teaches children; but he teaches them by using content. Considerable uniformity in the placement of content has developed in schools throughout the country. There seems to be most uniformity in topics to be taught at the primary level; greater variation occurs at the intermediate and upper elementary school levels. An analysis by Michaelis of 121 courses of study developed since 1944 revealed that the social studies, by and large, begin with the child's immediate environment of the home, school, and neighborhood, and gradually widen to include community, nation, and world.[25] The middle grades deal primarily with regions. Regional types are identified in the fourth grade and attention is given to life in these regions. The fifth and sixth grades deal largely with regions of the United States, developing both historical and geographic aspects. Then, for part of the sixth and in the seventh grade, attention is focused upon life in other countries and continents. In the eighth grade, the development of the United States and its world status predominates.[26] Perhaps this eighth-grade emphasis is the result of the general desire to assure study of our nation for the many children who drop out of school at completion of this grade.

Analysis of Sequence

It is remarkable that so little has been done to identify the organizing elements which underlie the development of sequence in social studies. In an analysis of the curriculum guides of eight school systems, Sand was able to find organizing elements (concepts, values, skills) defined explicitly in only one.[27] However, in studying the social studies practices of four school systems, he found sequential development of concepts in all four, of values in only one, and of skills in two.[28] He found, too, that the primary grades ranked first, the intermediate grades second, and the high school third in the sequential development of the elements he studied.[29] It is of great interest that the school level which traditionally claims greatest concern for children and least concern for subject matter *per se* should be doing the best job of developing content materials sequentially. Could it be that we lose concern both for the sequence of child development and the underlying concepts in subject matter as we progress upward through

---

[25] *Op. cit.*, p. 19.

[26] Federal Security Agency, Office of Education, Division of Elementary Education, *Social Studies Courses of Study,* XVII (April, 1949), 2.

[27] Ole P. Sand, "Continuity and Sequence in Social Studies Curriculums" (Ph.D. dissertation, Department of Education, University of Chicago, 1948).

[28] *Ibid.*

[29] *Ibid.*

the grades? The analysis of grade units conducted by Michaelis and listed earlier would suggest that basic organizing elements in the social studies are lost sight of in the maze of unrelated, discrete topics proposed for study in the upper elementary grades.

Some Elements Identified. It is essential that an elementary school faculty determine for itself those elements that are to be built upon consistently through the grades. In one school, analysis might involve separate treatment of each subject conceived of as a social science—history, civics, and so on. In another, it may be necessary to identify those elements to be developed through the fusion of history, geography, and citizenship. In still others, the process may involve systematic identification of the basic values, skills, and understandings involved in achieving effective, satisfying human relationships.

It will be helpful to any curriculum committee working on this problem to realize that any program of social studies will include the following five aspects:

1. Persistent problems of social living important to all people, wherever they might live.
2. Recognized ways of dealing with these problems varying according to forms of government and kinds of social values held. (Cooperation vs. competition; democracy vs. autocracy; etc.)
3. Areas in which people and problems are found. These areas may be geographic, political, climatic, or cultural.
4. The ideas, concepts, or generalizations which man's experience has found valuable for dealing with his social problems. (Subject matter.)
5. The intellectual processes by which man has gathered, recorded, tested, and used his understanding of himself and his world to deal with his problems of human relationships (use of tools; *e.g.,* language, maps, charts, globes, group processes, etc.).

As teachers examine this list, they will recognize that areas (the expanding world—home, school, community, regions, Europe, Asia) are most commonly used as a basis for planning sequences in social studies. It should be recognized, however, that generalizations and social studies skills might also be major themes for a social studies program. Similarly, the persistent problems of living can be used to develop continuity. Actually, all five have their proper place in planning for adequate sequential development in the social studies program of the elementary school.

By way of illustrating the possible results of such a study, the elements and the classification of these elements produced by committees of teachers in the Louisville, Kentucky, elementary schools are presented here.[30] The organizing elements running through the grades have been grouped into three categories: understandings and concepts; habits and skills; attitudes, appreciations, and interests. The theme to be developed sequentially throughout the program is as follows: "The child becomes acquainted with the social pattern of action and thought."[31] This theme is related to the maturation of children by beginning with experiences close to the child in the kindergarten (home and school) and leading out to the more remote world relationships by the sixth grade.[32] The sub-themes for each of the seven levels illustrate this as follows:

Kindergarten: The child at home and at school.
First Grade: The child and his relationships in his home and at school.
Second Grade: The child and his relationships in his community.
Third Grade: The child and his relationships in his city.
Fourth Grade: People and their environment.
Fifth Grade: The people of the Western Hemisphere and their world relationships.
Sixth Grade: The people of the Eastern Hemisphere and their world relationships.[33]

The deepening of understanding through the grades is illustrated here by selecting one concept having to do with individuality and dependence patterns, which is built upon at each successive level:

Kindergarten: The place of the individual in a social group.
First Grade: The interdependence of the individual and the group.
Second Grade: The need for health and safety regulations.
Third Grade: People who live in our city have some needs in common with people everywhere.
Fourth Grade: Three common needs of mankind are food, clothing, and shelter.
Fifth Grade: The nations of the Western Hemisphere depend on each other and on the Eastern Hemisphere for ideas, goods, and services.
Sixth Grade: People of various races and nationalities throughout the world have common needs and interests.[34]

Similarly, habits and skills are reinforced through the grades. One

[30] Louisville Public Schools, *A Tentative Course of Study for Social Studies in the Kindergarten and Primary Grades,* Bulletin 8, Part 1; *Social Studies in the Elementary School Curriculum: Intermediate Grades,* Bulletin 8, Part 2 (Louisville, Kentucky: September, 1947).
[31] *Ibid.,* frontispiece.
[32] *Loc. cit.*
[33] *Ibid.,* pp. 1-10.
[34] *Ibid.*

item from each level is selected by way of illustrating skill in communication:

Kindergarten: Listen purposefully.
First Grade: Communicate his ideas to others.
Second Grade: Give directions clearly and certainly.
Third Grade: Make simple reports.
Fourth Grade: Participate intelligently in discussion and listen attentively and courteously when others are speaking.
Fifth Grade: Do individual and group planning.
Sixth Grade: Exercise his responsibility in keeping the discussion moving consistently toward a conclusion.[35]

It is obvious from the above, that activities are to be selected in each grade with a view to developing communicative skills as one objective. In the same way, provision is made for the sequential development of attitudes, appreciations, and interests. Again, we select one item from each grade level to illustrate expanding interest in and appreciation for human achievements:

Kindergarten: An interest in school.
First Grade: An interest in the achievements of other members of the home and school groups.
Second Grade: An appreciation of the contributions made to his welfare through the industry and efforts of his neighbors.
Third Grade: An interest in the contributions of Louisvillians, in the fields of science, art, literature, music, education, industry, and government.
Fourth Grade: A sympathetic attitude toward all peoples for their efforts in adjusting their lives to their immediate environment.
Fifth Grade: An interest in the contributions of the people of our neighboring countries to aesthetic, cultural, and spiritual expression.
Sixth Grade: An attitude of sympathetic interest and an open-mindedness toward the problems, achievements, and future development of our world neighbors.[36]

The identification of basic organizing elements underlying the social studies is essential if any meaningful curriculum organization is to be attempted. And, ". . . without organization, learning experiences are isolated, chaotic, and haphazard."[37] Insight into the under-

[35] *Ibid.*
[36] *Ibid.*
[37] Ralph W. Tyler, "The Organization of Learning Experiences," *Toward Improved Curriculum Theory,* Supplementary Educational Monographs, Number 71, Virgil E. Herrick and Ralph W. Tyler, eds. (Chicago: The University of Chicago Press, 1950), p. 50.

standings, skills, and attitudes to be developed through the grades is as necessary to the teacher who draws heavily upon children's experience as it is to the teacher who depends to a large degree on organized bodies of subject matter.

Some Organizing Principles. One of the most commonly applied principles in the social studies is the chronological. Epochs are studied in their order of appearance. Or, the history of communal living is traced. Or, perhaps, the contributions of great scientists, explorers, and writers through the ages are studied. It is difficult to keep the application of this principle compatible with the sequences of child development. To be logical, this approach must start at the beginning —when time concepts are but poorly developed in children.

Another principle is that of beginning with experiences close to the personal life of the learner and then moving out into the home, then into the school, then into the community, and ultimately into the state and nation. Both Sand[38] and Michaelis[39] found this principle most commonly applied in the curriculum guides they examined. One suggested weakness of this principle, however, is that many aspects of the geographically close environment are profound in their complexity. Tyler suggests that children may more easily understand the primitive culture of the Indian or the Eskimo than the complex organization of their own local urban community.[40]

Still another principle of sequence involves beginning with the simple and moving to the complex. Difficulty of application here stems from trying to differentiate what is simple to the learner from that which is complex.[41] This is particularly true of the social studies where attitudes and values—themselves complex phenomena—are considered. Yet a program of social studies which does not help children examine and constructively develop their attitudes and values about themselves and their social relationships is failing to consider an important area of objectives.

38 *Op. cit.*
39 *Op. cit.*, p. 22.
40 *Op. cit.*, p. 65.
41 In this connection, Kelty reports that teachers listed the following topics, in order, as most difficult for fifth-graders to understand: making the new government, new government begins work, revolution in the South, revolution in New England, revolution in the west, colonial government, kinds of government, revolution in middle states, causes of Civil War, Civil War political leaders, Civil War military leaders, Confederacy, narrative of Civil War, years following the Civil War. See Mary Kelty, "The Middle Grades Program: Articulation with the Upper Grades," *The Study and Teaching of American History,* Seventeenth Yearbook of the National Council for the Social Studies, Richard E. Thursfield, ed. (Washington: National Council for the Social Studies, 1946), p. 214.

Much research remains to be done. The application of organizing principles which apply only to subject matter is not enough. Nor does insight into principles of human growth and development and of learning suffice. It is likely, too, that no single organizing principle will be found adequate in providing for sequential learnings in the social studies.[42]

SOCIAL STUDIES ACROSS THE GRADES

A teacher in a given grade finds himself in the position of having to tie in to what has gone before. This necessitates, first, identifying the sequential elements being developed throughout the grades, and, second, establishing meaningful relationships among these elements, so that patterns are formed. The teacher may use as his point of departure textbooks, topics, units, or children's experiences.

Departure Points in the Improvement of Learning and Teaching in Social Studies

Textbooks. No single caricature may be drawn of the teacher who uses the textbook as the organizing center for learning. Some begin and end with it. Others keep it as a handy reference. Still others scarcely refer to it as they work with children. However, because of the assumptions that must be made about a textbook, close allegiance to it can scarcely result in creative teaching in the social studies.

Frequently the textbook approach hampers movement from one form of curriculum organization to another. Teachers hesitate to attempt broad fields or fusion approaches without the security of a book similarly organized. As a result, the teacher tends to stay reasonably close to the logical organization of the geography or history text even when the course of studies and the report card use the term "social studies" to indicate fusion of the two subjects. Fortunately, according to Michaelis, very few elementary school programs use only this approach at the present time.[43]

Topics. Again, finding points of departure at a given grade level by use of topics varies as much as practice through textbooks. Preston identified seven plans currently in operation for assigning topics among the various grades.[44] These ranged from history, period by period, and geography, region by region, to a "planless" procedure by

---

[42] See Gordon N. Mackenzie, "Organizing Elements of the Curriculum," *Toward Improved Curriculum Theory, op. cit.,* p. 53.

[43] *Op. cit.,* p. 14.

[44] *Op. cit.,* p. 44.

which topics emerge and are selected for study by the group. However, he identifies one type based on generalizations which might well run right through the grades.[45] Three of the generalizations he lists are these:

> Man is a social being capable of changing.
> Interdependence among peoples is furthered by communication and transportation.
> For effective living, man needs food, clothing, and shelter.[46]

In the first, the understanding to be developed through the grades is clear, but the topics to be selected as points of departure in a given

Beloit Public Schools, Beloit, Wisconsin

"HOW MUCH FOR THIS PUMPKIN, FARMER BROWN?"

grade are not. In the second and third, the topics of communication, transportation, food, clothing, and shelter stand out clearly as learning-teaching centers to be used in developing the two major understandings. Generalizations of this kind, then, would be very helpful to the classroom teacher if they specifically highlighted promising topics to be used in developing given concepts. The major criticism of

45 *Ibid.,* p. 49.
46 *Ibid.,* pp. 51-52.

most procedures employing the topic approach is that topics too frequently bear little relationship to one another.

Units. Michaelis lists separate-subject units, correlated-subject units, and comprehensive social studies units in increasing order of preference.[47] This preference is in line with Rivlin's rejection of separate school subjects in unit teaching[48] and the concept of Wesley and Adams that the social studies unit is focused upon some significant process or social relationship.[49]

Experiences. Using the social experiences of children as a point of departure may involve the use of textbooks, topics, and units. However, the focal point is the experience itself. From an incident in the child's life, or the question he asks, or the problem he is struggling with, we seek out the textbook, we propose study topics, or we set up the framework for a comprehensive unit. Subject matter is no less important; it is simply used differently. For instance, an extensive study of churches and religions grew out of one group's own experience in church attendance. Free discussion in the seventh grade at Moultrie, Georgia, produced questions such as these:[50]

1. Why do I go to one church and my friends have to go to another?
2. Do people go to the same kinds of churches all over the United States?
3. What kinds of worship services are held by different churches in different places?
4. What do different church groups believe?

Seeking to find answers to these, the children selected topics for study, some of which were:

1. Ideas and beliefs of our own churches, particularly in regard to modes of baptism.
2. Kinds of worship services held at different churches in Moultrie.
3. Types of architecture and kinds of church buildings in Moultrie.
4. History of our churches.

Studying these topics led youngsters not only to the textbook, but to many other books as well.

A good point of departure for teaching social studies in a given grade merits an affirmative answer to each of these questions: Will it

47 *Op. cit.*, pp. 32-34.
48 Harry N. Rivlin, *Teaching Adolescents in Secondary Schools* (New York: Appleton-Century-Crofts, Inc., 1948), p. 109.
49 *Op. cit.*, p. 221.
50 From material submitted by the teachers of the Moultrie Elementary Schools.

further the skills, understandings, and values sought in the social studies? Is it related to the maturity level of the children? Does it have "lead-on" possibilities? Does it buttress learnings sought elsewhere in the program?

SOCIAL LIVING IN SCHOOL AND CLASSROOM

A social studies program conceived only in terms of the activities carried on under the name of history or geography, or of some fusion of subjects, is very limited, indeed. Many of the most powerful social learnings are those which occur in conjunction with daily living in the classroom, in the hallways, and on the playground.

Using the process of living together in the classroom as an organizing center for learning involves several major considerations. In the first place, we need to take inventory of the various activities having educational promise. These include getting in and out of the room, taking care of coats and other belongings, managing equipment and supplies, using hallways, lavatories, drinking fountains, playgrounds, and so on.

Sarah Groves faced these considerations with her second-grade class.[51] She was dissatisfied with existing confusion in the lunchroom, in conducting housekeeping duties, and in getting ready to go home. She started with the fundamental assumption that the growth and learning of children are facilitated when they accept responsibility. Then, she helped the group to decide upon a satisfactory seating arrangement for planning sessions. Finally, sixteen chairs and nineteen movable desks were drawn into a circle. The children next set up some standards for planning procedures. These included talking one at a time, listening when someone else is talking, keeping in one place until the session is ended, being pleasant to one another, and so on. It was agreed to have a planning session each morning.

Three big projects, in line with the teacher's concerns, were begun. After two weeks, a group evaluation session revealed the following agreements on improvement:

1. Keeping crumbs and paper off the floor.
2. Formal, quiet talk at tables.
3. Reasonable order on way to cafeteria and other rooms.
4. Removing paper from trays.

However, dissatisfaction was expressed by the group in regard to the following:

[51] From material submitted by the staff of Garden Hills School, Atlanta, Georgia (Emma Burnett, Principal).

1. "Ganging-up" on one person on playground.
2. Breaking up other children's games on the playground.
3. Getting wraps.

Four months of planning, followed by action and evaluation, produced group and individual changes to an amazing degree. An increasingly large number of boys and girls carried on individual study. Cafeteria conduct no longer was a cause for concern. Attitudes toward others on the playground improved markedly. Considerable skill was achieved in arriving at decisions without taking a vote, and group discussion had become a satisfactory way of disposing of most class problems.

This class succeeded not only in practicing basic social skills, but also in reaching a level of self-discipline that facilitated all learning and teaching. These emergent outcomes far exceeded the outcomes Miss Groves had in mind initially.

Student Organizations and Activities

The many activities of a non-academic nature sponsored by elementary schools sometimes have been described as extracurricular. These include student councils, junior town meetings, assembly programs, clubs, intramural teams, and the variety of special-interest groups found in most schools. But if we accept the definition that ". . . the curriculum for each child is the sum total of all his experiences which are in any way affected by the school,"[52] then such activities hardly could be called *extra*curricular. In practice, these activities are the proving ground for the application of insights and understandings pertaining to the way people treat other people.

School Projects

The social studies are like other aspects of the curriculum in that, in program building, consideration must be given to children, society, and subject content. That is one reason why large-scale projects, not necessarily planned as part of the social studies program, have much to offer in furthering the aims of the social studies. One of the ways to develop "we-ness" instead of "me-ness," and a feeling of personal involvement in the otherwise impersonal remoteness of the school, is through participation in group projects of school improvement. Personal needs, societal realities, and appropriate content are brought into meaningful relationship.

52 J. Murray Lee and Dorris May Lee, *The Child and His Curriculum* (New York: Appleton-Century-Crofts, 1950), p. 199.

Some of the desirable characteristics of such school projects are the following:

1. The activity should contribute to the attainment of over-all school objectives.
2. Clearly stated goals for the project should be established by the group to guide planning, action, and evaluation.[53]
3. These goals should be developed cooperatively, with all members participating.
4. Maximum participation on the part of all should be sought throughout all activity.
5. The relationship between what is being done and the established goals should be clear at all times.
6. Critical thinking should be encouraged throughout, ideas being accepted or rejected in the light of accepted criteria.
7. Sound problem-solving procedures should be used throughout.
8. The teacher should be a guiding member of the group.
9. Student benefit should be paramount, and school publicity only a by-product.[54]
10. Evaluation for progress toward goals and for possible unplanned concomitants should be a continuous process.
11. The activity, or various phases of it, should be brought to a recognized conclusion before interest has waned. Too often, school projects die a slow, neglected death. Successes warrant a celebration and failures at least a decent burial and post-mortem.

RESOURCES FOR TEACHING THE SOCIAL STUDIES

All teachers of social studies should recognize that their children, audio-visual materials, texts, and library resources are important aids to effective teaching in social studies as in all other instructional areas. Chapter 16 describes more completely than is possible here how these resources can be selected and used to further effective learning.

Community Resources

Community considerations are particularly important in the social studies, and, in the lower elementary grades, community concerns constitute both learning content and instructional resources.

Teachers themselves may take inventory of what the community offers. One such inventory was conducted by the DeKalb County (Georgia) teachers in their annual summer workshop.[55] Similarly, the

---

[53] Michaelis, *op. cit.*, p. 159.
[54] Rivlin, *op. cit.*, p. 388.
[55] DeKalb County Schools, *Report of the DeKalb County Summer Workshop* (Decatur, Georgia: DeKalb County Board of Education, 1951).

staff and students of many high schools in the country conduct community surveys as part of their schools' self-evaluation process for accreditation. The results of such surveys offer valuable data about the community for classroom use.

Mrs. Pickert's fourth-grade class decided to take its own inventory.[56] The group had decided on community study rather than study of foreign countries, and presented such reasons as the following for taking the inventory:

1. We will know the names and locations of streets in case signs are broken down.
2. We will be able to help strangers if we know the streets and businesses.
3. Learning our community first will help us in learning about other countries.
4. I would like to compare our community with other places.
5. Most of the work would be done at school. I would rather work at school than at home.

Information was gathered through direct visits, from answers to letters written to business concerns, and from a questionnaire sent to parents. The thoroughness of the job resembled a government census and overwhelmed the teacher. She had anticipated neither the enthusiasm of the children nor the comprehensive nature of their work.

The question might well be raised as to whether or not such a project warranted the time spent on it. Had the collection of data been the sole end, the answer would probably be no. But the teacher wisely used the project as an organizing center for learning. Language skills were developed through writing of letters, preparing reports, reading replies, summarizing materials, and so on. Spelling centered around the words being used daily. The purchase of stamps, numbering of streets and homes, and various compilations encouraged the development of number skills. Group work fostered desirable social relationships. Above all, community-consciousness was developed. For the balance of the year, classroom learning was enriched by the children's ability to draw upon the environment around them.

The social studies should and can be a vital source of learning for children, rather than the source of dissatisfaction reported by Jersild and Tasch in their survey of children's interests.[57] How the social studies program became a source of vital experience for one group of children is described in the next section.

56 From material submitted by the faculty of the E. P. Howell elementary school in Fulton County, Georgia (Minnie Howell, Principal).
57 Op. cit.

TEACHING AND LEARNING IN THE SOCIAL STUDIES

A Class At Work

Let us look at the way in which one teacher proceeded with her second grade class.[58] Let it be clear, again, that the following account tells of one highly desirable line of progression. Other teachers might have proceeded quite differently, but in equally sound ways. Miss Newbury's teaching background and classroom situation were not unique.

Forty-one children constituted the chief furnishings of her classroom. And they were pretty much like seven- and eight-year-olds everywhere. The group represented a range of nearly seventy I.Q. points. Some had virtually no reading vocabulary; others read at close to the fifth grade level. As individuals they were capable of the most vigorous physical activity at one moment, and the most profound lassitude not many minutes later. Displays of adorable or prankish behavior came and went with equal uncertainty. Taken as a group, or as individuals, they were enough to tax the patience, strength, mind, and ingenuity of any teacher—much like other children.

Finding a Point of Departure

As the breathless youngsters settled into their seats after recess, Miss Newbury decided to get at the background of what she had seen and heard.* Why were some people called "dirty greasers?" . . . Oh, because they eat greasy food. They're bandits, and they live in Mexico, and they steal horses and shoot people. They'll cheat you, and you can't trust them. The best thing to do is to shoot 'em . . . Well, Miss Newbury had gotten what she asked for, and it didn't sit very well.

When the outpour had died down, she moved in again with a quiet, half-to-herself comment . . . This is all very strange. I have an aunt who lives in Mexico . . . A gasp, a whistle, a skeptical snort, and then: You do? I'll bet she has a whole stack of guns. How many Mexicans has she killed? Does she have a big ranch? Has she seen any rustlers? Is it safe there? . . . Yes, it's just as safe as it is here. She doesn't live on a ranch. Her husband is an engineer. They live in very much the same way we do. I've visited them in Mexico . . . You have? . . . Eyes and mouths are wide open now, and Miss Newbury has undivided attention.

---

[58] The account that follows has been adapted from notes kept by Miss Josephine Newbury of the Center Hill School in Fulton County, Georgia, as she guided her second grade children in their study of Mexico (Mrs. M. V. Barnett, Principal).

* During recess, Miss Newbury had watched her group of children chase and "shoot" a bunch of "dirty greasers."

We Make Plans

Where do we go from here? This was the thought that momentarily troubled Miss Newbury . . . Perhaps you would like to find out some more things about Mexico. Perhaps you would like to write my aunt . . . Couldn't we visit her? . . . Yes, we could pretend. But we couldn't actually visit because it's too far . . . As far as Rich's? (a large store in Atlanta) . . . Laughter from the group and a voice: Lots farther, silly, a hundred times, a million times, a million, million times . . . No, not that far, Tommy, but it would take your daddy

University of Wisconsin Summer Laboratory School

UNDERSTANDING OUR NEIGHBORS THROUGH IMAGINARY TRAVEL

several days to drive there in his new car. Now, what are some of the things you would like to know about people who live in Mexico? . . .

As fast as the questions came, the teacher listed them on the blackboard:

1. What do the Mexican people look like?[59]
2. How do they talk?

[59] Actual phrasing and events are presented; however, space limitations necessitate condensation and abbreviation. Some readers may prefer the term "Spanish-American" to "Mexican." This will be the case particularly in the southwest portions of the country. However, the latter, rather than the former, was used by the group described here.

3. What do they eat?
4. How do they dress?
5. Do they fly kites?
6. What do they do in school?
7. How do they get places?
8. What kinds of work do they do?
9. What kinds of stores do they have?
10. How do they play? What do they play?
11. What are their towns like?
12. How can we be friends?
13. Do they go to Sunday school and church?
14. What can we do to help each other?

Miss Newbury's next question was not so productive . . . How might we discover some of this information by ourselves? . . . Five ideas came forth:

1. "Play like" we take a trip to Mexico.
2. Write letters to people in Mexico.
3. Read stories about Mexican children.
4. Look at pictures of Mexican life.
5. Enjoy seeing things that came from Mexico.

The Teacher Makes Plans

The children were still eager, even though the entire process had taken three times as long as those activities usually engaged in by the group. But Miss Newbury wanted both to maintain this enthusiasm and to take stock of the series of events that had occurred in such rapid succession. That afternoon and evening she did some thinking and some planning. She reviewed in her mind her over-all purposes and wrote down the following for the proposed study of Mexico:

1. To help the children begin to build a broader conception of the world.
2. To help straighten out the children's misconceptions about the Mexicans.
3. To help them discover the many ways in which Mexican children are like themselves.
4. To help the boys and girls find answers to their questions through their reading and other experiences.
5. To help them develop the ability to plan and select and to attack new activities in a spirit of research.
6. To lay a foundation for further study and research in which they will find rich experiences.

She knew that the proposed activity would fail unless materials suitable for the children were available. Much of this would be brought forth by the children themselves, but some things were needed immediately. Her research brought forth authentic Mexican objects as well as books and pamphlets.

BOOKS FOR CHILDREN—*Pancho* (Hader), *Manuella's Birthday* (Bannon), *Pepe and the Parrot* (Credle), *Pablo's Pipe* (Eliot), *Pancho and His Burro* (Gay).

FILM STRIP—*Children of Mexico* (Encyclopedia Britannica).

RECORDS—"Let's Fly to Mexico" and several recordings of Mexican music.

OTHER PRINTED MATERIAL—travel folders and guides, maps, globe, *National Geographic* magazines, pictures, newspapers.

EXHIBITS—wool rug, pottery, woven mats and baskets, ancient Aztec money, modern money, straw toys, schoolbooks, stamps, picture cards, silver jewelry, Mexican flag.

Then she went to her file of pictures that had been collected through the years. How many times this file had saved the day! Appropriate Mexican pictures were mounted and words and phrases that might be used in writing stories about them were printed on charts. Next, reading cards were made and filed according to subjects. Stories were printed in anticipation of the needs of slow readers. It was hard work, spread over several days, but it resulted in a rich supply of resources to be used when needed.

We Carry Out Our Plans

These materials were enough to begin with, and to stimulate the group. The children got the idea and the room took on a cosmopolitan air. At one time, seven sets of encyclopedias, brought by the children and richly illustrated, were in use. The materials were organized and the room rearranged. One large table in the center of the room was used for displaying globe, atlas, and objects of interest about Mexico. These objects were placed on display in groups of two or three at a time, rather than indiscriminantly. Centers of interest were set up for clay modeling, chalk work, painting, and sewing. Reading materials, pictures, and charts were placed on the walls and on shelves.

To satisfy herself that learnings appropriate for these children actually were taking place, Miss Newbury kept a record of activities. She then classified them along conventional subject lines in accordance with the course of study. Her classification and some illustrations of activities are listed here.

A. Language Arts
   1. Reading stories about Mexico in books and regular readers for pleasure.
   2. Reading for information from materials classified as the study progressed.
   3. Keeping a record of the imaginary trips to Mexico.
   4. Writing letters to people in Mexico.

5. Writing stories about interesting things learned.
6. Writing invitations for culminating fiesta.
7. Telling groups about what they have read and done.
8. Building "new word" lists for spelling and understanding.

B. Social Studies
   1. Becoming acquainted with maps, globe, atlas.
   2. Finding out about the homes, dress, food, customs, occupations, etc., of Mexico.
   3. Discovering more about transportation through study of ways of getting to Mexico.
   4. Making large picture map of Mexico.

C. Science
   1. Comparing the seasons.
   2. Comparing topography with own surroundings.
   3. Studying flowers, fruits, foods, animals.
   4. Studying some of the natural resources and the products of them.

D. Health and Physical Education
   1. Comparison of diets.
   2. Comparison of food handling and distribution methods.
   3. Discussion of the *siesta* period.
   4. Playing Mexican games.

E. Creative and Appreciative Arts
   1. Enjoying Mexican music.
   2. Learning simple songs in Spanish.
   3. Making up a simple song about an experience in Mexico.
   4. Creating a simple Spanish dance.
   5. Painting large pictures of Mexican scenes.
   6. Modeling in clay, decorating paper plates, making scenery for the *fiesta*, making costumes.

Mexican-centered activities did not dominate the entire day. In fact, some days went by without any direct attention given to this major activity. Less time than usual was devoted to various studies, however, because the study of Mexico involved every desired type of learning at one time or another. But not all the spelling, reading, science, and so on, pertained to Mexico. Since very little attention to number work was provided through the project, daily arithmetic lessons usually were held. A well-balanced educational diet resulted.

We Bring Matters to a Conclusion

Classroom life has a pulse. Wise teachers keep a sensitive finger on this pulse—in a number of places. When interest begins to wane (quarrels occur more frequently, building projects are abandoned, models are no longer attractions) and the material dealt with no longer promises rich returns, it is time to terminate the activity.

There is a great temptation to put on a show or to think of schemes that will enable each child to share in what every other child has done. It is a temptation to be resisted. Learning principles are violated when we expect youngsters to learn in a fifteen-minute report what other children mastered over a period of weeks.[60] Quality of learning should be fostered throughout the entire process. The culminating activity, then, should be a natural outgrowth, occurring while interest is still high, and requiring neither exhaustive preparation nor intense emotional demands.

The class itself produced the means for drawing the project to conclusion. When the children read about a *fiesta,* someone said, "Why can't we have a *fiesta?*" The idea won instantaneous approval. "Ramona's Patio" was chosen as the site of the great event. A program began to take shape, a date was chosen, and invitations to parents written. On the gala day, activities began with the class singing a Spanish lullaby. Then, they read the travel log that had been kept so carefully from day to day, and sang their original song, "My Little Burro." Their own Spanish dance was a gay finale. A Spanish-American menu of nut cakes, hard candy, and Mexican chocolate ice cream brought matters to a substantial conclusion. On display throughout were the scrapbook, picture book, story-charts, drawings, paintings, and table arrangements of Mexican exhibits. A mock battle on the playground one spring morning had produced far-reaching effects, indeed!

Some Unanticipated Values

Miss Newbury had set forth some rather specific goals. But, as she looked back over all that had occurred, she identified many values that had not been anticipated at the outset. She set them down as follows:

1. Children grew in their ability to work together congenially.
2. Children learned to take constructive criticism from one another.
3. Children began to assume more responsibility for direction of their own activities.
4. Children learned to become more resourceful.
5. Children learned to adjust to disappointment. (It was necessary to change the place of *fiesta* at the last moment.)

[60] Frequently, a mass of information is condensed into short space and read to the bored class. S. G. Brinkley, "Mental Activity in College Classes: Student Estimate of Relative Value of Ten Learning Situations," *Journal of Experimental Education* (June, 1952), summarizes a twenty-year study with college students in this regard. These students reported being least alert mentally, among ten common classroom learning situations, during the verbal reports of their classmates.

6. Children showed greater appreciation for school books.

7. Children had opportunity to do things on their own ability level. A sense of security was fostered, therefore, and interest maintained.

8. Some of the slowest children made some of the most important contributions.

9. There was carry-over into the home, older brothers and sisters actually participating in the work.

The reader may ask, "Was this social studies? Was it single-subject orientation, broad fields, or fusion?" These questions are scarcely relevant. The learning experience began, progressed, and concluded with the real concerns of people trying to live and work together harmoniously. "Social studies" is merely a classification to assure inclusion in the curriculum of certain types of human problems. Organization is useful only for revealing to a teacher and children how learnings considered today relate to what has gone before and what should follow, and for establishing a point of departure. The teacher is concerned with promoting desired changes in children, not with simple manipulation of subject matter. Did this teacher promote desired changes in children? Did subject matter play a subordinate but meaningful role?

IN RETROSPECT

In this chapter, the role of the social studies in the total elementary school program has been examined. Some of the basic understandings the writers have sought to develop are summarized below:

1. The social studies are concerned with problems of human relationships. These are the real problems of daily living faced whenever two or more people are called upon to play, work, or live together. Such problems abound in the lives of elementary school children.

2. The social studies draw upon any content material that offers promise for improving the quality of human living.

3. There is a surprising amount of agreement, in practice, over the topics actually covered through the elementary school grades. However, there is very little evidence to show that these topics represent sequential development of basic skills, understandings, attitudes, and values. A principle of organization applied most commonly in the selection of these topics is that of beginning with experiences close to the personal life of the learner and moving out into the home, school, and larger community.

4. In given grades, teaching practice reveals heavy dependence upon single textbooks, consideration of specific topics that may or may not be closely related to one another, various types of teacher

dominated or teacher-pupil planned units, or orientation around past and present experiences of children. Several types of such practice may exist in one school. However, in virtually every instance, some attempt is made to relate the social studies to other aspects of the instructional program.

5. Rich opportunities for social studies experiences in the elementary school are provided in the school and classroom living of boys and girls. Informal contacts in hallways and on playgrounds and the more formal activities of student government, assembly programs, clubs, teams, and so forth, are so vital in promoting social development that they deserve careful consideration in the total program of the school.

6. Resources for teaching and learning in the social studies are abundant and readily accessible. These include the realities of human growth and development and of learning, the teacher's educational background, an almost inexhaustible array of books, pamphlets, films, film strips, recordings, maps, globes, charts and models, and the many animate and inanimate offerings of the local and world community.

7. Both what and how children and teachers learn together are as important in the social studies as in other aspects of the elementary school program. The problems studied should be of real concern to children, not trimmed with an artificial frosting to hide their unsuitability for the human palate. Children and teachers should participate in planning, implementing plans, and evaluating both process and product. The entire learning-teaching enterprise should reflect progress in desirable inter-personal relationships, and be accompanied by satisfactions of an abiding nature for all concerned.

BIBLIOGRAPHY

Cunningham, Ruth, et al., Understanding Group Behavior of Boys and Girls. New York: Bureau of Publications, Teachers College, Columbia University, 1951.

Estvan, Frank J., "The Relationship of Social Status, Intelligence, and Sex of Ten and Eleven Year Old Children to an Awareness of Poverty." Unpublished Ph.D. dissertation, Department of Education, University of Chicago, 1948.

Foshay, Arthur W., and Kenneth D. Wann, et al., Children's Social Values. New York: Bureau of Publications, Teachers College, Columbia University, 1954.

Goodlad, John I., "Sequence of Learnings in Elementary-School Social Studies," Viewpoints on Educational Issues and Problems. Thirty-Ninth Annual Schoolmen's Week Proceedings. Philadelphia: University of Pennsylvania, September 10, 1952.

Hilliard, Pauline, *Improving Social Learnings in the Elementary School.* New York: Bureau of Publications, Teachers College, Columbia University, 1954.

Jersild, Arthur T. and Ruth J. Tasch, *Children's Interests and What They Suggest for Education.* New York: Bureau of Publications, Teachers College, Columbia University, 1949.

Michaelis, John U., *Social Studies for Children in a Democracy.* Englewood Cliffs, N.J.: Prentice-Hall, Inc., 1950.

Moffatt, Maurice P., and Hazel W. Howell, *Elementary Social Studies Instruction.* New York: Longmans, Green, and Co., 1952.

National Council for the Social Studies, National Education Association, *Skills in Social Studies.* Twenty-Fourth Yearbook. Washington: The Council, 1953.

Peterson, Eleanor M., *Aspects of Readability in the Social Studies.* New York: Bureau of Publications, Teachers College, Columbia University, 1954.

Preston, Ralph C., *Teaching Social Studies in the Elementary School.* New York: Rinehart and Co., 1950.

Sand, Ole P., "Continuity and Sequence in Social Studies Curriculums." Unpublished Ph.D. dissertation, Department of Education, University of Chicago, 1948.

Smith, Joe., *Student Councils for Our Times.* New York: Bureau of Publications, Teachers College, Columbia University, 1951.

Tooze, Ruth and Beatrice K. Krone, *Literature and Music as Resources for Social Studies.* Englewood Cliffs, N.J.: Prentice-Hall, Inc., 1955.

Wesley, Edgar Bruce, and Mary A. Adams, *Teaching Social Studies in Elementary Schools,* rev. ed. Boston: D. C. Heath and Co., 1952.

THE
SCIENCE
PROGRAM

9

TO THE CHILD, THE WORLD IS A FASCINATING BUT
confusing place. He soon becomes aware of the
natural world of day and night, lightning and
thunder, growth and death. As he grows up, he is
introduced to innumerable man-made things
such as television, synthetics, "miracle drugs,"
radar, jet propulsion, and atomic power. His
job of trying to understand the world he lives
in is not easy. As one six-year old complained,
"Atoms, atoms, even the radio talks about atom's
hats."[1]

Teachers realize how much help children need

[1] Gerrit C. Zwart, "Suffern Meets the Challenge of Atomic
Energy," *New York State Education*, XXXVII (March, 1950),
436.

in order to understand the physical and biological phenomena surrounding them. This is the field of science, and *some* of it is bound to creep into the elementary school program. How much emphasis should be placed on science in an already over-crowded schedule, or how the program should be organized, are moot questions. Many teachers feel unprepared to deal with science because of an unwarranted fear that it requires special methods and complicated apparatus.

SCIENCE IN ELEMENTARY EDUCATION

Instruction in elementary science takes many forms. In School A, it consists of a discussion about the "pretty stone" which Susie found on the way to school this morning, the tadpoles which John will bring to school tomorrow, and something which might come up next week or next month. Leaves, seeds, flower bulbs, cocoons, nests, can usually be counted on to appear sooner or later. Time to discuss these things is found during the sharing or current events period; individuals or groups may work on their projects after completing their regular assignments, or during their free time. Pupils and, sometimes, the teacher are hardly aware of the fact that they are "having science."

In School B, science classes meet regularly in a well-equipped science laboratory. In such a setting, a fifth-grade unit in electricity was developed as follows:[2]

Aware of the importance of helping children develop a sense of security in their environment, the teacher selected a unit on electricity to take care of many of the unknowns in the lives of her pupils. She introduced the unit with a discussion, in the course of which the following questions were raised:

Why do lights go on when you push a button?
Where does electricity come from?
Why does an electric iron get hot?
How are light bulbs made?
Why do lights sometimes fail to come on?
What are fuses?
What do batteries have in them?
What are good conductors of electricity?
What makes electricity dangerous?
What makes bells and buzzers work?
Why do we see sparks when we stroke a cat's fur in the dark?
What causes lightning?

With these questions in mind, the children proceeded to find the answers. They read, observed the teacher do experiments, performed individual experi-

[2] Illa Podendorf, "Elementary Science and Society: A Fifth Grade Unit in Electricity," *School Science and Mathematics,* XLVII (June, 1947), 549-554.

ments, and thought about and discussed the things they had seen, read, heard, and done.

Experimentation was stressed in the belief that this is one of the most important science experiences for children. Fortunately, these pupils had a good store of equipment available, such as: dry cells, small light bulbs and sockets, buzzers, bells, motors, telegraph sets, telephone sets, a large spool of copper wire, screw drivers, single and double-throw switches, push buttons, a small amount of mercury, brass and iron rods, a sheet of zinc, electro magnets, a question board, a box to serve as a house, and a small generator.

Activity cards were prepared giving instructions and assistance for 29 experiments which the children performed individually. The following are examples:

1. Connect a cell, a light, and a single-throw switch.
4. Connect two cells, a light, and a push button.
5. Use one dry cell, a small lamp bulb, and one piece of insulation wire, and make the bulb light.
8. Connect a buzzer, two dry cells, and a push button.
12. Show in any way that you choose that iron, brass and zinc are good conductors of electricity.
15. Make a list of things which are good conductors and a list of things which are not good conductors. Be sure you have at least ten things in each list.
17. Connect a telephone transmitter, telephone receiver, and two dry cells. See page 33 in "Electricity" for help.
24. Connect a buzzer, a cell, and two push-buttons in such a way that the buzzer will ring when either button is pushed.
26. Connect two telegraph sets and two cells so that messages may be sent from one person to another.
28. Wire the house so that a bell will ring from either the front or back door.
29. Make plans for and wire a complicated set up of your own.

Toward the end of the unit, discussion periods were set aside to answer each of the questions raised in the introduction of the unit. At this time, the teacher stressed the important concepts of electricity.

The teachers of School C do not teach science either as a part of the ongoing experiences of children or as a subject. Science is taught in conjunction with other subject areas. How science makes its contribution to other content fields is well illustrated in the following account of a fifth-grade unit on "Water Life and the Fishing Industry."[3]

This unit had its beginnings in a previous study on transportation when the change in motive power of fishing vessels was discussed.

Weighing the possibilities of such a unit, the teacher noted the following:

A. *In Science*: (Only partially reported here)

Maintaining aquaria, balanced and otherwise
Comparing fishes with other water animals such as mammals

---

3 California State Department of Education, *Science in the Elementary School* (Sacramento: The Department, 1945), pp. 205-237.

Observing plankton organisms, the microscopic plant and animal forms that
provide food for many fishes

Studying plant and animal life along the seashore

Studying specialized structures of fishes and other water animals for moving
and breathing

Learning about tides, and their causes

Learning about the principles of floating and buoyancy

Getting acquainted with problems of conservation

Becoming acquainted with common fresh-water animal and plant life

B. *In Social Studies*: (Only partially reported here)

Becoming acquainted with the fishing centers of North America

Learning about the life of a New England Fisherman

Studying California's coastal fishing

Studying the salmon industry with emphasis on the canning of salmon

Learning about the button industry

Studying fishing as a sport

Learning about government protection and conservation of fishes

Getting acquainted with problems concerning ownership of the fishing
industry

Learning something of the problems of labor

Studying the problems of marketing

C. *In other activities*:

Art and construction

Oral and written English

Arithmetic problems

Map and chart work

The availability of materials for this unit was also investigated. In the school
environment were: aquaria, specimens, pictures, films that could be ordered; and
from the high school science department: compound and binocular microscopes,
test tubes, aquarium jars, a life history set, and some living material. The surrounding locality offered a fish hatchery, a river, a dam which had a fish ladder,
the municipal lake, mountain streams. The city library presented a wealth of
books, magazines, and visual aids.

In his preliminary planning, the teacher set up the following outcomes:

1. The development of a habit of scientific thinking: the habit of making closer
and more careful observations, a greater desire for all relevant facts, and for
more carefully drawn and more accurate conclusions.

2. An aggressive attitude toward solving problems; a strong desire to work things
out.

3. A knowledge of the importance of the fishing industry and an understanding
of its relation to the welfare of many people. Appreciation of workers. Knowledge and appreciation of some of the activities of the government.

4. The securing and reinforcing of certain specific abilities in traditional fields,
particularly in written and oral English.

5. An increased ability to proceed in independent research in so far as skills
allow.

6. An appreciation of the value of co-operative planning and execution, not only in the classroom work but in dealing with the greater social and scientific problems.

Various class, group, and individual activities were engaged in during a ten-week period. Library usage was learned in selecting books for the classroom library. Problems of temperature, evaporation, feeding, aeration, cleaning, and providing sufficient plant life were solved in maintaining aquaria. Letters were written to obtain information. (A fish-hatchery project was abandoned when it was discovered that the season of the year was not favorable for obtaining eggs.) Visits were taken to a near-by fish hatchery, and the ocean shore. Oral and written reports were prepared. A fishing-products map and various charts were made. Interesting arithmetic problems were derived from various bulletins on fishing. Specimens of sea life were collected and exhibited. Various art activities, such as individual illustrations and a group frieze, were encouraged. A period for sharing experiences was a daily event. The unit was culminated by a "convention" representing fishermen, owners of fishing establishments, the government, and customers to discuss problems of conservation, prices, and wages.

Elementary Science Is General Science

Although the three schools described above differ in the ways in which they deal with science, they have one characteristic in common. In each case, content has been drawn from a number of branches or organized fields of science. Rather than specializing in one area, such as botany or physics, elementary science deals with the basic concepts of all science fields, and is, therefore, referred to as *general* science.

In a study of 46 science courses of study, published between 1940 and 1948,[4] not one was confined to a single science area. Several combined a limited number of science areas; 41 included material from practically all the physical and biological sciences. An analysis of the distribution of units listed in fifteen of the above courses of study which were organized on a topical basis is shown in Table 1. From this table, it may be seen that general science, rather than specialized courses in science, is the rule in elementary education.

Status of Elementary School Science

Unlike the 3 R's, whose place in the elementary curriculum has been assured almost from the beginning of public education, interest in elementary science has fluctuated down through the years. This is well illustrated by the history of science teaching in Cleveland.

No subject in our school program has undergone such mutations as elementary school science. This subject in the form of natural history was taught in upper

4 An unpublished study made by Frank J. Estvan under the direction of Virgil E. Herrick for use in the Field Program of the Committee on Surveys and Field Services, Department of Education (Chicago: University of Chicago, 1948).

TABLE 1

DISTRIBUTION OF TOPICS IN MAJOR SCIENCE AREAS[5]

Science areas	Topics in Grades						Total no. of topics	Per cent. of total
	1st	2nd	3rd	4th	5th	6th		
1. Physics and chemistry	32	28	31	27	25	37	180	25
2. Earth and sky	26	28	28	35	28	30	175	25
3. Animal life	28	28	25	26	25	17	149	21
4. Plant life	19	20	16	18	21	14	108	15
5. Human life	12	9	8	6	10	19	64	9
6. Miscellaneous	1	6	6	7	5	7	32	5
Total	118	119	114	119	114	124	708	100

grades of certain of our public schools from their organization, and in all by 1850, but was dropped from the course in 1853. Elementary school science was reintroduced in 1857 in the form of object lessons for the lower grades. The science work was broadened in 1870 and physics was added for the sixth and seventh grades. This was, however, omitted from the new course of study of 1880. Effort was again put forth in 1893 to give science instruction an important place in the schools. This course was carried forward for ten years, when in 1903 the instruction in the upper grades was eliminated and that for the lower simplified and joined with language, . . . with no separate place upon the program . . . from 1903 to 1926, there was little elementary science taught in Cleveland. In 1926, however, a committee prepared a tentative outline in elementary science.

With the establishment of the curriculum center for elementary science at Doan School in February, 1928, the subject was given a definite place in the program of the schools.[6]

In the quarter of a century which has elapsed since elementary schools have recognized the importance of elementary science, there has been a growing concern for this area of instruction. An analysis of state curriculum guides available in 1949 revealed that 17 states had prepared separate courses of study in science. The investigators noted that "the publications for elementary science, for the most part, have been prepared recently. All those analyzed, with the exception of one, were prepared during or since 1941."[7] There is a tendency for some school systems to require the teaching of at least one science unit

[5] *Ibid.*, p. 5.

[6] Cleveland Public Schools, *Science Course of Study; Cleveland Elementary Schools* (Cleveland: Board of Education, 1948), p. 1.

[7] G. G. Mallison and K. E. Anderson, "A Survey of State Syllabi for Science," *Science Teacher*, XVI (February, 1949), 40.

in each grade. In other schools, this concern takes the form of time stipulations. Teachers of the Buffalo schools, for example, recommended that from 45 to 50 minutes per week be devoted to science teaching in each of the elementary grades. It is interesting to note, that "in no case should the amount of time be decreased; only in very unusual cases should the time be increased."[8]

Although science is receiving more attention today in elementary schools than in the past, it has not achieved the status of a "basic" subject. In many states it is strongly recommended by professional circles, but legally designated an "optional subject." Forward-looking schools, however, are finding ways of doing something constructive about meeting the science needs of boys and girls.

Purposes of Elementary Science Instruction

Science education in the elementary school is directed toward the development of: (a) understanding and appreciation of man's physical and biological environments; (b) scientific attitudes and methods in the solution of problems; and (c) effective use of science learning resources.[9]

In order to help boys and girls solve problems in their environment, a functional understanding of scientific principles governing such broad areas as the following should be developed:[10]

The Universe: Study of the stars, the sun, the moon, the planets and their interrelationships; causes of day and night, seasonal changes, tides, eclipses, and (less completely) of the vastness of the Milky Way and of Galactic systems beyond our own.

The Earth: Origin, formation of mountains, weathering of rock into soil, erosion, volcanism, prehistoric life, and the forces that are changing and have changed the earth.

Conditions Necessary to Life: What living things need in order to exist, how they are affected by changes in the environment and the struggle for existence.

Living Things: Variety, social life, adaptations for protection, life cycles of plants and animals, how they obtain food, their economic importance, and man's influence upon nature.

8 Buffalo Elementary Schools, *A Beginning Guide for Teaching Science* (Buffalo, New York: Board of Education, n.d.), p. 5.

9 Glenn O. Blough and Albert J. Huggett, *Methods and Activities in Elementary School Science* (New York: Dryden Press, 1951), pp. 11-13.

Harrington Wells, *Elementary Science Education in American Public Schools* (New York: McGraw-Hill Book Company, Inc., 1951), pp. 43-44.

10 National Society for the Study of Education, "Science Education in American Schools," Forty-sixth Yearbook, Part I (Chicago: University of Chicago Press, 1947), pp. 75-76.

Physical and Chemical Phenomena: Common chemical and physical phenomena such as light, sound, gravity, magnetism, and electricity; changes in matter; and phenomena associated with radiant energy and atmospheric changes.

Man's Attempt to Control His Environment: In gardens, on farms, in orchards; inventions and discoveries; use of power and of materials; his control over living things; his study of places he cannot reach directly; and other such topics.

University of Wisconsin Summer Laboratory School

WEATHER AND CLIMATE AFFECT OUR LIVES

To understand and cope with their problems effectively, boys and girls must approach them "scientifically." They must cultivate the habit of studying problems objectively; to be more concerned with *the facts* than with personal biases. They need to know how to obtain information, ways of analyzing evidence, and how to test conclusions based on their data. Knowledge of resource materials in science, competence in laboratory procedures, and ability to accumulate and organize data from a variety of sources are indispensable study aids.

Science Programs

Variety, if not innovation, characterizes elementary programs. As has been suggested, most science programs consist merely of a collection of topics which do not necessarily bear any relationship to one another. Other programs are based on major science concepts. A third type of program combines science with other instructional areas.

Topical Approach. Among the first to be utilized, the topical approach is still one of the most prevalent types of science programs. It has assumed various patterns, depending upon the basis used to select topics. A few schools have given children's interests the highest priority in selecting topics or problems.[11] Some have used the seasons as the organizing principle for science activities.[12] Very common is a collection of topics whose suitability for a particular grade level has been tested over the years.[13] A modification of the latter is a plan known as spiral serialization, involving a repeated return to each field for further development at succeeding grade levels.[14]

Science Concepts. A reaction to the seemingly unrelated topics which constituted elementary science programs was a movement in the early thirties to organize science in terms of its major principles.[15] Key generalizations of science are analyzed, and their constituent con-

11 Galveston Public Schools, *Handbook for Elementary Grades* (Galveston, Texas: Board of Education, 1944). The 1950 revision is organized in terms of experiences and concepts.

12 Iowa State Department of Public Instruction, *Iowa Elementary Teachers Handbook*, Vol. 5, Science and Nature Study (Des Moines: The Department, 1943).

Montana State Department of Public Instruction, *A Course of Study for Rural and Graded Elementary Schools* (Helena: The Department, 1942).

Vermont State Department of Education, *Suggested Courses of Study and Teachers' Manual in Science* (Montpelier: The Department, 1942).

13 Cleveland Public Schools, *op. cit.*

Glen Falls Public Schools, *Elementary School Science Syllabus,* Vol. I and II, rev. (Glen Falls, New York: Board of Education, 1948).

West Virginia Department of Education, *A Handbook for Teachers of Elementary Science* (Charleston: The Department, 1941).

14 El Paso Public Schools, *Tentative Course of Study for Elementary School Science* (El Paso, Texas: Board of Education, 1944).

New Orleans Public Schools, *Tentative Course of Study in Elementary School Science* (New Orleans, Louisiana: Board of Education, 1941).

15 New Hampshire State Board of Education, *Program of Studies Recommended for the Elementary Schools of New Hampshire: Science, Grades 1-6* (Concord: The Board, 1944).

New York State Education Department, *Science, A Program for Elementary Schools; Grades 1-6,* Bulletin No. 1224, rev. (Albany: The Department, 1942).

Rockford Public Schools, *Developing Democracy: A Curriculum Guide, Elementary Schools* (Rockford, Illinois: Board of Education, 1945).

South Dakota Department of Public Instruction, *Course of Study for Elementary Grades* (Pierre: The Department, 1943).

cepts allocated to the various grades in order of their logic. Thus, the development of major ideas in science is cumulative throughout the grades.

In some instances, an attempt is made to "accent" this continuous expansion of generalizations by designating a grade theme, as is often

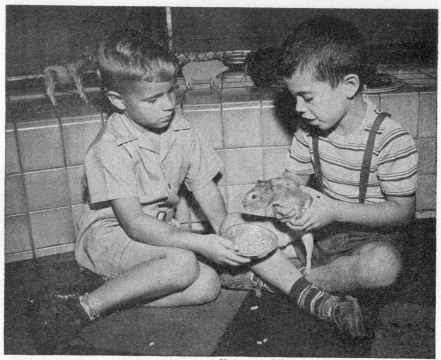

University of Wisconsin Summer Laboratory School

LEARNING RESPONSIBILITY THROUGH ANIMAL CARE

done in the social studies.[16] This might be "birds of our community" or simply "animals." When used, the theme is generally a matter of emphasis or a point of departure, rather than a guide for selecting all topics or activities for a particular grade.

Combining Science with Other Subject Areas. This group of programs includes all those plans in which science is considered in relationship to other subject areas. In its simplest form, it is merely the attempt to teach certain science units when they "fit in" with certain

[16] Eugene Public Schools, *Science Course of Study, Grades 1-6* (Eugene, Oregon: Board of Education, 1946).

Louisiana State Department of Education, *Revised Course of Study in Science for the Elementary Schools,* Bulletin No. 465 (Baton Rouge: The Department, 1941).

other social studies or health units; the respective subjects still retain their identity.[17] One step beyond this is the fusion or integration of science with some other content area, such as health, mathematics, or, most often, social studies.[18] A further step in the direction of integration is taken in those programs which select and use science knowledge and thinking processes on the basis of their importance in dealing with the persistent social problems all adults and children face.[19] Similar to these programs, but giving greater rein to teacher-pupil planning for identifying and planning worthwhile experience, are plans in which the needs or persistent problems of children define the science understandings and abilities to be taught.[20] In these programs, science loses its identity as a subject.

Selection and Grade Placement of Science Topics

There is little agreement about the selection and grade placement of topics in elementary science instruction. An analysis of 15 courses of study, summarized in Table 1, revealed that from 28 to 36 different topics were allocated to each of the elementary grades in this composite group of outlines. Wide variations were also found when topics in the various science areas were analyzed. For example, 22 different units were listed in the area of physics and chemistry. In no case did a topic appear in as many as half the course outlines. More than half of the topics appeared in only one course of study.

The grades in which certain topics appeared in these same 15 courses of study are summarized in Figure 1. Topics which received about equal emphasis throughout the grades were: (a) magnetism and electricity; (b) air, wind, and airplanes; (c) machines and tools;

17 Cincinnati Public Schools, *The Intermediate Manual*, Curriculum Bulletin 125 (Cincinnati, Ohio: Board of Education, 1945). The 1954 revision is organized in terms of concepts and experiences.

18 Los Angeles County Schools, *Course of Study for the Elementary Schools of Los Angeles County* (Los Angeles: Office of the County Superintendent, 1944).

Orange Public Schools, *Social Studies—Science, Language Arts in the Fourth Grade,* Curriculum Bulletin 504 (Orange, Texas: Board of Education, 1946).

19 New Mexico State Department of Education, *Curriculum Development in the Elementary Schools of New Mexico,* Bulletin No. 2, rev. (Santa Fe: The Department, 1947).

Santa Barbara County Schools, *Santa Barbara County Curriculum Guide for Teachers in Elementary Schools,* Vol. 2 (Santa Barbara, California: Office of the County Superintendent, 1940).

Virginia State Board of Education, *Course of Study for Virginia Elementary Schools,* Grade I-VII (Richmond: The Board, 1943).

20 National Committee on Science Teaching, *Redirecting Science Teaching in the Light of Personal-Social Needs* (Washington, D.C.: American Council of Science Teachers, N.E.A., 1942).

(d) water; and (e) gardening. Topics emphasized at the respective grade levels were as follows:

FIGURE 1

GRADE DISTRIBUTION OF SCIENCE TOPICS [21]

Science areas	Grades					
	1	2	3	4	5	6
1. Physics and chemistry (25% of Total)	———— magnetism and electricity —————————— ———— air, wind, airplanes —————————— ———— machine and tools ————— ——— ———————— ——-—— water —————————————— ——— heat ——— ———					light sound
2. Earth and sky (25% of Total)	seasons & weather ———— earth and universe —————— rocks & minerals earth formation & changes					seasons & weather
3. Animal life (21% of Total)	———— animal life —— —————————— ———— insects —————— ———— birds ———— pets ——					
4. Plant life (15% of Total)	———— plant life —————————— ———— seeds —————— — trees ———— ———— gardens———————————————					
5. Human life (9% of Total)	health safety ———— food ————————					health safety alcohol & narcotics
6. Social and miscellaneous (5% of Total)	— interdependence of life —————— — conservation ——— ——— —— man's use of nature classifying ——— life and growth ——					

Primary grades (1 and 2)	Intermediate grades (3 and 4)	Upper grades (5 and 6)
pets	heat	light
insects	rocks and minerals	sound
seeds	insects	earth formation
food	birds	and changes
man's use of nature	interdependence	trees
	classification	alcohol and
	and growth	narcotics
		interdependence
		conservation

In short, Figure 1 indicates that the same science topics appear in practically every grade of the elementary school. Some receive about

[21] Unpublished study by Estvan, *op. cit.*, p. 12.

the same treatment throughout the grades; a majority are given special emphasis at different levels. On the whole, however, there is little agreement in the grade placement of science topics. These findings are similar to the ones reported earlier by Hillman[22] and Gilbert.[23]

ORGANIZING ELEMENTARY SCIENCE INSTRUCTION

If science instruction is to be effective, activities, materials, concepts, and thought processes have to be organized around some center which has significance for children and is valid for science. Three common bases have been used in the development of many elementary school science programs, namely: 1) the interests of children about themselves and their physical and biological world; 2) the important concepts of science; and 3) the emergent needs of children. Illustrations of these three ways of organizing science programs are presented below.

An Interest Approach. In their 1944 handbook, the teachers of Galveston took the position that science programs should be based on one of the primary motivations for turning to science: the child's curiosity about the world in which he lives. For these teachers, the major objective of science was to satisfy children's interests as they develop "naturally through actual contact with mysteries of nature instead of through a prescribed course of study for each item taken up formally and apart from real experience.[24]

To accomplish this aim, teacher and pupil must decide in terms of their particular interests and inclinations what they wish to study at any particular time. The teacher's encouragement and attitude of learning and investigating, it is believed, will help the child to understand and appreciate the material being considered.

In giving such high priority to interests, the assumption is made that children's interests are not only worthwhile, but that they furnish the clue as to "what" and "when" to teach. Recognition is also given to the highly motivating character of interests, and the belief is held that interest begets interest. Coverage of the field of science is regarded as being of lesser importance; or else, it is assumed that the developing nature of children's interests will ultimately provide for adequate scope. In short, once the basic criterion of satisfying the

22 James E. Hillman, *Some Aspects of Science in the Elementary Schools,* Peabody Contributions to Education, Nos. 8-14 (Nashville: George Peabody College for Teachers, 1922).

23 Alice Gilbert, "Science Content in the Elementary School," *School Science and Mathematics,* XLIII (November, 1943), 769-774.

24 Galveston Public Schools, *op. cit.,* p. 88.

child's science interest is met, no prescriptions are made about the scientific phenomenon to be examined, or the content and processes to be utilized.

For the satisfaction of the "here and now" science interests of pupils, as opposed to interests "in general," at least three conditions must be met: First, the teacher must make a determined effort to know what these science interests are. Noting what boys and girls read, do at home, bring to school, etc., will give her valuable insights about their concerns. Secondly, children must be given opportunities to express their interests orally and in writing, formally or informally. Lastly, pupils and teacher must discriminate among the various interests represented in the classroom, selecting those which lead to a broadening and deepening of science pursuits and to the cultivation of new interests by individual members of the group.

Most elementary schools do not use children's interests as the primary or sole basis for determining the selection and organization of science materials. Regardless of how the science program is organized, however, all approaches to this problem consider children and their interests and questions as excellent vehicles for motivating and developing science activities.

Organizing Around Science Concepts. Many teachers are of the opinion that the most effective organization of science programs is that which is based on the continuous development of major science understandings or generalizations. These major science ideas are set up as the *content* objectives of science instruction in a manner, described by Craig, which involves:[25] (a) setting up criteria for the selection of science objectives; (b) obtaining science objectives satisfying these criteria; (c) evaluation of these objectives by educators, laymen, and children for their importance; (d) examining treatises on science to determine how these objectives can be analyzed into their constituent elements; and (e) assigning these subordinate concepts as specific objectives to various grade levels on the basis of logical development.

In contrast with the interest approach, therefore, a "concept" program gives highest priority to *content*. In this case, however, content is not narrowly defined as facts and knowledges, but includes science

25 Gerald S. Craig, *Certain Techniques Used in Developing a Course of Study in Science for the Horace Mann Elementary School;* Contributions to Education, No. 276 (New York: Bureau of Publications, Teachers College, Columbia University, 1927).

National Society for the Study of Education, *A Program for Teaching Science,* Thirty-first Yearbook, Part I, Chapter X-XI (Bloomington: Public School Publishing Company, 1932).

principles, generalizations, understandings, and concepts—all of which are used synonymously in general practice.

Three broad generalizations were identified by the teachers of Rockford, Illinois as being focal points for all science teaching. These were analyzed to include the following major understandings:

I. Life on earth consists of plants and animals.
   A. Plants and animals are useful to man.
   B. Plants and animals need air, sunshine, water, and food.
   C. Plants and animals have many ways of protecting themselves.
   D. Plants and animals prepare for winter.
   E. Plants and animals reproduce themselves.

II. Man has found ways of using energy to do the world's work.
   A-D (Four major understandings about machines and inventions)
   E-F (Two major understandings about magnetism and electricity)

III. The earth is a part of a great solar system and of a still more vast universe.
   A-E (Five major understandings about the earth's surface)
   F-J (Five major understandings about atmosphere)
   K-N (Four major understandings about the solar system)

These major understandings are developed through a number of specific concepts allocated to the various grades. Examples of the subordinate concepts necessary to develop the five understandings included in the generalization that life on earth consists of plants and animals, are as follows:

GRADE 1

Animal Concepts

2. All animals need air, sunshine, water and food.
6. Some animals prepare for winter.
   a. By storing of food—ants, bees, squirrels.
   b. By thickened coats—dog, sheep.
   c. By migration—birds.
   d. By hibernation—frogs, snakes, bears.
7. Animals reproduce themselves.

Plant Concepts

2. Plants need air, sunshine, water and food.
7. Plants change with the seasons, through seed dispersal by wind, water, animals, and man.

GRADE 2

Animal Concepts

2. Animals are protected from the cold by storage of food, thicker fur, migration.
3. Animals are protected by nature—polar bear's fur is white like its surroundings.
5. Birds help man by eating insects which would destroy food.
9. Birds hatch their young by heat from their bodies.

Plant Concepts

1. Plants undergo a definite life cycle.
3. Plants are adapted to seasonal changes.
6. Fruit grows from flowers.

University of Wisconsin Summer Laboratory School

CHILDREN LEARN ABOUT ANIMALS FROM ANIMALS

GRADE 3

Animal Concepts

1. Animals move from place to place to get food and water.
4. Water animals need food and air just as land animals do.
7. Animals build homes for protection.

Plant Concepts

1. Plants need food.
2. Plants make their food in the leaves. To make food they need water, sunlight, and air.
4. Plants have means of protection against enemies, weather, and climate.

GRADE 4

Animal Concepts

1. Some kinds of animals live in communities and cooperate with one another.
2. Animals and men depend upon others of their kind and each other for many things.
9. Many animals deserve protection because of their value to man.

Plant Concepts

1. Plants are essential to us. They give us food, clothing, and shelter.
3. Plants help hold soil to the earth.
6. Plants reproduce in several ways.

GRADE 5

Animal Concepts

2. All animals must eat at times during their lives in order to grow in size, heat, and repair their bodies.
3. Most animals are constantly in danger of being caught and killed by other animals.
4. Some animals change their color with the seasons.

Plant Concepts

1. Many plants make their own food.
3. Plants supply great quantities of food for man and animals.
5. In order to keep our fields and woods beautiful, we should protect and conserve our flowers and trees.

GRADE 6

Animal Concepts

7. Some animals are armed with weapons, such as teeth, claws, etc.
8. Other animals are protected by armor, such as shells, hard wings, scales, etc.
10. There is great need for the protection of animals if their kinds are to continue.

Plant Concepts

2. Plants that have flowers and bear seeds are the most varied, useful, and numerous of all the major groups of plants.
3. Only green plants can make their own food.
4. Plants and animals depend on each other.[26]

This type of approach to science instruction is based on three assumptions. First, competent people can agree as to the major generalizations of science. Second, it is possible to determine the logical sequence for developing the various sub-concepts for each major science principle. Third, teachers can relate these concepts to the interests and concerns of boys and girls.

Actually, attempts to identify major science concepts have not led to as uniform results as one would expect. Two studies[27] showed marked disagreement with Craig's pioneering effort. Examination of courses of study based on this approach also reveals considerable diversity in the major concepts selected as a basis for organizing the program. New York State, for example, uses the following six:

1. There are many kinds of living things on the earth.
2. Earth conditions are changing.
3. Matter and energy are subject to many changes.
4. The earth is a small part of the universe.
5. Plants and animals survive many changes.
6. Living things are interdependent.[28]

[26] Rockford Public Schools, *op. cit.*, pp. 6-8.
[27] W. C. Croxton, *Science in the Elementary School* (New York: McGraw-Hill Book Company, Inc., 1937), 109.
Martin L. Robertson, "The Selection of Science Principles Suitable as Goals of Instruction in the Elementary School," *Science Education*, XIX (February, 1935), 3.
[28] New York State Education Department, *op. cit.*, opposite p. 8.

Attempts to discover a "natural" sequence of concept development have produced several grade-placement studies. Two investigators[29] of the early twenties found that children of the fifth grade and below did not assimilate real principles of science, and that their knowledge of elementary science was largely restricted to observational and factual material. Later studies[30] disclosed that pupils in all grades of the elementary school have the ability to generalize. From his experience in teaching a unit on the concept of light and energy change, Haupt concluded that:

1. Such a generalization can be used as the basis for progressively complex instruction in successive grades.

2. Children at all ages can and do generalize. They differ in the complexity of the associations of concepts and the experiences involved.

3. At all levels, pupils approached a correct understanding of the generalization.

4. At lower levels, presentation of relatively complex ideas resulted in more erroneous ideas than vaguely correct ideas.

5. Content from all the sciences can be used to develop generalizations.[31]

Thus it would seem that whether or not pupils generalize is to some extent dependent upon whether or not methods of teaching provide them with opportunities to practice scientific thinking.

Organizing Science Programs Around Needs of Children. The child development movement has produced considerable thinking to the effect that science should be organized in a way to help children solve their problems of "growing up" in our culture.

Basic to the needs approach is the definition of children's problems. One of the most comprehensive attempts to define them was made by the National Committee on Science Teaching in cooperation with nine other national or regional science groups. Problems were conceived of as those needs or "desirable directions of growth and reason-

[29] Hanor A. Webb, *General Science Instruction in the Grades,* Contributions to Education, No. 4, Part II (Nashville: George Peabody College for Teachers, 1921).
James H. Hillman, *op. cit.*

[30] W. C. Croxton, "Pupils' Ability to Generalize," *School Science and Mathematics,* XXXVI (June, 1936), 627-634.
George W. Haupt, "First Grade Concepts of the Moon," *Science Education,* XXXII (October, 1948), 258-262.
Martin L. Robertson, "An Investigation of the Relative Effectiveness of the Two Methods of Teaching Elementary Science," *Science Education,* XVI (February, 1932), 182-187.

[31] G. W. Haupt, *Experimental Application of a Philosophy of Science Teaching in an Elementary School,* Contributions to Education No. 633 (New York: Bureau of Publications, Teachers College, Columbia University, 1935).

able achievements, at the individual's level of development, which make for his welfare and that of our society."[32] The Committee recognized that there are needs peculiar to individuals and to localities, but that more often it is the intensity of the need or the situation in which it must be met that varies.

The position advanced by the National Committee on Science Teaching highlights several additional differences between the needs approach and the ones previously described. What is studied in this kind of program does not necessarily have to be classified in the physical or biological realms. The focus of attention is upon the child's needs or problems, and not on science *per se*. As a corollary to this course of action is the necessity for dealing with all content areas and their appropriate techniques which have a bearing on the problem, and not solely with the area of science. Lastly, it is assumed that more effective controls of behavior have been developed in this type of approach, because the child has actually had practice in learning how to solve his own problems.

PROBLEMS OF SCIENCE INSTRUCTION

Some teachers are reluctant to teach science, because they fear that they are not well enough versed in the ideas or principles of science, or because of uncertainty regarding the "special" methods and materials which may be necessary. A consideration of the science experiences described in the beginning of this chapter indicates that Teachers A, B, and C were required to deal with science content, and to utilize techniques and materials which were not always the same as those for other academic areas. This does not mean, however, that the problems they faced were unique to the teaching of science, or that they were insurmountable.

Developing Scientific Thinking. In examining the units developed by teachers A and B, we are impressed by one characteristic which they had in common. *Children were seeking answers to questions which they had helped to formulate.* This is the essence of what is called scientific thinking. It is not limited to any single area of experience, such as science, any more than "cooperation" is a form of behavior developed solely in the social studies.

Scientific thinking, or the scientific method, is basically a careful attempt to solve a problem. This is not a unitary trait or characteristic which can be developed by admonishing children to "think carefully." It involves recognizing and defining the problem, suggesting

32 National Committee on Science Teaching, *op. cit.*, p. 12.

and examining hypotheses, drawing and testing conclusions. Many specific skills compose each of these sub-processes. One description included the following kinds of behavior:

1. Sensing significant problems
   a) Sensing situations involving personal and social problems where science knowledge and skills can be profitably used
   b) Recognizing specific problems in these situations
2. Defining problem situations
   a) Isolating the single major idea of the problem
   b) Stating the problem (question) in definite and concise language
   c) Selecting the key words of a problem
   d) Defining key words as a means of getting a better understanding of the problem
3. Studying the situation for all facts and clues bearing upon the problem
   a) Learning to recognize valid evidence
   b) Recalling past experiences which bear upon a problem
   c) Isolating elements common in experience and the problem
   d) Using experimental procedures suitable to the solution of a problem
   e) Locating source materials
   f) Using source materials
   g) Solving mathematical problems necessary in obtaining pertinent data
   h) Making observations suitable for solving a problem
   i) Using talks and interviews as sources of information
4. Making the best tentative explanation or hypothesis
   a) Selecting important factors related to the problem
   b) Identifying the different relationships which may exist between the factors
5. Selecting the most likely hypothesis
   a) Analyzing, selecting, and interpreting relevant data
   b) Judging pertinency or significance of data for the immediate problem
   c) Recognizing weaknesses in data
   d) Using resourcefulness in proposing new hypotheses
6. Testing the hypothesis by experimental or other means
   a) Checking the hypothesis with the recognized authorities
   b) Devising experimental procedures suitable for testing the hypothesis
   c) Organizing data
   d) Rechecking data for errors in interpretation
   e) Applying the hypothesis to the problem to determine its adequacy
7. Accepting tentatively or rejecting the hypothesis and testing other hypotheses
8. Drawing conclusions
   a) Using the hypothesis as a basis for generalizing in terms of similar problem situations[33]

An integral part of the scientific method is scientific attitude. It is characterized by an intellectual curiosity and eagerness for discovery

[33] National Society for the Study of Education, *op. cit.*, pp. 145-147.

that is objective and open-minded. There is a withholding of judgment, coupled with a willingness to accept "tested" reality. Judgments
and conclusions are regarded as tentative and subject to change in the
light of additional evidence. In behavioral terms, this means that one:

1. Looks for the natural causes for things that happen:
   a) Does not believe in superstitions, such as charms of good or bad luck.
   b) Believes that there is no connection necessarily between two events just
      because they happen at the same time or one after the other.
2. Is open-minded toward work and opinions of others and information related to his problem:
   a) Believes that truth never changes, but his ideas of what is true may change
      as he gains better understanding of that truth.
   b) Revises his opinions and conclusions in the light of additional reliable
      evidence.
   c) Listens to, observes, or reads evidence supporting ideas contrary to his
      personal opinions.
   d) Accepts no conclusions as final or ultimate.
3. Bases opinions and conclusions on adequate evidence:
   a) Is slow to accept as fact anything not supported by convincing proof.
   b) Bases his conclusions upon evidence obtained from a variety of depend-
      able sources.
   c) Searches for the most satisfactory explanation of observed phenomena
      that the evidence permits.
   d) Sticks to the facts and refrains from exaggeration.
   e) Does not permit his personal pride, bias, prejudice, or ambition to per-
      vert the truth.
   f) Does not make snap judgments or jump to conclusions.
4. Evaluates techniques and procedures used and information obtained:
   a) Uses a planned procedure in solving his problems.
   b) Seeks to use the various techniques and procedures which have proved
      valuable in obtaining evidence.
   c) Seeks to adapt the various techniques and procedures to the problem
      at hand.
   d) Personally considers the evidence and decides whether it relates to the
      problem.
   e) Judges whether the evidence is sound, sensible, and complete enough to
      allow a conclusion to be drawn.
   f) Selects the most recent, authoritative, and accurate evidence related to
      the problem.
5. Is curious concerning the things he observes:
   a) Wants to know the "whys," "whats," and "hows," of observed phenomena.
   b) Is not satisfied with vague explanations of his questions.[34]

At all levels of education, therefore, the teacher's goal should be to
develop greater competence in the making of discriminating judg-

[34] *Ibid.,* pp. 147-148.

ments and critical thinking. The field of science provides exceptional opportunities for experience in this kind of problem solving. Many problems in this area are of such a nature as to encourage experimentation with concrete materials, or observation of the "real thing." Scientific methods and attitudes can be the concern of all teachers, regardless of the particular subject or grade they happen to be teaching.

Securing and Utilizing Materials for Teaching Science. A common characteristic of the units on electricity and water life were the many avenues used to get at the problem. A great variety of materials were used. To teachers who are accustomed to relying upon books as primary resources, this may pose several problems.

One enthusiastic teacher, when he found only three books on astronomy available in his small school, used the library resources of a neighboring community. The children took up the search, and brought various kinds of reading matter from their homes. As a class, they wrote letters for free and inexpensive pictures, charts, and bulletins. A trip to the museum of a nearby city was taken. A film was ordered. Toward the end of the unit, one pupil asked, "What's the name of the star that's over there about eight o'clock at night?" It was then that this inexperienced teacher realized that the sun, the moon, and the stars had been there all the time!

For just as science is all about us, so are science materials. In studying machines, for example, bricks and a board, or a see-saw in the playground make good levers. Erector sets and mechanical toys brought from home will illustrate many principles. Machinery in the school workshop can be examined. The lowly can opener and egg beater from home kitchens are examples of certain machines. The surroundings can be explored for opportunities to observe machinery being used in road repair, farming, and construction.[35]

Complicated apparatus and techniques, it has been found, tend to confuse the child—and the teacher. The illustration may be more complex than the idea to be developed. The trend is toward simple experiments with materials and objects which are familiar to children. Are we studying rain? To find out where the water goes, let us "experiment" by placing water in a dish or hanging a wet cloth up to dry. After a shower, let us watch the water run off the ground, dig down into the ground to see if some of it has soaked into the soil, or watch the sidewalks get dry. Shall we become rainmakers? A teakettle (not a flask), a hot plate (not a Bunsen burner), and a pie tin (not a

[35] Glenn O. Blough and P. E. Blackwood, "Materials for Solving Science Problems," *Childhood Education,* XXVI (March, 1950). 312.

condenser) will do.[36] Many useful publications have appeared recently showing teachers how to perform science experiments with simple and inexpensive equipment.[37]

For materials, teachers are urged not to overlook the general equipment of the school. A globe and a projector can be used to illustrate the earth's circle of illumination. A survey of storage spaces usually unearths quantities of odds and ends. A resourceful teacher can make good use of "junk." Children, too, are being given opportunities to share in the construction of simple apparatus, models, and containers. Most spectacular is the growing interest in audio-visual aids.[38] Pictures, advertisements, and cartoons with science implications are being systematically collected and filed for ready reference. Science by radio and television is here.[39] Some schools are making intensive community surveys in order to capitalize on out-of-school science resources. Evaluation of basic texts and supplementary science books is a well-established practice.[40] More and more school groups are preparing resource units to help their teachers. In many cases, great reliance is still placed upon high school science departments for the specialized equipment occasionally needed. Such simple items as thermometers, magnifying glasses, test tubes, dry cells, battery motors, and even a magnet kit and a microscope are becoming standard equipment in an increasing number of elementary schools.

Improving Teacher Attitudes About Science. Basic to the improvement of science teaching is the development of proper teacher attitudes towards science and science instruction. Indifference and insecurity can be overcome, and a readiness to "try" science awakened, once the teacher forms convictions about the importance of doing something about science. Teachers can increase their adequacy to

[36] *Ibid.,* p. 311.

[37] Charles K. Arey, *Science Experiences for Elementary Schools,* Practical Suggestions for Teaching No. 4 (New York: Bureau of Publications, Teachers College, Columbia University, 1942).

Paul E. Blackwood, *Science Experiment Books for Children,* Selected References No. 14 (Washington: Office of Education, May, 1948).

Carleton J. Lynde, *Science Experiences with Ten-Cent Store Equipment* (Scranton, Pa.: International Textbook Company, 1941).

Bertha M. Parker, *Science Experiences: Elementary School* (Evanston, Ill.: Row, Peterson & Company, 1952).

[38] Clyde K. Miller, "Science Materials in Action," *See and Hear,* V (March, 1950), 28-31.

[39] Catherine Dillon, "The Museum with a Voice," *Childhood Education,* XXVI (March, 1950), 316-321.

[40] California State Department of Education, *op. cit.,* pp. 273-418.

Paul E. Kambly, "The Elementary School Science Library," *School Science and Mathematics,* L (March, 1950), 209-212.

deal with science by engaging in some of the activities suggested by Blough and Huggett:

1. Read science materials both on the children's level and on your own—such as this book. Keep it on your desk for ready reference.

2. Do some of the "things to do" that this book and others suggest, such as "going to see," observing, collecting. After you get started, you may be surprised at your own enthusiasm.

3. Do some of the experiments yourself. They are not difficult, and many of them are very interesting. They make it real.

4. Find a junior-high-school science teacher and ask his help. It will do each of you good to know what the other is doing. You can exchange ideas and make use of each other's background.

5. Find out whether your state, county or city has a course of study or bulletin on the teaching of science. It may be published under separate cover or as part of a bulletin on the total elementary-school curriculum. In either case it is bound to be full of teaching ideas.

6. Be sure to order the teacher's manuals that go with the textbooks used in your school. They are good sources of help that are often overlooked.

7. Watch current periodicals and other publications for articles about science teaching.

8. Try to arrange to watch another teacher working with children and science. You may get many good ideas in this way.

9. Avail yourself of any opportunity provided in your school to attend workshops, extension courses, or other in-service projects which can better equip you to teach science.

10. Be open-minded in your approach to the teaching of science![41]

IMPROVING SCIENCE EXPERIENCES FOR CHILDREN

In rethinking and reviewing the material of this chapter on science instruction in the elementary school, the reader will want to consider seriously the following points:

If every child is to develop a more adequate understanding of himself and of the complex and demanding world he lives in, then it is necessary that he gain in understanding of the important concepts of science, become skillful in using the scientific method in dealing with his problems, and gain in appreciation of the attitudes of intelligent questioning, demonstrable verification, and constructive action.

Science in the elementary school is not the prerogative of one branch of science; all areas of science knowledge and practice contribute to the questions, problems, and growing concerns of the elementary school child.

[41] Glenn O. Blough and Albert J. Huggett, *Methods and Activities in Elementary School Science* (Copyright 1951 by the Dryden Press, Inc. Reprinted by special permission), p. 5.

Science fundamentally is a way of thinking and acting. It is not the covering of topics in the science book or memorizing answers provided by the teacher. Scientific thinking is a way of seeing, defining, and dealing with problems in such a way that you can deal with them better the next time you face them.

Children are not able to ask questions, define problems, collect information and data, verify hunches and possibilities, and follow through on implications of present knowledge to other similar problems in 15 minutes a day, or even in 45 minutes a week. The time schedule of the school day will have to be related to the nature of educational programs being developed if science experiences for children are to be improved.

The phenomena of all the important concepts of science exist in the everyday world of every child. Every child and teacher can find appropriate applications in the world that exists around them if they will but open their eyes, observe carefully, and utilize resourcefully what they find.

Adequate materials and facilities, good library resources, and technical help are all important and valuable. Their utilization, however, is in the hands of a teacher who uses them as tools and helps to the more effective understanding of children. None of these resources can see, think, try out, generalize, predict, or use constructively the ideas and procedures of science. The children, with the teacher's help, will have the excitement, the satisfaction, and the security of doing this for themselves.

BIBLIOGRAPHY

Arey, Charles K., *Science Experience for Elementary Schools.* Practical Suggestions for Teaching No. 4. New York: Bureau of Publications, Teachers College, Columbia University, 1942.

Blough, Glenn O. and A. J. Huggett, *Methods and Activites in Elementary-School Science.* New York: Dryden Press, 1951.

Bruce, Guy V., *Science Teaching Today:* A Series of Practical Teaching Aids, Vol. I-VII. Washington, D.C.: National Science Teachers Association, 1950.

Burnett, R. Will, *Teaching Science in the Elementary School.* New York: Rinehart and Company, 1953.

California State Department of Education, *Science in the Elementary School.* Sacramento: The Department, 1945.

Craig, Gerald S., *Science for the Elementary-School Teacher.* New York: Ginn and Company, 1940.

Croxton, W. C., *Science in the Elementary School.* New York: McGraw-Hill Book Company, Inc., 1937.

Department of Elementary School Principals, *Science for Today's Children*. Thirty-second Yearbook. Washington, D.C.: The Department, N.E.A., 1954.

Garrison, Charlotte G., *Science Experiences for Little Children*. New York: Charles Scribner's Sons, 1939.

Heiss, E. D., E. S. Osbourn, and C. W. Hoffman, *Modern Methods and Materials for Science Teaching*. New York: The Macmillan Company, 1950.

Lynde, Carleton J., *Science Experiences with Ten-Cent Store Equipment*. Scranton, Pa.: International Textbook Company, 1941.

Parker, Bertha M., *Science Experiences: Elementary Schools*. Evanston, Ill.: Row, Peterson and Company, 1952.

Pitluga, George E., *Science Excursions into the Community*. New York: Bureau of Publications, Teachers College, Columbia University, 1943.

Wells, Harrington, *Elementary Science Education in American Public Schools*. New York: McGraw-Hill Book Company, Inc., 1951.

THE
ARITHMETIC
PROGRAM

.

10

AS WE ENTER A SIXTH GRADE CLASSROOM, WE HEAR
the teacher saying: "Open your books to page
293. Today we are going to learn how to divide
fractions. Look at the illustration at the top of
the page."

The example, $3/4 \div 7/8$, is placed on the
board for all to see.

The teacher continues: "The book says, 'to divide a fraction by a fraction, invert the divisor
fraction and multiply.' It's as simple as that! Just
invert and multiply. In this case, the divisor fraction is 7/8. The word 'invert' means simply to reverse the two numbers of this fraction. So, 7/8
becomes 8/7. Remember, the book says to invert

and then to multiply. So far we have done the 'invert' part and our example looks like this."

As she talks, the teacher writes "3/4 x 8/7" on the blackboard.

"Now—we already know how to multiply fractions. In case you have forgotten, let me remind you of the rule. We learned that all we had to do to multiply two fractions was to multiply the two numerators together, multiply the denominators, and then divide. Don't forget, though, that we should reduce the fractions or cancel whenever possible. In this case, you see that we can cancel by dividing the 4 of the first fraction and the 8 of the second fraction by 4."

Suiting action to words, the teacher now makes the example on the

blackboard look like this: $\dfrac{3}{\cancel{4}_1} \times \dfrac{\cancel{8}^2}{7}$

"Now that the necessary cancellation is done, all that remains is to multiply. 3 times 2 is 6. 1 times 7 is 7. The result is 6/7. Simple, isn't it?"

An analysis of this situation suggests the following weaknesses:

1. Arithmetic is here taught in almost total isolation from the realities of daily living, from the remainder of the total curriculum, from mathematical meaning, and from any consideration of children and how they learn.

2. The textbook appears to be the sole determiner of arithmetic instruction—it dictates what is to be taught and how it is to be taught.

3. Instruction begins with an abstract rule, rather than deriving the generalization from a series of related experiences.

4. Methods used reflect a teacher-telling, pupil-doing-as-told procedure. Elements of pupil experimentation accompanied by reflective thinking and discovery are almost completely absent.

5. Children are ignored, for the most part, in planning for and carrying out instruction. There is little evidence of any attempt to determine individual readiness or to provide the necessary background of experience for the new material being presented.

6. Practice (drill) is assigned in the absence of meaning, either in terms of understanding the technique involved, or of understanding why learning the particular skill is desirable.

The fact is that the above practices are typical rather than unusual. For example, Hamilton[1] found in a recent study of elementary classrooms that 86 per cent of the teachers followed textbook procedures in the teaching of arithmetic. The fact that such a large proportion of

[1] Jean F. Hamilton, "A Study of Textbook Material in the Field of Arithmetic" (Unpublished Ph.D. dissertation. Department of Education: State University of Iowa, 1950).

teachers allow their responsibility for organizing the arithmetic program to go by default to writers of textbooks constitutes at least one indictment of present programs in the elementary school. Furthermore, many studies[2] have established the weakness of present programs in terms of results achieved.

Beloit Public Schools, Beloit, Wisconsin

NUMBERS ARE PUT INTO BUSINESS

WHAT IS ARITHMETIC?

Arithmetic has been, and should be, defined in a variety of ways. A number of different points of view give meaning to what is meant by the term *arithmetic.*

First, arithmetic must be seen as a product of the mind of man—an invention conceived by man as he put his intelligence to work on those problems of daily living which demanded quantitative thought for solution. "The body of doctrine which we now know as arithmetic and a portion of which we teach to young children began as a response to human needs. . . . Giving names, tallying, comparing and

2 See, for example: M. T. Eaton, "Survey of the Achievement in Arithmetic of 11,348 Sixth Grade Pupils in 486 Schools in Indiana," *Indiana University School of Education Bulletin,* XX (March, 1944), 1-62.

combining actual groups, and counting—these, it is clear, must have been evolved to serve human purposes."[3]

Second, arithmetic is a language for recording and communicating thought about quantitative experience. Number symbols are essentially adjectives which may be attached to things to describe their quantitative characteristics. Symbols of operation may be interpreted as verbs in that they express action with numbers. As words of the English language must be related to experience for meaning, so arithmetical symbols must be related to experience for quantitative meaning.

Third, arithmetic is a logically organized system of interrelated ideas. For example, the basic principle of directional counting allows us to relate and tie together the operations of addition, subtraction, multiplication, and division. All are based fundamentally on the counting idea, with addition-subtraction and multiplication-division being, respectively, inversely related to each other.

Fourth, arithmetic is a way of thinking. Thinking about and with quantities is not a unitary ability. Hickerson, for example, proposes: "The three types of mathematical thinking may be expressed as: (1) representing with mathematical symbols the quantitative aspects of concrete situations, (2) computing, and (3) understanding the theory or science of mathematics."[4]

Fifth, arithmetic is part of what is commonly called social studies in the elementary school program. Quantity, and the necessity for dealing with quantity, pervade most aspects of human relationships. Teaching arithmetic in isolation from social context is difficult to justify under any circumstances.

Sixth, arithmetic is a science. As Buckingham puts it: "In addition to accretions motivated by human needs, the cumulative development of arithmetic has been due to inner growth, to accruals resulting from the deposit of original ideas. These increments to the original stock are due in the main to mathematical thought and research."[5] This again underlines the importance of the systematic structure of arithmetic, if the area is to be grasped with real understanding.

[3] B. R. Buckingham, "The Social Point of View in Arithmetic," National Society for the Study of Education, *The Teaching of Arithmetic*, Fiftieth Yearbook, Part II (Chicago: University of Chicago Press, 1951), p. 269.

[4] J. Allen Hickerson, *Guiding Children's Arithmetic Experiences* (Englewood Cliffs, N.J.: Prentice-Hall, Inc., 1952), p. 1.

[5] Buckingham, *op. cit.*, p. 272.

ARITHMETIC AND THE TOTAL INSTRUCTIONAL PROGRAM

No one questions arithmetic as one of the essential portions of the instructional program of the elementary school. In fact, "according to a recent survey, about ten per cent of every elementary-school child's time is devoted to direct study of the subject."[6] There is, however, some question as to what the relationship of arithmetic to the remainder of the instructional program should be.

Effective learning in arithmetic and other areas is based to a considerable degree on relationships of two kinds: (a) those which seek to tie the multiple learning experiences of children together into an understandable whole; and (b) relationships between school learning experiences and daily living. The teacher who wishes to promote such relationships through arithmetic instruction has several means available:[7]

1. Studying children in and out of the classroom to determine which aspects of the textbook are related to their past and present experience.[8]

2. Developing a number of experience units drawn from the daily living of children for use as vehicles in teaching arithmetic.[8, 9]

3. Utilizing real problems involving quantity as the basis for arithmetic instruction as they arise in school and in out-of-school situations.[9]

4. Emphasizing quantitative thinking as one important aspect of all areas of instruction.[10]

5. Organizing instruction around broad problems of living wherein arithmetic becomes but one of a number of major resources.[11] Teach-

[6] Herbert F. Spitzer, *The Teaching of Arithmetic* (Boston: Houghton Mifflin Co., 1948), p. 20.

[7] For more extensive discussion of means see:

L. J. Brueckner and F. E. Grossnickle, *Making Arithmetic Meaningful* (Philadelphia: John C. Winston Co., 1953), Chapter III.

Ernest Horn, "Arithmetic in the Elementary School Curriculum," National Society for the Study of Education, *The Teaching of Arithmetic*, Fiftieth Yearbook, Part III (Chicago: University of Chicago Press, 1951), pp. 8-21.

R. L. Morton, "The Place of Arithmetic in Various Types of Elementary School Curriculums," Conference on Arithmetic, *Arithmetic 1949* (Chicago: University of Chicago Press, 1950), pp. 1-20.

[8] R. D. Willey, "Use of Arithmetic in the Out-of-School Life of Children," *Mathematics Teacher*, XXXV (January, 1942), 23-28.

[9] G. M. Wilson, "Functional Problem Units," *Education*, XLIX (February, 1949), 327-385.

[10] H. Maguire, "Can Arithmetic Be Correlated with the Unit of Study?" *Mathematics Teacher*, XXXVI (May, 1943), 219-225.

[11] C. M. Williams, "Arithmetic Learning in An Experience Curriculum," *Educational Research Bulletin*, XXVIII (September, 1949), 154-162.

A STUDY OF HOUSING BRINGS IN ARITHMETIC

ers who become increasingly aware of the quantitative problems faced by youngsters, and who have sufficient ingenuity to translate such knowledge into learning experiences in the classroom, are essential to the improvement of arithmetic instruction.

THE PURPOSES OF ARITHMETIC INSTRUCTION

There is general agreement that the over-all aim of arithmetic instruction should be:

To develop in children the ability to do effective quantitative thinking in coping with situations of daily living both in and out of school.

The key words in this statement of over-all purpose are "quantitative thinking" and "situations of daily living." One uses the number system as a means for thinking about quantity in social situations. Quantitative thinking, then, is, or should be, the core of arithmetic instruction.

A clear understanding of the scope of the arithmetic program demands definition of the particulars necessary to the achievement of this major goal. Brownell's statement of purposes is one illustration of what such a sub-definition might look like. He proposed that arithmetic instruction should seek to develop:

1. Computational skill:
   Facility and accuracy in operations with whole numbers, common fractions, decimals, and per cents . . .
2. Mathematical understandings:
   a. Meaningful conceptions of quantity, of the number system, of whole numbers, of common fractions, of decimals, of per cents, of measures, etc.
   b. A meaningful vocabulary of the useful *technical terms* of arithmetic which designate quantitative ideas and the relationships between them.
   c. Grasp of important arithmetical generalizations.
   d. Understanding of the meanings and mathematical functions of the fundamental operations.
   e. Understanding of important arithmetical relationships, such as those which function in reasonably sound estimations and approximations, in accurate checking, and in ingenious and resourceful solutions.
   f. Some understanding of the rational principles which govern number relations and computational procedures.
3. Sensitiveness to number in social situations and the habit of using number effectively in such situations:
   a. Vocabulary of selected quantitative terms of common usage (such as kilowatt hour, miles per hour, decrease and increase, and terms important in insurance, investments, business practices, etc.)
   b. Knowledge of selected business practices and other economic applications of number.
   c. Ability to use and interpret graphs, simple statistics, and tabular presentations of quantitative data (as in study in school and in practical activities outside of school).
   d. Awareness of the usefulness of quantity and number in dealing with many aspects of life. Here belongs some understanding of social institutions in which the quantitative aspect is prominent, as well as some understanding of the important contribution of number in their evolution.
   e. Tendency to sense the quantitative as part of normal experience, including vicarious experience, as in reading, in observation, and in projected activity and imaginative thinking.
   f. Ability to make (and the habit of making) sound judgments with respect to practical quantitative problems.
   g. Disposition to extend one's sensitiveness to the quantitative as this occurs socially, and to improve and extend one's ability to deal effectively with the quantitative when so encountered or discovered.[12]

The wide acceptance of this statement of specific objectives is illustrated by its appearance as the major statement of aims in the recent

12 W. A. Brownell, "The Evaluation of Learning in Arithmetic," National Council of Teachers of Mathematics, *Arithmetic in General Education,* Sixteenth Yearbook (Washington, D.C.: The Council, 1941), pp. 231-232.

yearbook on arithmetic produced by the National Society for the Study of Education.[13]

BASIC INGREDIENTS OF THE ARITHMETIC PROGRAM

The general scope of arithmetic has been indicated in preceding discussions of the nature of arithmetic and its purposes. The intention here is to help the teacher see just what it is that she and children must pay attention to in developing an effective arithmetic program.

All programs of arithmetic worthy of the name must pay attention to the following basic ingredients at some point and in some way:

1. The decimal number system with its particular kinds of numbers and ways of dealing with them.

2. Important concepts of quantity and mathematical relationship.

3. Social situations demanding quantitative thinking.

These important aspects of an arithmetic program are interrelated. One way of picturing these relationships is shown in Figure 1, which points up a number of generalizations about the arithmetic program.

Basic Ingredients and Meaning in Arithmetic. The teaching of arithmetic for meaning has been emphasized recently in educational writings. Meaningful arithmetic, however, has signified different things for different people.

First, a rather large group of experts would have us believe that the most important meanings in arithmetic are those inherent in the structure of the number system.[14] Meaningful teaching would place consistent emphasis on concepts and relationships derived from a logical analysis of the number system and the operations used in dealing with number.

A second group of experts holds that arithmetic takes on meaning primarily from its function in daily living. These men insist that meaning in arithmetic comes from the situations of daily living which demand the use of number. Many would add that particular computational skills and abilities are best taught through the use of experience units organized around socially significant problems.[15]

A third point of view is that meaning in arithmetic must be established in terms of the child's ability to attach overt actions to symbols

[13] National Society for the Study of Education, *The Teaching of Arithmetic,* Fiftieth Yearbook, Part II (Chicago: University of Chicago Press, 1951), pp. 6-7.

[14] See, for example: W. A. Brownell, "Place of Meaning in the Teachings of Arithmetic," *Elementary School Journal,* XLVII (January, 1947), 256-265.

H. G. Wheat, "Why Not Be Sensible About Meaning?" *Mathematics Teacher,* XXXVIII (March, 1945), 99-102.

[15] See, for example, G. M. Wilson, "What Is Functional Arithmetic?" *Education,* LXV (April, 1945), 466-469.

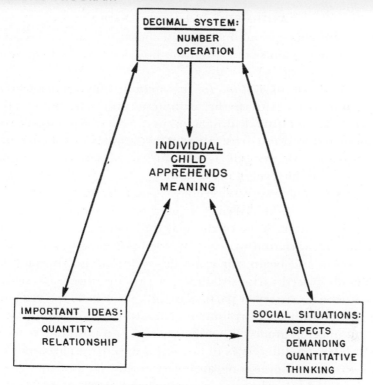

Figure 1. INTERRELATIONSHIPS OF THE BASIC INGREDIENTS OF
ARITHMETIC INSTRUCTION

of number and operation—to visualize what is to be done in concrete
terms.[16] This point of view stems basically from considering instructional method, rather than from considering what is to be looked at
in seeking meaning. The many writers who emphasize child discovery
of number facts and ideas through the manipulation of concrete objects represent this point of view.

The underlying idea is to have youngsters see sense in what they
are doing in arithmetic. Any point of view which emphasizes one particular ingredient of our arithmetic program to the exclusion of
others is unacceptable to the present authors. The problem of meaning in arithmetic, then, is essentially one of organizing instruction
around number system, basic ideas, and quantitative situations in relation to each other, in order to aid the child most in attaining insights for himself.

[16] For a clear presentation of this point of view, see H. Van Engen, "Analysis of
Meaning in Arithmetic," *Elementary School Journal,* XLIX (February, 1949), 321-329.

ARITHMETIC OVER THE GRADES

Having our conception of arithmetic—what it is, what it is for, and its essential ingredients—our attention now turns to looking at arithmetic over the grades.

Present Patterns of Arithmetic Instruction. The teacher who seeks to determine what pattern the arithmetic program should take by consulting the literature dealing with this problem is doomed to disappointment and probable frustration. Any examination of current proposals reveals little general agreement on gradation of arithmetic content, even at the level of major topics.

A comparison of relatively recent proposals by Wheat,[17] Brueckner and Grossnickle,[18] and Wilson[19] highlights the evident confusion regarding this matter. Some of the real differences among these three statements: (a) variation in recommended points at which particular instruction should begin; for example, addition and subtraction beyond ten are placed variously in grades two and three; (b) suggested points at which mastery of particular topics is to be expected; for example, some authorities recommend mastery of long division with whole numbers in grade six, while others would postpone it to grade seven or later; (c) differences in how far the study of particular topics should go; for example, one authority would confine the study of decimals to understanding when encountered, while others would develop all fundamental processes with decimals in organized fashion over several grades; and (d) differing beliefs regarding the relative importance of the basic ingredients of arithmetic; some emphasize the number system and the mathematical; others attach greater importance to quantitative situations and the social.

These and other differences point up the essential dilemma faced by the elementary school teacher. There are no readily available answers to such questions as: when should instruction on particular arithmetic content begin; for how long a period should particular items be taught; and when should children be expected to master certain aspects of arithmetic?

Possible Bases for Determining Patterns of Arithmetic Instruction

Teachers and school staffs have many resources available to help them determine what should be taught when and in what order in the

17 H. G. Wheat, "The Nature and Sequences of Learning Activities in Arithmetic," National Society for the Study of Education, *The Teaching of Arithmetic,* Fiftieth Yearbook, Part II (Chicago: University of Chicago Press, 1951), pp. 51-52.

18 L. J. Brueckner and F. E. Grossnickle, *Making Arithmetic Meaningful* (Philadelphia: John C. Winston Co., 1953), pp. 96-97.

19 G. M. Wilson, *Teaching the New Arithmetic* (New York: McGraw-Hill Book Co., Inc., 1951), p. 30.

arithmetic program. Possible bases for making such decisions include:

1. Analyses of current texts and courses of study to identify patterns of agreement.

2. Studies of the social usage of number.

3. Studies of children's use of number in ongoing experiences both in and out of school.

4. Logical analyses of the number system and its operations to pinpoint learning difficulties and mathematical relationships.

5. Studies of children's ability to perform and understand in arithmetic in relation to mental age and/or developmental status.

To use text and course analysis to determine the arithmetic program is a "counting-of-noses" technique. Justifying what we do in arithmetic in terms of "this is the way most are doing it" may merely lead to the compounding of error, unless it be assumed that all current publications offer a common best way for all children to learn arithmetic. That this assumption is false may be inferred from extreme differences in text[20] and course proposals, and from the obvious fact of individual differences among children.

Studies of social usage have indicated points at which the arithmetic experiences of children go far beyond the use made by the average person of number and operation in daily activities. For example, Dalrymple,[21] Russell,[22] and Cassell[23] have alerted us to possible overemphases in the teaching of fractions and fractional processes, decimals and decimal operations, and denominate numbers. Unfortunately, most of these studies have considered only arithmetic usage by *adults*. Furthermore, their attention is confined to how adults use the mathematics *they already know*, to the exclusion of how mathematics *might be used* if knowledge and awareness were to be extended.

Studies of child usage have been concerned with: (a) the arithmetic demands of other subject areas on children;[24] (b) arithmetic knowledge accumulated by children in pre-school years;[25] and (c) analysis of

20 R. P. Ulrich, "Grade Placement of Computational Topics in Arithmetic," *Elementary School Journal*, XLII (September, 1941), 50-59.

21 Charles O. Dalrymple, *Fractions in Business and Life*, (Unpublished Ph.D. dissertation, School of Education, Boston University, 1934).

22 G. B. Russell, "Decimal Usage in the Occupational World," *Journal of Educational Research*, XXXVIII (April, 1945), 633-638.

23 Mabel Cassell, *What Measures Do Children Know and Why?* (Unpublished Ph.D. dissertation, School of Education, Boston University, 1941).

24 R. D. Willey, "A Study of the Use of Arithmetic in the Elementary Schools of Santa Clara County, California," *Journal of Educational Research*, XXXVI (January, 1943), 353-365.

25 S. M. Mott, "Number Concepts of Small Children," *Mathematics Teacher*, XXXVIII (November, 1945), 291-301.

the daily living of children to determine experiences which demand quantitative thinking.[26] Awareness of possibilities for arithmetic instruction in other subject areas promotes more extensive application of number in school, but hardly provides a sound foundation for determining when particular aspects of number thinking should be taught. Definitions of what children know before they come to school constitute a sound developmental basis for knowing where to *begin* arithmetic instruction, but are useless in determining instruction over the grades. Analyses of the daily experiences of youngsters to determine actual uses of quantitative thinking seem to represent one of the most fruitful means for determining the what and when of arithmetic instruction.

Logical analyses of the number system and its operations provide us with much information useful in planning for arithmetic experiences. Such studies as that of Osburn[27] dealing with learning difficulties in long division should help teachers to anticipate probable difficulties and to arrange instruction to provide for their gradual introduction to children. Definitions of possible difficulties also indicate points to emphasize in instruction. Unless the arithmetic program is to be organized primarily around the number system and its operations, however, this basis for planning arithmetic programs must of necessity be relegated to secondary importance.

Finally, some planning for arithmetic instruction on the basis of the relationship of pupil performance in arithmetic to mental capacity and/or developmental status seems to hold considerable promise. This is attested by the extent to which the work of the Committee of Seven[28] has affected and changed patterns of arithmetic instruction in recent years. Their findings, however, dealt only with mental age necessary to *master* a given process or element of a process (indicating times when topics should be taught to completion), and did not consider when teaching should be initiated, nor over how long a period it should spread. Furthermore, there is some evidence[29] to show that the methods of instruction used are potent factors in determining the relative difficulty of particular arithmetic concepts.

26 D. E. Warren and W. H. Burton, "Knowledge of Simple Business Practices Possessed by Intermediate-Grade Pupils," *Elementary School Journal*, XXXV (March, 1935), 511-516.

27 W. J. Osburn, "Levels of Difficulty in Long Division," *Elementary School Journal*, XLVI (April, 1946), 441-447.

28 C. W. Washburne, "Mental Age and the Arithmetic Curriculum," *Journal of Educational Research*, XXIII (March, 1931), 210-231.

29 See for example, E. J. Swenson, "Difficulty Ratings of Addition Facts as Related to Learning Method," *Journal of Education Research*, XXXVIII (October, 1944), 81-85.

No one of the five bases for determining patterns of arithmetic instruction is sufficient unto itself. Analyses of current texts and courses of study provide us with a picture of what is now being done, and a means for placing a particular instructional program in the context of present practice. All other suggested bases can supply us with the necessary information for examining arithmetic programs critically to determine the directions that will bring about improvement.

Present Trends in the Teaching of Arithmetic

Clearly definable changes have been taking place in the arithmetic program in recent years. Some of the more important of these trends are:

1. A changing conception of the arithmetic program at the primary level of the elementary school.

We find increasing general agreement that primary arithmetic should be concerned with the development of basic concepts of number and operation on an informal *but planned* basis, rather than with helping children to achieve automatic mastery of the so-called basic facts of addition and subtraction. Without the security of the textbook (although some publishers provide primary supplements for those who want them), the primary teacher is faced with the task of seeking and capitalizing on children's quantitative experiences both in and out of school to promote necessary understandings of fundamental number concepts on a planned basis.[30]

2. A gradual shifting of certain portions of arithmetic content to higher grade levels.

Aside from shifts due to the postponement of formal instruction to later grades, a potent factor producing this upward movement has been gradual recognition that youngsters were being asked to master certain concepts at times when they were ill-equipped to do so. This realization is partly the result of study[31] devoted to the appropriateness of particular topics for given levels of mental maturity.

Mastery of the basic facts of addition and subtraction used to be expected of all children by the end of the second grade level; this expectancy is now usually postponed to the third grade on the assump-

[30] Excellent illustrations of primary instruction of this sort are contained in Edwina Deans, "Child Experience and the Development of Quantitative and Qualitative Concepts," Association of Childhood Education, *This Is Arithmetic* (Washington, D.C.: The Association, 1945), pp. 7-19.

[31] For details, see C. W. Washburne, "The Work of the Committee of Seven on Grade Placement in Arithmetic," National Society for the Study of Education, *Child Development and the Curriculum,* Thirty-eighth Yearbook, Part I (Chicago: University of Chicago Press, 1939), pp. 299-324.

tion that previous concern for basic number concepts will insure more rapid and effective mastery of basic facts at this later time. Furthermore, fundamental operations with fractions, the topic of percentage, and the computing of the volume of geometric solids are now generally taught a year or two later in the arithmetic program than previously.

3. The elimination of certain topics, or portions of topics, from the elementary arithmetic program.

Most recent eliminations from the arithmetic program have been due to the fact that many arithmetic topics fail to meet the criterion of actual use in daily living, either for children or for adults.[32] As a result, consistent efforts are being made (both in texts and courses of study) to eliminate: (a) computation with fractions having excessively large numerators and/or denominators;[33] (b) ragged decimals in decimal computation (e.g. $32.5 + 2.067 + .0034$); and (c) drill for mastery on such topics as division of fractions and computation with large decimals.

4. Spreading the teaching of certain major arithmetic topics and concepts over longer periods of school time.

For example, the topic of fractions is commonly dealt with throughout the elementary grades at gradually increasing levels of difficulty. The early years may serve to establish such basic fractional meanings as the part-of-the-whole idea, the part-of-a-group idea, and simple ratio in comparing groups. These, then, serve as a foundation for later consideration of addition and subtraction of like fractions, eventually followed by mastery of all processes with all types of fractions.

5. Increasing concern for mental and oral arithmetic as a necessary phase of instruction.

Perhaps the major share of computation carried on by children in arithmetic has been accomplished with paper and pencil. Wherever this has been true, the fact that daily living often requires one to compute in one's head has been ignored. Recognition of this fact requires a revamping of arithmetic and its instructional methods to insure frequent practice of computation on mental and oral bases.

---

[32] Justification for this statement is found in G. B. Russell, "Decimal Usage in the Occupational World," *Journal of Educational Research*, XXXVIII (April, 1945), 633-638.

R. D. Willey, "Use of Arithmetic in the Out-of-School Life of Children," *Mathematics Teacher*, XXXV (January, 1942), 23-28.

G. M. Wilson, "Social Utility Theory as Applied to Arithmetic, Its Research Basis, and Some of Its Implications," *Journal of Educational Research*, XLI (January, 1948), 321-337.

[33] One justification for this practice is found in: G. M. Wilson and C. O. Dalrymple, "Useful Fractions," *Journal of Educational Research*, XXX (January, 1937), 341-347.

Increased emphasis on such procedures demands corresponding attention to estimation and approximation as abilities to be developed by children—our concern is not always for *exact* answers, but often for rough approximations sufficiently accurate to meet the needs of particular number situations.

6. A broadened conception of the nature and place of problem solving in the arithmetic program.

Problem solving in elementary arithmetic has too often been limited to computational exercises in word form, with such so-called "problems" serving primarily to give practice in the fundamental operations.

This situation is gradually changing. Problems are being used as important centers of attention around which arithmetic instruction may be organized. Problems of increased complexity and breadth are being included in the arithmetic program. Units organized around the school store, constructing a playhouse, planning a party, and the like are becoming increasingly common in arithmetic instruction.

The necessity for going beyond the text in providing problem activities in arithmetic is underlined by Dexter.[34] Her analysis of word problems in a recent text series indicated that three out of five were one of the following types: samples to serve as guides to the solution of similar problems, exercises requiring only the reading or writing of numbers, questions requiring fact responses, and purely artificial situations. Most of the remaining problems were classified as possible situations, but as unlikely to occur in most communities. Less than 1 per cent of all problems were classified as real in the sense that they were pertinent to child experience and interest.

7. Increasing use of more varied instructional materials.

Arithmetic of the past too often had as its only instructional materials the textbook, the workbook, the blackboard, and paper and pencil. Recent years have seen rapid and prolific development of a tremendous variety of aids for teaching arithmetic—manipulative materials for a range of purposes and levels, films, film strips, charts, demonstration devices, and the like.[35] Objects of all kinds to be counted and handled thoughtfully, simple abaci for discovering and demonstrating number facts, geometric forms, pocket devices for

[34] C. E. Dexter, "Analysis of Written Problems in a Recent Arithmetic Series," *Education*, LXV (April, 1945), 488-490.
[35] For a selective and recent summary of instructional materials in arithmetic see F. E. Grossnickle, C. Junge, and W. Metzner, "Instructional Materials for Teaching Arithmetic," National Society for the Study of Education, *The Teaching of Arithmetic*, Fiftieth Yearbook, Part II (Chicago: University of Chicago Press, 1951), pp. 155-185.

teaching place value, number charts, fraction wheels and boards, collections of typical measuring devices—these and more are commonly available to teachers of arithmetic. The vast majority of aids can be self- or child-produced for a few pennies from materials readily at hand.

8. Changing emphases in evaluating progress toward arithmetic goals.

Although we still have a long way to go in improving evaluation in arithmetic, significant changes in classroom practices are gradually taking place. First, a broader range of arithmetic objectives is being evaluated. Second, many more procedures of evaluation are being used than pencil-and-paper tests. Third, teacher and standardized pencil-and-paper tests are being improved. Fourth, there is greater effort being made to bring the child into the evaluation process. Fifth, evaluation is becoming an important part of the teaching-learning process.

SOME PRINCIPLES OF INSTRUCTIONAL METHOD IN ARITHMETIC

Methods of teaching arithmetic at all levels should be designed to provide opportunities for children to: (a) make exploratory approaches to new quantitative situations to determine the nature of problems to be resolved and to establish need for working on them; (b) think for themselves in discovering possible means for solution, in trying and comparing alternatives, and in arriving at the best possible means of solution at their own levels of maturity; and (c) draw their own conclusions in the form of generalized concepts, rules, and relationships springing from their own very real experiences.[36] The implications of this statement for arithmetic classrooms are many.

First, the role of the learner must be an *active,* rather than a passive, one—he must share in decisions made regarding the what, how, why, and next steps of arithmetic learning experiences. This means that demonstration-imitation procedures no longer suffice in the teaching of arithmetic.

Second, instruction must be focused on real problems related to the quantitative needs of children. When this is done, children have

[36] Research support for what follows is found in studies such as:

L. W. Harding and I. P. Bryant, "Experimental Comparison of Drill and Direct Experience in Arithmetic Learning in a Fourth Grade," *Journal of Educational Research,* XXXVII (January, 1944), 321-337.

E. J. Swenson, "Organization and Generalization as Factors in Learning Transfer, and Retroactive Inhibition," *Learning Theory in School Situations,* University of Minnesota Studies in Education, No. 2 (Minneapolis: University of Minnesota Press, 1949), pp. 9-39.

centers of attention about which they can and will want to be active.

Third, thinking used to arrive at major concepts, understanding of relationships, general rules for dealing with number situations, and the like, will be predominantly inductive rather than deductive. Our intent here is not to advocate that *all* arithmetic be taught inductively, but to insist that induction has too long been neglected as a major method for developing arithmetical generalizations in meaningful fashion.

Fourth, means for facilitating problem solving activities and reflective thinking must be available to children. Texts, reference books, manipulative materials, models, charts, measuring devices, and a host of other materials all have a place in the arithmetic classroom as resources for children in their problem solving efforts.

Fifth, differences in levels of maturity reached by children at a particular time must be recognized and accepted by teachers of arithmetic. Differences can be accepted and capitalized on via such procedures as: (a) selecting quantitative problems for instruction which are sufficiently broad to provide opportunities for children to participate in their solution at their varying levels of maturity; (b) varying level of performance expected of a child in terms of where he is in his arithmetic development, and focusing on progress made over time in evaluating the results of instruction; and (c) striking a balance among individual, small group, and total group activities in relation to the patterns of need present in a given classroom.

Sixth, the classroom which focuses on exploration, discovery, and generalization must pay attention to the quality of personal relationships which exist in this classroom. If we expect children to explore freely within the limits of their abilities, to "stick their necks out" in suggesting tentative solutions, to feel free to verbalize what arithmetic experiences mean to them, then it becomes important that the relationships present be the kind which promote constructive participation.

Seventh, instructional method must seek to tie together the basic ingredients of arithmetic. Social situations within which children can explore and discover quantitative problems demanding new mathematical facts, skills, and abilities for their solution—these may be the beginning points of instruction. These new number needs then lead to further exploration of ways and means for handling them designed to discover adequate techniques for solution. From these activities come opportunities to generalize important ideas of mathematics from experience for both the number system itself and its social context. This is meaningful arithmetic.

Eighth, practice for mastery will follow the development of meanings through exploration-discovery-generalization procedures.

The arithmetic classroom which exhibits these characteristics of instructional method is a learning laboratory in the true sense. To demonstrate that the average teacher can bring about conditions of this kind, let's look at a third grade arithmetic class in action.

A THIRD GRADE STUDIES THE POST OFFICE[37]

In making a study of the post office over time, this third grade class had learned much about how the post office serves the community, including uses of arithmetic such as the cost of mailing letters in different ways and the relation of cost to weight of letters and parcels. At valentine time the class decided to sell stamps needed for mailing valentines to children in the school. In discussing this as a possible project, the need for accuracy in computing stamp costs and in making change was brought out. This led to the realization that the group had not as yet learned the multiplication facts with three. The teacher helped the children to see that they could either make a list of the costs of any number of 3-cent stamps from 1 to 9 to refer to, or that they could learn how to find the costs of different numbers of stamps for themselves. The latter was decided upon as the immediate goal.

Instruction began by asking children to show different ways of finding out how many 3 threes are. This elicited a variety of responses. One child arranged 3 groups of three pennies each on his desk and counted them one by one to get the answer while the others watched. Another illustrated a quicker method by counting the pennies by threes. Still another went to the blackboard, drew three rows of small circles, and counted them one by one.

Pupils were then asked to suggest how the answer might be found without using objects or pictures. One pupil suggested adding three threes; another counting by threes. A third said that he knew that 2 threes are 6, so 3 threes are 3 more or 9. The class agreed that the last method was best because it saved time, after considering the alternatives.

This general method was then used to find the product of 4 threes. The solution accepted by the class was: "We know that 3 threes are 9; so 4 threes are three more than 9, or 12." Pupils were asked to demonstrate the correctness of this solution by using concrete objects, then drawing, then by addition. In a similar way the facts for 5 threes, 6 threes, and 7 threes were developed. The facts for 8 threes and 9 threes were derived through use of the general method only as evidence of understanding of the generalization involved.

As the several products were discovered, they were listed in tabular form on the blackboard. This summary was used as the basis for bringing out relationships among the listed products. One child pointed out that each product was 3 greater than the preceding product, and 3 less than the product following. An-

[37] Adapted from: L. J. Brueckner and F. E. Grossnickle, *How to Make Arithmetic Meaningful* (Philadelphia: John C. Winston Co., 1947), pp. 15-17.

other saw that 4 x 3 was twice as much as 2 x 3. These and other pupil comments underlined the systematic nature of the listed facts.

Children were then asked to apply their results to finding the cost of different numbers of stamps. They then went on to suggest original problems using these facts which were not related to stamps. They were encouraged to work out answers in some way when they could not recall facts immediately and then to check their answers by referring to their summary list.

When it became evident that most children really understood the facts that had been developed, a variety of practice exercises was provided to help the class to master them. Many children who wished to participate in the selling of stamps in the class post office practiced on their own at odd times. The teacher constantly checked methods used by pupils to obtain their answers and encouraged them to discard inefficient procedures for more mature techniques as understanding grew.

Even this brief description of a series of arithmetic learning experiences at a single grade level clearly illustrates adherence to most, if not all, of the proposed principles of instructional method in arithmetic. The only principle which cannot be seen operating explicitly in this description is that which has to do with the quality of personal relationships. However, one may certainly infer that this was an important consideration in the mind of this teacher from the ease with which suggestions came from the children and the important role played by children in making decisions.

SOME SPECIFICS OF INSTRUCTIONAL METHOD IN ARITHMETIC

The following discussion centers in turn on instruction with whole numbers; the teaching of fractions, decimals, and per cents; and the development of problem solving abilities. In each case, an attempt is made to bring out and answer the kinds of questions usually asked by classroom teachers.

The Teaching of Whole Numbers

Perhaps the most frequent plaint of arithmetic teachers is, how can they teach the so-called basic facts of addition, subtraction, multiplication, and division to children in a way that will insure both understanding and eventual automatic mastery? Research provides neither a complete nor a well-defined answer to this question. To improve this aspect of the arithmetic program, the following suggestions may be helpful:

1. Make sure that children come to their study of the basic facts with an adequate background of experience.

No child should be plunged into a beginning study of addition and subtraction facts who does not possess reasonable competence in the counting process and a fair grasp of the fundamental meanings which may be attached to whole numbers.

2. In presenting the basic facts over time, instructional procedures should generally move through a series of well-defined stages: (a) encountering the need for facts in real situations; (b) exploring ways and means of obtaining answers through concrete means (*i.e.,* the manipulation of actual objects); (c) recording discoveries made through picturing the thinking done via semi-concrete representation; (d) expressing the number fact in words; and (e) representing the fact in symbolic terms.

3. The basic facts should be so organized for teaching as to take advantage of and emphasize the relationships which exist among them.

There are several kinds of relationships which are helpful in thinking about organizing basic facts for instruction: (a) relationships among the fundamental operations; (b) number families stemming from a particular number; (c) relationships inherent in proximity of one number to another in the number series; and (d) the relationship of reversals in number facts (*e.g.,* $2+3$ and $3+2$).

4. Postpone the teaching of the zero facts until needed.

This suggestion stems from two current notions: (a) that it is extremely difficult to develop the meaning of zero in terms of its use in actual situations with children, and (b) zero facts are not really needed until the child moves into addition, subtraction, multiplication, and division involving the teens and beyond.

5. Teach the "easy" facts first; follow with the more difficult facts.

What evidence there is seems to indicate that "easy" basic facts include: (a) sums to 9 or below; (b) subtraction facts with minuends of 9 or less; (c) the doubles (*i.e.,* $3+3$; $4—4$); (d) products involving 1, 2, 3, 4, 5 as multipliers and multiplicands; and (e) division facts involving 1, 2, 3, 4, 5 as quotients and divisors. When basic facts are taught meaningfully, however, order within groups of easy or difficult facts is probably immaterial.

6. Organized tables of basic facts should be an end-product, rather than a beginning point.

The building of tables by children can be a very useful way to summarize completely what is known, and may then serve as a reference tool in intensive study leading to automatic mastery.

7. The technical vocabulary of the processes should be de-emphasized in the early stages of instruction in the basic facts.

We may speak of combining groups rather than addends; say "how many in all," rather than "what is the sum"; "take away," rather than "subtract"—this vocabulary describes clearly the essential meaning of what we are trying to do and thus aids the child to understand the processes in the early stages of arithmetic instruction.

8. Children must be provided with specific study procedures at the point when automatic mastery of basic facts becomes desirable, after the development of thorough understanding.

The availability of a variety of procedures from which a child may select in carrying on his own intensive study is highly desirable. This implies that no one procedure is equally suitable for all children, but that every child must have at least one means for achieving desired mastery. Some may find individual flash cards useful; others may prefer simple oral games involving cooperative effort; still others may work best with a say-write-repeat procedure.

Adding Upward or Downward. Whether children should add upward or downward is probably a relatively unimportant methodological question, although it is one often asked by teachers. There is some evidence to support adding downward as somewhat superior, but *only* in beginning experiences with the process. As soon as checking in both addition and subtraction work is emphasized, and children encounter addition in the horizontal form, the question becomes superfluous.

Take-Away Method in Subtraction. The evidence regarding relative superiority of the several subtraction methods is conflicting and inconclusive; some studies support one method, others support another. If understanding is important, the subtractive process must be rationalized with children. It is recommended, therefore, that subtraction be taught on a take-away, decomposition basis in order to handle the problem of borrowing in meaningful fashion.

The Long Division Form. There is considerable agreement that the long form of division should be introduced from the very beginning of children's work with this process, and most particularly when uneven division is first encountered with one-figure divisors. This procedure is justified on the bases that: (a) it develops readiness for using the long process in later encounters with more complicated division problems; (b) beginning errors can be more easily spotted; and (c) it brings early checking into play (*i.e.*, in $3\overline{)7}$, the question of how many 3's in 7 is answered directly when the long form is used).

Estimation of Quotients. One of the most difficult aspects of arithmetic for children to learn (and for teachers to present) is the estimation of quotient figures in long division with two-figure divisors and more. Most discussions of this question are limited to two-figure divisors alone, and to consideration of two common methods: the "apparent" method and the "increase-by-one" procedure. Supporters of the respective methods conflict sharply. Until convincing evidence is forthcoming, the present writers recommend that children become familiar with both procedures.

Carrying and Borrowing. The extent to which a child experiences difficulty in understanding and performing the necessary carryings and borrowings of addition and subtraction depends to a large degree on his understanding of two fundamental mathematical concepts. First, it is virtually impossible for him to understand what happens in either carrying or borrowing unless he first possesses a very clear understanding of the meaning of *place value* in our decimal number system. Furthermore, he must have grasped the basic notion that all arithmetical operations are essentially *regrouping* for the purpose of simplifying quantitative situations by expressing results in the standard terms dictated by decimal notation. If these two ideas have been emphasized from the earliest beginnings of arithmetic instruction, few children should have trouble in understanding what it is that is being carried, or that carrying is merely an extension of the kind of regrouping first encountered in establishing the meaning of the teen numbers (*i.e.,* interpreting 15 as 1 ten and 5 ones).

The Use of Crutches. Among the commonly recognized crutches used are the writing of small numbers above in carrying and borrowing, the use of the caret (∧) to facilitate decimal point placement in long division with decimals, and the teaching of cue words in dealing with word problems. Many crutches go unrecognized as such; for example, the child who counts on his fingers, who resorts to drawing a picture of a numerical situation, who remembers a number fact through recourse to manipulation of concrete objects. A reasonable point of view in this connection would seem to be that children should be allowed all possible aids to understanding and performance; the criterion of use should be whether more effective learning results. At the same time, one must recognize that most crutches are not essential to mature arithmetical performance and, in actual fact, may eventually block further progress in efficiency with numbers. This being so, it seems clear that the use of helpful crutches while the child is working at a relatively immature level of performance is commendable, but that the discarding of such devices should be strongly encouraged as soon as he moves to a point of being able to operate with some confidence without them.

The Teaching of Fractions, Decimals, and Per Cents

We are coming to realize that the beginning years of the elementary school can provide a solid foundation for more intensive work with fractions in the later years. Small children can achieve a beginning grasp of two basic meanings of a common fraction: as one or more equal parts of a whole, and as one or more of the equal parts of a group. Naturally these initial contacts with fractions should be confined to such small unit fractions as $\frac{1}{2}$, $\frac{1}{3}$, $\frac{1}{4}$, and should be centered in work with real objects and with very common measures. Early experiences with coins in activities centering around the toy store, the post office, and the like, can provide opportunities for developing fractional concepts and a beginning understanding of decimals.

Commonly, teaching practices in arithmetic reveal a frightening lack of concern for the essential relatedness of fractions, decimals, and per cents. These ought not to be seen as isolated enterprises, for most of what we need to know and achieve in the study of decimals and per cents is based fundamentally on ideas already encountered in the study of common fractions.

Every teacher of arithmetic must recognize that any fraction can take on any one of four different meanings, depending on the context in which it is encountered. These are the part-of-a-whole and part-of-a-group ideas mentioned above, and also the fraction as an indicated division (first encountered in simple problems of uneven division), and the fraction as a ratio used to express relative size of two groups or amounts. The latter idea will probably not be introduced until the upper grades.

The importance of establishing the respective meanings of numerator and denominator, the terms of the fraction, in relation to these four fraction meanings cannot be overemphasized. For example, in interpreting $\frac{3}{4}$ in terms of the part-of-a-whole idea, the child must understand that the 4 indicates the equal number of parts into which the whole is divided and the 3 the number of those equal parts wanted. If they do not comprehend such ideas, children experience considerable difficulty in seeing clearly the applications of fractions in daily living.

The question of which fractions to teach, considered briefly earlie⁻

in this chapter, is subject to generalizations about which most would agree:

1. Fractions with large denominators probably should receive only incidental attention, if they are treated at all.

2. Emphasis should be placed primarily on a limited number of fractions (denominators of 2, 3, 4, 5, 6, 8, 10, 12, 16 as a suggested minimum), as these account for close to 100 per cent of all uses of fractions in daily living.

Rationalizing the Division of Fractions. Traditionally, division of fractions has been taught by rule: Invert the divisor fraction and multiply. Recently a method involving equalizing the denominators of the fractions has gained considerable support (*i.e.,* $3/4 \div 5/6 = 9/12 \div 10/12 = 9/10$). This has the advantage of employing the principle of likeness which makes for easier rationalization should such be desirable. Some argue that fractional division occurs so infrequently in daily living as to make time spent rationalizing a waste of effort.

Cancelling. The terms *cancel* and *reduce* can have insidious effects in teaching fractions, because their common meanings of "cross out or get rid of" and "make smaller," respectively, do not convey what is involved at all. In this connection, the writers recommend that in all cases of "cancellation" in multiplication of fractions, and of "reduction" both upward and downward (*i.e.,* $1/2 = 2/4$; $6/8 = 3/4$), emphasis be placed on the fact that these are actually specific applications of the so-called Golden Rule of fractions: Both numerator and denominator of a fraction may be multiplied or divided by the same number (except zero) without changing the value of the fraction.

Decimal Fractions. Research indicates that decimals are seldom used in real life except in connection with money, since we characteristically make our measurements on fractional bases. This has led many writers to suggest that this aspect of arithmetic be de-emphasized at the elementary school level. Some have gone so far as to advocate limiting the study of decimals to understanding and appreciation alone, with no computation with decimals being taught. It is unlikely that this extreme position will gather many supporters, for there is much in decimals to help fill in the total picture of our number system and how it operates; this alone justifies some emphasis.

Percentage. The topic of percentage, while closely related to fractions and decimals (per cents being merely a special kind of fraction with a constant denominator of 100), is somewhat different because of the direct uses to which per cents are put. The development of per cents as numbers was the direct outgrowth of a need for some means of comparison on a ratio basis to allow for direct comparison among the ratios themselves; thus, percentage is essentially a social concept attached to and used primarily in business and comparative statistics. Per cents are never used directly as numbers in computational procedures, but rather must be changed to equivalents in fraction or decimal form. Thus, the essential problems of teaching percentage are: (a) establishing the basic meaning of per cents for interpretive purposes; and (b) developing ways and means for converting fractions, decimals, and per cents from one to the other. Percentage as a topic is now generally taught systematically at seventh grade and beyond. However, children have frequent need to interpret per cents as ratios in their reading long before this point is reached (*e.g.*, Brazil produces 65% of the world's coffee crop).

Typically the work in percentage at the upper grade levels centers around business applications such as profit and loss, interest, and the like. These applications give rise to three general types of percentage problems which in turn have led to the development of the so-called "case method" for dealing with them. What little evidence there is indicates that percentage can be taught successfully and with meaning without recourse to this arbitrary classification into cases. Dependence on past insights derived from similar problem types in working with fractions is probably more meaningful, and serves to emphasize the essential relatedness of fractions and per cents.

The Teaching of Problem Solving. One of the most difficult methodological problems faced by teachers of arithmetic is that of helping children to develop increased ability in problem solving.

The large number of studies[38] which have compared two or more of the common methods taught to children to aid them in problem solution have failed to establish that any one method is distinctly superior—the evidence is conflicting and inconclusive. Only two things seem clear: (a) slow learners seem to derive some benefit from prescribed means of attacking problems; and (b) providing the learner with some helps in attacking problems is better than giving no help at all. For arithmetic teachers this suggests a *multiple* methodological approach to problem solving with children. This demands, of course, that every arithmetic teacher familiarize himself with common problem solving techniques, such as the so-called formal analysis method (asking a series of set questions as: what is asked for, what is given,

---

[38] An excellent summary of research to 1944 appears in: H. C. Johnson, "Problem Solving in Arithmetic: A Review of the Literature," *Elementary School Journal*, XLIV (April, 1944), 396-403, and XLIV (May, 1944), 476-482.

what processes are needed?); dependencies methods designed to help children clarify the relationships found in a problem via graphic, pictorial, and/or tabular means; and associational methods utilizing "models" for the solution of problems containing similar elements.

A second group of studies has attempted to discover characteristics of word problems which make some more difficult for children than others. The range of factors studied has included: (a) relative familiarity of the problem setting; (b) imaginative versus straightforward conventional settings for problems; (c) interrogative versus declarative sentence structure; (d) vocabulary difficulty; and (e) presence or absence of extraneous detail in word problems. As one might logically expect, word problems based on situations drawn from the known experiences of children and stated in simple language without extraneous detail in interrogative form tend to be easier for children to solve.[39] The effect of imaginative settings on problem difficulty remains in doubt.

Studies of factors associated with high and low achievement in problem solving have identified a number of specifics which differentiate among children. These are neatly summarized by Brueckner and Grossnickle[40] as follows:

1. In such psychological factors as general mental ability, delayed and immediate memory, language level, and general reading ability, the differences between good and poor achievers in problem solving are highly significant in favor of the good achievers.

2. The differences in skill in fundamental operations and ability to estimate answers also are highly significant in favor of the good achievers.

3. The differences in four basic reading skills peculiar to arithmetic as a special field (steps in problem analysis; finding the key question of the problem; estimating answers to problems; ability to read graphs, charts, tables) and in range of information about arithmetic also are highly significant in favor of the good achievers.

Finally, research has provided us with information as to the effectiveness of certain techniques for helping children to achieve greater success in solving word problems. Study has been made of such procedures as: (a) use of exercises requiring only that children select the

39 See for example:
  G. A. Kramer, *Effect of Certain Factors in the Verbal Arithmetic Problems upon Children's Success in the Solution* (Baltimore: Johns Hopkins Press, 1933).
  H. M. White, "Does Experience in the Situation Involved Affect the Solving of a Problem?" *Education,* LIV (April, 1934), 451-455.
  40 L. J. Brueckner and F. E. Grossnickle, *Making Arithmetic Meaningful,* (Philadelphia: John C. Winston Co., 1953), p. 514.

correct processes demanded by problems; (b) additional practice in computational skills needed in problems used; (c) practice in estimating answers; (d) the use of "cue" words and phrases; (e) direct instruction in the common terminology of arithmetic; (f) having children build their own problems; (g) oral reading and discussion of word problems, followed by silent reading with emphasis on the specialized reading skills of arithmetic; and (h) requiring pupils to re-state problems in their own words. What evidence there is, and it is quite meager, tends to support the use of a pattern of helps such as those suggested above in problem solving activities with children.

A FINAL WORD

Improvement of instruction in arithmetic will come about when teaching staffs embark on cooperative efforts designed to:

1. Provide the classroom teacher with workable definitions of each of the three basic ingredients of arithmetic: the number system and its operations; the key ideas of quantity and relationship; and possible social situations in which quantity is predominant.

2. Open up opportunities for intensive study of the relationship of the basic ingredients to each other.

3. Encourage teachers to examine alternative patterns of arithmetic instruction critically.

4. Facilitate classroom experimentation in seeking patterns of arithmetic instruction best adapted to the given school situation. These efforts should produce a greater realization of the pervasiveness of number in daily living both in and out of school, and recognition of the fact that dealing with number and operation in isolation from basic mathematical concepts and points of application is sterile arithmetic instruction. Assuming these outcomes, the individual classroom teacher becomes the key to change for the better in arithmetic programs.

BIBLIOGRAPHY

Brueckner, L. J. and F. E. Grossnickle, *Making Arithmetic Meaningful.* Philadelphia: John C. Winston Company, 1953.

Buckingham, Burdette R., *Elementary Arithmetic: Its Meaning and Practice.* Boston: Ginn and Company, 1947.

Clark, John R. and Laura K. Eads, *Guiding Arithmetic Learning.* Yonkers: World Book Company, 1954.

Hickerson, J. Allen, *Guiding Children's Arithmetic Experiences.* Englewood Cliffs, N.J.: Prentice-Hall, Inc., 1952.

Hollister, George E. and Agnes G. Gunderson, *Teaching Arithmetic in Grades I and II.* Boston: D. C. Heath and Company, 1954.

Morton, Robert L., *Teaching Arithmetic in the Elementary School. Volume I: Primary Grades.* New York: Silver Burdett Company, 1937.

———, *Teaching Arithmetic in the Elementary School. Volume II: Intermediate Grades.* New York: Silver Burdett Company, 1938.

National Council of Teachers of Mathematics. *Arithmetic in General Education,* Sixteenth Yearbook. Washington, D.C.: The Council, 1941.

National Society for the Study of Education. *The Teaching of Arithmetic,* Fiftieth Yearbook, Part II. Chicago: University of Chicago Press, 1951.

Spencer, P. L. and Marguerite Brydegaard, *Building Mathematical Concepts in the Elementary School.* New York: Henry Holt and Company, 1952.

Spitzer, Herbert F., *The Teaching of Arithmetic,* 2nd ed. Boston: Houghton Mifflin Company, 1954.

Stokes, C. Newton, *Teaching the Meanings of Arithmetic.* New York: Appleton-Century-Crofts, Inc., 1951.

Wheat, Harry G., *How to Teach Arithmetic.* Evanston: Row, Peterson and Company, 1951.

Wilson, Guy M., *Teaching the New Arithmetic,* 2nd ed. New York: McGraw-Hill Book Company, Inc., 1951.

THE HEALTH,
PHYSICAL EDUCATION,
AND RECREATION
PROGRAM

11

THE IMPORTANCE OF HEALTH HAS LONG BEEN recognized. But the organization of school programs to explore health knowledge, develop health skills, and provide health services is a comparatively recent phenomenon. Practice ranges from "free" play and a morning "clean-hands check-up" to the well organized and supervised health, physical education, and recreation programs of schools in all sections of the country.

THE HEALTH PROGRAM
IN SCHOOL AND COMMUNITY

Effective Cooperation in Health Education

In general, the school is responsible for health education, the home for health care, and the community for health promotion.[1]

[1] J. Murray Lee and Dorris May Lee, *The Child and His Curriculum* (New York: Appleton-Century-Crofts, 1950), p. 576.

While this statement theoretically clarifies the function of the three major agencies responsible for the health of boys and girls, in practice such a clear-cut distinction is not easily made. Children suffer to the degree that gaps exist between the points where the function of one agency leaves off and the function of another begins.

Cooperation among community health agencies in conducting the total health program may be identified at a number of levels.

1. Information is shared. The school informs the home about regulations pertaining to inoculations, medical certificates, observed deficiencies in children, and so on. The home sends notes explaining absences, provides medical reports, and gives data concerning past illnesses. The public health agency provides information concerning epidemics, available resources, and health precautions. The whole program is a non-personal sort of operation.

2. Mutual responsibilities are defined and assumed. The information-sharing process continues. But each agency attempts to assist the others in doing their respective jobs. The home makes it easier for the school to keep down epidemics by keeping Johnny home and having him medically approved before going back to school. Public health agencies assist the school in periodic check-ups. The school assists in the community health campaigns. However, each group may see only a part of the child. Each may not see the total job to be done and the way the parts are related to one another.

3. All agencies join forces behind a common purpose—to improve the total health picture in the community for all the children of all the people. Each agency sees its particular phase of the work in relation to all other phases. Johnny is at the center of the entire process.

Figure 1 shows home, school, and public health department operating at each of these three levels. In the first diagram, each is broadcasting but, like a radio station, each does not know whether or not anyone is receiving. In the second, contact with the others has been established, but each has its own line of communication and each sees a different child. In the third, common lines of communication have been set up and all three together see the same child.

Cooperation at this third level is rare. But more and more communities are exploring ways of uniting their resources into coordinated efforts in health improvement. Health councils, pre-school conferences, and community health inventories represent three such efforts.[2]

---

[2] The extended school program (eleven and twelve months) is an illustration of home-school-community cooperation that involves health education. See Chapter 3.

Community Health Councils[3]

In some communities, agencies have secured effective cooperation through the establishment of community health councils. Such councils are appropriate for both the small rural community and the large

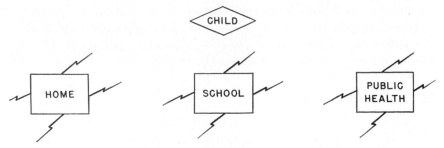

A. INFORMATION IS MADE AVAILABLE. NO COMMON
FOCUS UPON THE CHILD

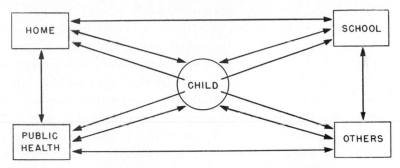

B. CERTAIN MUTUAL RESPONSIBILITIES ARE DEFINED.
EACH SEES ONLY PART OF THE CHILD

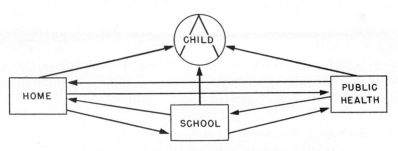

C. ALL JOINED TOGETHER BEHIND A COMMON PURPOSE
Figure 1. LEVELS IN COOPERATION FOR HEALTH EDUCATION

[3] The community health council is just one type of coordinated community health effort. For others see: Delbert and Oberteuffer, *School Health Education* (New York: Harper & Brothers, 1949), pp. 375-382; American Association of School Administrators, Twentieth Yearbook, *Health in Schools* (Washington: The Association, 1942), pp. 301-306.

urban center. Organization may be very simple; for example, a teacher, a parent, and the county health nurse may make up the council in a small rural community. Or, in a large metropolitan center, the following may be included in the organization: school principal, public health physician, dentist, school nurse, school health coordinator, psychologist, guidance specialist, nutritionist, janitor, representative of the student council, representative of the Parent-Teacher Association, and teachers of physical education, biology, home economics, and special education.[4]

Pre-School Conferences

The work of the Lena Cox Elementary School in Atlanta illustrates admirably what can be accomplished through the spring conference for parents of pre-school children. Each spring the community is surveyed to determine the number of children likely to be entering the first grade the following September. Early in May, the parents of these children are invited to the school. A dental hygienist, public health nurse, nutritionist, the principal, first grade teachers, parents, and a representative from a local teacher education institution participate. The teachers of this school maintain that not only does greater conformity with desirable health practice result, but also that incidence of disease and absence are reduced in early school years.

Another promising practice in cooperative health education is the pre-school conference for teachers, which often includes parents. The pre-school conference offers a unique opportunity for schools and school systems to plan with parents and community health agencies for improved health education. Sources of communicable disease and how to eliminate them, when and how to conduct health and dental examinations, the respective roles of home, school, and public health agency in dealing with outbreaks of disease, and health precautions in athletics, are all appropriate discussion topics. More than one community health survey has had such beginnings.

Community Health Inventories

School curriculum committees cannot get very far with any comprehensive program of improvement without identifying the health needs of boys and girls and the health problems of the community. This was soon discovered in Moultrie, Georgia, by a committee of

4 National Committee on School Health Policies, *Suggested School Policies* (New York: Health Education Council, 1945), pp. 8-10.

teachers who worked as a group on a curriculum reorganization program throughout the elementary school.[5]

The work of this group formed the basis for a three-year study begun in 1939. In cooperation with the Commission on Teacher Education of the American Council on Education, the Moultrie Elementary Schools joined the Colquitt County Schools and the Moultrie High School in a study of health, recreation, and home problems. A planning committee was set up, consisting of classroom teachers and principals, the county health officer, the county health engineer, board of education members, ministers, patrons, and a consultant. Testing for hookworm resulted in treatment for 106 children and the virtual disappearance of hookworm cases. Plans for immunization against typhoid fever, smallpox, and diphtheria were successfully carried through. A dental clinic for indigent children was established. Ear and eye clinics followed in later years. The health curriculum kept pace with community effort.

This illustration brings out two essential factors. First, real change comes as the result of careful planning and research, and intelligent action based on findings. And second, while the process of health improvement may be initiated by any interested agency, it can be carried through at a high level of success only when all other agencies affected become purposefully involved.

Coordinating the Community Health Effort

An effective community program of health and safety requires coordination of the efforts of schools, health departments, welfare agencies, clinics, police department, and the like. Analysis of cooperative efforts at such places as Baltimore, Maryland; Washington County, Tennessee; Calhoun County, Michigan; and Hartford, Connecticut suggests a number of guiding principles linked to success.

1. Any plan of cooperation requires a delineation of the activities of the participating agencies and of the individuals within the agencies.
2. Any participating agency must retain administrative control of its own activities.
3. Cooperation in the school health program requires a recognition of the professional nature of education, as well as that of the health-medical sciences.
4. There is no single best plan for the coordination of agencies in the health program of the school.

5 From material submitted by the Moultrie Elementary Schools. The material used here is taken from a report prepared by Mrs. Juanita H. Doster and Mrs. Jane G. Comer.

5. In successful joint programs the democratic process of group thinking is important.

6. The development of community organization in a democratic society requires continued, patient, and persistent effort.

7. As cooperative activities succeed and increase in scope, there often develops a program requiring the efforts of some one person to draw the activities together and to see that the program as a whole moves toward the general goal.[6]

THE SCHOOL AND HEALTH EDUCATION

The school's function as defined here is two-fold: the development of health knowledge, habits, and skills; and the provision of health services.

Health Knowledge and Healthful Behavior

Teaching for the development of health knowledge has suffered from our failure to see the relationship between present activities and ends sought. We too often forget that the test of health information is its application in healthful living. There is no evidence to suggest that the possession of health facts alone makes a significant difference to the health practices of boys and girls.

There is some evidence, however, to indicate that youngsters can relate themselves meaningfully to problems in the health area and that consequently, health knowledge will be developed and applied. The Willimantic Study is a case in point.[7] Three hundred and eighty-five children, grades four through eight, in St. Joseph's and St. Mary's Parochial Schools in Willimantic, Connecticut, took part in the study. The children recorded the nature and quantity of their food on a daily diet sheet. They then rated their diets, using the National Food Guide;[8] a rating of thirteen for any given day indicated an adequate diet for that day. By using an arbitrary dividing point of 9.0, a "poor-diet" group of 247 and a "better-diet" group of 138 were designated. It was discovered that the better-diet group was absent significantly less during the year, had only half the dental deficiencies, and achieved slightly better in school. Of course, it is impossible to designate causal relationships on such evidence.

The interest developed in the children is of great significance. They all sought to improve their dietary habits. Science lessons con-

6 American Association of School Administrators, *Health In Schools,* Twentieth Yearbook (Washington: The Association, 1942), pp. 306-309.

7 Viola Everitt and Martha Potgieter, "Food Habits and Well-Being of School Children," *Elementary School Journal,* LII (February, 1952), 344-350.

8 Bureau of Human Nutrition and Home Economics, United States Department of Agriculture, Leaflet No. 288 (Washington: Government Printing Office, 1946).

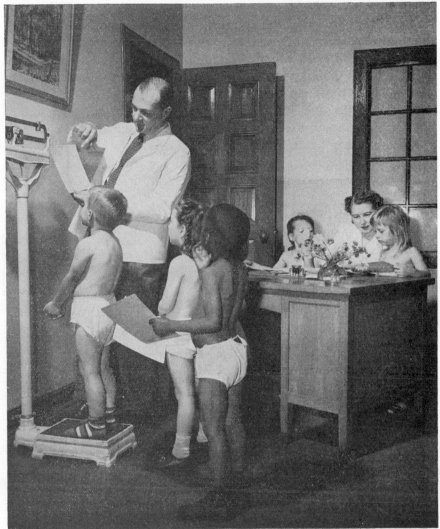

The University School, Ohio State University

HEALTH SERVICES ARE PART OF A SOUND PROGRAM IN HEALTH, PHYSICAL, AND RECREATION EDUCATION

centrated on food and nutrition, experiments with chicks were conducted, and various health projects were initiated. A second diet survey showed an improvement of 50 per cent in the average diet rating. Health knowledge, increased understanding, and healthful behavior were tied together in a meaningful way.

Maintaining a Healthful Physical Environment

In many schools over the country, youngsters read, write, or talk about good posture while sitting in desks that make practicing their lessons impossible. In others, youngsters strain to read blackboard charts outlining the structure of the human eye. There still are schools where boys and girls do daily calisthenics in dusty, ill-ventilated classrooms. An appallingly large number of our elementary schools fail to come up even to minimum standards of health and safety. Some are beset by neck-cricking drafts. Others are lighted only by single light bulbs dangling from the ceiling of each room. Still others have inadequate window surface, or dingy, faded blackboards.

The discrepancy between an unsuitable physical environment and the goals of learning becomes particularly apparent in teaching for the development of health knowledge, habits, and skills. Teachers and administrators everywhere must take stock of their environment and project plans for improvement.[9]

Using Existing Facilities

Nothing could be more inappropriate than a "book program" for the learning of health knowledge, habits, and skills. Centers for learning exist abundantly in and about the school. Lighting, ventilation, lavatory facilities, water supply, sewage disposal, upkeep of building, lunchroom sanitation, and heating are all centers for investigation within the school building. Outside the school building in the community are many other centers for the development of health knowledge, habits, and skills.

The idea that teachers and administrators should take stock of the learning environment has been repeated several times in this volume. In the area of health education, at least two broad questions should be asked: (1) In what ways may this environment be made compatible with the good health practices we are seeking to develop? (2) What resources exist in the school and community environment which may be utilized in creating positive learning experiences for boys and girls in the elementary school?

[9] Helpful guides to aid in this process include the following: Elementary Classroom Teacher Association and Elementary School Principals Association, *Self-Evaluation in the Elementary School,* Elementary School Bulletin No. 11 (Trenton: State of New Jersey Department of Education, 1946); Illinois Association of School Boards, *Characteristics of a Good School,* The School Board Reference Library, Pamphlet No. 7 (Springfield, Illinois: Illinois Association of School Boards, February, 1947); Southern Association's Cooperative Study in Elementary Education, *Evaluating the Elementary School* (Atlanta: Commission of Research and Service, 1951).

PROVIDING SCHOOL HEALTH SERVICES

Scope of School Health Services

The scope of school health services rendered will vary from place to place, not only according to local interest, but also according to the supplementary facilities available.

Take for example, the Hans Christian Andersen school at Askov, Minnesota. The story of what was done at this school in a small, rural community reads like a fairy tale, indeed.[10] At first, no dental facilities were available in the local community. Then, ideas began to take shape in a few kindred minds. A suite of rooms in the school was turned into a dental office, and a teeth-saving study for 300 school and pre-school children got underway. One phase of the study involved a thorough examination with X-ray and sodium fluoride treatment for children aged three, seven, ten, and thirteen. The second phase was dietary in nature. Initial motivation for the children was provided through the purchase of four white rats.[11] Two were fed on what was considered to be an optimum diet for humans; one on a typical Askov diet (mothers of Askov children are noted for being exceptionally fine pastry cooks); and one on soft drinks, candy, cookies, and cake. The first two thrived during the six-week period; the local stereotype began to look poorly; and the fourth barely survived the experiment. The children were impressed; and extensive study into the effects of the diets, especially on teeth, got underway. The third and fourth aspects of the four-way program were mental hygiene and dental care.

The ten-year study is still going on. Teachers, six dentists in Pine County, and interested citizens have found a way to have a top-flight dental program for boys and girls where no facilities previously existed.

Role of School in Providing Health Services

What should be provided in school health services? When does a school cease to become an educational institution and become involved in the field of medical care? The following list is proposed as a

10 Subsequent details are from an article by Netta W. Wilson, "A Four-Way Program in Dental Care," *Journal of the American Association for Health, Physical Education, and Recreation*, XXI (January, 1950), 13, 36-38.

11 Schools all over the country have found rats useful in nutrition studies. Literal-minded folks sometimes object to the validity of these studies on the grounds that diets will not necessarily affect children in the ways they affect rats. While this may or may not be true, it does not detract from the motivational value to be derived. If rat studies result in the children's increased interest in nutrition and improved dietary habits, then they serve their purpose.

suggestive guide in seeking answers to these questions. These are the characteristics of a well-planned health service:

1. Accumulation of health records from at least the time the child enters school. Communication with parents should provide the pre-school and perhaps pre-natal history.

2. Careful school observation of children by teachers. Teachers must be so well aware of the normal appearance of their children that they recognize abnormalities immediately.

3. Periodic, carefully-planned, physical examinations.

4. Consultation with parents about the results of physical examinations and about any irregularities noted through teacher observation. Conferences are recommended.

5. Consultation with parents regarding any school conditions likely to endanger the health or safety of their children.

6. First-aid treatment, and emergency medical and dental services. There are times when the first phone call must be to a physician and the second to the parent if a life is to be protected.

School Health Examinations for Children

Unless teachers really *see* their pupils, they fail to fulfill the major part of their function as school health observers. Casual observation may lead to more careful scrutiny when unusual appearance is noted. The formal morning inspection is of questionable value. Not only is it sometimes embarrassing to children, but in addition it frequently has the bad psychological effect of suggesting that the items checked are of no further concern for the rest of the day. Teachers should keep such matters as the following under careful observation: standing and sitting posture, skin color and blemishes, coughing, sneezing, and sniffling, what and how much is eaten, distance of book from the eyes, turning the head to hear, condition of eyes, changes of clothing, temper outbursts, crankiness, attitudes toward others, restlessness, moodiness, and so on. The teacher's job is to note unusual symptoms and to see that appropriate referral-type action is taken.

Formal health examinations have a real place in school life. Ideally, these are team projects involving child, parent, teacher, and various professionally trained personnel—physicians, public health nurses, dentists, dental hygienists, and psychologists. Some communities are learning that a teacher-nurse combination constitutes an effective screening team where the budget is limited, and a valuable supplement to periodic examinations by specialists (See Figure 2). The trend today is to have children immunized and examined by the family physician before entering school. A thorough examination is then given every three or four years with dental inspection occurring more frequently.[12] While professional services are likely to increase, the teacher must never abandon the role of constant observer of the health of school children.

Records and Reports

An integral part of any school health service program—or, for that matter, any health education program—is an adequate system of records and reports. A detailed health history record of the pre-school period should accompany the child into school. This should cover both the personal and family history of the child.[13] Essential data should then be recorded on a health record card that will accompany the child throughout his school life. Ideally, a health folder should be maintained for each child. It should contain not only this permanent record card, but also check lists for teacher observation, forms for recording the results of special examinations such as the dental survey, and notations concerning conferences or reports sent to the home. Sample forms are available in many places.[14]

One multi-purpose card proving itself useful is Wetzel's grid.[15] It is designed to appraise a child's height-weight relationship according to his body type, rather than on the basis of norms derived from the general population. Other useful devices are available from the National Education Association and the American Medical Association. These growth charts can do nothing about what they reveal. They merely expedite the job of teacher, parent, nurse, and doctor in identifying growth problems.

HEALTH, PHYSICAL EDUCATION, AND RECREATION IN THE CURRICULUM

Health knowledge, health skills, health values, can be justified only through their tested relationship to the maturation and continued healthful existence of human beings. This statement implies that

12 George M. Wheatley and Grace T. Hallock, *Health Observation of School Children* (New York: McGraw-Hill Book Co., Inc., 1951), p. 11.

13 For a list of items to be covered, see American Association of School Administrators, *op. cit.*, p. 3.

14 See for example, Fred C. Ayer, *Practical Child Accounting* (Austin, Texas: The Steck Co., 1949), p. 61; American Association of School Administrators, *op. cit.*, pp. 30-31, 43, 46; Delbert Oberteuffer, *School Health Education* (New York: Harper & Brothers, 1949), pp. 219-222.

15 "Grid for Evaluating Physical Fitness in Terms of Physique (Body Build), Developmental Level, and Basal Metabolism." The grid is published by NEA Service, Inc., 1200 W. 3rd St., Cleveland, Ohio.

elementary-school health programs should be oriented closely around the real life concerns of boys and girls. It is essential, then, that the teacher know what these concerns are.[16]

Strang and Smiley propose that the child should have learned the following by the time he leaves the public school:

1. To keep himself healthy and clean.
2. To protect others from colds and other communicable diseases.
3. To render first aid in case of illness or accident.
4. To be able to care for the sick, prepare wholesome food for the family, and take care of infants and small children.
5. To obtain the best medical and dental care that he can.
6. To value social health measures, including health insurance and hospital service plans.
7. To appreciate the history of health progress and to keep in touch with new discoveries that are being made.[17]

The teacher will be prepared to deal with these proposed outcomes when he is well-informed about the following:[18]

1. The social, economic, and cultural background of the community and of the child.
2. Health conditions peculiar to the local environment.
3. Facilities for the prevention and treatment of illness in the community.
4. The individual health condition of each child.
5. The daily behavior of each child.
6. Expressions of health interest and concern on the part of children, parents, and fellow teachers.
7. Tests of health knowledge, and attitudes and results derived from their use.

Physical Activities in the Grades

The Need for a Planned Program. The fifth-grade teacher, arms folded, stood at the top of the bank that sloped to the playing field. Below her, twenty boys charged up and down the field involved in a game that had the ear-marks of soccer but was contaminated somewhat by both basketball and football. A lusty kick sent the ball to one end of the field, followed by the yelling horde. Another stalwart foot

[16] See Denver Public Schools, *Health Interest of Children* (Denver, Colorado, 1947).
[17] Ruth M. Strang and Dean F. Smiley, *The Role of the Teacher in Health Education* (New York: The Macmillan Company, 1941), p. 93.
[18] Adapted and expanded from American Association of School Administrators, *op. cit.*, p. 62.

promptly sent the ball sailing in the opposite direction. The on-rushers skidded to a stop, wheeled, and were off again. And so it went on—the long kick and the mad rush.

"When do the other rooms get their recess?" inquired a visitor.

"Oh, we all have recess at the same time. But this isn't recess. This is our physical education period. I like to spend it this way. Boys and girls this age like free play, you know!"

Yes, boys and girls like "free" play. But this travesty scarcely could be described as free play. Free play involves freedom of choice. Furthermore, it brings with it a set of ground rules developed by the group, especially with youngsters of this age. And it prefers to do without the observation of non-participating adults. There is no place for the disinterested teacher-spectator in today's schools.

> Let us remember that guidance of immature learners by more mature teachers is one of the distinctive marks of an educational enterprise. Physical education is not a free play period during which children are turned loose on a playground.[19]

Basically, physical activities are directed towards health improvement and maintenance. But, whereas health is a means to the attainment of other ends, physical activities may be carried on as ends in themselves.[20] The physical education and recreation aspects of the total health program contribute significantly to the several goals of that program. They have been found particularly useful in:

1. Developing basic motor skills used not only in recreational life, but also in carrying on normal life processes.

2. Providing young people with knowledge of and proficiency in recreational activities for both present and later living.

3. Encouraging the development of desirable moral values, respect for the rights and privileges of others, and skill in associating with other people.

4. Providing the enjoyment and satisfaction that come from pleasurable creative and aesthetic activity.

Developing Basic Motor Skills Through Physical Activities. Basic motor skills used in normal life processes include walking, running, hopping, skipping, jumping, and leaping. Skills to be applied in all sorts of games are catching, throwing, kicking, volleying, serving, and

---

19 Department of Rural Education and American Association for Health, Physical Education, and Recreation, *Physical Education in Small Schools* (Washington: National Education Association, 1948), pp. 11.

20 Helen Fahey, "Physical Education in the Program," *Childhood Education,* XXIX (April, 1953), 379.

bowling.[21] Boys and girls of the intermediate grades show a remarkable readiness for perfecting these skills. The rapid-growth period of early childhood is completed for almost all of them; the early adolescent growth spurt is not yet begun. Growth is proceeding at a steady pace that permits integration and refinement in development. The gang spirit then dominant lends itself well to application of skill in group games. Coupled with these favorable elements is a strong personal drive during the late childhood period to exceed one's own previous performance. Three or four ten-year-olds will spend free hours each day trying to exceed the height of the best jump of the previous day. Practice in distance running, in throwing for distance and accuracy, in broad-jumping, in batting, in pitching, alternate with one another. Usually one form of activity will predominate for several weeks within one gang, only to be replaced with another, carried on with equal intensity.

The kind of teacher-assistance that yields observable results stems from knowledge and judgment in at least the following three areas:

1. Knowledge of correct form or varieties of correct form in the specific skill being taught.

2. Legitimate expectancy in, and concern for, the development of the skill in each child.

3. Effective teaching procedures in guiding learning of the skill.[22]

Jones, Morgan, and Stevens suggest the following teaching procedures in developing skills:

1. Know what is to be taught and what standards of performance are to be emphasized.

2. Attempt to find among the group a child who naturally performs or approximates the skill to be taught.

3. Guide the class in evaluating the elements of correct form displayed by the skillful performer, and establish the standards of achievement toward which all may strive.

4. Permit everyone to attempt the new skill. Allow sufficient time and space for practice, so that some success, no matter how limited, may be achieved by everyone.

5. Evaluate the achievement that has been made during the lesson by considering the individual's own progress commensurate with his ability, and by restating the goals toward which the group may continue to strive in the next practice period.

6. When progress of the class is increasingly manifest, apply the skill in more complex situations such as in games and rhythmic activities.

[21] See Edwina Jones, Edna Morgan, and Gladys Stevens, *Methods and Materials in Elementary Physical Education* (Yonkers, N.Y.: World Book Co., 1950), p. 22.
[22] *Ibid.*, p. 20.

7. Avoid drudgery, praise honest efforts, and encourage the individual. Provide enjoyment for the children by offering a variety of related activities.[23]

Developing Moral Values Through Games. Teamwork is applied democracy. Performance is enhanced in relation not only to individual improvement, but also in relation to group improvement in pulling together. Group games provide boys and girls with an opportunity to test fundamental human values for themselves. They are able to *perceive* the relationship between ends and means. It is in clarifying this relationship that insightful leadership yields rich returns. What is our goal? Is it to win? If it is, then learning how to push, to pull, and to trip at the right moment so as not to be seen may be appropriate activity for the attainment of that goal. Is it to win under certain conditions? If it is, then these activities are no longer appropriate. But, also, if it is, then reward is possible only when a victory is won. Learning that occurs when boys and girls are guided in selecting the values by which their behavior will be governed, and in weighing the consequences of observing or violating these values, is learning that persists. The physical activities carried on by boys and girls of elementary school age are rich in potentialities for teaching moral and spiritual values.[24]

Competitive Athletics in the Elementary Schools. Teamwork implies teams, and teams suggest competition. The matter of athletic competition for boys and girls of elementary-school age is one that is much disputed. The protagonists for such competition claim values in enhancing the ego of shy individuals, developing group loyalties, providing wholesome emotional outlets, and giving incentive for body development. The antagonists point to the danger of over-exhaustion, the development of a disproportionate value system, manipulation of young people for ends that are not their own, and many others.[25] A reasonable position to take is that under certain carefully controlled conditions, a limited amount of competitive athletic activity among elementary school boys and girls may yield

23 *Ibid.,* pp. 35-36. See also pages 25, 30, and 33 for suggestions in teaching throwing, jumping, and running. Pages 44 to 50 list helpful activities for developing fundamental skills. See also pages 51 to 60 for self-testing activities, 61 to 76 for stunt suggestions, 94 to 130 for games, and 209 to 224 for recreational games that are both passive and active in nature.

24 At this point the reader will find it well worth his while to refer to the publication of the Educational Policies Commission, *Moral and Spiritual Values in the Public Schools* (Washington: National Education Association, 1951).

25 For an analysis of several arguments, see Eldon D. Brinley, "Interschool Athletics for Elementary School Youngsters," *Journal of School Health,* XXXIII (September, 1953), 209-215.

worthwhile returns. Similarly, under poorly controlled conditions, competition in athletics may be carried to excess, and gravely endanger the well-being of boys and girls.

The question of whether or not competitive athletics are or are not beneficial for elementary school children probably cannot be answered in the absolute.[26] There are many variables. Perhaps the problem is taken care of when educational workers seek intelligent answers to the following questions:

1. What kind of recreational program best facilitates the motor skill development, social development, physical well-being, and personal satisfaction of ALL children?

2. What background of training and experience must educational workers have had if they are to provide effective leadership for such a program?

3. What do growth characteristics of certain age groups suggest for group and individual play?

4. What do growth characteristics of certain age groups suggest for precautions against physical strain?[27]

5. To what degree is competition a natural outgrowth of the activity itself and of the present development of boys and girls?

6. To what degree will competition promote or impede attainment of the educational values sought in the program?

7. To what degree do goals, activities, and outcomes reflect constantly the welfare of boys and girls, rather than the selfish ends of adults?

Developing the Creative and Aesthetic Through Rhythms. Suggest to a group of five-year-olds that they listen carefully to a recording and then respond to what they hear with body movements. Some listen to the music intently, begin to respond to it, and then move about the room becoming more and more free in their movements as the idea begins to take hold and as joy in expression increases. Others pay very little attention, gazing abstractly about the room. Ultimately, they may get up to imitate others but their movements are haphazard and uncoordinated. Perhaps the music is meaningless to them. Perhaps the music suggests no specific physical responses to

[26] For a penetrating analysis of the problem, see Report of the Joint Committee on Athletic Competition for Children of Elementary and Junior High School Age, *Desirable Athletic Competition for Children* (Washington: American Association for Health, Physical Education, and Recreation, 1952).

[27] For standards on physical fitness of boys for athletic competition, see "Report of Committees on Standards of Physical Fitness for Students Who Engage in Competitive Athletics," *Journal of School Health,* VIII, No. 3 (March, 1943), 57. For girls, see *ibid.,* p. 83.

University of Wisconsin Summer Laboratory School

ALL ABOARD FOR EUROPE

it. Readiness both to hear rhythm and to respond to it are dependent upon physical, mental, social, and emotional growth.

The principle of individual differences is very evident in children's responses to rhythmic impulses. No two individuals will sense the rhythm nor express it in the same manner. It is therefore important that no child will be hurried into some form of response before he has had adequate opportunity to develop an awareness of the rhythmic elements involved.

Thought and feeling must precede physical expression. For this reason the child must be given ample opportunity to listen quietly to the accompaniment until its message is translated into the urge to respond through muscular action. The resultant physical activity will more likely be a vital creative expression embodying not only bodily response but a satisfying emotional and mental reaction as well.[28]

Creative teaching recognizes in rhythmic activities far more than response to metre alone. Children quickly catch and interpret the mood of what they hear. They become responsive to harmony and melody. Consequently, a wide range of accompaniment must be provided. Percussion instruments are excellent for establishing the basic beat. The piano is helpful because of its versatility in stimulating response to metre and mood. For teachers who want carefully selected materials, excellent recordings are available.[29] Teaching

[28] Jones, Morgan, and Stevens, *op. cit.*, p. 132.
[29] For example, "Rainbow Rhythms," prepared by Nora Belle Emerson and T. E. McDonough. These may be ordered through P. O. Box 608, Emory University, Georgia.

methods and materials must encourage, not stifle, creativity and spontaneity. A period each day of mimetics, folk games, or dancing, depending upon the age and interests of the children, will provide a refreshing and satisfying phase of the daily program.

Physical Activities and Child Development. The publication of the National Education Association, *Physical Education in Small Schools,* does such a fine job of relating physical activities to growth characteristics that several pages of it are reproduced here.[30] The outline below should serve as a useful guide in planning the physical education and recreation curriculum for the complete scope of the elementary school. The original list has been cut in the interests of conserving space.

CHARACTERISTICS AND NEEDS OF CHILDREN

PRIMARY GRADES

Characteristics	*Needs*
1. Hunger for constant physical action.	1. Activities which encourage running, jumping, pushing, pulling, hanging, climbing, throwing, catching, striking, kicking, carrying, and so on.
2. Relatively slow development of the small muscles.	2. Activities requiring, first, whole-body movement; gradually introducing skills demanding eye-hand, hand-foot, and other coordinations.
3. Fatigue easily.	3. Short active play and relaxation periods, to maintain interest and avoid mental and physical fatigue. Frequent rest periods or changes of activity. Periods of "sitting still" (a strain to young children) should be short, and interspersed with periods of muscular activity.
4. Interest in activities requiring energy and motion, often of a noisy nature; love of chasing and being chased.	4. Chasing games in which free shouting is allowed; rhythmic activities, free construction and handwork periods.
5. Curiosity keen; like to investigate.	5. Creative activities.
6. Interest in rhythmic activities.	6. Rhythms to music, to songs, to percussion, to verse, and so on.

MIDDLE GRADES

Characteristics	*Needs*
1. Rapidly developing motor coordination.	1. Games, creative and folk dancing, stunts, self-testing and other activities developing increasing skills of wide variety. "Lead-up" games valuable.
2. Bodily growth and proportions change slowly.	2. Skills and tests of strength should be developed gradually, activities being adjusted to individual capacities.

30 *Op. cit.,* pp. 15-20.

3. Variations in size, weight, and coordination among individuals.

4. Antagonism to opposite sex, especially among boys, often present.

5. Interest in adventure and in the fantastic.

3. Classification of pupils on basis of capacity, without embarrassing those individuals who are less mature physically.

4. Girls' and boys' activities organized separately for some activities.

5. Play-writing and dramatization, puppetry, active and dramatic games, self-testing activities suited to the interests of the group.

UPPER GRADES

Characteristics

1. Rapid physical growth, often uneven in various proportions of the body, with resultant awkwardness and lack of coordination. Individuals vary widely in development.

2. Susceptibility to fatigue.

3. Increasing power of attention and interest in problem-solving challenges.

4. Emotions strong and not well under control.

5. Loyalty to gangs, clubs, and teams; strong desire to "belong."

6. Desire for excitement and adventure.

Needs

1. A program allowing for grouping of individuals in various ways for different types of activities, according to interest, capacities, and degree of coordinated skills. Care should be taken in all aspects of the program not to expose individuals who are clumsy and inept at certain activities to the ridicule of their classmates.

2. Although interest and attention can be more sustained than in lower grades, activities should not be too long continued. Periods may be longer, but activities should be varied between the active and the more restful types.

3. Games and other activities involving mental, as well as physical, skills are appropriate for this age group. "Lead-up" games of a higher type of organization, and quiet indoor games such as checkers, anagrams, card games, and others may be introduced. "Carry-over" activities—those which may be used profitably for recreation in adult life —are desirable parts of the upper-grade program.

4. Competitive games may arouse rivalry and even personal antagonisms. Every effort should be made to build standards of fair play, and of being a "good loser" and "a generous winner."

5. Team games are popular at this level and may be used frequently, but they should be safeguarded by changing the personnel of teams often, in order to avoid emotional clashes and to prevent the child who is not well socialized from being ostracized by a "closed" grouping.

6. Original dramatics and puppet plays, for both boys and girls, may offer much to satisfy this desire, if subjects and incidents are well chosen. Certain team games and individual stunts and contests are also valuable, if competition is keen but friendly.

Education for Safe Living

An educational program designed with safe living in mind promotes wholesome human values. In developing such a program, at least three kinds of values must be considered:

1. The legal and ethical aspects of the public school's responsibility for the children entrusted to it. Teachers and principals in the elementary school must demonstrate their regard for this trust to the degree that they become thoroughly familiar with legal provisions governing children's welfare and act within the framework of this knowledge.

2. Faculty concern for safety provisions. These provisions include removing plant conditions that threaten pupil safety, planning appropriate fire precautions, supplying safe athletic equipment, and assuring supervision at dangerous street-crossings.[31]

3. Pupil concern for one another. Development of consideration for others should not be left to chance. Teachers should plan for opportunities to bring appropriate pupil behavior above the level of "polite manners" to the level of reasoning and conscious performance. Why not push someone's face into the drinking fountain? Why not push three at a time through doorways? Not because the teacher says, "Don't!" but because harmless fun for all suddenly may become tragedy for all.

Understanding and Skill Are Developed in Programs of Safety Education

Concern for the safety and well-being of others is a thoughtful process. It may not always be brought about through direct experience. We can scarcely afford to let a child find out that moving automobiles are dangerous by having him run in front of one. But we are too content with talking in this area of safety, with telling what to do and then admonishing when practice defies our words. From their early years, children must be helped to understand the *why* of safe behavior and so guided in their practice of it that it becomes an integral part of their being.

Upon entrance to school, children should be led carefully over the school plant. Emergency alarm signals should be identified and explained. Procedures for entering and leaving buildings should be discussed and practiced. Older children should talk about their re-

---

[31] William C. Reavis, Paul R. Pierce, Edward H. Stullken, and Bertrand L. Smith, *Administering the Elementary School* (Englewood Cliffs, N.J.: Prentice-Hall, Inc., 1953), pp. 344-345.

sponsibilities to little children and then be guided into activities that call for demonstration. Understanding of the problem and individual skill in performance must go hand in hand. The curriculum must provide for both.

Education for Mental Well-Being

Every phase of our daily living affects, and is in turn affected by, our mental health. Obviously, then, school practices such as marking, reporting, and promoting; teacher attitudes towards children's values; the importance of learning to read; and infractions of school rules, profoundly influence mental health.

Understanding Pupil Behavior. People want to be understood and accepted by others. They want to be sure that their presence has a positive effect on this world and at least a few of its inhabitants. They want to love and be loved. They want to be able to do some of the things that gain the approval of others. And yet, children and adults alike frequently act as though they had no need for others and others had no need for them.

Actions frequently spring from physical appearance. Appearance is a dominant factor in determining peer-group popularity of pre-adolescent girls. Size often enters into one's feeling of adequacy. Glandular conditions that produce obesity or apparent laziness lie in back of much schoolroom listlessness. Personal skills or other physical characteristics that have been commercially exploited frequently produce a disproportionate sense of self-importance. Illness and accidents sometimes produce overdependence upon others, or an unwholesome "martyr-complex."

Children bring with them to school much of what they experience at home. Knowledge of high parental expectancy can create vicious pressures for school accomplishments. Homes broken by divorce or crippled by parental conflict are rich soil for rebellion and delinquency.

Frequently, disturbed children are unhappy because of major forces that seem so unjust. Membership in a minority group, growing up on the wrong side of the tracks, continually tearing apart friendship patterns to move with the family . . . these and many more environmental factors can be destructive influences in the lives of young children.[32]

32 For a detailed discussion of these and other causal patterns, see Fritz Redl and William W. Wattenberg, *Mental Hygiene in Teaching* (New York: Harcourt, Brace, and Co., 1951), pp. 116-145.

Teachers who understand children are in an advantageous position for helping children. Basic, then, to the mental health of children is an elementary school program designed to seek and use information about children in every activity designed for children.

We believe . . . that teachers who understand children think of behavior as being caused. They see a youngster's present actions as based upon his past experiences, as shaped by his present situation, and as influenced by his desires and hopes for the future. This view of human behavior holds that a child's actions can be understood if his relevant past experience is known, and if his desires and hopes for the future are taken into consideration. It also implies that every girl and boy is educable, that unacceptable behavior can be changed, and that desirable and effective action can be evoked.[33]

Providing a Wholesome Learning Environment. A wholesome learning environment operates within a framework that provides control and direction for the activities carried on within it. A framework too narrowly defined, or imposed arbitrarily from without, tends to restrict and limit progress towards self-discipline, a major goal of mental hygiene.[34] The inability of individuals to confine themselves to these limits frequently leads to rebellion. Rebellion fosters further impositions from without and, as the cycle progresses, further rebellion. The end product seldom is increased self-control.[35] A framework too losely defined, or not defined at all, fails to provide the security essential to good mental health. In the words of Redl and Wattenberg:

Beyond the days of infancy, restrictions are a part of living. Some are obviously necessary in school. Children are not injured by knowing what adults expect them to do and what their friends demand of them. In fact, within limits such realizations make for psychological health. It is as unpleasant to have grownups ignore you as to have them nag you all the time. A teacher who would let children do everything they wanted would leave them every bit as unhappy as one who had a rule for everything.[36]

Children in the elementary school must be given the opportunity to define the framework that will govern their classroom behavior and *be guided in the use of that opportunity.* They must be given

[33] Commission on Teacher Education, *Helping Teachers Understand Children* (Washington: American Council on Education, 1945), p. 8.

[34] See Percival M. Symonds, "Is Frustration Compatible with Good Mental Hygiene?" *Progressive Education*, XXX (February, 1953), 107-110.

[35] See Ronald Lippitt, "An Experimental Study of the Effect of Democratic and Authoritarian Group Atmosphere," *University of Iowa Studies of Child Welfare*, Vol. 16, 1940, 43-195.

[36] *Ibid.*, p. 321.

the opportunity to decide according to their present level of maturity. Providing a wholesome learning environment in the elementary school demands certain faculty agreements concerning the over-all framework of pupil control, as well as certain individual adjustments suggested by teacher and pupil personalities in the classroom.

Guidance in Problem-Solving. It is the nature of human beings to have problems. An individual's mental health is heavily dependent upon the adequacy of his solutions to personal problems. Many schoolroom problems are artificial to children. Frequently the real problems that the child brings with him to school and the imposed problems of the classroom clash to the degree that neither set is resolved. To do away with these schoolroom problems on the grounds that they are not real to the child is not the solution. Artificial though these problems may appear, the child needs to solve them satisfactorily in the process of growing up. A more logical approach appears to be to make a careful attack upon the problems of greatest reality to the child—problems that block normal learning in school.

The use of music, graphic art, and psychodrama, in the process of bringing deep-seated problems to a level of self-recognition and verbalization has been discussed elsewhere. (See Chapter 12.) Equally important are certain more direct counselling approaches. Evident interest in children and their problems, together with a reputation for respecting confidences, have put many teachers in guidance situations demanding the utmost skill in directive and non-directive counselling. Bullis advocates a direct attack on the personal problems of pupils, thus lifting the guidance function of the elementary school teacher to more than an incidental level.[37] Children are led to examine incidents involving human relationships, to read stories containing similar incidents, and then to relate these activities to people in their own lives. Gradually children come to volunteer their own feelings under typical conditions. They come to recognize the frequency with which other children experience feelings similar to their own, and to recognize that their problems are not unique.

The Effects of Teachers' Health

It is commonly accepted that the health of the teacher affects his attitudes and abilities; that his health directly affects the health of children; and that living and learning in the classroom are conditioned accordingly. It is obvious, then, that maintenance of sound

[37] H. Edmund Bullis and Emily E. O'Malley, *Human Relations in the Classroom* (Wilmington, Del.: The Delaware State Society for Mental Hygiene, 1947).

physical and mental health among teachers is an essential ingredient in program development.

Early studies by Hicks[38] and by Peck[39] revealed that about one teacher in six is concerned excessively over such maladjustment difficulties as irritability, chronic low spirits, extreme shyness, uncontrolled temper, and excitability. Bronson[40] reported 35 per cent of 51 teachers studied were emotionally maladjusted. The problem is not one of comparing the mental health difficulties of teachers with health problems of other vocational groups. It is, rather, one of maladjusted teachers being entrusted with the molding of young lives. ". . . the possibility is always present that the child in association with the emotionally maladjusted adult will acquire similar habits."[41]

Discussion of the health of elementary school teachers becomes truly meaningful when directed towards determining the relationship between the teacher and the quality of classroom living. One approach to protecting children's health is to keep teachers who have physical or mental difficulties from entering the classroom, provided we are reasonably sure of the way teacher characteristics affect classroom learning. But even after careful screening of persons considered ill-suited for teaching, we have little assurance that the conditions of teaching itself will not induce later teacher ill health. Kvaraceus reports, for instance, the hazard to mental health of a host of complex interpersonal relationships arising directly out of the teaching position and the ineptitude of some personnel in getting along with others.[42]

Children themselves appreciate teachers who provide an environment that offers security, individual success, and opportunities for personal and social adjustment.[43] The teacher as a person is a vital element of that environment.

[38] Frances R. Hicks, "The Mental Health of Teachers." Unpublished Doctoral dissertation, George Peabody College for Teachers, 1934.

[39] Leigh Peck, "A Study of the Adjustment Difficulties of a Group of Women Teachers," Journal of Educational Psychology, XXVII (September, 1936), 401-416.

[40] John A. Bronson, "Problem Teachers," Educational Administration and Supervision, XXIX (March, 1943), 177-182.

[41] Robert F. Topp, "Are Your Children 'Catching' Your Emotional Ills?" Wisconsin Journal of Education, LXXXV (December, 1952), 3-4.
In this connection see the early research of Paul L. Boynton, Harriet Duggar, and Masal Turner, "Emotional Stability of Pupils and Teachers," Journal of Juvenile Research, XXVII (October, 1934), 22-32.

[42] W. C. Kvaraceus, "Mental Health Hazards Facing Teachers," Phi Delta Kappan, XXXII (April, 1951), 349.

[43] Paul Witty, "An Analysis of the Personality Traits of the Effective Teacher," Journal of Educational Research, XL (May, 1947), 662-671.

Evaluating the Total Program—a Summary Statement

In summary, the total program in health, physical education, and recreation may be evaluated according to the presence of the following characteristics:

1. The school's commitment to healthful behavior is expressed in a succession of carefully planned activities embracing all children enrolled in it.

2. The school's resources serve to enrich the services of other agencies committed to health through a cooperative framework which has the child as its center.

3. All school activities are conducted in an environment conducive to physical and mental well-being.

4. Children learn health habits and principles through opportunities to practice, rather than merely reading or talking about healthful behavior.

5. School records provide a health history of each child that is accessible, understandable to parents and teachers, and of use both now and later in determining the adequacy or normality of essential growth patterns.

6. Physical activities are related meaningfully to the growth characteristics and interests of children at successive ages.

7. Time allotments are flexible, and needed supplies and equipment are available in line with this flexibility.

8. Supervisory and other special personnel place the general welfare of children above their various specialties, and are available in line with teacher and pupil needs rather than for administrative convenience.

9. All available resources are organized into an in-service program designed to provide personal skills and insights needed for carrying on an effective program.[44]

BIBLIOGRAPHY

American Association for Health, Physical Education, and Recreation, *Children in Focus*. Washington: The Association, 1954.

American Association for Health, Physical Education, and Recreation, *Developing Democratic Human Relations Through Health Education, Physical Education and Recreation*. Washington: The Association, 1951.

[44] For a list of characteristics of good programs in the various special fields of the elementary school, see Harold G. Shane and E. T. McSwain, *Evaluation and the Elementary Curriculum* (New York: Henry Holt and Co., 1951), pp. 277-278.

American Association of Colleges for Teacher Education, *Health Needs of School Children.* Oneonta, New York: The Association, 1954.

Andrews, Gladys E., *Creative Rhythmic Movement for Children.* Englewood Cliffs, N.J.: Prentice-Hall, Inc., 1954.

Bauer, Lois M., and Barbara A. Reed, *Dance and Play Activities for the Elementary Grades.* New York: Chartwell House, Inc., 1951.

Bernard, Harold W., *Mental Hygiene in the Classroom.* New York: McGraw-Hill Book Co., 1952.

Cowell, Charles C., and Helen W. Hazelton, *Curriculum Designs in Physical Education.* Englewood Cliffs, N.J.: Prentice-Hall, Inc., 1955.

Denver Public Schools, *Health Interests of Children.* Denver: School District Number One in the City and County of Denver and State of Colorado, 1947.

Department of Elementary School Principals, *Health in the Elementary School,* Twenty-Ninth Yearbook. Washington: National Education Association, 1950.

Department of Rural Education and American Association for Health, Physical Education, and Recreation, *Physical Education in Small Schools,* Elsa Schneider, ed. Washington: National Education Association, 1948.

Irwin, L. W., and J. H. Humphrey, *Principles and Techniques of Supervision in Physical Education.* St. Louis: C. V. Mosby Co., 1954.

Jones, Edwina, Edna Morgan, and Gladys Stevens, *Methods and Materials in Elementary Physical Education.* Yonkers: World Book Co., 1950.

McNeely, Simon A., and Elsa Schneider, *Physical Education in the School Child's Day.* Washington: Office of Education, Federal Security Agency, 1950.

National Conference on Physical Education for Children of Elementary School Age and the Athletic Institute, *Physical Education for Children of Elementary School Age.* Chicago: The Athletic Institute, 1951.

National Institute of Mental Health, *The Teacher and Mental Health.* Public Health Service Publication, No. 385. Washington: Government Printing Office, 1954.

National Society for the Study of Education, *Mental Health in Modern Education.* Chicago: University of Chicago Press, 1955.

Neilson, N. P., and Winifred Van Hagen, *Physical Education for Elementary Schools,* rev. ed. New York: A. S. Barnes and Co., 1954.

Oberteuffer, Delbert, *School Health Education.* New York: Harper and Bros., 1949.

Redl, Fritz, and William W. Wattenberg, *Mental Hygiene in Teaching.* New York: Harcourt, Brace, and Co., 1951.

Schlesinger, Edward R., *Health Services for the Child.* New York: McGraw-Hill Book Co., 1953.

Vannier, Maryhelen, and Mildred Foster, *Teaching Physical Education in Elementary Schools.* Philadelphia: W. B. Saunders Co., 1954.

Wheatley, George M., and Grace T. Hallock, *Health Observation of School Children.* New York: McGraw-Hill Book Co., Inc., 1951.

THE ARTS
IN THE
ELEMENTARY
SCHOOL

12

THE CHILD'S SCHOOL LIFE SHOULD BE CONDUCTED in an atmosphere rich in art in all its forms. How often do your children translate their feelings about Hallowe'en, Christmas, and Easter into dance form? How often do they say, "Let's draw what we feel," or "What would the giant's voice sound like on the piano?" Do they look for design in buildings, in snowflakes, in flower petals? How often do you read them a poem that captures the mood of a lazy spring afternoon? Too often, children are denied opportunities because we fail to grasp the potential of art form in improving the learning environment.

We are only beginning to see some of the ways

in which art in its many forms may be used as catharsis and therapy in the lives of children. Teachers in the kindergarten and primary grades are well aware of the power of music to soothe a restless or excited group. Handicrafts are playing a significant role in therapy programs for persons suffering from mental and physical exhaustion. There is some evidence to suggest that eliciting response to rhythmic stimuli provides an avenue to educational rehabilitation of spastic children. The next decade should provide some exciting insights into song, dance, finger paint, and ceramics, as liberating influences in the lives of boys and girls.

The Role Defined

A forward-looking program of appreciative and creative arts in the elementary school is designed:

1. To help the child find bases for understanding and appreciating art and art forms to provide deep satisfactions not only for the present but throughout a lifetime.

2. To help the child gain confidence in and satisfaction from such activities as singing, dancing, modelling, painting, writing, listening, and building.

3. To help the child find personally and socially appropriate outlets for tensions and creative urges.

4. To provide an environment conducive to the development of unusual artistic interest and aptitude.

5. To provide bases for the interpretive observation of child development.

6. To assist the child in his never-ending struggle to understand and cope with the complex environments and cultures that surround him, no matter how modest his contribution or how simple his way of life may be.

THE ARTS CURRICULUM

One goal of the elementary school is to develop confidence and satisfaction in and from the arts. We see children, therefore, becoming comfortable with a wide range of art forms. They draw, paint, build, listen, create rhythmic sounds and rhyming words, tell stories, model with clay, dance, sing, act, and mimic.

Another goal is to develop appreciation for, and understanding of, the outstanding creations of others. We visualize children examining great paintings, listening to symphonies, observing talented dancers, and attending concerts of many types.

The tendency to neglect the vast background of art in creative teaching has not only deprived the child of a wealth of pleasure but has limited his creative experience to his own efforts. Some art educators claim that the use of professional art, especially in the elementary grades, endangers the child's creativeness, but it must be a fragile kind of learning that is so easily corrupted.[1]

Still another purpose is to provide opportunity to reduce tension. We see teachers, then, building up a collection of records. Later, at specific moments, the age of the group, previous experiences of the children, and the prevailing mood, will enter into the teacher's selection of a record from this library.

Record players (equipped with earphones for individual listening), specially selected books, glee clubs, orchestras, choral groups, and even school radio stations (Elgin, Illinois, for example), do much to foster unusual abilities. Emphasis is put upon creating the environment in which talent may flourish, not upon selecting "events" for the gifted. Any special provisions constitute extension of, rather than substitution for, a program in creative-appreciative arts designed for all children.

Activities must be selected, too, for developing what might be called "interpretive" behavior. Their purposes are to develop the ability to see the order that exists about us, to identify harmony in nature, and to perceive beauty as value. Children need time for, and encouragement in, the reflective processes of interpreting the meaning of music, relating art forms to life around them, and exploring the meaning of life through poetic interpretation.

Using conventional classifications, it may be seen that the arts curriculum of the elementary school includes music, graphic and plastic arts, the dance, creative writing, literature, and drama in its various forms. In selecting specific learning activities, we give children opportunity to practice artistic skills deemed desirable, to identify and test basic values, and to deal with underlying concepts and understandings in the arts.

Organizing for Instruction

In organizing for instruction in the arts, two basic questions must be answered: (1) What underlying elements in the arts program may be identified to facilitate what is being done in the classroom today, building upon what has gone before, and laying the foundation for

[1] Victor D'Amico, "Creative Expression: A Discipline for Democracy," *Child Study,* XXIX (Fall, 1952), 11.

what is to come? (2) What centers may be identified for the organization of day-to-day classroom instruction?

Scope and Sequence. In partial response to the first question, it is possible to lay out the length and breadth of the arts program through an analysis of subject matter deemed appropriate for elementary school children. In graphic art, content includes color harmony, elements of design (compositional balance and unity), brush skills, and paint mixing. In creative writing, consideration is given to sentence structure, word meaning, expressive phrasing, and so on. Each subject area may be broken down into the elements of which it is composed.

These elements may then be arranged in some sort of internal order and relationship to one another. We may try, for example, to arrange them in order of difficulty. Selection of a topic, such as Ren-

University of Wisconsin Summer Laboratory School

GRACE AND COORDINATION ARE BY-PRODUCTS OF THE DANCE

aissance Art, is one way in which several basic ingredients of art as subject matter may be brought together for art as learning experience. The length and breadth of the arts program in the elementary school might be selected around a series of such topics—each drawn from the single field of art, and each carefully arranged through the grades so that, supposedly, the child will move from less to more difficult tasks and concepts.

At a more complex level, themes representing many elements drawn from several subject areas, and the many possible interrelationships of these elements, might be selected as organizing bases for the curriculum. In a theme such as "Man's Struggle for Freedom in the Present Century," for example, art and music disappear as separate subjects; but basic concepts in these fields are necessary for complete understanding of the main theme.

Although this kind of organization is important, we should not make a fetish out of it. Completely spontaneous opportunities for singing or dancing or play-acting should not be passed up simply because they do not fit into the "master" curricular plan. Likewise, purely routine but related activities, such as drawing pyramids when studying "Life Along the Nile" should be strictly avoided if no "feeling base" for expression has been developed.[2] Lowenfeld claims that such activities actually inhibit creativity and that the time used for them is more than time wasted; it is time spent in inculcating negative art attitudes and values.[3]

In recognition of the fact that learning organized around subject topics, units, and themes is frequently unrelated to the interests and maturity of the learners, some school people prefer to begin with the children, rather than the subject, as the organizing center. Neither approach can operate to the exclusion of the other. The initial focus may differ; but ultimately child and subject matter must be brought into harmonious relationship. With his eye on children, Gaitskell identified a sequence of developmental levels in painting derived from experimentation with thousands of pupils. From making scribbles, children move successively through the stages of naming scribbles, painting "me," painting "me" with others, and so on.[4] Lowenfeld also identified developmental levels in children's art

2 See Charles D. Gaitskell, *Art and Crafts in Our Schools* (Toronto, Canada: The Ryerson Press, 1949), p. 24.

3 Address by Viktor Lowenfeld at the Annual Teacher Education Conference of the Georgia Teacher Education Council, Athens, Georgia (January, 1951).

4 Charles D. Gaitskell, *Children and Their Pictures* (Toronto, Canada: The Ryerson Press, 1951), pp. 10-16.

products, relating them to normal intellectual, emotional, social, perceptual, physical, aesthetic, and creative growth, and suggesting appropriate art media, content, and technique.[5]

Lowenfeld uses this framework to arrive at a particular decision at the level of ongoing classroom instruction. He proposes no neatly-tied packages to be purchased by the teacher in the curriculum market and opened next morning to the eager hands and eyes of the child consumer. He guides the teacher to the creative teaching act, but in wise recognition of the nature of this act, leaves it to the participants. Although his analysis of the principles underlying an arts program is applicable to more structured curricula, his approach logically results in an emerging curriculum. Sequence emerges in developmental fashion from giving continuous attention to as many elements of the creative-appreciative process as can be synthesized and related at any given moment to the child's maturation.

This sounds superhuman, perhaps even chaotic. But when we keep in mind that integration is a unifying process, taking place in a child who is quite unaware of the involved preparations designed to make it happen, we become aware of order. The only chaos is that within the teacher's personality orientation when he attempts to do what he cannot visualize. It is likely that the best possible arts program will be the result of teacher decision based upon insight into the children, the creative-appreciative process, and the arts, rather than from office refrigeration and classroom thawing of curricular frozen foods.

Evaluating the Arts Program

Some of the questions that need to be asked in evaluating the total arts program are:

1. Does the program in each classroom give opportunity for children to practice all the different kinds of behavior implied in the objectives of the arts program? Teachers frequently feel insecure in various aspects of the arts and as a result tend to neglect those areas in which their deepest insecurities lie.

2. Are the opportunities provided in developing this range of behaviors the most productive possible? Of course, in an absolute sense, this is never knowable. But through experience the teacher will learn, for example, which records evoke free rhythmic expression or reduce tension.

3. How effective is the teacher in guiding the creative-appreciative

5 Viktor Lowenfeld, *Creative and Mental Growth*, rev. ed. (New York: The Macmillan Company, 1952).

process? Gaitskell offers two major questions, each with three sub-questions, for teachers to use in appraising their own work in art teaching. They are:

(a) Does the teacher respect the pupils as individuals?
    (i) Is each child encouraged to do original work?
    (ii) Are the pupils encouraged to use their own intellectual, emotional, and social experiences as a basis for the art and crafts programme?
    (iii) Does the teacher do her best to see that adequate supplies are available for children, and does she make sure that the supplies provided are suited to the needs and abilities of the individual members of the class?
(b) Does the teacher use effective teaching methods?
    (i) Does she appraise every art activity which she sponsors in the classroom by referring to the general aims of the art programme?
    (ii) Does she give sufficient guidance without interfering with the thinking of the pupils?
    (iii) Does she see that the pupils gain skill to express their ideas easily and naturally?[6]

4. What is happening to boys and girls *during* the program of art activities? This question merely expresses concern for the quality of the ongoing, day-to-day experiences in creating and enjoying.

Creative Teaching in the Arts

Each teacher can approach the learning-teaching process only from his own particular orientation. Very often, when exposed to other approaches, teachers only become insecure in their present techniques, rather than adept in new ones. They are worse off after than before exposure to the new ideas. The position taken in this volume is that teachers more often grow through broadening their present base of operations than through completely discarding their present practices. Shortcomings arise more from failure to see other possibilities than from deficiencies in whatever practices they are presently using.

In the pages that follow, then, three possible beginning points for teaching in the arts are identified. Teachers usually are found to be approaching their work from one of these three. But they should not stop there. In truly creative teaching, the teacher will use all three possibilities. The three dimensions of good teaching in the arts are:

1. *Children.* The teacher who is concerned first with children will ask himself: How can I help these children achieve the kind of emotional maturity that permits them to face their problems calmly and

6 Gaitskell, *Arts and Crafts in Our Schools,* pp. 55-56.

confidently? How can I help each child feel that he has a place of significance among these other boys and girls? But he cannot move far in answering such questions without considering the problems of how children learn and what they shall learn. Teachers may begin, then, to plan their arts teaching by thinking first about children. But they cannot proceed far before considering content, media, and the creative-appreciative process.

2. *The Creative-Appreciative Process.* The teacher may begin by asking himself: How are the range and depth of musical appreciation extended? What are the psychological bases of creativity? What are the processes involved in perceiving design, color, and harmony? But thinking about such matters cannot proceed far before one is forced to consider children and the relationship of their experience and maturity to the development of these learnings.

3. *Content, Media, and Product in the Arts.* The teacher may ask: When and how should patterns of dance steps be taught in the arts program? What is the place of grammar in the creative writing of children? Do musical classics have a place in the program? Again, the teacher cannot move far in answering these questions without considering the processes of creating and appreciating, and the development of young children.

The point of view espoused here, then, is that teachers may approach their teaching in the arts from any one of the dimensions enumerated. But their teaching will become increasingly effective to the degree that they consider and increase their understanding of all three.

Children as a Dimension in Planning and Teaching

There are many ways of approaching the arts program using children as the initial dimension. One way grows out of cross-sectional documentation of children's characteristics, a technique used extensively by Gesell.[7] Another draws upon the concept of basic human needs, a concept emphasized by Prescott.[8] Still a third uses developmental tasks, a concept that owes much of its clarification to Havighurst,[9] Tryon,[10] and others. Space prevents using all three of these

[7] Arnold Gesell and F. L. Ilg, *The Child from Five to Ten* (New York: Harper & Brothers, 1946).

[8] Daniel A. Prescott, *Emotion and the Educative Process* (Washington: American Council on Education, 1938).

[9] Robert J. Havighurst, *Developmental Tasks and Education,* 2nd ed. (New York: Longmans, Green and Co., 1952).

[10] In Association for Supervision and Curriculum Development, *Fostering Mental Health in Our Schools* (Washington: The Association, 1950).

approaches to understanding children to illustrate the use of children as a dimension in teaching.

Let us take one developmental task, "Learning One's Psycho-Socio-Biological Sex Role," and develop it in relationship to our other two dimensions in the arts programs.

Let us look at just a few characteristics of aesthetics which have significance for teaching and learning in the arts, especially when coupled with what we know about how children develop their sex role.

1. "All the arts in one way or another, to some greater or lesser extent, interpret life."[11]

2. "Aesthetic response is, precisely, response to the evocative values of organized pattern."[12]

3. "For only when an organism shares in the ordered relations of its environment does it secure the stability essential to living."[13]

"Yet it is an established fact that self-identification with the things we do is essential for any well-balanced individual, and self-identification with the needs of our neighbors is one of the most important assumptions for cooperation."[14]

4. True integration of experience can take place only in one being. We may get our deepest insights through interaction with another; we may achieve our deepest satisfactions in listening to a fine musical rendition when we are with those who are dear to us—but the final synthesis, the true integration, is a highly personal matter.

What we know about children, and what we know about the arts and art experience combine to show us the grain of the wood that is to be worked. In the seventh grade, we select a beautiful poem that portrays vividly an intense and moving love between a young man and a young woman. But it is too personal. It evokes an heterosexual pattern that is much too intimate. The girls blush and the boys squirm uncomfortably. We look again at our material and at its grain and texture. This time we select a rollicking tale of parties and hayrides, with swinging meter and teasing blank verse. Close, personal, face-to-face relationships are missing. Boys and girls do together what the boys and girls in the room are able to see themselves doing together. Life is interpreted. An aesthetic response of an appreciative

---

11 Irwin Edman, *Arts and the Man* (New York: W. W. Norton and Co., 1928), p. 33.

12 James L. Mursell, "How Children Learn Aesthetic Responses," *Learning and Instruction,* Forty-ninth Yearbook of the National Society for the Study of Education, Part 1 (Chicago: The University of Chicago Press, 1950), p. 183.

13 John Dewey, *Art as Experience* (New York: Minton, Balch & Co., 1934) p. 15.

14 Lowenfeld, *op. cit.,* p. 8.

Kathleen Moon and Fulton County (Georgia) Schools

USING APPROPRIATE MEDIA FOR GRAPHIC EXPRESSION

sort is evoked. Self-identification occurs, an experience takes place, and life is enriched.

In our seventh grade class, we decide to capitalize on our knowledge of developing heterosexual interests by encouraging dancing. We ignore the grain of the wood when we begin by pairing off for ballroom style. Youngsters struggling with the significance of the heterosexual relationship have their base for security pulled out from under them. They can not come to this new experience through the security of the group. They must face it alone. But set the stage for folk dancing, and we go with the grain. The groups merge, but the children retain a sense of identification with their own sex group. Close personal contacts with the opposite sex are brief, but they constitute significant bridges to adjustment in the pairing-off process that will come. Children identify with the needs of others and lay a foundation for the essential kind of cooperation implied earlier in the quotation from Lowenfeld. In the words of Neumeyer, ". . . the trilogue between medium, tool, and child becomes productive."[15]

[15] Alfred Neumeyer, "The Childhood Roots of Artistic Creation," *Childhood Education,* XXIII (January, 1947), 224.

The Creative-Appreciative Process as a Dimension in
Program Planning

It is quite conceivable that an elementary school teacher might approach the arts program from an almost purely aesthetic orientation. He says to himself, "There is so much beauty in the world. There is so much to enjoy. I want to make my children aware of it. I will stimulate their nerve-endings so that they will be keenly aware of sound, of flavor, of scent." Looking about him, he may be depressed at the insensitivity of others to the beauty he sees, hears, and feels.

It is difficult to realize how much of our diurnal experience is what William James called it, "a big blooming buzzing confusion." It is hard to realize how much of it is a semi-stupor. Life has often enough been described as a waking dream. But not much of it has the vividness, though a great deal of it may have the incoherence or the horror of a dream. For most people most of the time it is a heavy lethargy. They have eyes, yet they do not, in any keen and clear sense, see. They have ears, yet they do not finely and variously hear. They have a thousand provocations to feeling and to thought, but out of their torpor comes no response. Only the pressure of some animal excitement, instant and voluminous, rouses them for a moment to an impulsive clouded answer. Life is for most of us what someone described music to be for the uninitiate, "a drowsy reverie, interrupted by nervous thrills."[16]

This teacher's point of orientation is the creative-appreciative process itself; not children, nor art content, skills, or media. But, obviously, no teacher can carry on his philosophical preoccupation with his children's state of aesthetic oblivion without coming face to face with realities of child development and of media, process, or content in the arts.

Some of the basic understandings of aesthetics helpful in developing the learning-teaching process in the arts are:

1. The creative drive in mankind is secondary only to those basic drives directed towards self-preservation. To quote Neumeyer, "It is a surplus action of man's vitality as well as of child's vitality; it is an act of abundance."[17] In music, for example, it is possible that the babbling, rhythmic sounds produced by children between the sixth and ninth months of life constitute pleasurable use of sound, and may well be the beginnings of music and poetic appreciation.[18]

2. Aesthetic impulses take a three-fold mode of expression: origi-

---

[16] Edman, *op. cit.,* p. 15.

[17] Neumeyer, *op. cit.,* p. 222.

[18] There is evidence to suggest that these melodic sounds are used among children of many different racial cultures. See Mursell, *op. cit.,* p. 186.

nal creation in the form of a painting, symphony, or poem; repro-
duction of a creation previously formalized; and the enjoyment or
appreciation of the created or reproduced work.

3. To quote Mursell, ". . . aesthetic responsiveness . . . always
has the definite character of response to the evocative value of
pattern."[19]

4. The realities of the world around us—seen, felt, or sensed—inevitably pattern creative expression. The original basic drive, then,
is conditioned by all that surrounds and is made a part of the human
organism.

5. Evocative response is developmental. The conditioning process
that occurs can take place only in relation to the present insights,
themselves conditioned by past experience, of the individual involved.

6. This developmental process occurs as an integral part of the
organization of personality.

7. Participation is central to any concept of aesthetic response. Participation tends more frequently to be overt with children. With
adults it usually takes the forms of mentally reliving previous experience.

8. Refinement of aesthetic expression is essentially refinement of
human insight, which, in turn, expresses itself in improved sensitivity
to sound, color, and pattern or improved technique. Aesthetic expression, then, is educable.

The following remarks illustrate the practical classroom value of
these understandings of the creative-appreciative process when they
are considered with due regard to children and to process, content,
and media in the arts. This list of implications might easily be extended.

1. During the early phases of the pre-schematic stage, the teacher
should not concern himself with the child's development of form.
Rather, the teacher should direct his efforts towards both broadening
the child's acquaintance with expressive media and what they can do
for him, and deepening the child's associations between them and
his developing concepts of how he feels and what he thinks about
the world in which he lives. ". . . the educator has to help develop
the picture book of hieroglyphics."[20] And so the child learns the
satisfactions to be derived through expressing *how* he feels by apply-

19 *Ibid.*, p. 185.
20 Neumeyer, *op. cit.*, p. 224.

ing thick poster paint to absorbent paper with a bristle brush.[21] Similarly, clay, free dance, instrumentation, and music listening have potentiality for the encouragement of symbolic description.

2. Established criteria for the aesthetic qualities in creativity and appreciation have no place in the arts program. Children have their own individual aesthetic standards. Their preferences in pictorial representation, for example, correspond closely to their own productions.[22] Consequently, their aesthetic tastes tend to shift with their maturity.

3. Since the teacher's job is to assist in the process of establishing a dynamic relationship among self, media, and the thing, idea, or person to be described, he has a specific role to play in extending and clarifying the child's individual experience. This excerpt from Lowenfeld makes the point so clearly that no further analysis is necessary:

Once, during a visit in a first grade I saw children drawing just a line as a symbol for "mouth." Purposely I had a bag of candy in my pocket. After rattling the bag, I asked the children, "What do I have in my pocket?" "Candy," was the answer. "Do you think it is hard or chewy?" From the rattling the children deduced that it was hard candy. "Do you like candy?" was my question. "Yes," was the unanimous answer. Placing some candy on each child's desk, I asked them not to put it in their mouths until a given signal. "Now you may crush the candy, in order to find out how hard it is." And all the children bit the candy into pieces. After we had gone through the experience, I asked the children to draw "eating the candy." Every child in the classroom included the "teeth" in his representation. This *individual experience activated their passive knowledge.*[23]

4. Related to all three of these implications is what the teacher can do to help the child develop form for his interpretations. Again let it be emphasized that *the object is not to develop a certain form for a specific interpretation.* The purpose, rather, is to help the child see or feel what he can do with what he has to do it with. And so the child is given an opportunity to "get the feel" of bouncing up and down, dangling loosely from the center of his body, or hanging puppet-wise or slithering snake-like across a polished linoleum.[24] A rep-

---

21 Watercolor's fluidity has obvious advantages for expressing gay feelings. But, except in rare instances where a quick representation seems in order, the disadvantages outweigh the advantages. Primary-level children tend to become infatuated with the fluid characteristics of the medium, with the result that creative expression is replaced by mechanical activity characteristic of the scribbling carried on earlier by the very young.

22 John E. French, "Children's Preferences for Pictures of Varied Complexity of Pictorial Pattern," *Elementary School Journal,* LIII (October, 1952), 95.

23 *Op. cit.,* pp. 92-93.

24 Natalie Cole, *The Arts in the Classroom* (New York: The John Day Co., 1940), pp. 96-97.

ertoire of movements thus is built up, but it is not associated with anything specific, unless a relationship is established by the child quite as a by product.

5. But the child may be encouraged by the classroom setting to use his repertoire. The amateur choreographer presents his symbolic version of "Daddy coming home from work" or "Mommy and me collecting the eggs" or "We all go to Church." Or, the class listens carefully to recordings, selecting those arrangements that will best accompany their puppet show, "Saturday at Home."[25] Self, media, and individual conception of a condition, feeling, or object to be described are brought into harmonious relationship.

A Classroom Illustration

It is not possible here to consider all the arts—creative writing, painting, dancing, sculpturing, and so on—nor of all the various understandings, skills, and values that one might want to develop in each. It is possible, however, to show by use of an actual classroom illustration, how one teacher's program in music appreciation moved forward in attaining worthwhile educational goals.

Two points must be clarified. First, the desire to have eight-year-olds enjoy the best in music is not unworthy. It is a perfectly legitimate beginning concern. Second, the best in music need not fall on deaf ears, even those of eight-year-olds. The teacher's problem, begin where she will, is to bring medium, child, and classroom process into harmonious relationship until, to borrow again from Neumeyer, "the trilogue . . . becomes productive." Succeeding paragraphs are devoted to a description of how one teacher did just that in helping first-graders achieve through music some of the benefits previously listed.[26]

My children's families worked in a series of harvests and lived in labor camps and tents. The emotions of these children had been subjected to life in a family of as many as 10 persons in a single room, where the older members alternated between violent conversion at frequent revivals and equally violent backsliding.

The children cried at the least provocation, expected teacher to "whup" them for the smallest offense, and often wept at the relief of finding she did not intend to. . . .

Every morning at 10 the children had a glass of milk and a five-minute rest period. Once, while their heads were down on their tables, I put on a recording of Bach's *Air for the G String*.

[25] See Emma Dickson Sheehy, "From Movement to Dance," *Childhood Education* XXIII (January, 1947), p. 235.

[26] Katharine S. Taylor, "Autochthonous Approach to Music Appreciation," *Music Educators Journal,* XXXV (February, 1948), 17-19.

Before the music had ended, four children were asleep. Instead of having to hold the group down almost bodily for the necessary time, I had to say, "Shall we wake up now and see what is happening in our reading books?"

Flushed with this small success, I waited until they were all chattering noisily at lunch. Without comment, I played a Handel passacaglia. No one stopped talking, but the tension left their voices and mine. Not once did I have to ask that they keep their voices down.

University of Wisconsin Summer Laboratory School

EXPLORING THE USE OF SIMPLE TOOLS

That afternoon when they worked with clay, two children asked if I cared if we had music, and we did have it for the whole last hour of that day.

This chronology is literal truth. Here was idyllic release for the children's tension and mine and the solution, therein, to most of my discipline problems.

As the days went by, I played Beethoven's piano sonatas, his cello sonatas with piano accompaniments, Schumann's piano works, Schubert's soaring melodies. The children loved them.

Gradually, I added a few instruments and got to more elaborate chamber music. No music could better have suited my purpose. The almost standard four-movement form of the trio and quartet covers all classroom moods and activities.

The playing time was increased greatly tho gradually. We had the lively first movement of a quartet or quintet with social studies activities to begin the day. We progressed to the andante movement for milk recess. During lunch, we repeated the first two and continued through the entire sequence of four movements . . .

Only an excerpt from this wonderful real-life classroom story is reproduced here. Miss Taylor goes on to tell how Lorraine took off her shoes one day and danced "what the music told her to do," and how other children gradually followed suit. She related the insight into the works of different composers achieved by these children; they learned to "recognize" music, even if they did not know the names of the composers. Miss Taylor concludes with a series of don'ts that made themselves apparent to her as she worked with these children, which might be helpful to others:

1. Don't talk about the music. Nothing is more meaningless than a story of the great deaf man with the white beard. Let the music tell his story.

2. Don't name the music and expect children to recall titles. When a child likes something so much that he wants to hear it again, he will learn the reason for remembering its title.

3. Don't force any child to participate in the creative activities of the others. . . .

4. Don't invade his privacy by asking him what he has seen or heard or tried to express.

5. Don't subject a child to the emasculated arrangements of the classics which are appearing labeled as children's music. The themes of the masters to some degree are simply folk music, elaborated. Unless a child is hearing the real harmonies of Bach or Beethoven or Mozart, he is not hearing their genius. He has a right to hear them, and can if he is prepared.

6. Don't forever limit the scope of a child's experience in hearing music by setting words to the themes from the classics . . . consider carefully whether you may be setting up a Mickey Mouse to attract attention to a Michelangelo, and whether it will not be Mickey who is remembered.

7. Don't be afraid to allow a child to feel the intensity of your own enjoyment of the music.[27]

We have seen that a teacher may begin from his present point of orientation—to children, to the nature of learning, or to process, media, and content in the arts—and proceed with confidence in his planning and teaching. But his competence increases to the degree that he increases his understanding of each dimension and improves the relationships achieved among them. Such is creative teaching.

UNDERSTANDING CHILDREN THROUGH THE ARTS

The arts serve as vehicles for increased understanding of children in at least two different ways. First, they provide excellent means for

27 *Ibid.*, p. 197.

observing the behavior of children. Second, because the free, creative expressions of children are projections of their personalities, art products offer revealing insights into the more complex factors of the children's organizations.

Observation of Children

Child study programs in recent years have refined the anecdotal technique as a device for recording the behavior of children over a period of time. It is highly desirable that anecdotes of activities in the arts program be recorded, since creative-appreciative behavior lies so close to the roots of personality orientation. Examine this anecdote, for example:

I walked into a first-grade classroom about mid-morning. A wide range of activities was being carried on. One small group was working with the teacher. Other children were busily engaged, some singly, some in pairs and small groups. One chubby youngster was engrossed in creating a work of art. A large sheet of slightly absorbent paper was propped on an easel. On the ledge at the foot of the easel were several pots of thick, calcimine-type paint, and a pan of water. "Chubby" was deeply involved, painting and then standing back to examine the results. I walked over to him. Without looking up, he spoke quietly, almost to himself, "This is a tagger. He's in the jungle. He's jumping from tree to tree. I read about him this morning." The "tagger" was a large dark blob with smaller dark blob, presumably the head. Each blob was somewhat oval-shaped. Then "Chubby" dipped his brush into the pan of water, then into the paint without squeezing out the excess water. He proceeded to pass the brush, with swirling strokes across the body of the "tagger." The paint, too thin to be absorbed quickly, ran down from the body in several straight columns. Without looking up, "Chubby" commented, "Hey, look! This tagger's got legs!"

This is a most revealing anecdote, but it acquires interpretative meaning only in the light of a series of anecdotes taken from many aspects of "Chubby's" daily existence.

Children's Creative Products

The stories that children write or tell, the content of their poems, what they say they think about when they listen to music or look at pictures, help us to understand children. Although the music and the pictures are not themselves the children's creative products, their reactions to them have all the elements of creativity and consequently are projections of the real self.

Teachers sometimes ask if it isn't dangerous for people like themselves, often lacking an extensive psychological background, to use

University of Wisconsin Summer Laboratory School

CREATIVE DANCING ENCOURAGES RESPONSE TO MUSIC AND RHYTHM

such complex media for personality interpretation. It should be pointed out, first, that the helpful classroom leads that are derived from such material owe as much to careful observation as to deep insightful interpretation. It should be pointed out, also, that teachers ought not to spend hours of their time probing for psychological connotations in the creative products of children. To keep constant lookout for persisting patterns or for the very unusual and bizarre is all that can reasonably be expected. The danger of abuse or misuse of children's creative products in interpreting their behavior is minimized when sample products are observed over a period of time, when evidence collected is weighed in relation to evidence from other sources, and when tentative hypotheses, rather than remedial panaceas, are formulated.

THE ARTS AS THERAPY

This section deals with only three aspects of the therapeutic possibilities of the arts: as catharsis in the daily lives of normal children, in treatment and rehabilitation of the handicapped, and as media in the removal of persistent blocks to learning.

Catharsis in Children's Daily Living

There are few teachers in the primary grades who have not marvelled, some time or other, at the soothing effect of a particular piece of music on a tired and irritable group of children. Music in the kindergarten is as basic as a mother's lullaby beside the cradle. Unfortunately, as we progress through the grades, the arts are used less and less in this basic cathartic way. Perhaps this is because we get more and more concerned with developing school bands, training glee clubs and choral groups, and putting on dance performances.

We read earlier in this chapter Katharine Taylor's wonderful story of her journey into musical appreciation with twenty-five transient first-graders. The writer is able to draw from his own experience a similar incident involving a classroom of incarcerated delinquent boys, ranging in age from ten to eighteen years. We were able to move from jazz classics such as "Stardust" and "Begin the Beguine" to light concert and even opera, and back again—some of us getting lost in the process, to be sure. But worldlywise poses faded into relaxed reflection, intergroup hostilities changed to friendly banter, and more than once, faces lined prematurely with inner conflicts softened into untroubled sleep.

Illustrations such as these, repeated in the experience of tens of thousands of teachers, point to the undeniable fact that the arts have an unmistakable place in easing the tensions of modern living, tensions that are absorbed into the nervous systems of children as well as adults.

Therapy with the Handicapped

Explorations into the use of the arts as therapy in the rehabilitation of handicapped children are largely of a "case" nature. We have to guide us only the anecdotal accounts of people who have directed such programs in hospitals and special schools, special classes in regular schools, and in classrooms containing the normal range of children, many of whom suffer from some degree of handicap. Schorsch,[28] Deakins,[29] Uden,[30] and Berndt,[31] respectively, describe their work in dealing with hospitalized children, most of whom were seriously

[28] Sister M. Josepha Schorsch, "Music Therapy for the Handicapped Child," *Education*, LXX (March, 1950), 434-439.

[29] Edna Deakins, "Music for the Mentally Handicapped," *Illinois Education*, XXXVIII (March, 1950), 256-257.

[30] A. V. Uden, "Music and Dancing for the Deaf," *Volta Review*, LI (August, 1949), 366-368.

[31] Kurt H. Berndt, "Therapeutic Value of Music in School," *Music Educators Journal*, XXXVI (November, 1949), 25-27.

crippled, mentally handicapped children segregated in classrooms of
regular elementary schools, or deaf children; and with social misfits,
mentally inferior children, and physically inferior children in regular school programs.

Commenting on her experiences with the hospitalized handicapped,
Schorsch concludes:

> These children, more than any others, need music in the therapeutic sense of
> the word. They are socially, mentally, physically, and spiritually in need of its
> influence. Music can provide for them the emotional outlet that is necessary for
> happy living. It helps to promote a feeling of self-respect and well-being. It often
> assists in the development of stability and physical coordination which is charac-
> teristically lacking in them. . . . In its use with the physically handicapped, it
> helps to compensate for deficiencies and to promote a spirit of endurance and
> patience. . . . Both the physically and the mentally handicapped welcome it as
> an avenue of expression and as a much-needed emotional outlet.[32]

Deakins points out that mentally handicapped children frequently
have poor motor coordination and defective speech. Of course, such
associations lead us to suspect that many mentally handicapped children, so-called, really are not deficient in intellect, but rather are
blocked in their performance. Both motor coordination and speech
are improved through listening, participating, and creating. For the
speech defective, singing words is frequently an avenue to speaking
them.[33]

The work in this field permits of at least three significant generalizations:

1. Creative-appreciative activities are essential, not merely supplementary, aspects of the daily living of youngsters who present unusual
problems of social adjustment, mental development, and physical
handicap. Such activities not only enrich the daily living of these
children, but also hold promise for rehabilitation.

2. The essential factors in programs for handicapped youngsters,
as Deakins points out,[34] are essentially those inherent in any instructional program-knowledge of the pupil that includes a teacher with a
well integrated personality and appropriate instructional techniques.

3. The specific techniques appropriate for dealing with the handicapped offer significant cues for dealing with all children. The teacher
of the handicapped is forced to use "doing" methods—ones that em-

32 *Op. cit.,* p. 439.
33 *Op. cit.,* pp. 256-257.
34 *Op. cit.,* p. 256.

phasize the essentials of learning—when other teachers will be satisfied with just telling or showing. Deaf children "hug" the organ to "feel" sound. Would it not be helpful for normal children to "feel" sound in the same way?

The Arts and the Teacher

Few elementary teachers are artists in their own right. Many of those now teaching have had no formal background in such subjects as music education and art education.[35] But, increasingly, state certification requirements, frequently worked out with the teacher preparing institutions, are calling for one or more courses in the teaching of art and music.

Paramount in its influence upon the arts program, it would seem, is a teacher's insight into the complex process of a child's self-identification with an art object or a creative process, and the resulting reorientation of personality. For a teacher to be able to guide this process along positive lines is of fundamental importance. To do so in the elementary school does not necessitate artistic talent on the part of the teacher. It does require sensitivity, a sense of timing, and a willingness to accept children's standards. There is little doubt, of course, that given these characteristics, possession of talent would be a most desirable supplementary asset for enriching the total program, since teachers of unusual personal ability can do much to stimulate and encourage those children who themselves show artistic promise. It is not the purpose of the elementary school to develop genius; at the same time, the program of the elementary school should be such that genius can take root and thrive.

Guidance and the Teacher

The pictures children draw, the poems and stories they write, the rhythms and dance steps they create, come out of their experience. The teacher can do much to see that they have wide and varied experience, and ample opportunity to interpret in many ways what they experience. Therefore, we visit places—the parks, the art galleries, the museum, old buildings, railroad stations, the docks, churches and synagogues, zoos and aviaries and aquariums—we plan for what we will see, and we talk about what we saw. But since we can't visit

---

35 In a survey of 507 elementary teachers of Colorado in 1946, Mohr found that one-third had no courses in methods of teaching music during their preparation for teaching or in-service. See Estell Elgar Mohr, "Music Teaching Problems of Colorado Elementary School Teachers." Unpublished Doctor's dissertation, Stanford University, 1946.

everything we need to know about, we have vicarious experience through pictures, movies, film strips, radio, and television. And then we draw what we saw, what we did, or what we thought. Of course, we don't all draw the same thing. Somebody draws the boat pulling out from the pier; someone else only the flag at the stern; and someone else a small boy waving from the dock.

Sometimes we need to examine how we "feel" about what we saw, or how someone we're trying to draw might feel. Was the little boy sad who was waving from the dock? Sometimes we must get the "feel" of the action by doing it. Let's see, then, how the little boy looked when he waved. Here, you do it to see how it feels. This is the kind of experimental "feeling-base" that teachers are able to help children find in the creative-appreciative process.

The matter of specific guidance is particularly significant when we recognize the balance that must be maintained between avoiding stereotyped repetition on the one hand, and avoiding pushing the child into producing what his experience cannot yet guide on the other. As Boylston points out, a crooked chimney in a painting simply means that the child has not observed sufficiently to know that it must stand upright.[36] The position of the chimney will adjust itself when the child's observation adjusts itself. Perhaps we could aid this developing process by drawing children's attention to a series of upright posts supporting a handrail leading from the sidewalk down to the playing field, by observing a water tower on a hillside, or by examining the chimney of a house that stands beside a tall building. Notice that the guidance involved directs the observation process, not the creative act. We ask the child to observe closely; we do not sketch in the chimney as we think it should look. Or, we ask, "Is there a story about this?" not, "What is it?"[37] As Mursell so well points out, "Skill in any art should be regarded as refinement of insight, and it should be so treated pedagogically."[38]

The question of refinement of skill can be dealt with largely on the basis of purpose. The work of the elementary school has little to do with the development of skill in the arts as an end in itself. Even if skill does develop, our knowledge of the learning process tells us

36 Elise Reid Boylston, "Creative Expression and Child Art," *School Arts*, XXXXVII (May, 1948), 295.

37 Lenore M. Batchelor, "Children's Expression," *School Arts*, XXXXVII (May, 1948), 6a.

38 "How Children Learn Aesthetic Responses," *op. cit.*, p. 189.

that skill is best acquired through a variety of projects that emphasize the activity, rather than skill as an end. "Skill and techniques evolve from creative learning, and the child becomes conscious of his own need for further techniques when he learns creativity."[39]

Absolute standards for judgment of product, likewise, have no place in the elementary schools. How can we, as teachers, judge the child's product when we see differently, feel differently, and relate ourselves differently to the creative stimulus? As both Mursell[40] and Lowenfeld[41] point out, our evaluations should be based only upon the effect of creative activity upon the child. The process may be judged as inadequate when the child cannot confront himself in his creative expression with his own experiences, or when imitative pursuits block the child's creative efforts. The process is adequate when the child reveals his own independent thinking through expression of his own ideas in his own way.

One of the greatest enemies of an adequate process is the child's own quest for approval and the subtle classroom stimulants to this pursuit. Criticism constitutes misapprobation. To avoid it, some children will seek to conform at any price. Obviously, then, one needs to think carefully about the use of criticism of the product or the process of children's creativeness. Equally dangerous is the teacher's praise for the works of some children and her "no comment" for others. As Metcalf so well points out, the absence of comment is in such instances an act of damnation rather than an instance of neutrality.[42] Because of the presence—virtually inherent in classroom structure—of children's drive for approval, teachers must take conscious steps to build an atmosphere of complete and unconditional acceptance of whatever a child creates.

An actual classroom incident in creative writing serves to illustrate many of the points made concerning the teacher's role in guiding creativity. This excerpt is about Tim, an eleven-year-old in the fourth grade with only a 2.3 grade placement on the Stanford Achievement Test. His teacher told the story. The talking was in whispers in order that other children would not hear or be disturbed.

---

39 Beatrice Perham, *Music in the New School* (Chicago: Neil A. Kjos Music Co., 1941), p. 16.
40 *Music and the Classroom Teacher*, p. 273.
41 "Self-Confidence Through Creative Work," *Progressive Education*, XXVI (January, 1949), 77.
42 Lawrence E. Metcalf, "Must Teachers Be 'Neutral'?" *Educational Leadership*, X (October, 1952), 22-25.

Tim handed the teacher a folded paper and quickly went to his seat . . . Tim had written his first poem!

> I like spring.
> It is cool.
> The trees are like kites
> In the sky.
> I like spring.

"I wonder if there are other things that you enjoy in spring," asked the teacher.

"I like the birds," answered Tim.

"What do you like about the birds?" asked the teacher.

"I like to hear them sing," said Tim. "The birds sing a song to me."

"Would you like to say in your poem that you enjoy the birds?" asked the teacher.

"I could say, 'The birds sing a song to me and I feel happy.' "

"Let's read your poem again," suggested the teacher. She quietly read the lines again. "When you said, 'I like spring. It is cool,' were you thinking about the cool air?"

"Yes," answered Tim. "I don't like hot weather. I wanted to say, 'The air is cool' in my poem, but I didn't know how to spell 'air'."

"Don't worry about spelling, Tim, when you are writing a poem or story. Write the words the way they sound to you. I can help you to spell the words correctly later."

The teacher read:

> I like spring.
> The air is cool,
> And the trees are like kites
> In the sky.
> The birds sing a song to me
> And I feel happy.

"I enjoy reading your poem," said the teacher earnestly. "You have caught the spirit of spring. I think the other boys and girls would like you to share your poem with them."[43]

The following significant factors in successful guidance of the creative process may be readily identified from the foregoing:

1. The teacher accepted without qualification the child's creative product.

2. She helped him, through leading questions, to relate himself even more specifically to the experience he was attempting to express.

3. In so sharing, she established a mutual bond of trust of a kind particularly significant for many children like Tim who are our potential early drop-outs.

[43] Mary E. Bowers, "The Picture in His Mind," *Childhood Education*, XXIII (January, 1947), 218-220.

4. She placed technical matters—in this instance, spelling—in their appropriate place without creating the impression that such matters are of no significance whatsoever.

5. She led Tim a step further in his creativity; but the final product contained only his interpretations and verbalizations of them.

6. She contributed to Tim's sense of worth by making it very clear that she thoroughly enjoyed his interpretation and that others likewise would be enriched by it.

Lowenfeld so well sums up our philosophy regarding this whole question of teacher guidance and the several sub-questions posed that a lengthy quotation is felt to be justified here:

A child who has developed freedom and flexibility in his expression as a result of correct stimulation for self-expression will be able to face new situations without difficulties. . . . Thus, it becomes clear that any use of imitative methods, like the use of tracings or coloring of patterns in commercial color books, will not only restrict the child in his freedom, but will inhibit him in his own creative expression. He will become dependent on such patterns, not only in his creative work, but also in his thinking, as the one cannot be separated from the other. From that it becomes self-evident that self-expression leads finally to the emphasis of the free individual, and, therefore, to the truest and most precious attribute of democracy. Imitation, however, stresses dependency and blind obedience. Therefore, self-expression, in my opinion, is one of the most powerful educational weapons in a time which needs to collect all its forces for a survival of democratic thinking.[44]

The Teacher and Supervision

Two basic questions pertaining to the teacher and supervisory services are dealt with here: (1) What is the function of supervision in relation to the elementary-school teacher and classroom; (2) Is elementary-school instruction in the arts benefited when this function is fulfilled?

Regarding the first, it may be safely said that much of present-day supervision is not directed towards the function for which it was conceived.[45] Supervision is designed, fundamentally, to provide support, advice, and assistance to the classroom teacher who, in turn, is responsible for the arts program of his classroom. Supervisors in art and music who spend the bulk of their time in dealing directly with children in the classroom are not performing the function for which they are intended. In fact, they are usurping the role of the classroom

[44] "Self-Confidence through Creative Work," p. 76.
[45] See Andrew M. Banse, "Whither Music Supervision in the Elementary School," *Music Educators Journal*, XXXVI (September, 1949), 48.

teacher. Supervisors and specialists cannot know all the children and their creative processes in the many classrooms they supervise. Consequently, they are in no position to guide the aesthetic activities of these children.

Too often the supervisor's direct contact with children is motivated by a desire to make a good showing artistically in the community. First, the supervisor holds "try-outs" in individual classrooms. From these, unusually talented youngsters are selected and segregated for special training by the supervisor. All this activity culminates at the end of the year in a performance for parents, teachers, children—and, of course, the supervisor.

Frequently the supervisor feels compelled to step into the teaching spotlight because of recognized shortcomings in the work of the classroom teacher. But when the purpose is to teach the children, rather than to help the teacher, the supervisor is espousing a short, rather than a long-range view. The supervisor's role embraces the following types of activities:

1. Assistance to teachers in overcoming the insecurities many of them have in relation to the arts. This calls for high-level supervisory counselling, frequently of a non-directive sort.

2. Providing materials, devices, practical suggestions, and ideas to help the classroom teacher do a more effective job.

3. In-service education embracing such specifics as demonstrations, clinics, institutes, workshops, and so on.

The supervisor fulfills the function for which supervision was created when he focuses his attention upon assisting the classroom teacher. Direct work with children is justified only when it is a means to attainment of this fundamental end.

SOME KEY IDEAS

Summarizing here all that is in this chapter is impossible. But an attempt may be made to pull out some of the key ideas.

1. In spite of excellent programs in almost every part of the country, the creative and appreciative arts have scarcely been tapped as productive media in the lives of boys and girls in the elementary schools.

2. The central purpose of the arts program is to provide children with a vehicle to wholesome personality development and enriched living.

3. Teachers may approach their programs in the arts from one of three points of orientation. These include: recognized growth needs and developmental characteristics of children; aesthetics in the creative-appreciative process; and the arts as a field of study with its appropriate content, media, and techniques. It is perfectly legitimate for teachers to begin their planning with any one of these dimensions in the learning-teaching process. But it is essential, likewise, that teachers consider the other two dimensions, regardless of where they begin, if they are to move forward in the central objective of art instruction in the elementary school.

4. The arts program in its various creative and appreciative components, creatively conducted, facilitates catharsis, and even aids in therapy and rehabilitation for boys and girls.

5. The teacher's role is essentially one of stimulating evocative response, refining children's insights about their surrounding environment and their relationship to it, and refining the expression of this insight.

6. In the elementary school, the classroom teacher is responsible for guiding the total development of boys and girls. Specialists and supervisors play a significant role only to the degree that their activities facilitate increasingly better teacher direction of the learning process.

BIBLIOGRAPHY

Cole, Natalie R., *The Arts in the Classroom*. New York: The John Day Co., 1940.

D'Amico, Victor, *Creative Teaching in Art*. Scranton, Pa.: International Textbook Co., 1942.

Gaitskell, C. D., *Art and Crafts in Our Schools*. Toronto, Canada: The Ryerson Press, 1949.

———, *Children and Their Pictures*. Toronto, Canada: The Ryerson Press, 1951.

Grant, Parks, *Music for Elementary Teachers*. New York: Appleton-Century-Crofts, Inc., 1951.

Landeck, Beatrice, *Children and Music*. New York: William Sloane Associates, Inc., 1952.

Lowenfeld, Viktor, *Creative and Mental Growth*, rev. ed. New York: The Macmillan Co., 1952.

Mursell, James L., *Music and the Classroom Teacher*. New York: Silver Burdett Co., 1951.

Myers, Louise Kifer, *Teaching Children Music in the Elementary School*, 2nd ed., Englewood Cliffs, N.J.: Prentice-Hall, Inc., 1956.

National Society for the Study of Education, *Music Education*. Thirty-fifth Yearbook, Part II. Bloomington, Illinois: Public School Publishing Co., 1936.

Pepper, Stephen C., *Principles of Art Appreciation*. New York: Harcourt, Brace and Company, 1949.

Read, Herbert, *Education Through Art*. London: Faber and Faber, 1943.

Winslow, Leon Loyal, *The Integrated School Art Program*. New York: McGraw-Hill Book Co., Inc., 1949.

PART FOUR

DIRECTING,
ORGANIZING,
AND
EVALUATING
THE TOTAL
SCHOOL
PROGRAM

ORGANIZATION AND
ADMINISTRATION
FOR THE
EDUCATIONAL PROGRAM

13

ORGANIZATION AND ADMINISTRATION IN THE ELE-
mentary school exist to help provide the best
possible learning environment for boys and girls.
Organization and administration do not themselves provide instruction; they simply facilitate
it. Early pages of this chapter deal with what is
to be organized and administered: school size
and enrollment, trends in organizational patterns, school plant, personnel, and certain realities of the school's social setting. Attention is
then given to some of the problems involved in
effective school organization. Finally, problems
of administering the education program are discussed, with special emphasis on the principal's
leadership role.

PRIMARY FUNCTIONS OF ORGANIZATION AND ADMINISTRATION

This chapter's title sets its theme: organization and administration are *for* the instructional program. This is a theme not always borne out by practice in elementary schools. In fact, both past and present practice provide ample evidence that curriculum and instruction frequently are handmaidens of fixed structure and rigid administration. At the negative end of a continuum, organization and administration may actually impede the development and continuous improvement of a coherent program of instruction. At the positive end, they may serve to bring all elements of the educational enterprise into functional relationship one with the other.

The following are among the general functions of organization and administration:

1. Organization and administration provide the structure within which the educational needs of the community are observed, analyzed, and translated into school policy and program development.

2. Organization and administration crystallize the setting within which children strive for maximum development. How the setting is determined has much to do with whether children work and play in an environment which is safe and supportive, or whether they struggle in a setting that fosters undue tension, creates unnecessary barriers to growth, and endangers physical well-being.

3. Organization and administration determine in large measure the degree to which a sound educational program can be developed in a given educational situation.

4. Organization and administration have much to do with "efficiency" in the use of space, time, and money—with promoting optimum use of space, time, and money in relation to the instructional ends sought.

5. Organization and administration must encourage continuous professional and personal development of staff personnel to the end that the instructional program may provide increasing benefits to children.

THE SETTING FOR ORGANIZATION AND ADMINISTRATION

There are certain conditions—local, regional, and national—over which the individual school has limited or no control, although they profoundly influence its organization and administration. Certain of them—particularly school enrollment, school size, relatively fixed organizational patterns, buildings, experience and professional preparation of administrators and teaching personnel, and what the community feels the school can or cannot do—require some discussion here.

Enrollment and Teacher Supply

The fact that there were not enough classrooms and teachers to take care of the unprecedented increases in elementary school enrollment following World War II hovered like a cloud over all postwar plans for providing improved education for America's boys and girls. It is always difficult to engage school superintendents in planning for curriculum improvement while they are on the losing end of the battle for more buildings and teachers with which to staff them. Ahead of them lies the unhappy prospect of an annual increase of at least one million children in pupil population until a total of more than thirty millions in elementary schools is reached in 1960. To meet this crisis aggressive steps must be taken to provide (1) vastly expanded school budgets, (2) extensive building programs, and (3) greatly increased numbers of adequately prepared teachers.

School Size

Organization and administration are governed to a considerable degree by the size of the elementary school in which they function. At mid-century, only slightly more than 6 per cent of all elementary school teachers were in one-teacher schools, even though 29 per cent of all schools were one-room buildings. But nearly 90 per cent of Kentucky's schools, to cite one example, had three rooms or less.[1] One has only to visit any medium-size town in America to find elementary schools of thirty or more teachers. Similarly, consolidated schools of comparable size are located in many areas classified as rural. School size simplifies or complicates administration, dictates some aspects of organization, influences school-community interaction,[2] affects faculty relationships. The tremendous range in size complicates any written treatment of the problems involved. In recognition of the uniqueness of certain problems in organizing and administering small schools, a section of this chapter is devoted exclusively to schools of three rooms or less.

[1] Statistics cited based on "Statistics of State School Systems" *Biennial Survey of Education in the United States, 1948-50* (Washington, D. C.: Office of Education, 1950).
[2] Maurice F. Seay, "Consolidation: Barrier to Development of Community Schools," *Educational Leadership* X (May, 1953), 486-488.

University of Wisconsin Summer Laboratory School

MANY ACTIVITIES TAKE PLACE IN THE SAME CLASSROOM

Present Organizational Patterns

Elementary schools throughout the nation operate within an organizational structure over which they exercise little individual control. Traditionally, in the South the elementary school has been a seven-year unit, with four or, more recently, five years constituting the secondary school unit. New England schools have been characterized by an eight-year elementary school unit. Six-year units are predominant in the West and Middle West and have been gaining in popularity throughout the nation.[3] Organizational patterns tend to remain stable for long periods of time because of the magnitude of

[3] In 1948, approximately 68 per cent of 1732 cities of 2,500 population or more followed a six-grade-unit pattern; in 1910 practically no cities had this type of elementary school. See William C. Reavis, Paul R. Pierce, Edward H. Stullken, and Bertrand L. Smith, *Administering the Elementary School* (Englewood Cliffs, N. J.: Prentice-Hall, Inc., 1953), p. 167.

cooperative planning that must go into changing them. School faculties seldom seriously question the structure within which they find themselves.

School Plant

The school plant directly affects certain administrative and organizational arrangements. School sites and buildings are with us for a long time. Facilities once considered adequate no longer satisfy present standards; for example, thirty square feet of floor space per pupil are now recommended, in contrast to the fifteen once considered satisfactory.[4] Recognizing the rapidity with which both buildings and people get out of date, some educators have suggested (not entirely facetiously) that the complete faculty, and the plant as well, be retired every thirty years!

Preparation of Administrative and Teaching Personnel

The elementary school principal is becoming an increasingly well educated person by academic standards. The present-day prototype holds a master's degree; twenty years ago he had not completed four years of college. Improved conditions surrounding the elementary principalship have resulted in increasing numbers of qualified persons regarding the elementary school as a permanent career, rather than as a stepping-stone to the secondary school. This upgrading of the elementary school principalship has had much to do with improving the quality of administration and organization.

Not too long ago the possession of a degree by an elementary school teacher was a rare phenomenon. While some improvement in the training status of elementary teachers has occurred, too many still lack sufficient training (either professional or cultural) to be fully qualified for their work. Of 468,445 teachers in 32 states reporting in 1955, approximately 68 per cent had more than 120 semester hours of preparation, about 26 per cent had 60 to 119 hours, and 6 per cent had less than 60 hours.[5] Thus, thinking in the area of school administration and organization must be tempered by a consideration of the readiness of relatively untrained teachers to develop and carry out plans for a sound instructional program.

4 "School Plant and Equipment," *Review of Educational Research*, XXI (February, 1951), 31.

5 N.E.A. Research Division, "The 1955 Teacher Supply and Demand Report," *Journal of Teacher Education*, VI (March, 1955), 36.

Realities of the Social Setting

The setting within which the school operates has been described in the first three chapters. Some of the specifics—national, regional, and local—which profoundly influence elementary school organization and administration include:

1. Tremendous population shifts—rural to urban, region to region —which make accurate estimates of pupil enrollment and building needs impossible. Military and non-military industrial developments, which completely upset normal school development and planning in certain sections of the country, play a major role in these population shifts.

2. The steady march of industry into sections of the community which formerly were strictly residential.

3. Traditional segregation of pupils along race, sex, or religious lines, especially when such traditions are being subjected to legal or philosophical scrutiny.

4. The amount and value of taxable property within the district served by the elementary school.

5. The value attached to formal education by the citizens of the community.

The foregoing are just a few of the realities which must be recognized in organizing and administering the elementary school. To some degree they can be modified. To some degree they modify what can be done.

Organizing the Educational Program

The way in which a school is organized affects the instructional program of the elementary school in a number of ways. Three of the most significant of these relate to:

1. The classification of pupils as they progress year-by-year and level-by-level through the elementary school;

2. The allocation of teachers at each step in this progression;

3. School-wide provision, apart from special provisions within classrooms, for the individualization of instruction.

This section is devoted to these three problems and to the special case of the small rural school. The self-contained classroom versus departmentalization as one problem of organization is also discussed.

Vertical Organization

"Vertical organization" refers here to the means used to identify stages of school progress of children from the time they enter to the time they leave the elementary school. Traditionally, this purpose has been served by grade designations. When a dozen or more children were sent to the village school house to learn to "read, write, and cipher," grade organization was superfluous. But when school attendance laws, diversified curricular offerings, and heavily populated communities came into being, school administrators sought a convenient way of classifying the huge enrollments which poured into school buildings. One grade for a year of progress was the answer.

Other school practices fell into line with the graded system created. Teachers were assigned according to grade, and become first or third or fifth grade teachers. The content of instruction was divided into amounts deemed appropriate for each grade. Since these amounts were usually determined by a trial-and-error approach to an adequate diet for the mythical "average" child, special provisions became necessary for those toward the upper and lower ends of the ability curve. Unusually gifted children "skipped" a grade or participated in "enrichment" activities. Slow learners repeated grades. Courses of study and textbooks were prepared to fit the graded structure. The more practices were geared to graded plans, the more difficult it became to shift any part of the machinery without stripping the gears. This crystallization around the graded plan of vertical organization clearly illustrates how aspects of school organization can become formidable determinants in the shaping of educational programs.

In modern America, graded plans are the predominant pattern of organization for the elementary school. Advantages accrue from the fact that it is convenient to classify children, subject matter, texts, and teachers according to grade levels. Graded plans, however, make dealing with the problem of individual differences and developing a continuous instructional program over the grades difficult. Much research has shown what happens to children as a result of school practices which stem from grade classification plans.

Some educators believe that adaptation to graded structure can never be a good solution to the problems of individual differences and program continuity. Tear down the original structure and start over, they say! One tangible outcome of such thinking is the ungraded plan, represented most commonly by the primary unit. The primary unit usually embraces the conventional first three grades; occasionally kindergarten is added to make a four-year unit.[6] In Milwaukee, chil-

6 For more extensive treatment of ungraded plans of school organization, see John I. Goodlad, "Ungrading the Elementary Grades," N.E.A. Journal, XLIV (March, 1955), 170-171; and, "More About the Ungraded Unit Plan," N.E.A. Journal, XLIV (May, 1955), 295-296.

dren entering school normally may expect to enter the fourth grade six semesters later, but the length of time for some may be seven or even eight semesters.[7] Throughout the period of time, grade levels and promotions are non-existent; children simply proceed from task to task at the rate which seems best for them. With this type of ungraded plan, the elementary school may be divided into an upper and a lower unit, or into a single unit representing the complete spread of years embraced by the elementary school. Theoretically, elimination of grades may eliminate the lock step created when children, subject matter, and teachers are meshed together at fixed grade levels. The result desired is that all children will progress as normally and rapidly as possible in all areas of development through a continuous instructional program. Mere change in structure, of course, unless coupled with fundamental changes in the organization of the instructional program itself, cannot bring about such a result; structural changes merely provide opportunities for these more fundamental changes to occur.

Horizontal Organization

When we examine any vertical unit—be it a single grade or a unit embracing several years—for divisions or organizational plans within that unit, we are considering horizontal organization. Present practice reveals the following:

1. *Teacher Per Group Plan.* Elementary schools in the United States have moved away from departmentalization. Where departmentalization does exist, it usually is applied to the upper elementary grades.[8] A teacher per group per grade is the predominant pattern in elementary school organization, although variations exist in all major sections of the country. In such a pattern, the third grade teacher is responsible for a third grade class throughout the school day for the full school year. The basic assumption behind this kind of plan is that one teacher is best able to see the total development of each child in proper perspective. He is able to plan a program that properly balances rest and activity. He is able to relate troublesome be-

---

[7] Emil F. Faith, "Continuous Progress at the Primary Level," *Phi Delta Kappan*, XXX (May, 1949), 356-359.

[8] In a study of 63 cities in five major geographic regions of the United States, Dunn reported the extent of departmentalization for three decades as follows: 1920-29, departmentalization ranged from 5 per cent in the primary grades (1 to 3) to 37 per cent in grade 6; 1930-39, from 7 per cent in primary grades to 33 per cent in grade 6; 1940-49, from 3 per cent in primary grades to 18 per cent in grade 6. See Mary Dunn, "Trends in Instructional Organization in City Elementary Schools from 1920 to 1949." Unpublished doctoral dissertation, University of Pittsburgh, 1951.

havior in the afternoon to a morning incident. Most educators are agreed that a single teacher for a group of lower grade children is desirable.[9] There is much less agreement about the higher levels.[10]

2. *Departmentalized Plans.* Departmentalization occurs when teachers are assigned according to certain curricular divisions, usually subjects or fields of study. In its mildest form, teachers are assigned to a single school or group of schools to teach designated areas of the curriculum. One teacher, then, may spend full time teaching music in three elementary schools. In its extreme form, all teachers in a given school divide the program according to their various special competencies; one teacher handles social studies throughout all or several grades, another takes arithmetic, and so on. This practice is found most commonly in those schools that include the seventh and eighth grades. It seldom is found below the fourth grade or in primary units.[11]

Organizing for Individualized Instruction

School people realize that school organizational plans do not and cannot in themselves do the instructional job. Plans at the over-all school level have been devised, from time to time, however, to organize instructional time and materials in relation to the learning tasks of the individual pupil. Experimental programs have sought to attain, for example, one or more of the following objectives related to individualization:

1. To permit each child to select from a range of appropriate activities the particular activity of interest to him;

2. To permit each child to move from task to task in relation to his individual readiness;

3. To provide the individual child with an appropriate balance of drill and creative work, while making the utmost use of space, people, equipment, and materials.

Most of the experiments have suffered from preoccupation with certain objectives at the expense of other important ends. The multiple-track plan, for example, developed at various times in St. Louis, Detroit, Santa Barbara, Baltimore, and Cambridge, encouraged aca-

---

9 See Henry J. Otto, "Curriculum Issues in Elementary Education," *Educational Leadership,* VII (October, 1949), 21-25.

10 For an extensive summary of *pros* and *cons,* see Harlan H. Hagman, "Shall We Departmentalize?" *Nation's Schools,* XXVIII (July, 1941), 30.

11 For a more extensive analysis of the problem, together with a helpful bibliography, see Mary Dunn, "Should There Be Any Type of Elementary School Organization?" *Elementary School Journal,* LIII (December, 1953), 199-206.

demic progress within the child's ability, but lost sight of important
social goals. Although a child could be shifted from track to track,
such shifts were based on achievement in general rather than on
progress in specific aspects of attainment. This plan tended to negate
the differences in attainment apparent in a single individual at a
given time. Search's experiment at Pueblo late in the nineteenth century, and Burk's at San Francisco early in the twentieth, provided
both for some individualization in the selection of program and for
individual progress, but did not provide adequately for social development and social learnings. The Winnetka plan attempted to
overcome this social deficiency by providing two periods per day for
individual instruction in the basic skills, and two for group and creative activities. But it proved difficult to relate skills to meaningful
applications. The Dalton plan, more complex in its conceptual
framework, sought to maintain a delicate balance among individual
freedom in program development and in budgeting time progress
according to individual readiness and ability, and participation in activities requiring cooperation and social interaction. Pupils took on
"contracts," specifying designated amounts of work to be completed
within a specified time. The program suffered partly because the pupils' contracts tended to become compartmentalized, and partly because completing the contracts often overshadowed the real products
of learning. The Dalton plan has been criticized, too, on the grounds
that it developed undue pressure on the children seeking to complete
contracts.[12]

In spite of such criticisms, these were sincere and forthright attempts to overcome some of the difficulties inherent in the lock-step
of graded structure. These experiments made it emphatically clear
that there is nothing sacred about existing elementary school structure. Too many school principals and superintendents assume that
grade levels and/or departmentalization are hallowed trusts to be pre-
served at all costs. Decisions about the kind of instructional program
desired must precede decisions on implementing organizational
plans. Future changes in curricula, instruction, and school policy may
well demand a thorough overhaul of the elementary school's organiza-

[12] For further discussion of these experiments, see George C. Kyte, *The Principal at
Work* (Boston: Ginn and Co., 1952), pp. 159-165; Paul B. Jacobson, William C. Reavis,
and James D. Logsdon, *Duties of School Principals* (Englewood Cliffs, N. J.: Prentice-
Hall, Inc., 1950), pp. 405-406; Willard S. Ellsbree and Harold J. McNally, *Elementary
School Administration and Supervision* (New York: American Book Co., 1951), pp.
86-95.

tional framework. The basic question is, "What should organization do to facilitate the construction and operation of a sound educational program?"

Organizing Space in Relation to Personnel

Since World War II, construction of new classrooms has not kept pace with increased enrollments. As a result, class size has increased markedly and available space per pupil has decreased proportionately.[13] It is of utmost necessity that all available space be put to optimum use. Conditions are not optimum when a classroom is left empty for a portion of the day while pupils use other facilities.

Wirt's platoon plan, developed first at Bluffton (Indiana), then at Gary, was an attempt to utilize room space to optimum advantage in relating materials and teachers to the curriculum. The curriculum was divided into the basic academic subjects and laboratory activities, half the student body being engaged in each at any given time, and each half interchanging its location with the other half at intervals throughout the day. A mid-century report indicated that only 8 per cent of city schools use platooning, and more than half of these intend to abandon the plan.[14] Compartmentalization of subject matter is a primary criticism of this plan. Some critics claim, also, that children in the elementary grades thrive best when they have their own classroom home base throughout the day.

Concerned over the relatively small number of teachers in relation to need, the Fund for the Advancement of Education sought better means for using available teachers. Funds were made available to Central Michigan College of Education, in collaboration with the public school system of Bay City, Michigan, to support a five-year experiment to test the possibilities of using "aides" as a means of extending the effectiveness of teachers. Eight control rooms, and eight experimental rooms using teachers' aides with 50 per cent more children, were set up. Careful observation demonstrated that children received more individual attention from the teacher himself when he was assisted by an aide than when only the teacher was present. An interest-

13 For a discussion of trends in class size and of class size and room space as factors in the learning-teaching process, see John I. Goodlad, "Room to Live and Learn," *Childhood Education*, XXX (April, 1954), 355-361. For a discussion of organizational provisions and other aspects of the problem, see *Educational Leadership*, XII (October, 1954). The entire issue is devoted to "packing them in."

14 National Education Association, "Trends in City School Organization, 1938 to 1948," *Research Bulletin*, XXVII (February, 1949), 17-18.

ing by-product of the program is that some of the teachers' aides have been attracted to the teaching profession.[15]

Two shifts of youngsters per day are part of the experience of many teachers, particularly those who teach or who have taught in metropolitan centers. Many elementary schools house more children in neighboring churches and halls than in the school building itself. One suggestion, heard frequently, for alleviating the space and teacher shortage is the twelve-month school year with an accompanying twelve-month teacher contract.

Criteria for Elementary School Organization

Organization is a means to the accomplishment of other ends. It is best evaluated, then, on the basis of how well it facilitates the accomplishment of the desired ends. The following criteria may be helpful both in appraising the effectiveness of present organizational patterns and in projecting new structures.

A. Pupil Personnel
  1. Accounting—Organization must expedite the essential process of accounting for pupils: maintaining and using essential individual progress and health records, compiling vital statistics of attendance, quick location in case of emergency, and so on.
  2. Classification—Organization must facilitate the classification of pupils in groups best suited to what is known about them and their transfer from group to group when deemed desirable.
  3. Observation and analysis—Organization must permit individual observation and collection of data over time, and analysis of these data in total perspective.
  4. Development—Organization must encourage total development of the individual, no one aspect being developed at the expense of another.

B. Curriculum and Instruction
  1. Sequence in learning—Organization should facilitate a continuous view of the entire elementary school curriculum. It should foster building on what has gone before in preparation for what is to come, rather than the crystallization of discrete units piled one on top of the other.
  2. Relatedness in learning—Organization should facilitate easy

[15] For further discussion of this and similar experiments, see Fund for the Advancement of Education, *A Report for 1952-1954* (New York: The Fund).

grasp of the breadth of the curriculum and the relatedness of its component parts.

3. Flexibility—Organization should permit reorganization and adjustment of the curriculum without the need for a complete structural overhaul for each curricular revision.

4. Creativity in instruction—Organization should permit the teacher to introduce innovations in his teaching method and special provisions for the needs of individual pupils without serious upheaval in total school structure.

C. Time, Space, Materials, and Equipment

1. Time—Organization should encourage optimum use of the school day for instructional purposes. Conditions are not optimum when pupils must walk from one end of the building to the other when changing activities.

2. Space—Organization should encourage optimum use of space facilities at any given time. Conditions are not optimum when certain rooms not in use for part of the day are in heavy demand for the rest of the day.

3. Materials—Organization should help bring pupils and the materials they need together at the appropriate time. Conditions are not optimum when three classes must have access to the same library books at the same time.

4. Equipment—Organization should facilitate maximum utilization of minimum equipment for the jobs to be done. Conditions are not optimum when three movie projectors must be purchased to do the work of one properly scheduled.

D. Teaching and Supplementary Personnel

1. Teacher-per-group allocation—Organization should provide a teacher for each group of pupils. This makes it possible for each child to know at least one staff member who may see him as a total human being and who is responsible for his guidance.

2. Teaching relief—Organization should make possible some plan whereby each teacher is free to take time out from his group for at least a twenty minute period, preferably twice daily.

3. Supplementary instructional personnel—Organization should encourage optimum use of supervisory and other special personnel. Conditions are not optimum when specialists remove children or groups of children from ongoing classroom activities directed by the regular teacher.

4. Non-teaching personnel—Organization should encourage use of the services of non-teaching personnel throughout the full contracted time of employment. Conditions are not optimum when a janitor employed from 8:00 to 5:00 sits idly from 9:00 to 3:00 while waiting for classrooms to clear so that he may pursue his duties.

E. Administrative Personnel

1. Routine—Organization should facilitate the orderly, systematic, and economic performance by the administrator of those routine matters having to do with the operation of the school. Conditions are not optimum when the principal must spend half of his day attending to the mechanics of moving groups of children through the building.

2. Leadership—Organization should free the principal for performance of his essential leadership role and should help him to establish priorities in regard to those aspects of the program needing his attention in a leadership capacity. Conditions are not optimum when the sheer weight of maintaining the present operation prevents analysis of its shortcomings.

F. Basic Administrative Considerations

1. Financial—Organization should provide for optimum use of the educational dollar, whether the per pupil cost of education per year is $100 or $600. Conditions are not optimum when they necessitate duplication of space, materials, and equipment, none of which is used more than a small fraction of the school day.

2. Managerial—Organization should encourage orderly management of the educational enterprise. Conditions are not optimum when there is confusion in lines of authority and delegation of responsibility.

3. Public relations—Organization should facilitate communication between the school and the community of which it is a part. Conditions are not optimum when the progress of children from unit to unit of the structure is accompanied by violent parental repercussions.

The preceding list of criteria might well be used as a set of guidelines in appraising the effectiveness of organization in a specific school. Space does not permit applying these guidelines to the various types of school organization in existence. The reader might want to check the school he best knows against them. One type of school organization that fares rather well when such criteria are applied is the self-contained unit.

A Point of View: The Self-Contained Unit

The self-contained unit is not defined here as one teacher instructing the pupils of a certain class in all the studies of that grade.[16] Self-contained units need not be organized vertically into grades. Nor is the self-contained unit taken here as one side of an either-or argument between departmentalization and a teacher per class. Rather, a self-contained unit characterized by the following essentials is recommended:

1. One teacher is responsible for the total welfare of a given group of children. This does not mean that he necessarily does all of the teaching. He may turn the group over to the librarian for part of a day. During one period of the week some of his children may get special instruction in band, others in arts and crafts, others in photography. A recreational director may take charge of the group regularly for part of three days during the week. *But the regular classroom teacher participates in planning such activities; knows what goes on at these times; and exchanges information with his colleagues.* Preferably, the children spend most of the school day—three-fourths of it is sometimes recommended—with their assigned teacher.[17]

2. Supplementary personnel work toward goals agreed on in cooperation with the particular school and self-contained classroom with which they are associated. The resource person is at the disposal of the group, rather than the children being at his disposal.

3. All information collected about a given child is readily accessible to the teacher of the unit to which that child is assigned.

4. Individuals and groups are not limited by circumscribed content allocated on an arbitrary grade basis; curriculum planning depends on present status and readiness to move on. As children progress from one self-contained classroom to another, what they do is determined more by what has gone before than by what has been laid out in advance.

5. Individuals and groups may explore problems fully, unblocked by arbitrary divisions of subject matter or inflexible time schedules.

16 See Van Everie Kilpatrick, *Department Teaching in Elementary Schools* (New York: The Macmillan Company, 1908), p. 8.

17 See Henry J. Otto, "Curriculum Issues in Elementary Education," *Educational Leadership,* VII (October, 1949), 21-25.

6. Instructional materials account for the range of abilities and interests of the group, and do not represent merely the mythical average. For example, a few copies of many different books of varying levels of difficulty are available, rather than enough copies of the same volume for all children in the group.

7. The room is supplied with most essential items of equipment. Ordinarily, additional equipment needed is brought to the children, instead of the children being brought to the equipment.

The self-contained classroom is home base for a teacher and the particular group of children assigned to it. The only justifiable criterion for assigning other teachers or for otherwise tampering with the unity of the basic group is the welfare of the individuals in it. When children must be removed from the group temporarily for such purposes as special instruction, every attempt is made to keep such children in constant communication with the home group. Communication and association of the home group with other school groups are fostered constantly in order to avoid the creation of individual, isolated cells. Self-contained classrooms are not associated with particular vertical and horizontal organizational plans.

Organizing the Small Elementary School

There is nothing essentially different about organizing the small elementary school. But the thousands of elementary school teachers who teach in one, two, and three room buildings are faced with some problems which stem from school size. Several of these problems grow out of attempts to apply traditional compartmentalization of grades and subjects to the small school:

1. *The Problem of Several Grades in a Classroom.* Having several age levels in the same room does not create a unique instructional problem. It simply accentuates the range of individual differences normally present in any classroom. The spread in achievement increases as groups of children progress through the elementary school. By the fifth grade, one may expect a range of from three to ten years in achievement in particular instructional areas. Adding other grades merely extends an already great range somewhat further. The instructional problems remain essentially the same.

2. *The Problem of Arbitrary Subject Matter Demarcations.* When several grade levels exist in a classroom, it is utter folly to try to teach each subject to each grade group. Such an approach led one of the writers to attempt fifty-six periods per day during his first unenlight-

ened year in a one-room school enrolling children from eight grade levels!

3. *Materials Classified by Grades.* The problem of dealing with individual differences is complicated to even greater degree in small schools by the grade classification of reading materials. The slow reader, age twelve, resents use of the second grade reader when children several grades below him are using what he knows to be more advanced material.

4. *Transfers.* Teachers in small schools are hesitant to abandon grade demarcations when they know some children will transfer to larger elementary schools where grade classification is used.

Solutions to these and other problems created by the traditional artificiality of school organization lie not merely in abandoning the "chopped salad" pattern, but also in a changed point of view toward children and the entire instructional program. First of all, individual differences must be looked upon as educational assets rather than hindrances to be eliminated. If a teacher examines the true characteristics of his group and fosters the human individuality he finds, rather than attemping an impossible compression of children into convenient classifications, many organizational problems fade away. This statement is applicable to teachers everywhere, regardless of school size. Secondly, grade levels can be broken down as children tackle all-school or classroom projects, with individuals selecting their own appropriate problems, and teachers guiding according to individual need. Subject lines will often disappear in dealing fully with broad worthwhile problems which serve as centers around which instruction is organized. Materials may be selected with an eye to the range and diversity of differences among children, rather than in terms of the lock-step of graded organization. Both theory and practice must be *organized for education,* not for adaptation of school practice to a long-standing organizational structure which cannot stand critical appraisal.

Administering the Educational Program

The essential problem in school administration is to bring instructional elements—pupils, teachers, principal, auxiliary personnel, plant, materials, and community—into a functional relationship which preserves the parts and produces a smoothly operating whole. Such an enterprise is characterized by the following:

1. *Pupils are guided effectively into, through, and from the elementary school.*

a. Pre-school orientation procedures help to prepare the child for school, to acquaint the parent with school problems and procedures, and to insure necessary school provisions—space, teachers, materials—for entering children.

b. Information pertinent to the child's welfare and usable by school personnel is collected and maintained for convenient use.

c. Conditions and services essential to the child's well-being are provided.

d. The most promising curriculum designs are fostered and maintained.

e. The most effective instructional procedures are encouraged and facilitated.

f. Reporting procedures respect the personal integrity of the child and provide the parent with the information he wants and is entitled to have.

g. Procedures of pupil classification promote both child welfare and teaching efficiency.

h. Pupils move into the secondary school with a minimum of interference with continued progress.

2. *Teachers conduct their work effectively under conditions which promote maximum personal well-being.*

a. Their work with children is conducted without unnecessary interruption.

b. There is minimum outside interference with, and interruption of, classroom procedures.

c. They are protected from administrative chores not directly associated with classroom teaching.

d. They are protected from having to deal directly with community pressure groups who would influence the nature and course of learning.

e. They enjoy wholesome conditions of comfort and cleanliness in plant facilities.

f. They are encouraged to prepare for and accept positions of special responsibility and recognition suited to their abilities and interests.

g. Interpersonal relationships are so fostered that rivalry and hostility among faculty members are virtually non-existent.

h. They enjoy personal security in regard to salary, sick leave, and retirement.

Briggs, Thomas H. and Joseph Justman. *Improving Instruction Through Supervision*. New York: The Macmillan Company, 1952.

Chamberlain, Leo M., rev. by Leslie W. Kindred, *The Teacher and School Organization*, 2nd ed. Englewood Cliffs, N. J.: Prentice-Hall, Inc., 1949.

Dougherty, James H., Frank H. Gorman, and Claude A. Phillips, *Elementary School Organization and Management*, rev. ed. New York: The Macmillan Company, 1950.

Elsbree, Willard S. and Harold J. McNally, *Elementary School Administration and Supervision*. New York: American Book Co., 1951.

Englehardt, Nickolaus Louis, *Planning Elementary School Buildings*. New York: F. W. Dodge Corp., 1953.

Jacobson, Paul B., William C. Reavis, and James D. Logsdon, *The Effective School Principal in Elementary and Secondary Schools*. Englewood Cliffs, N. J.: Prentice-Hall, Inc., 1954.

Mackenzie, Gordon N., Stephen M. Corey, *et al., Instructional Leadership*. New York: Bureau of Publications, Teachers College, Columbia University, 1954.

Otto, Henry J., *Elementary School Organization and Administration*, 3rd ed. New York: Appleton-Century-Crofts, Inc., 1954.

Reavis, William C., Paul R. Pierce, Edward H. Stullken, and Bertrand L. Smith, *Administering the Elementary School*. Englewood Cliffs, N. J.: Prentice-Hall, Inc., 1953.

Reeder, Edwin H., *Supervision in the Elementary School*. Boston: Houghton Mifflin Co., 1953.

Shane, Harold G., and Wilbur A. Yauch, *Creative School Administration*. New York: Henry Holt and Co., 1954.

Southern States Cooperative Program in Educational Administration. *Creative Educational Leadership for a Changing Region*. Nashville, Tennessee: George Peabody College for Teachers, 1953.

Southern States Work-Conference on Educational Problems, *Developing Administrative Leadership for our Schools*. Tallahassee, Florida: State Department of Education, 1952.

Southern States Work-Conference on Educational Supervision, *Educational Supervision, a Leadership Service*. Charleston, West Virginia: Southern States Work Conference, 1955.

Wiles, Kimball, *Supervision for Better Schools*, 2nd ed. Englewood Cliffs, N. J.: Prentice-Hall, Inc., 1955.

THE LEARNING-TEACHING DAY

14

THE INEXPERIENCED TEACHER IS PREOCCUPIED FIRST with keeping the class busy. But soon he comes to see that the *quality* of pupil activities is of primary concern. Discussion of the factors influencing the quality of the learning-teaching day constitutes the heart of this chapter.

FACTORS PRE-CONDITIONING THE INSTRUCTIONAL DAY

The individual teacher is less likely to build a program around the problems of children when he thinks that it is necessary to "cover" a list of suggested topics in the course of studies, or that the principal expects him to give attention to

certain topics at specific times. Similarly, it is difficult for many teachers to correlate subject materials that are isolated in the course of
studies; to use children's interests when the course of studies presents
topics for study; and to move forward sequentially when no total
school planning for continuity is being undertaken. Real or imagined
rigidity in the total school program, real or imagined restrictions on

Kathleen Moon and Fulton County (Georgia) Schools

A GOOD LEARNING-TEACHING DAY PROVIDES FOR INDIVIDUAL
AS WELL AS GROUP ACTIVITIES

teacher initiative, continuous or sporadic faculty attention to curriculum building—all these profoundly affect the way a teacher will operate in the classroom.

The teacher therefore must seek answers to questions such as these: How much freedom do I really have? Do I have to cover these topics or may I use other topics that seek to develop the same skills and values? What are my responsibilities to the teachers of lower and higher grades? To my children? Where and to what degree do my values clash with certain school and system values that seem to have only traditional and sentimental validity? The answers will usually show the teacher who seriously considers these matters that he has much greater freedom than he may have believed.

Community Mores and Relations

The years since World War II have witnessed a heartening revival of public interest in schools—their philosophy, purposes, activities, testing programs, and reporting systems. Unfortunately, this interest has been capitalized upon by men seeking financial gain or the national limelight. The current clash of ideologies will be wholesome if it produces a thorough twentieth-century re-appraisal of the great common school experiment.[1] But there have been some dangerous splinter movements where attempts have been made through vicious scare techniques to develop minority viewpoints into the national viewpoint.[2] And many teachers—in fact, large numbers of teachers— have "scared." Individual teachers, nevertheless, have stood upon their feet again and again to speak out for what they believe to be good for children, and therefore good for America. The danger is not that teachers will re-examine, or even change, their viewpoints when they are under attack—but that they will cease to act in accord with what they believe.

The day-to-day planning of the teacher, then, is profoundly influenced by the fact that our schools are being subjected to criticism and attack, both thoughtful and irresponsible. This criticism affects the kind and amount of attention he gives to the traditional fundamentals, and whether he avoids or deals with controversial issues. It

[1] For an anthology of criticisms, *pros* and *cons,* of public education in America today, see C. Winfield Scott and Clyde M. Hill, eds., *Public Education Under Criticism* (Englewood Cliffs, N. J.: Prentice-Hall, Inc., 1954). Scott and Hill have selected a wide variety of articles previously published in professional and lay journals and organized them so that articles of a given type, or which relate to a given issue, are grouped together.

[2] See T. M. Stinnett, *Teacher Education at the Crossroads* (Florida: Southern Council on Teacher Education, University of Florida, 1954), p. 9.

also affects *how* he deals with these issues—actively or passively, insipidly or fervidly, as an educator or a propagandist. Obviously, then, the character of the daily program is affected directly both by the ideological controversies raging in the larger community, and the teacher's reactions to them.

Community, School, and Classroom Facilities

The quantity, quality, and variety of facilities for teaching and learning available in the classroom, school, and community do make a difference in the nature of the educational programs provided for children. Some teachers are resource-poor in the midst of plenty; others are resource-rich in a desert. Nevertheless, two teachers of equal ability and creativity will do jobs differing in effectiveness because of differences in available facilities.

A few simple questions about school, classroom, and community resources will quickly indicate some of the daily activities that are or are not possible:

1. Are gymnasium, auditorium, and lunchroom separate; or is there one central all-purpose room?

2. Is there one dark room for showing film and film strips, or can every room be quickly adapted for this use?

3. How much playground space is available and how accessible is it?

4. To what degree can desks and tables be moved and re-arranged?

5. Do more than one teacher and one group of children share a single classroom?

6. What industrial and commercial plants exist in the community, and how accessible are they?

7. What other community agencies—health, welfare, and recreation—exist and are accessible?

Answers to dozens of questions like this will prescribe certain limits to the instructional day. Teachers are advised to take inventory of facilities *with* children. Out of their exploration may come not only a sense of the bearing these resources have upon learning and teaching, but also of their potential use as instructional toe-holds.

These three areas—the curriculum and its planning, community mores and relations, and instructional facilities—are only examples of the many factors that pre-condition the instructional day. The way the teacher relates himself to them, consciously or unconsciously, affects the quality of day-to-day learning and teaching.

THE TEACHER'S SPAN OF CONTROL

Beginning teachers are overwhelmed by their broad array of responsibilities and the many different things to which they must attend. Experienced teachers, regardless of the working patterns already established, struggle continuously with the problem of knowing what to pay attention to. It is a problem, essentially, of differentiating first between the relevant and the irrelevant, and then of embracing the relevant in such a way that order results in the daily program. Teachers are expressing concern with this problem when they say: "How can I possibly teach these children anything and keep them quiet at the same time? There just isn't time to add anything else to the school day. You can't teach forty children crammed into a hatbox shared by another group in a double session!"

Elements Encompassed in the Teacher's Span of Control

The teacher's major considerations in planning and conducting the daily enterprise are presented below in a sort of check-list form. They operate in constant relationship—a moving, shifting relationship—throughout every activity in the day. When the day gets out of balance sometimes even to the point where it is in danger of disinte-

Beloit Public Schools, Beloit, Wisconsin

MODELS BRING EXPERIENCE CLOSER TO REALITY

grating into a chaotic shambles, one or more of these factors is sure to be the source of the trouble. A smooth, satisfying day is the result of the neat interlocking of parts. Some of these parts, discussed from the viewpoint of what is desirable, are presented below.

The Teacher's Control of Self. The teacher feels comfortable in the particular technique being used.[3]

The teacher's analysis of self in relation to technique reveals:

those things he can now do reasonably well;

those things he cannot do and feels he cannot attempt to do at this time;

those things he cannot do but feels he must learn to do if he is to become the teacher he wants to be.

Experimentation with a new procedure is governed by the principle that it may be checked and withdrawn safely before the "point of no return."[4]

The teacher is sufficiently relaxed about present commitment to method to be able to regard new ideas as a challenge to exploration rather than a threat to personal security.

The teacher sees sufficient relationship between ends and means to avoid panic or blind conformance in the face of popular new fads and frills.

The teacher introduces changes one at a time into parts rather than into all of the program, with proper regard for all factors that must be encompassed in his span of control.

The teacher is sufficiently relaxed to recognize that not all teachers do the same things equally well, and that no teacher succeeds equally well with all children.

NOTE: The teacher is more likely to have this control of self when she teaches in a setting free from interpersonal rivalry and hostility. The tone established here by administrative leadership is most significant.[5]

A Pervading Sense of Direction in the Teacher's Span of Control. The teacher has given sufficient thought to the meaning of the

---

[3] See Harry N. Rivlin, *Teaching Adolescents in Secondary Schools.* (New York: Appleton-Century-Crofts, Inc., 1948), pp. 67-68. Rivlin makes the statement, "It would be ideal if every teacher could do everything perfectly. Since he cannot, each teacher should take full advantage of what he does do well."

[4] See Herbert A. Thelen, "The Experimental Method in Classroom Leadership," *Elementary School Journal,* LIII (October, 1952), 76-85. Thelen expresses the same idea this way: "The principle is that the risk taken by the leader should not be greater than his ability to remedy the situation if the action turns out to be mistaken."

[5] For further development of this idea, see Fritz Redl and William W. Wattenberg, *Mental Hygiene in Teaching* (New York: Harcourt, Brace and Co., 1951), pp. 405-409.

school's goals to be able to visualize the kind of behavior changes (education) he is trying to develop in children.

The teacher's sense of direction supports, rather than blocks, a sense of direction possessed by the children; activities are planned and conducted in the light of mutual agreement on ends sought.

The teacher is able . . . "to distinguish between large major purposes, which give direction to the whole episode, and specific and immediate teaching purposes, which are used to move toward the accomplishment of the larger objectives."[6]

NOTE: A pervading sense of direction is more likely to prevail in a classroom when both the teacher and the children actually are participating in goal setting.[7]

An Understanding of Children in the Teacher's Span of Control. The teacher has some insight into the specific conditions which block or expedite the learning of particular children in the group.

The teacher is able to differentiate among those diversions and distractions which seriously impede the learning process and those which may be accepted as a natural concomitant of social interaction.

The teacher approaches dislocations in the daily program with a cause-seeking, rather than a punishment-giving, outlook.

Content and Materials in the Teacher's Span of Control. The teacher has a general grasp of the major contributions or concepts of a given field of study.[8]

The teacher has some considerable insight into the basic elements around which daily activity is to be organized—the concepts, skills, and values sought for in children as they learn.[9]

Textbooks and other source materials are used because of their appropriateness in achieving goals; they are not "to be covered" as though such coverage were, of itself, education.

Space in the Teacher's Span of Control. The teacher sees a relationship between the kind of activity being carried on and the space desired and available for that activity.

---

6 Virgil E. Herrick and James Knight, "Child Study and the Improvement of the Educational Program," *Elementary School Journal,* LI (March, 1951), 374.

7 For an extensive analysis of many aspects of pupil-teacher planning in the classroom, with much detailed descriptive material, see Alice Miel and Associates, *Cooperative Procedures in Learning* (New York: Bureau of Publications, Teachers College, Columbia University, 1952).

8 For further elaboration of the relationship between a subject field and a concept to be developed, see Gordon N. Mackenzie, "What Should Be the Organizing Elements of the Curriculum?" *Toward Improved Curriculum Theory,* Supplementary Educational Monographs Number 71, Virgil E. Herrick and Ralph W. Tyler, eds. (Chicago: The University of Chicago Press, March, 1950), p. 57.

9 For further elaboration, see *ibid,* p. 63-64.

The teacher sees possible relationships between pupil behavior and space appropriateness.

The teacher guides children in exploring possibilities for improving seating arrangements, storage space and its use, unused space in other parts of the building, and so on—all in relation to what the group wants to accomplish.

NOTE: Many elementary schools have moved so far from ideal conditions of room space and class size[10] that teachers readily become discouraged in seeking to use procedures that seem to require greater opportunity for group movement. It is encouraging to note, however, that many teachers see the significance of doing what they believe to be best, even with modifications, instead of resigning themselves in dispirited fashion to what appear to be insurmountable handicaps.[11] These teachers are able to report continued enthusiasm in their daily work—and sufficient satisfaction to cope with the potential discouragement of overcrowded conditions.[12]

Time in the Teacher's Span of Control. The teacher sees the significant learning involved in children planning their use of time:

Children's planning of time use is both a desired life behavior, and a means to effective conduct of the daily program.

Wise use of time is a learned behavior; ". . . children do not come ready-made with ability to make good use of time in school."[13]

The teacher sees time in relation to both short-term and long-term goals:

Time spent early in the learning-teaching process in taking care of what may be later persistent problems is time well spent.

A productive school year is really a composite of productive school days.

The teacher is able to plan and account for multiple outcomes in relation to specific time usage:

It is entirely possible that adequate attention may be given to spelling, for example, in the course of a day, even though no specific time is assigned to it.

There are many learning outcomes—critical thinking, concern for

10 See John I. Goodlad, "Room to Live and Learn: Class Size and Room Space as Factors in the Learning-Teaching Process," *Childhood Education,* XXX (April, 1954), 355-361.

11 Robert H. Anderson suggests ways local communities are meeting their needs for adequate school housing in "Each Community Must Face Its Own Problems," *Educational Leadership,* XII (October, 1954), 23-29. See also other articles in this issue.

12 For some encouraging anecdotal accounts, see "What Does Crowding Do?" *Childhood Education,* XXX (April, 1954), 365-373.

13 Alice Miel and Associates, *op. cit.,* p. 24.

the rights of others, humility, language skills, to name only a few—
that are best achieved with other learnings, rather than in separate
periods of time specifically devoted to their attainment.

The teacher is able to see a significant relationship between time
spent or to be spent and the kind and/or level of learning sought:

Early practice in a given learning activity produces a rate of progress that may easily be deceptive; progress slows down as the learner
moves upward on the learning curve.

The way time is distributed often is as important a factor in learning as the amount of time spent; short periods of practice distributed
over several days may be more productive than a long period of practice in a single day.

NOTE: There never is enough time for everything a teacher would like
to do. There usually is enough time to pay attention to those things
we believe to be truly significant. It would seem, then, that the
teacher's basic job is to determine which things are sufficiently important to warrant expenditure of time for their accomplishment.[14]

It will be seen from the foregoing that virtually all elements of the
school day are in some way encompassed in the preceding discussion
of "span of control." The illustrative sub-points, however, do not
cover certain problems in sufficient detail. Most of the subsequent
pages deal with these problems in different ways and in more detail.

TIMING AND PACING

When to begin an activity is the problem of timing. How fast to
move forward with an activity is the problem of pacing.

Timing

Billy is all steamed up about the new bus terminal going up across
from the theatre . . . Should I, the teacher, use this interest as a
starting point in studying transportation now, even though such a
unit is planned for next spring? Miss Green is going to be showing
that movie on salmon fishing tomorrow . . . Should I use it, too, and
save having to re-order it later, even though we aren't ready to make a
study of salmon fishing right now? We're studying New England now
in our social studies, but the stories and poems we are reading are all
about Mexico . . . Should I substitute New England stories for these
stories of Mexico? Susan suggested we make up a dance to go with
the poem . . . Should we practice it now or wait until this afternoon

14 See Earl C. Kelley, "What Dare We Leave Out?" *Educational Leadership*, XI (January, 1954), 209-213.

when we'll be able to use the gym? These questions have to do with timing the learning enterprise.

The first question is related to using children's interests; the second to selecting materials; the third to selecting content; the fourth to arranging for space. Obviously, there are no absolute answers to such questions; no answers that will apply to all contexts in which the

Beloit Public Schools, Beloit, Wisconsin

COMMUNICATION IS A PERSISTENT PROBLEM OF HUMAN RELATIONSHIPS

questions arise. But we should have enough insights at this point into the factors involved to suggest ways of arriving at solutions.

Two criteria are important in the timing involved: the readiness of the group; and the relationship of the topic proposed to the sense of directions possessed by teacher and pupils.

Pacing

The presence of thirty-five little energy systems—each differing from all the rest in capacity for movement and in present operating efficiency—poses for the classroom teacher one of the most perplexing and frustrating instructional problems. This problem is essentially one of helping each group member moving forward at the pace which is right for him. Pacing requires that the teacher be aware of the progress patterns previously exhibited by each child, and of both past and present deviations from his patterns.

An analysis of current practice suggests that there is greater school provision for present attainment differences than for present rate differences. School people still keep children back for failure to reach certain norms or standards. They also group children in terms of their recognized differences in attaining the concepts or skills sought. But elementary school daily schedules—which should be relatively free from artificial time divisions—are still set up primarily around the idea of so much time per subject per day. All teacher planning, then, must accept and account for the fact that pacing a child is a completely individualized problem, even when group membership is reduced to two pupils.

Listed below to illustrate the pacing problem are a number of instructional conditions which do not maintain proper pacing of children's progress. After each example is listed one of several possible cues to detecting cause. Finally, a remedy is suggested. This parallel arrangement of problem, cause, and remedy should not be taken literally. The items merely illustrate the pacing dilemma, and offer hints to be explored through trial-and-error experimentation.

Problem	Possible pacing difficulty	Possible remedies
1. Ted, with a record of high academic attainment for his three previous years in school, begins to disturb children around him soon after tackling seatwork.	Ease with which Ted completes tasks leaves him with much free time on his hands, and high energy output keeps him from sitting still after completing a task.	a) Walk around to Ted soon after seatwork begins and suggest other study to do. b) Arrange for supplementary activities of a constructive sort. c) Let Ted move ahead in area of study quite apart from progress of others, but spending equivalent amount of time each day.
2. During shift from arithmetic to reading, Sidney displays temper, slamming pencils and banging books, generally disturbing the class.	Sidney enjoys arithmetic but he is a plodder, moving slowly and accurately. He resents being pulled from enjoyable, uncompleted work to engage in less enjoyable studies.	a) Suggest to Sidney that he skip the first few arithmetic problems, since they do not present difficulty to him. b) Change the schedule so that another activity enjoyable to Sidney follows arithmetic. c) Analyze Sidney's reading problem with a view to determining cause of reading disability and lack of interest.

3. Unusual amount of cheating, questionable absences, or tenseness and irritability breaks out in the classroom.	The class is moving too quickly into new studies without sufficient readiness, and with insufficient guidance in assuring that children know how to do each successive problem.	a) Take a spot survey by observing children's classroom performance, questioning group, interviewing parents. b) Administer standardized achievement tests and relate results to difficulty of regular classroom work. c) Examine arbitrariness of daily schedule with a view to more pupil involvement in planning. d) Institute daily and weekly planning sessions to keep constant classroom check on pupil insight into group progress.
4. Bobby just isn't trying any more. Most of the time he won't even attempt to get down to business, but listlessly passes the time away.	a) Bobby has for so long been over his head that he under-aspires, assuming without trying that he could not succeed. b) Bobby for so long has breezed unchallenged through his work that he has lost all interest and is bored with the whole business of school. (There should be very little difficulty in selecting one of these over the other as a possible hypothesis.)	a) Begin immediately to differentiate tasks for Bobby, being certain to arrange for immediate success experience, stressing assured success over level at attainment until Bobby's interest begins to return. b) Introduce Bobby to a few new differentiated tasks with a statement concerning their difficulty; continue to provide at least some activities of unusual challenge, to the extent that personal time limits permit.
5. The last 10 to 15 minutes of the cafeteria lunch period is marked by fussing, fighting, and general confusion, even though most children are still eating.	The rapid eaters are finishing first and time lies heavily on their hands while they wait for the others.	Observe the eating habits of the group carefully and then send the children into the cafeteria in such a way that slow eaters eat first.
6. The school council is disintegrating; children's decisions are frequently vetoed by the principal, and the student body is generally dissatisfied with council decisions and their implementation.	a) The realm of the council's jurisdiction has not been defined. b) Problems that lie beyond the interest and understanding of elementary school age children are being submitted to the council. c) Legislative, judicial, and executive functions of the council have been neither differentiated nor defined.	a) Hold sessions between representatives of the pupils and of the faculty to determine appropriate council functions in line with pupil maturity. b) Analyze problems to differentiate the meaningful from the meaningless for children of this age. c) Remove disciplinary activities completely from the council's jurisdiction.

7. Mixed sex group activities in the fifth grade are leading to intense girl-boy rivalries.	Boys and girls are being expected to associate and work closely together when drives for identification with own sex group are strong.	a) Be sure that groupings do not call for close working together of a few boys with a few girls. b) Keep sexes separated so far as small group activities are concerned until sociometric studies provide leads for experimental groupings.

Learning Timing and Pacing

Obviously both timing and pacing, in addition perhaps to other factors, are involved in each of the incidents outlined above. It is probable that timing and pacing are key factors in differentiating the good teacher from the poor one, the experienced from the inexperienced. There is no magic formula for learning them. Good timing and pacing involve learning innumerable details and synthesizing them into the right decision at the right moment.

Some factors and conditions significant for good timing and pacing are:

1. Learning activities are introduced when both pupil interest and readiness are at the optimum.

2. The total time spent on a given activity approximates the interest time span of the children.

3. Learnings are arranged so that they support one another, and promote learning.

4. Time spent on activities that are too easy or too difficult is minimal. The teacher is alert to cues in this regard, and is quick to guide pupils to more worthwhile tasks.

5. Periods of lag due to quick completion of activities or to frustration because of inadequate time are likewise minimal. Provisions are made for enrichment, or for shortened assignments and increased time, depending upon need.

6. Classroom activities are obviously free from hurry and bustle and yet productive activity moves steadily ahead. Each child has significant jobs to do *all* day; he moves easily from activity to activity, there is a marked absence of "orders" from the teacher, and a minimum of dilly-dally. There is time for wholesome relaxation, for laughter, and for doing the things that seem important right now that are productive of rich learning. Above all, in a setting of wise pacing and timing, the teacher is poised and relaxed, alert to individual welfare, and ever moving forward toward clear objectives.

Achieving a Balanced Daily Program

The final achievement of a well-balanced school day is a cooperative pupil-teacher enterprise. But before, during, and after the time that children and teacher engage in planning, the teacher must keep a constant watch on what is happening to assure the presence of certain elements which may be of little concern to children and not readily perceived by them. Significant considerations are:

1. Subject matter as an instructional dimension must constantly be related to more fundamental curricular components: the concepts, skills, and values which underlie the educational enterprise.

2. The areas of living through which fundamental concepts, skills, and values are developed must encompass the children's complete range of day-to-day, week-to-week problems.

3. Available time is conceived in terms of multiple possibilities for organization, rather than as a fixed daily program.

4. Continuous formal and informal evaluation is sensitive to present time balance and imbalance, and leads to appropriate adjustment.

Balance Among Organizing Components of the Curriculum

A balanced daily program does not necessarily result from devoting so much time per day to each instructional area, in line with the particular scheme of curricular organization being followed. It is the result of ascertaining that certain fundamental elements receive consistent and persistent, but not necessarily daily, attention.

The teacher considering the problem of balancing the daily program will want to go far deeper than the relative superficiality of questioning such as: Did we spend thirty minutes today on arithmetic? Did we get in a spelling period? Have we spent enough time on Norway? Instead, he should ask: To what extent are these children relating mathematical aspirations to the realities of our world and to living? To what extent are we deepening habits of awareness in relation to the place of letters in words, and words in communication? Are these children grasping the significance of natural forces in the way of life developed by a group of people? In effect, is subject matter contributing in a significant way to individual behavior changes expressed in a comprehensive list of educational goals?

Comprehensive Attention to Areas of Living

Like the day of the adult, the day of the child falls into major divisions, determined by his needs and his interests, which are the need to play, to rest, to eat, to work, to learn new things, to enjoy companionship, and to attend to personal concerns. Once the modern teacher envisions the curriculum as a sequence of life experiences, and planning as a manipulation of these experiences to meet the needs of children, the making of a daily program becomes comparatively easy.[15]

A comprehensive school day, then, finds children learning concepts, deepening skills, and developing values in relation to living in the natural, social, and scientific world around them. Not all areas will be dealt with every day, and no one area will dominate for any great length of time.

In analyzing the kind of day that should emerge from the planning envisioned in this and the preceding section, certain operational guidelines emerge:

1. Each phase of the day is planned with a view to the total range of behavior changes sought, and no phase of the day is conceived of as being merely busywork, space filler, or time waster.

2. Each phase of the day is planned with a view to extending practice in the various phases of human living.

3. It is recognized that a single area of living may well have potential for extending every kind of behavior contemplated.

4. It is recognized that some essential skills are not adequately practised through classroom social living, and that provision must therefore be made for special practice sessions.

5. It is recognized that school at best represents only a segment of a child's daily living, and that behavior in other than school situations cannot be predicted accurately.

Time and Its Distribution

The problem of available time in the classroom is akin to that of available time in our own hurried lives. There seems to be so much to do and so little time to do it. But differences among schools, as among people, are apparent. Many small rural schools still seem to have time for a wide range of living, often carried on at what appears to be a leisurely pace. But the big urban elementary school may easily become a place of pressures, of time schedules, and of machine-like organization. In such settings it is difficult for many children to "find themselves," to cushion their tensions, to establish a satisfying daily rhythm.

The first essentials regarding wise time usage relate to the teacher's

[15] Kate V. Wofford, *Teaching in Small Schools* (New York: The Macmillan Company, 1946), p. 91.

perception of the school year. He must see the school year ahead as it really is: a succession of seasons that have significance for instruction, a succession of breaks that drastically cut the length of time available, and a series of unknowns that will cut the school year even more. He must then perceive which series of time units are relatively unbroken and therefore adaptable to certain kinds of instruction. Such thinking and planning reduces the possibility of the group's moving into an extensive unit a week before Christmas, just as it reduces the danger of an ominous lull just before a holiday period.

A second group of essentials relates to the teacher's grasp of instructional dimensions in relation to time dimensions. If he sees the school day as so many available hours to be divided up into so many pieces to accommodate so many subjects, he might as well reconcile himself to a chronic complaint of too little time. Each unit of time has multiple possibilities for effective use. Single goals, single functions, single activities, must not be balanced off against single units of time on a one-to-one ratio. Each time unit must be viewed by the teacher as being subject to geometric analysis. In this light, a minute in a classroom of thirty-five children must be thought of as thirty-five minutes multiplied by the number of learning concerns that can be encompassed at any one time.

A third group of essentials in considering time usage is that of the teacher's personality organization. As mentioned earlier, the teacher does much to set the timing and the pacing. A teacher who already is "off balance" by the time the school day starts probably will make poor decisions in regard to timing and pacing. Children are quickly affected by evidences of disorganization in the teacher and lose their normal sense of rhythm in the day's activities. They too become pushed off balance. Under such conditions, time is not used to best advantage.

A fourth group of essentials in time usage relates to the number of people who share the instructional day. One group is the children. The other is the teachers. A teacher cannot individualize an instructional day for forty children in the same way that she can for twenty-five. Different perceptions of time usage may be called for. Similarly, time usage and instructional techniques must shift when class size moves upward.

Certain guides for action may be drawn from an analysis of problems in ordering time:

1. The teacher's planning in regard to time should be narrowed

gradually from yearly to weekly units, and finally to daily units of hours and minutes.

2. Time sequences are subject to many different kinds of analysis. Consideration of a given time unit should embrace:

a. the possibilities for varied pupil activity;

b. the variety of basic concepts, skills, and values that may be developed in that unit;

c. the possibilities that the particular time expenditure involved will eliminate the need for other time expenditures.

3. A teacher's personal time schedule must be put in order if he is to be a positive influence in developing time schedules with children.

4. Many aspects of the curriculum may be developed without providing separate time for them. For instance, spelling generally is taught best within the natural content of other activities, rather than in separate prescribed periods.

5. All personnel who work with children in the instructional enterprise must come together to consider their total, as well as their individual, time allocations in relation to the passage of daily and weekly time.

Evaluating Program Balance

Earlier in this chapter, the significance of each teacher identifying for himself those concepts, skills, and values which underlie instruction and curriculum was stressed. A list of these objectives can be most useful in appraising program balance. This list can be used not only to evolve an over-all picture of class progress, but also to an individual's distribution of activity. Such a list can then be related to the areas of living through which basic learnings have been developed. Figure 1 shows the possibilities of relating basic learnings to the areas used for their development. A chart like this might be used for a total class or for an individual. It is by no means complete; it suggests only a few items to give the teacher ideas for developing such a chart for himself.

The amount of cross-checking possible in such a chart depends entirely upon *what* had transpired in the classroom and *how* the learning enterprise had been conducted. Naturally, more spaces would be filled in in considering the total class than in appraising the activity of a single individual.

Brief attention must be given to the role of parents. Parents can readily understand a chart such as the foregoing and stand to profit much from discussing it with the teacher. Discussion soon dispels parental fears aroused by children's comments to the effect that, "We haven't studied geography for ten days," or, "We never have a spelling lesson."

FIGURE 1

CHART FOR RELATING AREAS OF ACTIVITY TO AREAS OF
FUNDAMENTAL LEARNING IN EVALUATING PROGRAM BALANCE[16]

Basic areas of Learning	Areas in which classroom activities were conducted			
	Group work	Recreational Reading	Computational Activities	Graphic and Plastic Art
1. Understanding of personal strengths and weaknesses	X	X	X	X
2. Recognition and respect for the rights of others	X	X		
3. Skill in group discussion	X			
4. Understanding of democratic traditions	X	X		
5. Appropriate social attitudes toward various levels of socio-economic status	X			
6. Understanding the effect of seasonal changes on the habits of people		X		X
7. Skill in simple measurement of distances			X	
8. Setting up tentative hypotheses about causes of surrounding phenomena		X		

FINDING APPROPRIATE ORGANIZING CENTERS FOR LEARNING AND TEACHING

The teacher who must prepare lessons anew for each time segment of each instructional day *ad infinitum* is in for a dreary, demanding, never-ending, out-of-class school life. His behavior might well be compared to a rower who pauses long enough for the boat to stop after

[16] See Ralph W. Tyler, *Basic Principles of Curriculum and Instruction*, Syllabus for Education 360 (Chicago: The University of Chicago Press, 1950). The chart used here is an adaptation of one proposed by Tyler, on page 32, for checking behavioral against content aspects of educational objectives.

each stroke. Some days will be like this in even the best managed class-room—all activity seems to have slowed to a stop simultaneously. But, ordinarily, one activity should stimulate another in such way that the teacher spends most of his time helping children make wise choices instead of dreaming up things that might possibly be of interest to them.

Use of Effective Organizing Centers

Chapter 6 described the nature of the organizing centers which are helpful to children and their teacher in relating and developing the instructional activities of a given class or school day. Organization always relates the important aspects to be considered to some organizing point, which gives both unity and stability to the organization.

Organizing centers, as has been pointed out, must have the characteristics of importance, accessibility, breadth, organizing capacity, and developmental potentiality if they are to be helpful to children and teachers in coordinating their educational activities.

PLANNING IN THE CLASSROOM

This section deals more specifically with the actual process of daily planning, especially as it involves children. It is a first principle of program planning that children be involved significantly in the process.

Beginning Where We Are

In beginning where we are, it is important to know how far we have come. This is partly a teacher activity. He knows some things because of his incidental observation of the group the year before. He can find out much more by talking with the previous teacher. A recording system which maintains anecdotal-type data is an invaluable aid.[17] But much functional information can be gained from the group itself.

Knowing what problems of planning children are already accustomed to solving helps us to determine our level of approach. Too little challenge may lead to regression; too much to frustration. Elementary school children are capable of assuming responsibility, and they grow in self-dependence to the extent to which they have opportunities to assume it.

17 For instance, the Parker School District, Greenville, South Carolina, maintains such records on all children from the time they first come to school.

The Teacher and Planning Procedures

The teacher, too, must begin where he is. Many teachers after an enlightening course in child study or a visit to an activity-centered classroom want to jump in with both feet. Perhaps everything they have been accustomed to doing seems out of line with their changed point of view. The result may be that these teachers swim so far from familiar shores that they cannot regain them or any other shores. Until rapport has been built up, children are not likely to throw a life-belt to a sinking teacher. The danger is that if we try new procedures and fail miserably, we are not likely to blame ourselves. It is so much more comforting to blame the procedure. But we may not try again. The old rut is so deep and comfortable, and the experience of almost drowning so frightening, that we stick doggedly to our old ways. The answer lies in trying one thing at a time just enough at a time.

For example, the fifth-grade teacher who begins the year by conducting tours of the plant, must provide also for other activities. To do nothing but plan, carry out, and evaluate in relation to tours is asking for trouble. Fifth-graders require much more varied activity than this. Let us assume that this teacher always has conducted his class along somewhat formal lines, with a definite time period assigned each day for each subject. He is now disturbed by the artificiality of his procedure and wants more life-like activities. He probably would do best to retain most of his former organization and incorporate a block of time for more free planning together. Usually, too, it is best to provide this block of time in relation to that area of the curriculum in which the teacher feels most comfortable. At any rate, it is essential that the teacher feel at home in what he is doing. Feelings of personal inadequacy are soon sensed by a group of children, and then the group too begins to feel insecure in its operations.

Planning an Initial Schedule

It usually is best, except for the unusually skilled teacher, to plan the first week or so of the term rather carefully. There are several distinct advantages in this:

1. The resulting orderly school day frees the teacher for many of the mechanics involved in getting school underway.

2. Generally speaking, youngsters react favorably to an orderly beginning. A wholesome atmosphere may result.

3. By providing a framework, the teacher is able to learn about the

present development of his group before determining the level of participation to be expected.

4. The security of his framework permits the teacher to begin careful experimentation with new procedures. A pre-determined schedule is always there to fall back upon if planning with children does not prove fruitful at first.

5. Children's horizons of what a school day can be like may be expanded. When children are asked to choose, they can choose only from what they know. If children are asked what games they would like to play, they are able to suggest only the three they already know. The job of the teacher is to help them find a fourth. Thus, carefully planned school days which are exciting and interesting for children provide readiness experiences for future planning. As children are brought more and more into the planning process, they have more and more to bring to it.

Teachers are often disappointed at the paucity of ideas contributed when children are first asked to participate in the planning process. But it would be well to look at the backgrounds of these children. How sterile has their school experience been? How exciting do we expect suggestions of fifth-graders to be when they have spent four years of their school lives in carrying out assignments and listening to presentations? We must help them to find more exciting paths to learning. A teacher cannot afford to be a spectator in the learning process. She must be one of the group, leading sometimes, guiding sometimes, following sometimes, but always a member of the group.

The "orderly" school day mentioned above does not imply rigidity. It implies rather, a program worked out with some logic behind it.[18] It should include some time set aside each day for planning or evalu-

[18] For the reader who is interested in examining schedules worked out by others, the following references are included:

Fay Adams, *Educating America's Children,* 2nd ed. (New York: Ronald Press, 1954). See pp. 106-107 for sample daily schedules.

Ilse Forest, *Early Years at School* (New York: McGraw-Hill Book Co., Inc., 1949). See pp. 82-88 for schedules from nursery school through the second grade.

J. Murray Lee and Dorris May Lee, *The Child and His Curriculum,* 2nd ed. (New York: Appleton-Century-Crofts, Inc., 1950). See pp. 256, 257 for outlines of three schedules—for a one-room rural school, for a fifth grade, and for intermediate grades.

Freeman G. Macomber, *Child Development in the Elementary School* (New York: American Book Co., 1941). See pp. 2-13 for programs contrasting a conventional with a progressive classroom.

For a discussion of daily and weekly plans, see John U. Michaelis, "Making Plans for Teaching," in John U. Michaelis and Paul R. Grim, *The Student Teacher in the Elementary School* (Englewood Cliffs, N. J.: Prentice-Hall, Inc., 1953), pp. 82-111.

Kate V. Wofford, *op. cit.* See pp. 101-102 for a daily plan of work for a one-room school comprising 22 pupils, grades one through eight.

ating work. It would not, however, necessitate teacher-domination of program planning. It might include a quiet, story-telling period following lunch. It would not require that the teacher tell all the stories.

Providing for Continuous Planning

The program carefully planned in advance by the teacher is merely a means of getting started. The teacher, even of the very young, wants to bring children more and more into the planning process. There are many ways of doing so, depending upon the teacher, the group, and other circumstances. One way is to select an area of the program in which the teacher feels particularly secure and which offers unusual opportunities for planning with children. Motivation for planning may be provided for by a field trip, a movie, an unusual moth brought to class, and so on. The alert teacher, quick to see the relationship to over-all purposes, stimulates questions that deserve answers. A large block of time is allocated for the study of children's problems. The rest of the schedule goes on as before, but for one period of time each day careful plans are made together.

Another scheme is to set aside a free period, usually at the beginning of the day, for planning all the day's activities. With older children longer periods may be set aside once each week during which the activities for the entire week are planned. Short daily periods are used for evaluation. In Helene Critchett's second grade class in the Avondale Elementary School, Avondale Estates, Georgia, children and teacher assemble together at the end of each day. With the teacher in the corner and children fanned out close around her on the cleanly-scrubbed square of linoleum, events of the day are passed in review. No day would be complete without this intimate powwow.

Whatever the means used, the day's work should be conducted in such a way that children participate in the very heart of the planning process. It is so easy to let children take care of a few necessary details at the periphery of the learning process—such as regulating temperature and cleaning the boards—and then to rest assured that they have a meaningful role in conducting the day's activities. There probably are some activities in the daily program of the elementary school that should be initiated and carried through entirely by the teacher. There are others that warrant mutual assumption of responsibilities. There are still others that should be carried on with little guidance from the teacher. It is well for the teacher to identify activities in each category with a view to extending pupil participation. One way to do this is to keep a diary for a week or more, recording every activity of each school day. An illustration of this is a running account kept by sixty-six teachers and the student teachers who had been placed with them.[19] Observation for a four-hour period in each classroom revealed the following activities, grades one through three:

Conducting devotional

Singing with children

Participating in drives for bonds, stamps, tinfoil, paper and coat hangers

Observing the weather

Playing outdoor games

Teaching folk games

Listening to records

Planning a party with children

Teaching reading to several groups at one time

Eating with children in cafeteria

Free play with assorted materials

Reading poetry to children

Creating rhythmic exercises

Teaching writing

Helping children with number skills

Teaching children to write paragraphs

Helping children to learn to spell

Leading a discussion of current events

Helping children to learn to live with others

Studying records of children

Assisting in the compilation of records of children

Helping children take care of pets

Making stories about specimen brought in for science table

Talking informally with children

Having rest periods for children

Assisting the local health officer in his examination of children

Conducting science experiments

Making charts and flash cards for word drills

Planting seeds in an indoor garden

Helping children with dictionary study

Collecting lunch money

Making attendance records

Selecting materials for individuals

Visiting the public library

Making inventories of communicative skills

Developing a procedure for the study of a group problem

Showing a movie

Editing a newspaper

Teaching the orchestra family

Helping a pupil analyze his own folder

Teaching choral reading

Holding conferences with individual children

Encouraging children to experiment with different art media, wood, clay, papier-mâché textiles

Guiding children in the use of workbook

Helping children improve table manners

Helping children appreciate good lighting and adequate ventilation

Teaching the basic steps in nutrition

Writing thank-you notes

Using an encyclopedia for more information about frost and sleet

Planning and directing free time

Reading charts about excursions

Attending student council meeting

Administering tests

Making puppets

Playing out stories

Conducting indoor recess

Checking Sunday School attendances

Listening to the free conversation of children

Teaching a child to use a flute

Helping children with milk and cracker time

Planning and giving assembly programs

Administering first aid

Planning a committee meeting with P. T. A. members

Planning with children and teachers for Dad's Night

It would be an easy matter for the teacher preparing an inventory to distribute the activities into the three classifications given in the preceding paragraph. Then, he might decide that a larger part in planning certain of these activities should be assumed by the group

[19] Data collected by the Georgia Teacher Education Council in its study of preparation programs for primary teachers, 1951.

and proceed accordingly. Subsequent check-ups would reveal the progress made.

A basic principle in providing successful continuity to planning is that those affected by changes should have a vital part in effecting these changes. Children, like adults, want to play a role in that which affects them; to be in the "inner circle." Strong bonds of understanding, made strong by mutual sharing, result in a smooth-running classroom. Steady learning does not just happen; it is planned for.

Trends in Daily Planning

Teachers must not blindly follow innovations in school and classroom organization. A particular organization is used because it expedites a particular kind of learning in a particular situation. It may have application to other situations; it may not. The trends in planning reported below are presented here only because many people in today's schools are finding certain kinds of organizational procedures helpful. The reader should use or adapt them only as they are appropriate for his particular teaching situation in the elementary grades.

1. *Increased emphasis on planning in relation to what we know about children.* Utilization in planning of what we know about energy patterns is a case in point. With young children, we know not only to keep intense working periods short, but also to expect a range of interest span within any given group.

2. *Increased emphasis upon including children in the planning process.* A framework for realization of pupil-teacher planning is established by setting aside special periods of time for planning and evaluation. The length of time to be planned for, depth of evaluation attempted, and so on, will vary with the maturity of the group.

3. *Increased stress on the social element.* There was a time when only teacher-pupil interaction found expression in the classroom. Children talked to the teacher or not at all. Present organization calls for increasing opportunity to work together in groups. More and more, classroom furniture is planned so that a number of small working groups may be established quickly.

4. *A school day visualized as a sequence of life experiences.* In the modern school one does not merely pass through a succession of subject "periods." Opportunities are provided for play, rest, work, food, and bodily elimination, under conditions closely approximating those normally experienced in daily living outside the classroom.

5. *Activities of the day are related to behavioristic goals.* The

school of today cannot afford to center its program around passing interests. Outstanding teaching means doing that which is best for children, not merely that which is good. Teachers and children must have before them goals which imply behavior to be developed. What is the skill, value, attitude, or concept we're after?

6. *Decreasing attention to subject sequences.* Research has discredited the idea that we are mentally most alert early in the morning and therefore should tackle those subjects thought to involve the most complex intellectual processes. Not long ago, visits to thirty different elementary classrooms first thing in the morning probably would have revealed thirty classes hard at work on arithmetic.

7. *Increasing subject synthesis.* This is in keeping with the trend to provide more life-like experiences. Life experiences do not divide themselves neatly into subjects. The process of living involves solving many problems which draw upon several areas of knowledge. It is ridiculous to deal with the historical background of Mexico in the morning and its geographic realities in the afternoon. It is equally ludicrous to concern ourselves with the history of New England and the geography of Brazil in the fall and then turn to the history of Brazil and the geography of New England in the spring.

8. *Flexibility and large blocks of time.* Flexibility permits a group to capitalize on current happenings, adjust itself to interruptions, and continue an activity while interest is still high. Learning in America still begins and ends too much with the ringing of bells. Large blocks of time lend themselves well both to flexibility and increased synthesis of subject matter.

9. *Movement away from daily periods allotted to each area of the curriculum.* There was a time when teachers and children would have had a deep feeling of guilt, or relief, if a formal spelling period had not been held sometime during the day. Now there is increasing emphasis upon occasional evaluation periods to determine what is being learned and what adjustments need to be made.

10. *Establishment of major work centers.* This is in keeping with the emphases upon social development and upon large blocks of time embracing a variety of activities. Lane recommends the following: art center, clay table, music table, library corner, workbench, gas plate, sink, science table, small portable stage, games table, typing table, bulletin board, simple playhouse, and provision for block play.[20]

11. *Emphasis upon making the impersonal and the inanimate mat-*

20 Robert H. Lane, *The Teacher in the Modern Elementary School* (Boston: Houghton Mifflin Co., 1941), p. 130.

ters of routine. There was a time when youngsters responded, like trained animals, to a series of numbers. "One" meant stand up, "two" meant left turn, "three" meant forward march, and so on. Now, insight into why a certain kind of behavior is desirable is sought. But an informal room does not mean a disorganized room. There is no place for procedures which permit materials and supplies to be left anywhere in the room, paint brushes to be left unwashed, and so on. Children should be guided to see the importance of having tools strategically placed, of having equipment ready for use, and of arranging work space so that it does not interfere with that of others.

It should be recognized that trends are very general phenomena. Some of the best practices in today's schools were to be found in some classrooms of thirty years ago. On the other hand, some of the practices long since decried as being inappropriate to a changed philosophy go on daily in today's classrooms.

Some Guiding Ideas

This chapter has been organized around several guiding ideas, some of which have been introduced through the creation of separate sections. Other ideas appeared at various times without special announcement. All of these major ideas are brought together here as a summary of the significant considerations in the learning-teaching day.

1. Before a teacher and a group of children come into the classroom, a host of factors inside and outside of the building already have conditioned much of what ultimately will go on in that classroom. Most of these factors have been discussed in other chapters.

2. The moment a teacher and a group of children come into the classroom, a set of dynamic relationships is set in operation by the immediate interplay of certain classroom realities. The teacher's vision of what these interrelationships mean, his actual grasp of them, or his failure to grasp them are referred to as his "span of control."

3. The teacher's daily successes and failures are as much a result of *when* something is done as it is of *what* is done. The subtle blending of factors encompassed in the span of control is vital to good timing. Likewise, good pacing—moving individuals and groups along at just the right speed—results from skillfully holding back a little here and pushing quickly ahead there.

4. At first glance, good timing and pacing appear to be qualities a teacher "just has." In reality, they come from careful attention to a host of details over the years. Their presence marks not merely "ex-

perience," but the difference between having five or ten years of thoughtful, creative experience, or one year's experience over and over.

5. A good school day is a balanced school day. But this balance is not likely to be achieved just by assuring oneself that so many minutes per day are allotted to each of so many subjects. A balanced program is achieved by making sure that the basic organizing elements of curriculum and instruction are dealt with through classroom activities embracing all areas of a child's daily living.

6. All of us are plagued in our living and our working by time—its lack, organization, and steady passage. The key to satisfying use of time in teaching and learning is to think of time as having multiple dimensions, and activities as having multiple functions.

7. A teacher and a group of children must organize learning around centers which have significance, are accessible, have breadth and scope, are capable of being related to other learning, and may be moved forward. These centers are intangible (even when made of solid marble!) in that their possibilities as organizing centers for learning are seen in all aspects of significance only by their user. Such centers are commonly found in ideas, materials, collections, exhibits, places, and people.

8. Timing and pacing take on special significance in the process of planning daily programs with children. Children who have not participated in teacher-pupil planning must be introduced to it gradually and carried along in terms of their readiness for increased responsibility. But the desirability of such shared responsibility must always be held high as an educational goal.

9. Maintaining pupil control is reduced to minor significance when school days are: a) planned by teacher and children thinking together; b) thought of in relation to the demands of children's energy system; c) well balanced in regard to selection of activities; d) organized around centers that move the group readily from activity to activity. The teacher's perspective on personal strengths and limitations, and on what constitutes rich classroom living, is a crucial determinant in the school days that finally occur.

10. Constant evaluation is essential if the many considerations in adequate classroom planning are to be present in proper relationship to each other.

Each day in a school year is like a page in a book. If it is carefully planned in relation to the whole, it becomes a meaningful part of a volume. If it is carelessly planned, or not planned at all, it becomes only a series of sentences or a jumble of words. The page may be ripped out with very little effect upon the story. Each page in the book—each day in the year—has a part in determining the quality of the final product.

BIBLIOGRAPHY

Association for Childhood Education International, *Helping Children Live and Learn*. Washington: The Association, 1952.

Association for Supervision and Curriculum Development, *Creating a Good Environment for Learning* (1954 Yearbook). Washington: The Association, 1954.

Brogan, Peggy, and Lorene K. Fox, *Helping Children Learn*. New York: World Book Co., 1955.

Burrows, Alvina Trent, *Teaching Children in the Middle Grades*. Boston: D. C. Heath and Co., 1952.

Bush, Robert Nelson, *The Teacher-Pupil Relationship*. Englewood Cliffs, N. J.: Prentice-Hall, Inc., 1954.

Cunningham, Ruth, *et al.*, *Understanding Group Behavior of Boys and Girls*. New York: Bureau of Publications, Teachers College, Columbia University, 1951.

Forest, Ilse, *Early Years at School*. New York: McGraw-Hill Book Co., Inc., 1949.

Lane, Howard, and Mary Beauchamp, *Human Relations in Teaching*. Englewood Cliffs, N. J.: Prentice-Hall, Inc., 1955.

Miel, Alice, *et al.*, *Cooperative Procedures in Learning*. New York: Bureau of Publications, Teachers College, Columbia University, 1952.

Thomas, R. Murray, *Ways of Teaching in Elementary Schools*. New York: Longmans, Green and Co., 1955.

Weber, Julia, *My Country School Diary*. New York: Harper & Brothers, 1946.

POLICIES AND PRACTICES IN MARKING, REPORTING, AND PROMOTING

15

WHAT MARK DID YOU GET? DOES YOUR DAD WHIP you if you get a bad report card? Did you pass? Children in America have asked these questions of one another for generations. And, for good reason, they are asking them still.[1]

That all school children, their parents and their teachers are so personally affected is evi-

[1] An average rate of nonpromotion of approximately 10 per cent for all elementary grades was reported by Hollis L. Caswell, *Non-Promotion in Elementary Schools* (Nashville, Tennessee: George Peabody College for Teachers, 1933), pp. 24-25. There has been a marked downward drop in recent years, but the percentage is still substantial particularly in the first grade. See Fred E. Harris, *Three Persistent Educational Problems: Grading, Promoting, and Reporting to Parents* (Lexington, Kentucky: Bureau of School Service, College of Education, University of Kentucky, 1953), p. 9.

dence enough of the significance of marking, reporting, and promoting. The fact that many of our policies are so inconsistent with our educational beliefs points to the need for careful study and subsequent overhaul of practices in these areas.

The term *marking* is used throughout this chapter to signify the process of assigning marks or scores to the work, accomplishments, or development of children, both on a day-to-day and a long-term basis. It is not used to mean the more comprehensive process of record keeping, inasmuch as marking is only one part of this process. *Reporting* in this chapter, refers specifically to communicating with parents or guardians regarding school progress. *Promoting* and *nonpromoting* refer here to the act of moving a child to the next grade or retaining him in his present unit of the school's organizational structure.

Some Guiding Principles in Marking and Reporting

Appraising pupil progress and reporting that progress to parents must be governed always by concern for individual welfare. No marking device, no reporting system, and no scheme of regulating pupil progress, however expeditious and understandable, which endangers individual welfare is acceptable. A marking device, then, that is very sparing of teachers' time but destructive of pupils' self-respect is not acceptable. Similarly, a reporting system that is acceptable to parents but overly demanding of teachers is not adequate. A set of principles governing ends and means, and applying to both marking and reporting, is presented here. Later in the chapter, certain specifics related to each practice are analyzed in the light of these principles.

1. *Marking and reporting must be related directly to progress in those areas of human behavior defined in the accepted educational goals.* The teacher, then, has an immediate reference point to determine significant areas of development for evaluation. Similarly, child, parent, and teacher can focus together upon both progress in a given area and within the range of areas worthy of examination. What to mark and to report is answered by "What are we trying to accomplish?"

2. *The wide variation among children in velocities of development must be recognized by any sound system of marking and reporting.* Educational practices must encourage both full exercise of this individuality and acceptance of its normality. How to mark and to report becomes, in part, the answer to "What ways best reveal and encourage individual progress toward accepted goals?"

3. *The different velocities of development apparent within any one child must be recognized and fostered.* Progress in one area cannot be presumed from knowledge of progress in another. Educational pronouncements that affect all of the child cannot be made on the basis of evidence that reflects only part of him.[2] Marking and reporting indices that lump a wide range of progress into a very few categories are of questionable value.

4. *The evidence used for determining progress must be clearly related to the area being examined.* In the absence of criteria that are valid and objective, appraisal of a youngster's attainment in arithmetic, for example, may be affected by such important but inappropriate factors as personal neatness, pleasant disposition, spoken English and the like. It is essential, therefore, that the kind of behaviors to be assessed be identified and that a body of objective data related to these behaviors be collected.

5. *Marking and reporting should embrace a range of characteristics that is no greater than the range of available data.* If teachers have no data pertinent to the physical development of children, they are not prepared to make decisions relative to it, even though the school's purposes include physical emphasis. They should refrain from reporting physical development until such time as adequate data are available.

6. *The processes of marking and reporting must be diagnostic and constructive.* The difference between modifiable and unmodifiable behavior is crucial here. The energies of children need to be directed toward changes that result from learning rather than toward those that are the product of maturation alone. Marking and reporting, then, are essentially guidance processes. Children must be guided toward acceptance of such realities as physical stature and toward wholesome dissatisfaction with variables that can be changed through their own efforts.

7. *Marking and reporting are cooperative endeavors that can be successful only in an atmosphere of mutual understanding.* This means, for one thing, that children and parents must be "in on" the selection of criteria to be used. Mutual understanding develops when all affected have a voice in the process. This presupposes a faculty that is able to plan and work together. Involvement of children in all phases of the reporting process is assumed. And, finally, parents who are "close" to the school are essential to success.

[2] John I. Goodlad, "As We Know, So Must We Do," *Childhood Education*, XXIX (October, 1952), 66.

Lou Gardner

WHEN A FELLER NEEDS A FRIEND

8. *Marking and reporting must respect individual integrity*. This principle is particularly significant because educational goals embrace much more than subject matter achievement. It is one thing, for example, to receive an "F" for arithmetic; it is quite another to get "F" for personality. People tend to be more sensitive about what they are than about what they do. Marking and reporting must be something we do *with* people, and not *to* them.[3]

The Temptation of Absolute Criteria. When the purposes of elementary education were narrowly confined to areas of subject matter attainment, when learning was viewed as knowledge of subject matter rather than changed behavior, and when much less was known about the differing velocities of child development, recording and reporting progress or percentages of a theoretically possible 100 seemed the logical thing to do. Hosts of such marks were collected and averaged in order to report to parents at regular intervals throughout the year.

It might be argued that such a system has an "absoluteness" about

[3] Maurice Troyer, *Accuracy and Validity in Evaluation Are Not Enough,* (The J. Richard Street Lecture for 1947) (Syracuse, N.Y.: Syracuse University Press, 1947), p. 12.

it. It is impersonal and objective, permitting clear separation of pupil-teacher relationships and pupil achievement. "You may not be doing very well in arithmetic but that doesn't change how I feel about
you." Unfortunately, the problem is not quite so simple. A word is
spelled either correctly or incorrectly, but teacher judgment goes into
the initial selection of words. Given a thousand words from which to
choose two test lists of one hundred each, it is possible to prepare lists
that differ widely in difficulty. A score of 83 on one list may be the
equivalent of 96 on the other. Similarly, a score of 76 in arithmetic
may be the equivalent of 92 in spelling. This problem of objectivity
becomes increasingly acute where criteria of excellence are even less
well defined. What one teacher thinks is good composition, for example, constitutes "sloppy thinking" to another. Instead of a single
unchanging measuring stick, there are many. The standard shifts
from teacher to teacher and from subject to subject.

Numerical marks transferred to a report card, then, are really quite
meaningless—and are particularly dangerous because most people
think they know what they mean. Teddy is "good" in spelling and
"bad" in arithmetic because his marks are 92 and 73, respectively. Actually, 89 is the lowest mark in the group for spelling this month and
78 is the highest for arithmetic. Jean didn't do too well last year; her
marks were almost always low. But this year, she's making wonderful
marks. Actually, this year's teacher has much lower standards than
last year's.

It is not surprising, in view of these obvious deficiencies, that the
use of percentages in marking and reporting had practically faded
from the elementary school scene by mid-century.[4] But a clear-cut
alternative was not and is still not universally accepted.

Comparison with Group Achievement. There are some advantages
in knowing where a child stands in relation to a group on a given criterion. For one thing, a teacher who has such information is able to
make specific plans for individual differences. For another, children
who have shown little mathematical aptitude throughout the years (as
revealed by the records) may be helped in making intelligent vocational decisions.

The "ABC" system of marking and reporting developed, in part, as
a convenient means for expressing comparative standings. A mid-cen-

---

[4] "The Changing Report Card," *Educational Trend,* Issue No. 952 (New London,
Conn.: Arthur C. Croft Publications, 1952), p. 2. The system still has its exponents, however. A series of articles in *Collier's,* 1953-54, deplored at several points—and with more
than nostalgic emphasis—the passage of traditional marking and reporting systems from
the scene.

tury report revealed that nearly 60 per cent of 216 report forms used in selected elementary schools followed a four or five-point scale approximating the "ABC" type of reporting.[5]

All of the fallacies surrounding absolute, unchanging measuring sticks—discussed in the previous section—apply here as well. In addition, the kind of competition that is encouraged and the ultimate results of this competition deserve attention. Many argue that we live in a highly competitive society. Therefore, any marking and reporting system that removes the competitive element is "soft" and unrealistic. The race and the A's should go to the fittest. There is, however, an essential difference between the school's race and life's race. In life, we are relatively free to gravitate to positions commensurate with our abilities; to seek satisfactions and accomplishments in activities that lie within our capacities. Not so in school. Up to the age of 15 or 16, the child is in school whether or not he chooses to be; he is asked to compete whether or not he wishes to.[6]

An examination of the number of high or low grades received by children at upper and lower ends of the ability scale illustrates the basic unfairness of competitive school grades. By far the major proportion of unsatisfactory grades is received by children at the lower end of the ability scale, irrespective of effort. Under a competitive grading system, then, these children are forced to compete when their ability to compete is insufficient to provide either zest for the fray or a realistic chance for success. It is difficult to defend any marking system that, in application, cannot be reconciled with the objectives of education in a democracy.

Comparison with Own Achievement. Teachers who suffer with slow-learning children attempting to compete in the uneven struggle for competitive grades may prefer the alternative of marking and reporting for improvement or effort, while still retaining the familiar A B C. "Tommy isn't very bright in arithmetic," they may say, "but he works hard and steadily improves. He, instead of Billy, ought to get the A. Billy is bright enough and usually comes through with near-perfect scores on the tests, but he takes life easy and does not pay attention much of the time."

On the surface, such attitudes seem justified, but certain complicating factors must not be ignored. Billy may have discovered that he can "get by" quite nicely without paying close attention. His lack of effort and concern may be the direct result of the instructional pro-

5 *Ibid.,* p. 2.
6 See Troyer, *op. cit.,* pp. 5-6.

gram itself. In school systems insisting on minimum essentials of achievement for each grade, children at both ends of the ability range suffer. The slow child may find it impossible to attain the standards set within the time allowed. The bright child, on the other hand, may easily attain these levels, and then become listless and inattentive for want of a real challenge to his abilities.[7] Given the same incentive, then, Billy's effort and interest might equal or surpass Tommy's.

One difficulty in marking based on improvement arises in the actual application of such a criterion. It is readily apparent that improvement from a low point on a scale of proficiency is more easily accomplished than is improvement from a high point. It is much easier, for example, for one golfer to improve his score from 130 to 120, than for another to improve his score from 75 to 65. It therefore becomes extremely difficult to estimate how much improvement to expect from a particular child in any given time unit. Furthermore, to rate one person's improvement over another's when each began at a different point and has different potential for growth, not only is questionable practice but also is virtually impossible.

Still another difficulty arises from the traditional connotations attached to symbols used. In spite of all our efforts to define other meanings, an A still is translated to mean "best" or "top" or "superior." In practice, then, any other meanings are likely to be misinterpreted. Hence, the slow-learning child who enters high school with a record of straight A's based on effort or improvement is likely to be regarded as a "top" student. The resulting disillusionment for child, parents, and teachers brought about by return to group comparison at the high school level may produce greater ultimate harm to the child than would have resulted from the application of a competitive scale from the time of school entrance. It is not easy to sell a new story under an old title and cover. A, B, and C have been with us too long to be readily re-defined.

The use of such symbols as S and U in marking and reporting grew out of the desire to find a system more compatible with a philosophy emphasizing individual growth. Full acceptance of the range of abilities in a group and of the normality of that range demanded comparing a child's present performance with past performance and with ability. Theoretically, a slow-learning child who seemed to be working up to his full capacity would receive an S. Conversely, a bright

[7] Ralph W. Tyler, "Helen Is Smarter than Betsy," *NEA Journal*, XLII (March, 1953), 165-166.

child who lagged far behind his ability would receive U (regardless of his comparative position in the class).[8]

Obviously, an understanding of the supporting philosophy is essential to using, understanding, and accepting such symbols. The degree of understanding accompanying, for example, a shift from A B C to S and U has often been the determining factor in both the original acceptance and the later continuance of the changed system. First, teachers must understand that S is not necessarily equivalent to A and B; that a child receiving F under a system of group comparison might well receive S under a system considering only his own abilities. Secondly, parents must understand that a child receiving nothing but S grades on his report cards is not necessarily a genius. The failure to understand the basic premises differentiating one system from another has resulted, too often, in changed symbols but basically unchanged marking and reporting. The frequent result has been either a return to the old system in its entirety or a meaningless cloaking of the old in new raiment. In both instances, further improvement becomes more difficult to achieve than it was before the superficial shift in symbols occurred.

There are many variations of the S and U system. Sometimes, as in Lawrence, Massachusetts, checks are used.[9] Frequently, a refined scale using three or more divisions is employed. Des Moines uses four divisions: S—satisfactory, I—improving but not yet satisfactory, U—unsatisfactory, L—less satisfactory than last quarter.[10] Basic to the effective use and interpretation of symbols of this kind is concern for the individual's progress, and its appropriateness for him alone.

A Problem of Multiple Dimensions. It becomes obvious that the problem of marking and reporting has multiple dimensions. The need for several approaches rather than a single solution stems from the need to keep one's eye on range of educational goals, to consider the wide variations in children's developmental velocities, to give children constructive insights into themselves, to provide useful guidance services, and to give parents information that is meaningful.[11] It is important, now, to examine these dimensions and the considera-

8 Some of the difficulties involved in making these discriminations are discussed by Dorothy Rogers, "Common-Sense Considerations Concerning Report Cards," *Elementary School Journal,* LII (May, 1952), 519-520.

9 *Educational Trend,* Issue Number 952, p. 3.

10 *Ibid.*

11 For a discussion of functions to be served by marking and reporting, see William L. Wrinkle, *Improving Marking and Reporting Practices in Elementary and Secondary Schools* (New York: Rinehart and Co., 1947), pp. 30-35.

tions they raise in greater detail. Specific practice is then analyzed against this comprehensive background.[12]

The guiding principles presented earlier in the chapter stressed the significance of educational objectives for any evaluative activity. Functionally, goals must be defined in such ways that the behaviors sought are clear. Several of these guiding principles also refer to the child as a focal point in evaluation. "It is easy in the midst of test forms, class averages, and national norms to forget or lose sight of the essential purpose of all evaluation—to help the learner become increasingly more skillful rather than less."[13] It follows, then, that teachers must seek not only to make more valid and reliable observations of pupil behavior, but also to involve the learner consciously in the process. Essentially, evaluation is a *continuous* process, with joint pupil-teacher observations of desired changes in pupil behavior.

We cannot escape the question of standards, their derivation and application. In protest against the unthinking application of rigid, arbitrary standards in the past, modern education has swung, in many instances, away from *any* consideration of standards. The position taken here is that the question of standards must be dealt with, not side-stepped; the crucial issue becomes one of determining how to use them constructively:

. . . the determination of adequacy is not a simple task dependent on only one standard, but a multiple task dependent on the many appropriate and necessary standards against which all (social) behavior must be examined. The task to be performed, the comparison of his own performances, the comparison of particular skills within his own developmental pattern, the comparison of his behavior with those of his peer group, comparison with those of adults or with what adults expect—all are important and necessary appraisals of the same skill behavior. No one standard is ever enough to answer all the necessary questions being asked.[14]

Still another practical consideration in marking and reporting is that of parent involvement. Wholesome parent involvement is not merely a logical outcome of a point of view, but means, essentially, participation in a program of parent-teacher education essential to curricular revision and program advancement.

So many inter-related dimensions present formidable obstacles to

[12] Succeeding paragraphs in this section draw heavily from Virgil E. Herrick and Frank J. Estvan, "Evaluation of Skills in Social Studies," *Skills in Social Studies* (Twenty-fourth Yearbook of the National Council for the Social Studies, Washington: National Educational Association, 1954), pp. 246-261.

[13] *Ibid.*, p. 251.

[14] Herrick and Estvan, *op. cit.*, pp. 257-258.

the development of an adequate system of marking and reporting. The succeeding discussion, developed with positive directions in view, recognizes the fact that all constructive programs of change begin with intelligent recognition of present shortcomings.

Assuring a Sound Basis of Evidence

The word *marking* has been retained in this chapter because it connotes a process of making judgments that may be translated readily into marks for reporting to parents. In the light of the past few pages, marking in itself is inadequate. Needed, instead, is a body of evidence about children—gathered in an atmosphere of child-teacher understanding—that may be used for a variety of purposes.

Teachers, children, and parents must look together, therefore, for evidence that permits decisions regarding:

1. the relationship between individual attainment and its adequacy for that child at any given time.

2. the nature—continuity, variability, amount—of progress over time.

3. the character of total group performance.

4. the degree of error in those areas that permit absolute criteria.

5. the adequacy of individual performance in relation to the demands of the situation, needed modifications in performance, and the possibility of these modifications.

6. future patterns of behavior that appear appropriate to the individual in all areas of future performance.

The evidence collected may be divided into four categories according to potential use, all overlapping in large measure, but each containing certain data peculiar to the purpose of that category. Hence, the teacher builds up certain information that is shared with neither children nor parents. This may include test scores.[15] It most certainly will include those observations and tentative hunches that children or parents are not now ready (and may never be ready) to share. A second category contains information that is the joint property of child and teacher, but not of parent. Teachers are obligated to withhold information from parents whenever they commit themselves to children to do so. Experienced teachers come to learn also that it is wise to withhold certain information whenever they find instances of parents being unable or unwilling to use such information con-

[15] The controversial issue of giving parents the results of intelligence testing is discussed by Robert N. Walker, "Teachers, Tests, and Telling Parents," *Elementary School Journal*, LIV (November, 1953), 151-156.

structively. The third category consists of a body of information that teachers, parents, and children look at together. Often this takes the form of a cumulative folder into which teachers and children place test results, conference summaries, samples of work done, and so on. Finally, there is a fourth area of information that is rightly the concern of parents and teachers only. Information as to physical and health deficiencies, emotional and social problems, indices of capacity for learning is illustrative of this fourth area of information. Much of this is the sort that teachers and parents need in making their decisions but that children could not use constructively.

We have moved, then, in this chapter, away from a concept of marking that attempts to reduce complex behaviors to a number of abstract symbols. A body of evidence from which a number of related decisions can be made is recommended. Any attempt to communicate this evidence and its meaning to parents through symbols is subject to serious question. And yet, the bulk of our reporting practices attempt to do this very thing.

AN ANALYSIS OF CURRENT PRACTICE IN MARKING AND REPORTING

The history of marking and reporting in American elementary schools[16] has been marked by two types of concerns. The first has involved striving for some sort of symbol system to express as expeditiously as possible the child's per cent of perfect performance in defined areas, his progress in relation to other children, and/or the character of his individual performance. The second concern has been for finding appropriate means of reporting the child's progress to parents.

Devices and Techniques for Reporting

Reporting by Cards and Letters. The report card is the most commonly used form of reporting. Make-up of cards arranges from a single page containing several items relative to subject achievement, to booklets comprising pages of descriptive statements pertaining to mental, physical, social, and emotional development.

Generations of Americans grew up knowing a report card that listed eight or ten subjects, and that provided spaces for times tardy,

16 For a summary of trends, see Ida B. De Pencier, "Trends in Reporting Pupil Progress in the Elementary Grades, 1938-1949," *Elementary School Journal*, LI (May, 1951), 519-523.

absences, classroom conduct, and signature of parent or guardian. Earlier forms supplied a score—65, 83, or 76—for history, arithmetic, spelling, and so on, and a letter grade for deportment. Later varieties awarded A B C D E for subjects, supplied a space for comments by the teacher, and retained the conduct rating. Many of these later forms assigned numerical equivalents for letter grades. Emphases on subject achievement, competition, punctuality, and conformance with teacher-determined standards of classroom conduct usually were paramount.

The greatest advantages of reporting by card, obviously, relate to administrative expediency. Usually both the items to be covered and the reporting periods are fixed. And a card doesn't "talk back." The greatest disadvantages lie in the limited dimensions of pupil progress communicated.[17] Too often, after examining his child's card, the parent still knows little about his child's progress. Furthermore, he cannot carry on a conversation with the card to find out. Frequently, as a result, the parent goes to see the teacher to learn what he really wants to know. Teachers often use the report card as a means for bringing parents to school.

The letter type of report is an outgrowth of the printed card. In contrast to the latter, it stresses flexibility and informality. School systems reporting considerable success with its use, however, indicate the desirability of standardizing certain comments or of defining a framework within which to compose statements. Such standardization may range from as little as a few headings—physical development, work habits, social characteristics, and so on—with space for comments, to a long list of descriptive phrases from which the teacher selects those that are appropriate. Actually, such refinements represent a return to many features of the conventional card.

Letter-writing offers the possibility for establishing a close, personal link between teacher and parent. In addition, it frees the teacher from many system-wide regulations that may run counter to his classroom principles and practices. In use, it often encourages writing by both parents and teachers at the time most appropriate to the child's welfare rather than at certain designated periods of the year. However, writing letters that convey significant meaning is a time-consuming practice. Phrasing ideas to convey the exact thought

17 The significance of the reporting system as a means of communicating not only pupil progress but also the entire school program is discussed by Harold I. Judson, Betty Finley, and Madeline Hunter, "The Report to Parents," *National Elementary Principal*, XXXI (June, 1952), 27-33.

and to portray existing conditions is a challenging task from which many teachers would prefer to be spared.[18]

Reporting by letter presents certain hazards. Informality sometimes discourages frank presentation and consideration of basic issues. To avoid coming to grips with such issues, the teacher may resort to vague adjectives or sweeping generalizations. Such statements as "Susie is a precious child" or "Tommy's attitude has been most commendable lately" convey very little meaning. Then, too, the absence of restrictions or regulations in reporting may be construed as an open invitation to violate the basic principle that evaluation must be based on objective evidence. Freeing the teacher from the bonds of report forms should not free him from the basic principles and considerations underlying reporting.

Reporting by Conference. The parent-teacher conference lends itself well to application of the basic reporting principles developed earlier. Frequently this procedure is used in conjunction with the card or letter type of reporting. For the most part, the advantages and disadvantages of letter reporting are further intensified by the conference method. The hazards, too, are similar and, when adequate precautions against them are not taken, may produce even more devastating results.

The cumulative folder frequently becomes the focal point for the parent-teacher conference. Its contents provide the necessary data: samples of work, anecdotal accounts, and personal development sheets. The teacher need not function as an arbiter; he and the parent clarify, interpret, and plan together. The parent receives the satisfaction of being "inside" the educational process; the teacher achieves satisfaction in feeling that the time spent in reporting will yield dividends. Of considerable significance is the ease with which the conference is extended to include the child. When this level of reporting is reached, the principle of evaluation being something done *with* people is in operation.

One significant project in conference reporting was carried out by the teachers and parents of a Contra Costa school in California.[19] After a series of joint meetings under the auspices of the school faculty and the Mothers' Club, it was decided to substitute conferences for report cards. Several times each year, for three successive

18 Some helpful suggestions for writing letters to parents are presented by the Association for Childhood Education, *Records and Reports,* Washington, D.C., 1942, p. 16.

19 For the story of this project in action, see Association for Supervision and Curriculum Development, *Instructional Leadership in Small Schools* (Washington: The Association, 1951), pp. 53-55.

days at a time, the daily school session was shortened to 240 minutes. Parent-teacher conferences were held from 8:00 to 9:00 each morning, 2:00 to 4:30 each afternoon, and 7:00 to 9:30 one evening. Through careful scheduling, a mother of several children was able to complete all conferences in one visit. The evening session made it convenient for fathers to visit the school. Parent and teacher reaction to the plan has been extremely favorable. Subsequent recommendations have led to longer conference periods and more evening schedules.[20]

In any enterprise that involves large numbers of people, practices that initially have significant meaning often become routine and purposeless. It is important, therefore, that each parent-teacher conference have a purpose that concerns a child's welfare.[21] Otherwise, what is essentially a sound educational practice may soon deteriorate into a meaningless chore. A purpose that is stated, is positive, and is understood permits both parent and teacher to make necessary preparations. The teacher reviews Tom's folder to be sure of the facts. The parent thinks of questions that should be raised, and of information about Tom that may be of value. An anecdote about some positive element of Tom's work or disposition helps to establish rapport and to get the conference under-way. Often, a conference is moved along by stating tentative conclusions as questions such as, "Could it be that Tom's concern is . . .?" "Is this a problem we might help one another on?" In this way, generalizations never become accusations and the parent has no need to go on the defensive.

Conferences always should be summarized. "Are we agreed, then, that . . .?" "I'll get that information to you in a few days and, in the meantime, if you would. . . ." Often, the summary will indicate certain follow-up action. After the conference is over, the teacher should look back over it to judge its strengths and weaknesses and to project plans for improvement.[22] A written summary of what took place is helpful in assuring follow-up, improving conference procedures, and initiating later conferences.

[20] For a detailed account of recommended procedures, see Katherine D'Evelyn, *Individual Parent-Teacher Conferences* (New York: Bureau of Publications, Teachers College, 1950); Duluth Public Schools, *Holding Teacher-Parent Conferences* (Duluth, Minn., 1953); Elgin Public Schools, *Holding Teacher-Parent Conferences* (Elgin, Illinois, 1953).

[21] See Beatrice Ford Parker, "The Parent-Teacher Conference," *Elementary School Journal*, LIII (January, 1953), 271-272.

[22] For a list of evaluated questions in this connection, see Virgil E. Herrick and others, *The Parent-Teacher Conference* (Madison, Wisconsin: Virgil E. Herrick, 1954), p. 31. This reference includes a helpful bibliography on the parent-teacher conference.

The parent-teacher conference is no reporting panacea. Many school systems are discovering that it opens more lines of communication and permits broader bases for reporting—in effect, permits approximation of the desirable principles laid down earlier in this chapter. But more lines of communication and broader bases for reporting provide also the possibility for greater misunderstanding. The conference is a professional technique demanding professional skills. For those who would learn these skills, it offers much for improved reporting to parents.[23]

The Process of Changing Reporting Practices

During the past half-dozen years, thousands of schools and school systems have experimented with changed systems of reporting. The *NEA Journal* summarized the progress of nine school systems in different sections of the country: Aberdeen (South Dakota), Pimella County (Florida), Tuscaloosa (Alabama), Hillsborough County (Florida), St. Clair County (Alabama), Sarasota County (Florida), Boise (Idaho), Dickinson (North Dakota) and Tacoma (Washington).[24] From these and other reports, certain conclusions may be drawn about effecting both change and progress in reporting methods:[25]

1. Parent-teacher understanding that has been built up over the years facilitates attempts to improve reporting procedures. Reporting is one of those problem demons that is emotionally charged. Consequently, it is not a good initial problem for bringing parents and teachers together. Attack upon the reporting problem should grow naturally out of prior work on other mutual problems.

2. The reporting system should not reach the point of change until parents have had a clear voice in all aspects of the decision. Involvement in changed reporting practices is not a courtesy to be extended to parents at the whim of educators. It is a parental right—to be demanded of school people, if necessary.

3. Since it is virtually impossible to involve all parents in the process of change, or even to represent them properly, a program of

---

23 It should be recognized at this point that several devices, rather than a single avenue, for reporting to parents often is the answer. For one account of a reporting system embracing three types of contacts with parents, see Robert H. Anderson and Edward R. Steadman, "Pupils' Reactions to a Reporting System," *Elementary School Journal,* LI (November, 1950), 136-142.

24 "Making the Grade with Parents," *NEA Journal,* XLII (April, 1953), 214-216.

25 For a detailed account of how one school system attacked the problem of changing the reporting system see "Teacher, How Is My Boy Doing in School?" (prepared by Alfred W. Held), *A Report of a Study of Reporting Practices in Racine Public Schools,* Racine, Wisconsin (mimeographed).

readiness must be instituted for those who did not participate. Frequently, letters of explanation are the only means of communication that can be established.

4. Postponement of change because parents or teachers are not yet ready for it easily becomes procrastination unless a program of readiness is begun. The "right" time for change often is quite unrecognizable, and the "ripe" time has a way of becoming rotten overnight.

5. Any change involves much planning, much study, and much patience. It is essential, then, that any change undertaken be sufficiently important to warrant the time and effort involved. So often the symbols produced are different, but the old philosophy remains.

6. Any change must be given a fair trial.[26] Dissenting voices are often lost in the enthusiasm of a campaign. But, afterward, when the results produce no universal panacea, the disgruntled voice of protest may sound like the chant of an oracle. Backtracking from a few forward steps often does much more than wipe out the progress made. It entrenches practice at a point inferior to what it was before the change was first initiated.

7. Practice has an unfortunate way of getting out of step with ideas. Reporting practices must be under continuous evaluation, then, not only because better ideas suggest better practices, but also because new parents and new teachers demand new processes of orientation and communication.

TO PROMOTE OR NOT TO PROMOTE[27]

To promote or not to promote? That is the question that plagues teachers—several hundred thousand teachers—each June. And it is a question that has plagued them each year for decades. Had Rip Van Winkle been a teacher, and had he dozed off twenty years ago while deliberating the fate of thirty youngsters, he might have resumed his deliberations quite naturally on awakening today. Not a soul would laugh; not a soul would consider his activities bizarre. Only the thankful thirty, spared through Rip's somnolent sojourn, might re-

---

[26] For an account of how one school system evaluated the results of a change in reporting, see T. K. Muellen, "An Experiment in Reporting Pupil Progress," *Elementary School Journal*, LII (September, 1951), 42-44.

[27] Appreciation is extended to the Association for Childhood Education International and the University of Chicago Press for permission to reproduce extensively in this section from two articles written by John I. Goodlad: "To Promote or Not To Promote?" *Childhood Education*, XXX (January, 1954), 212-215; "Research and Theory Regarding Promotion and Nonpromotion," *Elementary School Journal*, LIII (November, 1952), 150-155.

joice that the belated decisions would have no bearing upon their lives.

Some claim that promotion scarcely can be considered a significant present-day educational problem. "Why, I seldom find it necessary to retain more than three children," they may add. Three children out of, say, thirty? That's 10 per cent. And 10 per cent amounts to between two and three million elementary school children in all of America. But it must be recognized that many schools promote all or nearly all pupils. Let's be very conservative, then, and say that only from one to two million elementary-school children are retained in their present grades each year. Promotion an insignificant problem? One could hardly agree.

Not to Promote

Why retain a child? Let us think through some of the reasoning that must lie behind a million decisions not to promote. We may not agree, but the following are some of the reasons often given to justify nonpromotion:

1. When promotion is assured, pupils are unconcerned about their school work, developing poor work habits and careless attitudes.

2. Bright children come to resent equal promotion rewards for work that is obviously inferior.

3. Because of the need for teachers to spend a disproportionate amount of time with slow-learners, the presence of these children in the room serves as a hindrance to progress. The range of achievement is widened and group homogeneity reduced.

4. Achievement levels are enhanced through the repetition of only partially learned material.

5. Immature children, through grade repetition, are more likely to find suitable play and work companions at the lower grade level.

6. The promoted slow-learner, unable to do the work of the grade, frustrated and discouraged, develops inferiority feelings which adversely affect his social relationships and personality development.

To Promote

There are many people who believe that slow-learning children should be promoted regardless of present levels of attainment. Again, we may not agree with the arguments put forth to support this position, but let's examine a few:

1. The possibility of nonpromotion is a threat that constitutes

negative motivation. Children learn best under conditions of positive motivation and therefore should be promoted.

2. Children distribute themselves from poor to excellent in each of the many school endeavors in which they engage, usually with only slight variations from child to child on the continuum. To average these attainments is unrealistic. To determine arbitrary cutting points for passing or failing demands a refinement in judgment that defies human capacities.

3. The presence of older, repeating children in a classroom decreases group homogeneity.

4. Learning is enhanced when children move on to new endeavors instead of experiencing the boredom of repetition.

5. Grade repetition results in over-ageness which, in turn, produces behavior problems requiring special disciplinary action.

6. Promotion retains approximately equal chronological age as a common factor and results in improved personal and social relationships.

It is vividly apparent that the two sets of arguments are virtually identical. Each claims for itself the same virtues and, for the other, the same vices. Now, for both to have equal merit is impossible. What are the facts?

What Research Says

About Promotion Practices and Achievement. Studies on the achievement of repeaters indicate that these children do no better than children of like ability who are promoted. This was suggested by Keyes more than half a century ago, when he reported that only 21 per cent of a large group of repeaters did better after repeating a grade than before and that 39 per cent actually did worse.[28] Arthur corroborated these findings when she matched a group of repeaters with a group of nonrepeaters on the basis of mental age and discovered that the former learned no more than the latter over a two-year period.[29] Klene and Branson equated children on the basis of chronological age, mental age, and sex.[30] Half were then promoted and half retained. On the whole, the promoted group profited more

---

28 Charles H. Keyes, *Progress through the Grades of City Schools* (New York: Bureau of Publications, Teachers College, Columbia University, 1911), p. 63.

29 Grace Arthur, "A Study of the Achievement of Sixty Grade I Repeaters as Compared with That of Nonrepeaters of the Same Mental Age," *Journal of Experimental Education,* V (December, 1936), 203-205.

30 Vivian Klene and Ernest P. Branson, "Trial Promotion versus Failure," *Educational Research Bulletin* (Los Angeles City Schools), VIII (January, 1929), 6-11.

than the nonpromoted group in regard to achievement in school subjects. Saunders' conclusion, in summing up an extensive survey of
studies into the effects of nonpromotion, is pertinent here:

> It may be concluded that nonpromotion of pupils in elementary schools in
> order to assure mastery of subject matter does not often accomplish its objective.
> Children do not appear to learn more by repeating a grade but experience less
> growth in subject-matter achievement than they do when promoted. Therefore a
> practice of nonpromotion because a pupil does not learn sufficient subject matter
> in the course of a school year, or for the purpose of learning subject matter, is
> not justifiable.[31]

About Promotion Practices and Homogeneous Grouping. For most
teachers, to secure a class of children closely approximating one another in all areas of development would be the realization of a teaching utopia. But it is questionable that this would be socially desirable,[32] let alone feasible.[33] As Burr points out, when groups are made
nonoverlapping in achievement for one subject, or even for a phase
of a subject, they overlap greatly in other subjects or other phases of
the same subject.[34] From a study of 46 schools with varying rates of
nonpromotion, Caswell[35] concluded that variability in pupil achievement is no less for schools with high rates of nonpromotion than for
schools with lower rates of nonpromotion—findings that are substantially in agreement with those of Akridge[36] and Cook.[37] Whether
or not homogeneous grouping is desirable or attainable, nonpromotion does not appear to reduce the range of specific abilities with
which the teacher has to cope.

---

[31] Carleton M. Saunders, *Promotion or Failure for the Elementary School Pupil?*
(New York: Bureau of Publications, Teachers College, Columbia University, 1941), p. 29.
These conclusions are in substantial agreement with the findings of William H. Coffield,
*A Longitudinal Study of the Effects of Nonpromotion on Educational Achievement in
the Elementary School* (Unpublished doctoral dissertation, State University of Iowa,
1954).

[32] Alice V. Keliher, *A Critical Study of Homogeneous Grouping in Elementary
Schools* (New York: Alice V. Keliher, 1930), p. 22.

[33] Willard S. Elsbree, *Pupil Progress in the Elementary School* (New York: Bureau of
Publications, Teachers College, Columbia University, 1943), p. 44.

[34] Marvin Y. Burr, *A Study of Homogeneous Grouping in Terms of Individual Variations and the Teaching Problem* (New York: Bureau of Publications, Teachers College,
Columbia University, 1931), p. 55.

[35] Hollis L. Caswell, *Non-Promotion in Elementary Schools* (Nashville, Tennessee:
Division of Surveys and Field Studies, George Peabody College for Teachers, 1933), pp.
44-46.

[36] Garth H. Akridge, *Pupil Progress Policies and Practices* (New York: Bureau of
Publications, Teachers College, Columbia University, 1937), p. 54.

[37] Walter W. Cook, *Grouping and Promotion in the Elementary Schools* (Minneapolis: University of Minnesota Press, 1941).

About Promotion Practices and Habits and Attitudes. Sandin reported that approximately 40 per cent of slow-progress (nonpromoted) pupils wished to quit school as soon as possible and that a like per cent—as against 14 per cent of regular-progress pupils—indicated that they disliked school and school work.[38] These findings support Farley's conclusions that the failing child, receiving less satisfaction from his work, tends to become discouraged and frequently antagonistic.[39]

About Promotion Practices and Discipline Problems. Research studies conducted by McElwee[40] and by Sandin[41] revealed a greater incidence of behavior considered troublesome among retarded children than among regular-progress pupils. Although these findings favor promotion over nonpromotion, further experiments with carefully controlled situations need to be conducted.

About Promotion Practices and Personal-Social Adjustment. Sandin used sociometrics, rating scales, check lists, observations, and interviews to study aspects of social and personal adjustment.[42] In general, he found that nonpromoted children tend to choose companions from grades higher than their own, to be pointed out by classmates as children who associated with pupils from grades other than their own, and to be discriminated against in the selection of study companions. Goodlad equated promoted second-grade pupils with nonpromoted first-grade pupils on the basis of chronological age, mental age, and achievement.[43] Considerable preliminary work was done in order to secure equivalent conditions in regard to such matters as teaching, enrollment, urban-rural location of schools, physical normality of the selected children, and socio-economic status of their families. The results showed a heavy concentration of differences in the area of peer group relationships favoring the promoted group. Three different types of data pointed to the general difficulty of the nonpromoted children in making satisfactory social adjustments. The

38 Adolph A. Sandin, *Social and Emotional Adjustments of Regularly Promoted and Non-promoted Pupils* (New York: Bureau of Publications, Teachers College, Columbia University, 1944), p. 125.

39 Eugene S. Farley, "Regarding Repeaters: Sad Effect of Failure upon the Child," *Nation's Schools,* XVIII (October, 1936), 37-39.

40 E. W. McElwee, "A Comparison of Personality Traits of 300 Accelerated, Normal, and Retarded Children," *Journal of Educational Research,* XXVI (September, 1932), 31-34.

41 Sandin, *op. cit.,* p. 97.

42 *Ibid.*

43 John I. Goodlad, "Some Effects of Promotion and Nonpromotion Upon the Social and Personal Adjustment of Children," *Journal of Experimental Education,* XXII (June, 1954), 301-328.

promoted children, on the other hand, tended to be more disturbed over their school progress and their home security—concerns that appear to be closely related.

The body of evidence in all of these areas forms a consistent pattern: undesirable growth characteristics and unsatisfactory school progress are more closely associated with nonpromoted children than with promoted slow-learning children. Conversely, slow-learning children who have been promoted tend to make more satisfactory progress and adjustment than do their peers who have been retained. But the greater incidence of differences favoring the promoted groups is counterbalanced, in part, by certain significant differences favoring nonpromoted groups or individual children. A recommendation for blanket promotions, then, does not rise logically from the research. Nevertheless, the fact remains—*Slow-learning children profit significantly more from promotion than from nonpromotion.*

Neither Promotion nor Nonpromotion the Answer

Simply to conclude from research that promotion is the more defensible of two alternatives is not the answer. Promotion is no universal panacea. It does not change a child's basic learning rate. It does not automatically provide the instruction needed for the range of abilities and attainments ever-present in any given class. Arbitrary grade norms for a field of study usually are approximated at a given time by less than half the children in that grade. A single child may be significantly above arbitrary grade norms in one area of endeavor, significantly below in another, and only slightly above or below in still others. Instructional and organizational practices and policies must facilitate a spread in academic attainment that will keep pace with increasing spread in mental age.

Neither promotion nor nonpromotion materially changes the natural heterogeneity of a group of six-year-olds, nine-year-olds, or twelve-year-olds. The teacher must make provision for those children who read well or poorly, are large or small, get along well with others or have difficulty sharing. Keeping back two or three children each year doesn't help her or her colleagues. It may lull her into thinking, for a few blissful moments, that she has a homogeneous group. Promotion and nonpromotion are merely the trappings of an educational era that should be long past.[44] They do absolutely nothing to ease or expedite the job of the teacher. They certainly do little for children.

[44] See Urban H. Flecge, "Catholic Education Needs a 'New Look,'" *America* (April 24, 1954), 98-99.

Several Answers—Not One

To promote or not to promote? What is the answer? There are several answers rather than one.

First, it must be recognized that most teachers in America today work in a system of grade classification requiring that children move step by step through it. Further, more courses of study, textbooks, and even teachers are organized around the grade concept. When children are brought together in groups of thirty and more under such a grade classification system, it soon becomes apparent that some children deviate so markedly in certain characteristics that the desirability of retaining them in the group is questioned.

Under such an organizational setup, retention of some children, while the group as a whole progresses to the next step, occasionally appears to be a logical solution.[45] In the face of ample research evidence, summarized earlier, to the effect that nonpromotion results in later adjustment of children less frequently than promotion, the teacher is cautioned to ponder carefully each instance of doubtful promotion. When he cannot say with conviction, "Knowing this child as I do, the chances for successful school experience next year and in subsequent years are greater if he be retained," then he is advised to give the child the benefit of any existing doubt and promote him. He can ill afford to ignore the body of research that is before him.

But, under such circumstances, the act of promoting or retaining is only the beginning. The repeater must be provided for. Simply to do over work that was inadequately done before is not the answer. The year with younger classmates must be filled with exciting challenges, not dulled with the repetition of activities long since wrung dry of interest and stimulation. To promote the slow-learner to tasks far beyond his comprehension likewise is not kindness. Whether slow-progress children be regularly or irregularly promoted, adequate subsequent provision for their needs is essential.

These are short-term answers to the promotion question. In a sense, they constitute tardy treatment for a very sick horse. Neither nonpromotion nor promotion is the real answer. Needed is an educational program that facilitates continuous progress for all children in each of the various aspects of their development.

[45] The important question, after the decision is made to retain a child, is how to provide for his needs in the instructional program. For the criteria used in one school to determine promotion and nonpromotion and the subsequent results of careful retention of some children, see Lawrence O. Loldell, "Results of a Nonpromotion Policy in One School District," *Elementary School Journal,* LIV (February, 1954), 333-337.

This need suggests elimination of the grade barriers that have given rise to a host of fallacious notions about pupil progress. Of these, the fantasy that children should arrive precisely at a given "norm" each June is the most preposterous. One attempt to eliminate grade barriers is the ungraded unit plan. This plan, usually designed to provide for continuous progress from kindergarten or grade one through the third grade, is no longer an educational day-dream. One report, prepared in 1954 and not purporting to be complete, revealed thirty school systems in twenty states to be experimenting with some form of the primary-unit plan.[46] Nearly all of these were organized after 1945.

One of the earliest experiments was initiated at the Maryland Avenue School, Milwaukee, in 1942, and was carried on for three years before any other school was encouraged to change from the traditional grade plan.[47] Within a decade, sixty-nine elementary schools in that city had introduced at least some elements of the initial experiment. The primary supervisor described the program as follows:

> The ungraded primary school is a means of making functional a philosophy that we have been talking about for years. It is a way of adjusting our teaching and administrative procedures to meet the differing social, mental, and physical capacities among our children. It is not a method of teaching or a departure from established procedures long used by our best teachers. It is, rather, and administrative tool to encourage and promote a philosophy of continuous growth . . .[48]

Ungraded plans are not the answer to all educational problems. They merely set an organizational structure within which more of our educational ideals may be realized. The merits and limitations of such plans must be fully understood by those who will use and be affected by them. It follows, then, that teachers and parents must think through a philosophy of continuous progress and the structure that is most compatible with this philosophy. The plan for continuous progress introduced in the Nathaniel Hawthorne School, University City, Missouri, for example, was brought about through much planning, discussing, and experimenting.[49] It was not introduced until parents and teachers agreed that it was worth a try. Perhaps years of

46 Prepared by Donald P. Mattoon, State Teachers College, Willimantic, Connecticut, and mimeographed for use by a discussion group, Ninth Annual Conference, Association for Supervision and Curriculum Development, Los Angeles, 1954.

47 Florence C. Kelly, "The Primary School Plan in Milwaukee" (mimeographed).

48 *Ibid.*, pp. 1-2.

49 For an account of this plan, see Fred E. Brooks, "A Faculty Meets the Needs of Pupils," *Educational Leadership,* XI (December, 1953), 174-178.

experimentation with such plans will show us at long last that grade barriers are as unreasonable above the third grade as they are for the first three grades.[50]

The obvious result, of course, is that promotion and nonpromotion simply will disappear from school practice—yes, even from our vocabularies. With the philosophy of continuous progress—and there is a vast difference between "continuous progress" and "social promotion" or any other kind of one hundred per cent promotion—firmly entrenched, and grade barriers no longer existent, to promote or not to promote no longer will be a question.

IN RETROSPECT

In conclusion, four broad areas of generalization should give direction to practices and policies in marking, reporting, and promoting:

1. Marking is an inadequate term applied to a complex process of appraising the performance of a child in such a way that the appraisal may be understood and used constructively by that child, helpful to the teacher, and readily communicated to the parent. This appraisal seeks to keep the following considerations in focus: the child's ability, his present performance in relation to past performance in the group, and the level of performance needed now and later. Obviously, no single marking device can serve all of these criteria adequately. The most promising devices, then, are those that provide a variety of data from which several different kinds of appraisal and prediction can be made.

2. Reporting is essentially the process of communicating pupil progress to parents. It is one of several immediate ends served by marking. Since communication always involves at least two persons, and since teachers and parents ideally perform the dual role of recounting and listening in reporting, conference-type reporting is likely to be most satisfactory.

3. Promotion is part of the total problem of placing children in groups so that most effective learning and teaching may take place. Our lock-step graded system has forced teachers to consider criteria for determining the rate at which children will move from unit to unit of this system. The evidence clearly shows that promotion is more defensible than nonpromotion. But, since the act of promoting or retaining itself creates problems, and since these problems grow

[50] For some suggestions based on an analysis of sixteen centers using some form of ungraded plan, see John I. Goodlad, "More About the Ungraded Unit Plan," *NEA Journal,* XLIV (May, 1955), 295-296.

largely from the existing lock-step system, newer proposals more compatible with continuous pupil growth are being suggested. The ungraded unit plan is one widely proposed solution that is now being tried out in many school systems.

4. Marking, reporting, and promoting are practices that have affected the lives of most living Americans. Attempts to change these practices are not likely to be ignored by people who view them as an integral part of school life. Furthermore, the success of these attempts depends largely upon their acceptance by parents. For practical reasons alone, then, school people cannot afford to ignore parental opinion in seeking change. But, of more importance, parents want and deserve to know how their children are doing in school. They want certain kinds of information reported in ways they can understand. It follows, then, that parents must be constructively involved in all processes designed to improve practices of marking, reporting, and promoting.

BIBLIOGRAPHY

Association for Childhood Education International, *Grouping . . . Problems and Satisfactions.* Washington: The Association, 1954.

——, *Reporting on the Growth of Children.* Washington: The Association, 1953.

Ayer, Fred C., *Practical Child Accounting*, rev. Austin, Texas: The Steck Company, 1953.

Cook, Walter W., *Grouping and Promotion in the Elementary Schools.* Minneapolis: University of Minnesota Press, 1941.

De Pencier, Ida B., "Trends in Reporting Pupil Progress in the Elementary Grades, 1938-1949," *Elementary School Journal,* LI (May, 1951).

Elsbree, Willard S., *Pupil Progress in the Elementary School.* New York: Bureau of Publications, Teachers College, Columbia University, 1943.

Foshay, A. Wellesley, "Interage Grouping in the Elementary School," Unpublished doctor's project, Teachers College, Columbia University, 1949.

Goodlad, John I., "Research and Theory Regarding Promotion and Nonpromotion," *Elementary School Journal,* LIII (November, 1952).

——, "To Promote or Not To Promote?" *Childhood Education,* XXX (January, 1954).

Harris, Fred E., *Three Persistent Educational Problems: Grading, Promoting, and Reporting to Parents.* Lexington, Kentucky: Bureau of School Service, College of Education, University of Kentucky, 1953.

Herrick, Virgil E., and others, *The Parent-Teacher Conference.* Madison, Wisconsin: Virgil E. Herrick, 1954 (mimeographed).

Sandin, Adolph A., *Social and Emotional Adjustments of Regularly Pro-*

moted and Non-promoted Pupils. New York: Bureau of Publications, Teachers College, Columbia University, 1944.

Saunders, Carleton M., *Promotion or Failure for the Elementary School Pupil?* New York: Bureau of Publications, Teachers College, Columbia University, 1941.

Strang, Ruth, *How To Report Pupil Progress.* Chicago: Science Research Associates, Inc., 1955.

———, *Reporting to Parents,* rev. New York: Bureau of Publications, Teachers College, Columbia University, 1952.

Wrinkle, William L., *Improving Marking and Reporting Practices in Elementary and Secondary Schools.* New York: Rinehart and Co., 1947.

INSTRUCTIONAL
RESOURCES AND
SPECIALIZED
SERVICES

16

THE DEVELOPMENT OF THE KIND OF EDUCATIONAL program described in the preceding chapters requires more than a building, a book, and a teacher. Just as parents call upon the assistance of a great number of specialists, so the teacher needs the help of specialists in providing the services and resources necessary to implement present-day educational programs for children.

The importance of adequate instructional resources and specialized services in insuring a well balanced and developed educational program for children makes it necessary for teachers and school administrators to think carefully about the following three questions:

1. Does the educational program of the school have the necessary definitions—objectives, sequence, teaching patterns, etc., to permit the effective selection and use of materials and special services? Too frequently the educational program is defined by the materials, not the materials by the educational program.

2. Do the teachers and, increasingly, the children have the skill and know-how to select, develop and use resources and special services in teaching and learning? We are all familiar with schools with excellent educational resources poorly used.

3. Are there adequate administrative provisions for budget, procurement, maintenance, storage, development, and use of educational facilities, so that children, good learning, and appropriate materials are together at the same place at the same time?

Many Kinds of Materials Are Used in Teaching

As an example of the profusion of materials used in present day teaching, consider the suggestions made for a social studies unit on "Pioneers of the West."[1]

1. *Background Materials*

   Teacher's books such as *The Old Santa Fe Trail, The Santa Fe Trail, The Forty-Niners, The Road to Oregon.*

   Lists of children's books available in school libraries, public libraries, or central book depository.

   Written units that have been developed by other teachers secured from local county curriculum offices, university training schools, etc.

   Teacher-written stories available for class use.

2. *Initiation of the Unit*

   Realia—Covered wagon models, pioneer dolls, spurs, powder horns, wooden pack saddle, flintlock rifle, candle molds, water pouch, shot pouch, bow, arrow, flint.

   Pictures—Showing activities at Independence, Missouri, life on the trail, Plains Indians.

   Children's books—*On the Oregon Trail, Buffalo Caller, Mighty Hunter, Tree in the Trail, The Story of the Great Plains, Yankee Thunder, Indians of the Plains.*

   Maps—Political map of the United States, trail map of the United States.

3. *Construction and Industrial Arts Materials*

   General needs—sawhorses or work benches, hammers, cross-cut saws, keyhole saws, coping saws, clamps of various sizes, jack planes, files, mitre boxes,

[1] Adapted from California Elementary School Principal's Association, *The Principal and Curriculum Building,* Twentieth Yearbook (Oakland, California: The Association, 1948), pp. 102-105.

braces, several sizes of bits, tri-squares, pliers, tin snips, a cart for storing and transporting tools from room to room, soft pine lumber.

For constructing Conestoga wagons—lumber ripped to various sizes ($\frac{1}{2}''$ x $4''$, $\frac{3}{8}''$ x $5''$, $\frac{3}{4}''$ x $\frac{3}{4}''$, and $\frac{1}{2}''$ x $\frac{1}{2}''$), two sizes of $\frac{1}{2}''$ lumber ($2''$ and $3''$), Osnaburg cloth or unbleached muslin for wagon tops.

For making models of flintlock rifles—lumber $\frac{3}{4}''$ to $1''$ thick, $6''$ wide, and approximately $30''$ long, broomsticks for barrels, $\frac{1}{4}''$ doweling for ramrods.

For utensils—$1\frac{1}{2}''$ x $5''$ soft pine for trenchers, $\frac{3}{4}''$ x $2\frac{1}{4}''$ for the spoons, etc.

For shot pouches—Osnaburg cloth or burlap.

For pioneer clothing—sheeting or cambric, package of commercial dyes, and a large granite kettle.

4. *Audio-Visual Needs*

A large map of the United States

A slide of an outline map of the United States, a still film projector or bel-opticon, heavy wrapping paper, chalk, and India ink—for children who may wish to make a trail map of their own.

Films such as "Candle Making," "Flat-Boatmen of the Frontier," "Pioneers of the Plains," "Pony Express."

Slides, film strips, stereoscopes.

5. *Musical and Rhythmic Activities*

Music books containing songs sung by the pioneers, as for example: *Junior Laurel, Music Everywhere, Our Land of Song, We Sing, Intermediate Music, Songs of Many Lands.*

A manual of directions for helping children develop folk dances in connection with the unit.

An album of folk dance records such as "Early American Folk Dances."

Record player, autoharp.

6. *Art Needs*

Water colors and various sized brushes, charcoal, poster paints, colored chalk, a fixative and sprayer.

Thus, we see that almost everything is material for teaching. The calendar hanging on the wall, the temperature of the room, or the mud puddles on the school grounds; the stone, leaf or "live exhibit" brought to school by a child; a newspaper item or radio broadcast; Johnny's father who is a gardener—all can make contributions to a school experience; all are learning resources.[2]

[2] For ways of classifying instructional materials see:

Norman Woelfel, "How to Start a Teaching Aids Program," *Nations Schools*, XLVII, No. 2 (February, 1951), 74.

Edgar Dale, *Audio-Visual Methods in Teaching* (New York: Dryden Press, Inc., 1946), Chapter 4.

THE SELECTION OF INSTRUCTIONAL RESOURCES

The selection of instructional materials is basically a simple problem. It involves: (a) deciding what is to be done; and (b) determining what is needed to do it. The first is related to pupil and teacher purposes. When these have been made clear, participants in the teaching-learning situation have some basis for deciding which activities are most worthwhile, and hence, which materials are necessary for carrying them out.

Criteria for Selection

Learning resources must be subjected to the same tests of suitability as learning experiences, because learning experiences are impossible without materials, and learning materials not related to learning experiences are valueless. All materials, whether they be books, audio-visual aids, arts and crafts, or community resources, must be evaluated in terms of the following five criteria:

1. *Instructional resources must contribute to educational purposes.* This is the fundamental principle upon which all educational decisions rest. Materials should not be selected merely because they happen to be near at hand, or because they are novel. They should be required for the achievement of particular objectives; their absence would seriously retard the kinds of development intended by the teacher. Materials should be selected, therefore, which will be related to the accomplishment of specific educational purposes, which will include all the necessary purposes to be considered, and which will deal with purposes at the level intended.

2. *Instructional materials must be pupil-oriented.* The content of educational experiences and materials must be geared to the interests and needs of pupils, and their difficulty level governed by the maturity of the children to be involved. Features such as teaching guides, glossaries, and study questions in instructional materials reflect the importance of means for providing for a range of individual differences.

3. *The content of learning resources must be valid.* Validity is more than a matter of accuracy, comprehensiveness, or recency. The question of bias in textbooks and other materials is of national and international concern. The American Legion, for example, adopted the following criteria for the evaluation of the loyalty factor as expressed in instructional materials:

a. In the study of democracy both its accomplishments and failures are examined.

b. In the treatment of the individual's relationship to government his obligations are stressed as well as his rights.

c. In the presentation of the bitter truths of the history of democracy, an attempt is made to present constructive recommendations for preventing recurrence of the undesirable results described.

d. The materials help students to develop their own methods of propaganda analysis to be applied to all situations.

e. In dealing with controversial issues both sides of the issue are fairly presented.[3]

4. *Instructional materials should conform to high technical standards.* The effectiveness of instructional materials depends as much upon form of presentation as upon the nature of the content. Style is more than being clear and "easy to read." Children's interest is held by story form dealing with people and action in lifelike situations. Humor helps. Such things as the color of a book and other details of format determine whether or not children will be attracted to a particular volume. Certain graphic techniques give maps, charts, and posters the power to tell their story clearly and concisely. Painstaking attention must be given to photographic techniques and script writing if movies and film strips are to provide realistic and rich experiences for boys and girls.

5. *Materials of instruction should be practical.* They should be economical in time, money, and effort. Busy teachers and limited school budgets rule out the probability of excessive demands in these respects. Economy, however, is more than a simple comparison of the cost of material A versus material B. It is a matter of values received compared to the expenditures involved. Neither is economy solely a matter of initial cost. Lack of durability may offset what first appears to be a decided saving of time, money or effort.

The above considerations clearly indicate the need for a great variety of instructional resources. No one teaching aid is most effective for achieving all the different objectives of a learning experience, or for all children in a class. The presence of a great variety of teaching materials is usually one index of an educational program broad in scope and individualized in character.

Process of Selection

Responsibility for the selection of instructional materials is sometimes assumed by principal, supervisor, librarian, or director of

[3] Floyd L. Haight, "Evaluation of Instructional Materials," *Educational Leadership,* VIII (March, 1951), 351.

audio-visual services. The assumption underlying this practice is that these people, by virtue of training and position, know educational resources and materials best. Putting this function in the hands of one or two "experts" is calculated to expedite the whole process of selecting, ordering, and distributing materials. Implied is the belief that the curriculum is sufficiently stable for these specialists to be able to predict needs and to decide what materials will be most useful for the total school program.

In other schools, materials are selected by committees of teachers. This plan is based on the assumption that teachers know children best. At the very heart of the educational program, teachers are in the best position to know children's needs and to see the relationship between these needs and the materials and facilities required to satisfy them. Over a period of time, moreover, they can test the usefulness of certain kinds of resources. The fact that the teacher herself conditions to some degree the instructional needs of a learning situation is another reason some advocate this approach. It is assumed that teachers know how to find out what materials are available, and how to select materials of proven value.

The best plan is to get people who know materials and who know children together to select desirable educational resources and materials. The knowledge each has is necessary in any adequate attempt to deal with this problem.

Adequacy of Resources

A perennial question facing school personnel at all levels is the one involving expenditures for instructional materials. To put it another way, when does a school have adequate materials? Standards for libraries,[4] audio-visual materials,[5] physical education equipment,[6] etc., have been set up by groups specializing in these areas. These

[4] Lucille F. Fargo, *The Library in the School,* 4th ed. (Chicago: American Library Association, 1947).

Committee on Post-War Planning, *School Libraries for Today and Tomorrow* (Chicago: American Library Association, 1945).

[5] Helen H. Seaton, *A Measure for Audio-Visual Programs in Schools,* Series II, No. 8 (Washington: American Council of Education, 1944).

Recommendations of the National Committee of Fourteen appear in *See and Hear,* III, Issue 5 (January, 1948).

[6] National Facilities Conference, *A Guide for Planning Facilities for Athletics, Recreation, Physical and Health Education* (Chicago: The Athletic Institute, 209 South State Street, 1947).

Simon A. McNeely and Elsa Schneider, *Physical Education in the School Child's Day,* Office of Education Bulletin 1950, No. 14 (Washington: Federal Security Agency, 1950), Chapter IV.

standards are largely based on opinion. Budget allotments for teaching resources in communities of similar size are sometimes used as a measure of the adequacy of expenditures being made. But this may not be useful, because situations are never identical with respect to the curriculum and the need for resources, and because present practice may not necessarily be "best." A more valid approach to the determination of adequacy might be made in terms of the utilization of materials. If teachers continue to ask for additional materials, there is some reason to believe that either a need exists or there is faulty distribution of resources. If, on the other hand, materials are lying around unused, the problem may be one of creating interest in their utilization or of replacing them with materials which are more appropriate or up to date.

UTILIZATION OF RESOURCES

The question is often asked: When is the best time to show a film: at the beginning of a unit, in the middle, or at the end? The answer is: All three, *depending upon the purpose*. Instructional materials are *means*, not *ends* in themselves. There is no virtue, for instance, in simply showing a movie. It must be shown for some reason. Exposure to certain experiences does not necessarily insure learning, least of all a particular kind of learning. It is the way in which material is utilized that will determine the effectiveness of the learning experience and the nature of what is learned. A flat picture, for example, may simply be used for decorative purposes. On the other hand, it may be used to illustrate certain art principles, to furnish background for the understanding of a poem or story, or to demonstrate the way in which living things adjust to their environment. When to use a teaching resource, therefore, depends upon the purpose toward which it is to make a contribution, and raises the corollary question of how it can best be utilized.

A General Approach

Many of the problems of the utilization of teaching resources are common to all materials.[7] First, the teacher must determine specifically what she wishes to achieve or, to put it another way, what changes she would like to make in pupil behavior. Secondly, after

---

[7] Stephen M. Corey, "Using Instructional Materials," *National Education Association Journal*, XXXVII (February, 1948), 100-101; and the same author's "What Audio-Visual Materials to Use? The Teachers' Decisions," *The Education Digest*, XV (October, 1949), 1-5.

identifying learning experiences which she believes will lead to the desired changes, she must then ask the question, "What materials are needed in order to engage in these activities, and what skills must I possess in order to guide these experiences intelligently?" This kind of pre-planning must be followed by the third step, creating a feeling of readiness on the part of pupils. Readiness for a learning experience is not the same thing as readiness to use a certain type of instructional material. The former is a reflection of pupil goals and purposes, while the latter means technique to facilitate their achievement. A committee, for example, may come to the realization that its report to the class would be more easily understood if parts of it were visualized. This does not automatically create a readiness for the use of a poster, slides, or dramatization; for their readiness depends upon past experiences with these media and a knowledge of their usefulness for the problem at hand.

Albert Cox

FOR THE BEST SERVICE, AUDIO-VISUAL EQUIPMENT MUST BE KEPT IN PROPER REPAIR

The fourth consideration in the utilization of resources is the experience itself. To be effective, distractions should be reduced to a minimum, and the experience must be satisfying to the learner. It must involve intellectualizing or generalizing from this and related experiences. The final step is for pupils and teachers to evaluate the effectiveness of their activities for achieving their goals. In this process, the appropriateness of materials and the manner in which they were utilized will loom large. Thus, the general methodology may be the same for all materials, although the utilization of various teaching aids will involve specific skills and techniques.

Textbooks

Although they recognize textbooks as being one indispensable aid to learning, most teachers agree that no single textbook can meet the demands of a changing curriculum and the various educational needs represented in their classrooms. In a situation where there is much teacher-pupil planning, no one source of information can possibly answer all the questions raised. Where the objective is to learn a prescribed body of content, no one textbook can be geared to the reading levels of all children constituting a class group.

The use of the textbook as a source of information is obvious. Just as one turns to a dictionary for help about the meaning or spelling of a word, so one turns to a science book for information about certain science problems, or to social studies books for understanding about certain historical events.

Another function of the textbook is to organize. Experiences centered around interests or problems are not calculated to present the major ideas of a subject area in logical order. The strength of the textbook is its characteristic sequential development of ideas within a book, and among the books constituting a series. Such a planned, systematic presentation of ideas can "help the student to organize and to intellectualize, that is, to make meaningful his experiences."[8]

There are several important aspects of desirable learning, however, that cannot be covered by textbooks. No textbook can think critically, generalize, or apply ideas to specific situations. The learner and the teacher must assume major responsibility for making sure these learning processes are a part of their educational experiences. Nor can a textbook determine the pace and nature of the movement of the learning process. There is no way for a textbook to spurt ahead, go

[8] Ralph W. Tyler, "The Place of the Textbook in Modern Education," *Harvard Educational Review*, XI (May, 1941), 338.

back and look, or slow down in promoting the learning and understanding of children.

Audio-Visual Materials

Pictures, slides, films, radio, recorders, and television are no longer considered novel school resources. But they are not supplanting teachers, textbooks, or learning theories emphasizing pupil activity. In short, audio-visual aids have established themselves in the sphere of educational resources as worthwhile, and requiring real teaching and learning effort.

Just as pupils are not expected to read all the books which are in the library, so most schools have given up the practice of presenting all audio-visual materials to all children. They are being used for a purpose, and this purpose governs all the decisions relating to their use. The careful selection of audio-visual materials, availability of the "right" material when needed, and previewing films and transcriptions to check on suitability are clearly indicated.[9]

Perhaps the most important aspect in the utilization of audio-visual resources is a constant evaluation, by teacher and pupils, of their effectiveness and of the methods used in their presentation. A record of children's reactions to a film under certain conditions of use, for example, may become the basis for further decisions regarding its selection and utilization.[10]

Community Resources

The emphasis upon life-like learning, as well as the community-school movement, has given impetus to the use of community resources in promoting the educational program of the school. In some cases, this is the only way that pupils can obtain specific information about community processes. In using community resources, there are many opportunities to develop planning, observation, recording, and interviewing skills. In addition to study skills, skills in human relationships develop when pupils, teachers, parents, and community representatives come to know one another as they work toward a common purpose.

Just as the use of audio-visual aids is predicated upon a knowledge of what is available, teachers who wish to capitalize upon the wealth of

[9] National Council for the Social Studies, *Audio-Visual Materials and Methods in the Social Studies,* Eighteenth Yearbook (Washington, D.C.: The Council, N.E.A., 1947).

[10] Donald C. Doane, *Classroom Use of Audio-Visual Materials,* Laboratory Manual (Los Angeles: University of Southern California, 1950).

Morgandale School, Milwaukee, Wisconsin

A FIELD TRIP FOR THE STUDY OF BABY ANIMALS

community resources must first know what exists in the community.[11] Individually or in groups, incidentally or through well-organized procedures, teachers are studying their communities. Observation, study of local records, interviews, and questionnaires are some of the techniques which yield valuable information on the basis of which various kinds of resources are cataloged and pertinent data noted.[12]

Whether resource persons come to the school, or the pupils take an excursion, the use of community resources rests upon careful plan-

[11] A "Handbook of Field Trips and Source People" has been put into the hands of every Dearborn, Michigan, teacher by the Department of Audio-Visual Instruction. It lists 140 places to visit and nearly 50 resource people. The form of the handbook and its contents were determined by a field trip committee of teachers working over a period of more than a year. For details, consult *See and Hear*, VI (January, 1951), 20.

[12] Edward G. Olsen, *School and Community*, 2nd ed. (Englewood Cliffs, N.J.: Prentice-Hall, Inc., 1954).

ning, development, and follow-up after children have had contact with the community agent or agency.[13] Planning is extremely crucial in the use of community resources. In few other teaching-learning situations is poor planning more disheartening to pupils and teacher, or more devastating to school-community relations. Whether the group assumes a relatively passive role, as in a conducted tour of a museum, or whether pupils actively seek out the resources available in order to find answers to questions previously posed, the problems of teacher guidance and control of the situation are somewhat different from those in a typical academic situation.

ORGANIZING FOR EFFECTIVE SELECTION AND USE OF MATERIALS

Learning resources are properly organized when the right materials are in the right place at the right time. Proper administration and organization must take into account the methods of selection, evaluation, and purchasing of materials; their proper cataloging, storage, and maintenance; their distribution and utilization; and the means for discarding outmoded materials so that a working collection is not weighed down by that which is useless.

The Classroom

The classroom is organized primarily for the utilization of materials. Classrooms seldom possess, therefore, adequate storage facilities. Materials necessary for particular classroom uses should be placed there on a temporary loan or expendable basis. What instructional materials should be placed in the classroom for permanent safekeeping depends on how frequently the resource is to be used and how important it is that it be continuously available. The primary consideration is that the home base for children be kept a "working base," rather than a museum.

The Instructional Materials Center

In many school systems, over-all responsibility for servicing the instructional materials needs of the schools lies in several departments, notably the library and audio-visual center. To lessen the red tape involved when teachers use a variety of materials, to foster coordination rather than competition among the various materials specialists, and

13 Henry C. Atyeo, "The Excursion in Social Education," *Audio-Visual Materials and Methods in the Social Studies,* Eighteenth Yearbook, National Council for the Social Studies (Washington, D.C.: The Council, N.E.A., 1947), Chapter 4.

to eliminate duplication of effort and expense, some larger school districts are establishing instructional materials centers. Newark, New Jersey; Portland, Oregon; San Francisco, California; Santa Monica, California; and Los Angeles, California have brought together in one center all the instructional resources formerly divided among various departments of the school system.[14] This decision is based on more than practical considerations. It is a recognition of the fact that various communication media are interrelated and interdependent; that good teaching involves the use of several approaches, rather than reliance on one.

The time has come now to put all instructional materials in their proper places and to train our teachers in their proper use. One way to do this is to integrate the various departments supplying instructional aids to classrooms into one unified center. Each teacher would come to look upon an instructional aids center as the place to which she must turn before undertaking any unit of work in order to find what learning tools will be of the greatest help.[15]

Integration of learning resources is being facilitated in a number of ways by instructional materials centers. Resource bulletins are devoted to the description and use of a great variety of resources, rather than being limited to one type. Emphasis is placed on the way these materials are used in *conjunction* with one another in the development of units of work. Resource files which attempt to locate all the materials which might be used in connection with a particular unit are prepared. These files include books for teachers and pupils; films; filmstrips; slides; transcriptions; free and inexpensive materials; field trips; and curriculum guides. Some centers distribute resource kits for teaching certain units on a loan basis. One on "Pioneer Life" might include such things as related pictures, charts, and maps; pamphlets and books; construction plans and recipes; realia and samples of work; film strips, slides, and recordings; reference lists of books and films. Throughout, the emphasis is on meeting the classroom teacher's needs for *specific* and *varied* materials which she can then use in an integrated fashion to achieve educational purposes.

The School Building

When several classrooms constitute a school, the building itself becomes an important organizational unit for instructional resources.

[14] Margaret I. Rufsvold, *Audio-Visual School Library Service* (Chicago: American Library Association, 1949), p. 3.

[15] Willard B. Spalding, "Integration of Instructional Materials," *The Educational Screen*, XXVI (September, 1947), 394.

Materials stored in individual classrooms are little used, seldom come to the attention of other teachers, and quickly fall into disrepair or disorder. When many teachers are purchasing or borrowing supplies, some method of coordination is necessary. Experience has shown that someone in each building must be in charge of the instructional resources used by the school population. Traditionally, this has been one of the functions of the principal. As the school increases in size, or activity in the field of materials increases, other personnel are delegated this responsibility, usually on a part-time basis. The teacher-librarian is most commonly found in elementary schools. More recently, the part-time audio-visual coordinator has made his appearance to service building needs.

There is at present a trend toward decentralizing distribution centers, both by extended loans to schools, and increased purchases by individual schools. This has created a greater concern for improving instructional resources, and for centralizing the materials function in each building unit. From the librarian's point of view,

Beloit Public Schools, Beloit, Wisconsin

THE SCHOOL LIBRARY IS A BUSY PLACE

Administering and distributing materials used in the audio-visual program is not a new phase in the school library, for . . . it comprises functions and services already provided for books and graphic materials. Thus when the individual school library becomes the school's materials center embracing all media of communication, it is merely extending its existing library program.[16]

Regardless of who is selected to coordinate instructional materials for a school building, this person should look to the staff for plans and policies. The improvement of teaching resources is everybody's business, and school organization should make it possible for everyone to be actively engaged in this program.

SPECIALIZED EDUCATIONAL SERVICES AND RESOURCES

Special Teaching Services

Several kinds of "special teachers" have made their appearance in elementary education. Most common are those specifically prepared to teach music, art, and physical education. At the upper grade levels there may be teachers of home economics, "shop," and, sometimes, agriculture. In certain fields, reading especially, there are special teachers to assist so-called normal children who are educationally retarded. As we have come closer to realizing the goal of educating all the children of all the people, teachers of *exceptional children* have come into being.

The functions of special teachers vary considerably depending on the classroom teacher's competence and the place given to the special field in the total school program. In general, the special teacher is able to help school personnel and the community visualize more broadly the possibilities of his field as they relate to the total development of children and community.

Special subject teachers make their contribution to the total educational program by working directly with pupils, reaching pupils indirectly by working primarily with the teacher, or by dealing with both teacher and pupil. An art teacher, for example, may come into the classroom one or more times a week and "take charge" of the class, or the class may move to the special "art room." In either case, the regular classroom teacher may serve as his assistant, may simply be an interested onlooker, or may not even be present in the room. The need for integrating the work of the special areas with the regular work of the classroom, and for providing continuing experiences in these areas, is leading specialized teachers to help classroom teachers

[16] Rufsvold, *op. cit.*, pp. 7-8.

carry on activities which they have initiated. An even higher level of correlation is brought about when the special teacher is available to the classroom teacher at every step in the development of a learning experience. In those cases where a number of schools in a wide area such as a rural county or a city district must be served, the special teacher often functions as a consultant to teachers, rather than attempting to instruct personally each and every pupil in these schools.

Remedial Teachers

To assist classroom teachers in helping apparently normal children who are educationally retarded, many school systems provide remedial teachers. These are master teachers who are highly skilled in diagnosing difficulties and in providing for individual differences in learning. Most common is the teacher of remedial reading.

Traditionally, the services of a remedial teacher were sought *after* the child evidenced symptoms of severe retardation. More recently the trend has been to call on such expert teachers for the *prevention* of learning difficulties. Attention is being focused on the improvement of the developmental program and the early detection of individual learning difficulties.

As the role of the remedial teacher changes, so do his relationships with the classroom teacher. Clinics conducted by specialists in the school building or in the central office to which pupils report periodically for diagnostic and remedial instruction are still common. When the emphasis shifts to include prevention, the remedial teacher is likely to spend less time in the clinic and more with classroom teachers as a consultant or helping teacher. In larger schools, remedial teachers may be placed in charge of so-called "opportunity" or "adjustment" rooms which are organized on a half-day or full-time basis for small groups of pupils whose general academic achievement is far below expectation. In some schools, children having language difficulties, or children who have experienced prolonged absence, are placed in such rooms in order to help them "catch up."

Teachers of Exceptional Children

Quite recently, a different kind of specialist has come into being to aid children who deviate considerably from "normal" in physical, mental, or emotional characteristics. Exceptional children, as they are commonly called, include

the blind and the partially seeing, the deaf and the hard-of-hearing, the crippled (including the cerebral-palsied), the delicate (including the tuberculous and the

Esther Bubley and THE SCHOOL EXECUTIVE

CHILDREN EXTEND THEIR CONCEPTS OF SPACE AND TIME

cardiopathic), the epileptic, the speech defective, the mentally handicapped, the mentally gifted, and the socially or emotionally maladjusted and delinquent.[17]

As of 1952-1953, laws authorizing or requiring local school systems to provide special educational services for one or more of these types of children had been passed in 48 states. The increase in enrollment of pupils in special schools and classes since 1947-1948 was 159,087 or 47 per cent, compared to an increase in public school enrollment of 17.4 per cent. The greatest per cent of increase took place in enrollments of speech-handicapped (480 per cent), the mentally retarded

[17] Office of Education, *State Legislation for Education of Exceptional Children,* Bulletin 1949, No. 2 (Washington, D.C.: Federal Security Agency, 1949).

(129 per cent), and children with special health problems (113 per cent).[18]

Teachers of exceptional children function in a variety of ways. Many speech correctionists, for example, spend one or more periods a week in each classroom during which time they take charge of instruction. Others seldom engage in classroom instruction, but serve as consultants to classroom teachers in helping children with speech difficulties. A clinic arrangement for exceptional children is common in large elementary schools. One or more rooms of the school are set aside to house special equipment, materials, and facilities where a special teacher can diagnose and instruct atypical pupils on an individual or small group basis. In schools organized on a departmental basis, teachers of exceptional children may be placed in charge of "home rooms" where they provide special help to a group of children for half a day. This makes it possible for the special teacher to meet with two groups, and for atypical pupils to be in mixed classes for the remainder of their school program. On the other hand, some schools segregate atypical students for the full day under the direction of a specialist. Physically handicapped, mentally retarded, emotionally disturbed, or gifted children are often taught on this basis. In large communities an entire school may provide special education for physically handicapped, mentally retarded, or gifted children.

Some communities are assuming responsibility for providing instruction to pupils who are hospitalized or confined to the home for an extended period. In such cases

The traveling teacher will see the child's teacher and plan with her—instructional materials will be provided by the child's teacher. The traveling teacher might bring a small projector and show the child films, filmstrips or slides. She may bring a tape recorder with greetings from her classmates. Certain lessons may be recorded and repeated for her benefit. The child may tell her classmates what she's been doing. She would have access to a radio and her listening should be guided and indicated by the teacher. Pictures may be brought to the child.[19]

Organizing Special Teaching Services

Analysis of home-room plans, special classes, special centers, and special schools reveals that no one organizational plan is best *per se* for meeting *all* the needs found in a particular teaching-learning sit-

[18] Office of Education, "Statistics of Special Education for Exceptional Children," *Biennial Survey of Education in the United States*, 1952-1953, Chap. V (Washington, D.C.: Federal Security Agency, 1954), p. 18.

[19] Leslie W. Johnson, "New Hope for the Homebound," *School Executive*, LXX (November, 1950), 153.

uation. Thus, any plan for organizing special teacher services must be related to the total educational experiences of children and must be so organized that:

1. various needs of children, teachers, and parents are taken into account.

2. the quality of human relationships among pupil, specialist, classroom teacher, and parents will be enhanced.

3. the total school experiencing of the child will be as nearly unified as possible.

4. similarities among children will receive more emphasis than differences.

5. practical considerations will not loom so large as to offset advantages accruing from certain practices.

Pupil Personnel Services

Many classroom teachers have available a number of special services which are referred to generally as child welfare, pupil personnel, or guidance. Such pupil personnel activities can be classified into three broad areas: health, psychological, and home services. Programs vary considerably from school to school, and the professional literature itself reflects lack of agreement on function and organization of pupil personnel services. In practice, pupil personnel work tends to be focused primarily on the individual pupil. Through his concern for the welfare of each child, the personnel specialist contributes to the realization of the objectives of the total educational program. His contribution is neither incidental nor peripheral, but an integral part of the total school effort.

Psychological Services

Psychological services are performed or directed by psychologists, psychiatrists, psychometrists, and counselors. These specialists may assist classroom teachers by administering tests requiring highly technical training, coordinating or centralizing child study activities, conducting case studies of children in need of help, analyzing and interpreting child-study data, identifying children in need of special attention or treatment, and referring children to out-of-school agencies when the nature of the problem is beyond the scope and facilities of the school. Sometimes assistance is provided in counseling with pupils and parents.

Psychological clinics can assist by making more refined diagnoses of personality maladjustments, accumulating and interpreting data from a wide variety of sources, and coordinating the efforts of a great number of people and agencies in school and out of school in resolving child problems.

Home Services

Certain personnel workers have the responsibility of working directly with the home. The earlier preoccupation of these workers with school census and attendance enforcement has gradually given way to more positive functions, and an emphasis on prevention rather than punishment. The "truant officer" has been replaced by "attendance workers," "visiting teachers," or "school social workers." While child accounting and attendance are still important, more and more effort is being devoted to orienting new pupils and parents to the school and to creating a full appreciation of the school's work in homes where school attendance has been casual. A broad conception of the function of the home worker is that of the social worker who has the time and techniques

to help the child who is indicating that he is having difficulty in his use of the school experience by such behavior as truancy, poor academic achievement in spite of good ability, aggressive hostile behavior, shy withdrawn behavior, stealing, thwarting authority. She will give this service through working with the child, the parent, and the teacher as well as through the use of other school and community resources.[20]

Providing visiting teacher service indicates a recognition of the close relationship between school success and adjustment, and home and community environment. Some children need individual help in order to benefit from their school experiences—often different from and in addition to the help which can be provided by the classroom teacher. The school social worker can interpret a child's needs from the broader base of school, home, and community factors, and make appropriate suggestions for both school and home programs. Through conferences he can help teachers and parents to see the nature of child problems, what the school can contribute to their solution, what responsibilities must be assumed by the home, and what assistance may be sought from other community agencies. In many cases, he is in the best position to coordinate the efforts of the several persons or agencies involved in helping the child.

[20] Opal Boston, "School Social Worker in Modern Education," *Understanding the Child*, XIX (January, 1950), 2.

As a representative of the school, the visiting teacher relies less on police powers than on good counseling techniques, and considers himself a part of the mental hygiene team rather than a law enforcement officer.

Principles of Operation of a Pupil Personnel Program

Because of the relative newness of many of the functions described above, the range of needs which they attempt to meet, and the need for coordinating many services, efforts to provide pupil personnel services become complicated. Assuming that these services are an integral part of the total school program, the following principles might govern the organization and operation of a pupil personnel program:

1. Pupil personnel services are most effectively administered when their organization is structured to meet the individual needs of pupils.

2. The success of a pupil personnel program in a school system is directly correlated with the vision and perseverance of the administrative officers.

3. In the process of focusing attention upon the development of the pupil, emphasis should be given to the preparation of teachers and administrators to use pupil personnel services appropriately.

4. Pupil personnel services will operate best when the specialist in one area has enough understanding and appreciation of the work of specialists in other areas to be able to recognize the appropriateness of referrals and relationships.

5. All individuals who operate in school guidance should have familiarity with classroom procedures and appreciation of classroom problems. In turn, the classroom teacher should have an understanding of pupil personnel services.

6. Effective coordination of pupil personnel services may be secured either by placing such services within a single administrative unit and/or by establishing adequate coordination among various individuals responsible for segments of the program, as long as policies and relationships are clearly defined.

7. Coordination of pupil personnel services is materially improved when each of the departments within pupil personnel services contributes pertinent materials to a single running record for each child. Confidential information should be protected and made available only through the person recording the information.

8. To minimize undesirable duplication of effort among the various personnel services, it is essential that the scope and nature of each service be clearly outlined and the jurisdiction of each clearly established.

9. The setting of the school and the educational levels of its pupils condition the administration and organization of the program of pupil personnel services that will be most effective in that school.

10. Responsibility democratically assigned works best when a specialist operates as a consultant—a staff relationship in pupil personnel services.

11. A counselor and other specialists such as nurses should have a staff relationship in a school system, regardless of size of school.

12. It is basic that responsibility for various aspects of pupil personnel services should be assigned to the best qualified member or members of the school staff, and that all should work as a team under a sound administrative policy.

13. The role of the teacher as a key person in the utilization of pupil personnel services for assisting pupils should be clearly defined.

14. When any specialist works with members of the staff in helping pupils, the specialist has responsibility for broadening their understanding.

15. It is a policy of the counseling service to give appropriate help in time to prevent difficulty rather than to wait until real scholastic or personal trouble has forced the student to the attention of the counselor.

16. Where community agencies serving families and children exist, the school staff concerned with pupil personnel services should establish clear lines of relationships with these agencies.

17. Policies supporting the activities of a school guidance program should emanate from the constituents of the school—teachers, administrators, laymen, youth—especially from those most affected by the program.

18. All specialists in pupil personnel services should have an opportunity to participate in total staff planning and assist in curriculum development designed to meet the needs of the pupils.

19. There should be continuous study and evaluation of the guidance organization, including personnel used, in terms of how well the needs of pupils are being met in the local situation.[21]

TYPES OF COMMUNITY GROUPS AND AGENCIES

In our culture, many groups or agencies have some relationship to children and their education. Olsen has classified such groups as institutions, formally organized groups, agencies, private enterprise, and informal groups.[22]

These groups operate on different levels of relationship to an individual school. Some are located in the immediate community. Others are state or regional organizations which render service through field personnel or highly active distributive centers. Those which operate on a national or international level render less personalized service to the classroom teacher, but can provide real assistance nevertheless, as witness the United States Office of Education in the Department of Health, Welfare and Education.

On the local level, the post office, fire department, and police department are firmly established as "helpers" in the primary grades of American schools. Further, teachers could not do justice to the health needs of their charges without the assistance of the public health de-

21 Federal Security Agency, *Pupil Personnel Services in Elementary and Secondary Schools,* Office of Education Circular No. 325 (Washington, D.C.: United States Government Printing Office, 1951), 12-13.

22 Edward G. Olsen, *School and Community,* 2nd ed. (Englewood Cliffs, N.J.: Prentice-Hall, Inc., 1954), pp. 57-60.

partment. The public library, welfare department, and departments of education are likewise invaluable sources of special kinds of service.

The Public Library

Few elementary schools have a well-stocked library staffed by a full-time professional librarian. Most elementary teachers, therefore, look to the public library for additional assistance. In sparsely populated areas, this often takes the form of bookmobile service[23] or periodic shipment of book collections from city, county, or state libraries. Some teachers take their classes to a district public library on regularly scheduled bus trips.[24]

As communities grow larger, children may find it possible to walk to the neighborhood library in groups or as a class. A goodly proportion of children's books may even be loaned directly to the school, and the public librarian may come at designated times to assist with the school's library problems.

In some cities under 70,000 population, public libraries have established branches in school buildings, the costs being shared by the library board and board of education. Larger cities may support school and public libraries on a common basis. Where this is true, public librarians may aid in extending school library services by performing certain technical tasks such as ordering, classifying, and cataloging books, as well as through loans which may be temporary or permanent.[25]

Social Welfare Department

A child's problem sometimes stems from certain family conditions which are beyond the scope of a public school program. In many communities, teachers can refer such cases to local, county, or state social welfare agencies which are organized to deal with them. If the problem is economic, they can secure employment for the head of the family or provide additional financial assistance when necessary. Where child-rearing practices are poor, where discipline is lacking or unduly harsh, parental education, enforced by supervision, may be

[23] Committee of State School Library Supervisors and ALA Library Extension Division, "Public Library Bookmobile Service to the Schools," *ALA Bulletin*, XXXXV, April, 1951 (Chicago: American Library Association, 1951), 131-132.

[24] Rheta A. Clark, "Public Libraries Will Cooperate," *Elementary School Libraries Today*, Thirtieth Yearbook, The National Elementary Principal (Washington, D.C.: Department of Elementary School Principals, N.E.A., 1951), p. 234.

[25] Agnes Krarup, "Cooperation in Pittsburgh," *Elementary School Libraries Today*, Thirtieth Yearbook, The National Elementary Principal (Washington, D.C.: Department of Elementary School Principals, N.E.A., 1951), pp. 217-222.

instituted. Occasionally, remediation requires the placement of children in foster homes or institutions.

In all such efforts to improve the primary living-base of the child, the school's responsibility goes beyond that of referral. The school history of the child, including physical factors and home relationships, are important kinds of information which social agencies need in order to be effective. Rearrangements in family living often require the suggestions and cooperation of the school. Welfare agencies are dependent, also, on the teacher's observations as one way to check the effectiveness of their program for rehabilitating a child. Furthermore, the teacher's acceptance and support of a child with problems requiring welfare aid is a potent factor in bringing about change.

Governmental Departments of Public Instruction

Every teacher has a number of educational agencies which can assist in the improvement of instructional procedures in the classroom. State Departments of Education and the United States Office of Education distribute free of charge, or at nominal expense, numerous bulletins dealing with basic points of view in education and current educational practice and trends. Their monthly journals and periodic bibliographies indicate sources of information on problems of current interest in educational circles or new techniques and materials for teaching. Where new ideas are being tried, State Departments may provide consultants to assist a school staff in developing the program or organize workshops centering around problems encountered.

COMMERCIAL AGENCIES

Business agencies are increasing their efforts to develop materials of educational value to schools. Blatant advertising of a trade name in materials is being replaced by a real attempt to educate teachers about the nature of the product and its wise use. Thus, a wealth of industry-sponsored pamphlets, charts, exhibits, and films are available to teachers upon request. In addition, companies generally encourage and welcome visiting school groups. In many cases, industry is giving as much time and thought to the management of its conducted tours as to other phases of its public relations program.

There is a growing tendency to call upon commercial personnel for consultant services. For example, schools embarking on the production of locally-oriented instructional materials must, of necessity, turn to local businessmen for many of the facts and figures. The extent to which this kind of cooperation can be secured is well illustrated in an acknowledgment made by Fresno County teachers, who prepared a series of bulletins describing the various industries of their area.

The Fresno County Superintendent of Schools is especially grateful to the following persons and concerns for supplying information, pictures, and expert advice in the preparation of this booklet—the third in a series of Community Life Booklets for Fresno County: Borden's Dairy Delivery Company, Fresno; Boston Land Company, New Haven; California Fig Institute, Fresno; Coca-Cola Bottling Company, Fresno; Elmer C. Von Glahn, Corcoran; Fortier Transportation Company, Fresno; J. E. O'Neill, Inc., Fresno; Jourdan Concrete Pipe Company, Fresno; Pacific Gas and Electric Company, Fresno; Peerless Pump Division, Fresno; Producers Cotton Oil Company, Fresno; San Joaquin Valley Poultry Producers Association, Fresno; Selma Dressed Beef Company, Selma; Standard Oil Company of California, Fresno; Sun-Maid Raisin Growers of California, Fresno; United Air Lines, Fresno.[26]

Business Education Day

Another consulting service rendered to schools by commercial agencies is in the area of vocational information or guidance. A common feature of these activities is a Business Education Day, or a Careers Day Conference at which representatives of various industries are invited to speak and answer questions about vocational possibilities in their fields. Such large-scale programs are usually reserved for high school students. There is a tendency, however, to bring this kind of information to the attention of students before they are seniors so that they can make wise decisions about their high school program. The upper elementary or lower secondary grades (7th-9th) are being increasingly regarded as the point at which such programs should be initiated in order to provide for continuity and development in vocational guidance. In such cases, the consultantship services of commercial personnel are important throughout the entire period of public education to give emphasis to vocational understanding and choice.

PRIVATE NON-COMMERCIAL AGENCIES

American community living is characterized by voluntary participation in a host of private non-commercial groups which have been organized to meet a variety of needs. Some are primarily interested in the promotion of better human relationships among the diverse ele-

[26] Fresno County Schools, *Growing Cotton in Fresno County*, Community Life Booklet Number 3 (Fresno, California: Fresno County School Board, 1949), 2.

ments found in most communities today. Others are intent upon service to the community of a social-civic nature. The development of moral and spiritual standards is the major goal of another group of institutions. In general, however, private non-commercial agencies exist to improve the quality of personal-social living in the community.

In keeping with this major purpose, many activities of these groups are of an educative nature, or depend upon the education of the community for their success. The success of a Safety Campaign sponsored by automobile clubs or chambers of commerce, for example, depends as much upon the education of adults *and children* as upon automobile inspections and rearrangements in traffic control. In this example, the common concern for the "safety" education of children brings to many classroom teachers a wealth of materials and services to enhance instructional activities in this area. The cooperation of the school, in turn, adds to the effectiveness of the community's safety efforts.

Parent-Teacher Association

Composed of parents, teachers, and other interested members of the community, the P.T.A. is often the first source to which the school turns for assistance. No agency is in a more favorable position to provide direct and constructive services to the ongoing experiences in the classroom. Almost universally there is great interest in public relations, which involves various means for disseminating information about the public school program and its needs. In addition, funds, materials, or personnel are provided to help teachers carry out certain activities. In more recent years there has been a trend for school staffs and P.T.A. groups to work cooperatively on basic problems dealing with all educational areas. This viewing of "school" problems in the context of the larger "educational" problems, results in mutual understanding, and in support by parents and teachers of better school and home programs.

Community Coordinating Council

Youth welfare community agencies often organize some kind of central steering committee or coordinating council to foster cooperation among various groups and develop a total program on a community-wide basis. Such a clearing-house organization is fashioned in terms of the resources at hand and the particular needs of the community. Representation generally includes all groups interested in providing better opportunities for children and youths: social agencies, recreation programs, civic and service clubs, churches, schools, courts and juvenile enforcement officials, and youth organizations.

As one of many groups taking part in the council, the school can exercise initiative and leadership in shaping its policies. As one of many youth-serving agencies, the school can cooperate in the total community effort, and receive the benefits resulting from such co ordination of activities.

SELECTION AND USE OF COMMUNITY SERVICES

The great array and endless possibilities of school services provided by governmental, commercial, and voluntary agencies presents the teacher with the problem of how to select and use these community services to best advantage. Any decisions will involve consideration of at least the following three criteria:

1. *Community services must contribute to educational goals.* Regardless of how desirable the services may be, no group should be allowed access to school children for the purpose of proselytizing or of opposing its selfish interests to the common welfare. Only those services should be utilized which contribute most effectively to the purposes for which public education has been designed.

2. *Community services must help to create a balanced educational program.* A school which does not avail itself of community services is likely to be highly academic and divorced from the concrete realities of community living. The utilization of community services will balance "studying something that has happened somewhere else" with "doing something about personal-community living now." If the use of community services becomes a fetish, however, it may throw the educational program off balance because (a) it bears no relationship to the ongoing activities of the classroom or (b) it is so over-emphasized that other worthwhile activities are displaced.

3. *Community services should not be overly stimulating.* A certain degree of emotion is required for optimum learning, and this is usually generated in the use of community services. In some cases, however, the use of community services is associated with conditions which overstimulate immature learners and results in much harm. Teachers must protect children from activities of a highly competitive nature or those which emphasize the spectacular and "showy."

DEVELOPING PUBLIC UNDERSTANDING AND SUPPORT

Parents' interest in textbooks and workbooks, school board policies about the nature and extent of special services, and the activity of lay groups in evaluating the work and cost of operating schools—all are evidences of a great interest in educational resources. This interest is coupled ofttimes with a considerable lag in educational thinking. To capitalize on interest, the school must provide opportunities for laymen to develop an understanding of the functions of educational resources and their contributions to classroom experiences. This is achieved best by making it possible for laymen to work with professionals on educational problems. One such workshop, jointly sponsored by a state education group and a university, included educators and parents from various communities who met to plan projects for their home communities involving child development and guidance practices in home and school.[27] Lay people must come to realize the need for many and varied educational resources, for cooperation in making materials and services available, and for the desire to secure adequate financial support for their maintenance. In the final analysis, improvement in materials of instruction and specialized services will depend upon the people for whom the schools are run.

SUMMARY OF THE BIG IDEAS

In thinking about the use of instructional resources and specialized services to enrich and improve the educational experiences children have in the elementary school, the following ideas are important.

1. The educational resources and specialized services must contribute to valid educational objectives. These objectives must be one of the important bases upon which educational services and resources are selected, developed, and used, rather than vice versa. Such services and resources should contribute and facilitate educational programs, not determine them.

2. Educational resources and specialized services must be child-oriented. Resources must be brought to children for their benefit and enrichment, not the children brought to the resource and service. Individual children provide the second important basis for determining the selection and use of materials and resources.

3. The educational resources and specialized services must be teacher-oriented. Their selection, availability, and use should be

27 Grace Storm, "Illinois Child Development and Guidance Project," *Elementary School Journal,* LII (September, 1951), 6-8.

related to the daily long term teacher-pupil activity of the classroom and educational program of the school. Organization and administration of resources and services must be clearly related to function.

4. The educational resources and services must be authentic. Authenticity here has two meanings. First, the information and activities involved must be accurate, pertinent, and authoritative. Second, the motive behind the development of the material or resources must be fundamentally educational in nature and in the public interest.

5. All educational programs can be broadened and enriched through the use of resources and special services. No school or program is sufficient unto itself.

6. Few schools and educational programs have fully exploited the resources and services available to them. Imagination and initiative on the part of educational and community leadership is a valuable resource too seldom fully exploited.

BIBLIOGRAPHY

Clapp, Elsie R., *The Use of Resources in Education.* New York: Harper & Brothers, 1952.

Dale, Edgar, *Audio-Visual Methods in Teaching,* rev. ed. New York: Dryden Press, Inc., 1954.

Department of Elementary School Principals, *Elementary-School Libraries Today,* Thirtieth Yearbook. Washington, D. C.: The Department, N.E.A., 1951.

National Council for the Social Studies, *Audio-Visual Materials and Methods in the Social Studies,* Eighteenth Yearbook. Washington, D. C.: The Council, N.E.A., 1947.

Olsen, Edward G., ed., *The Modern Community School,* Association for Supervision and Curriculum Development. New York: Appleton-Century-Crofts, Inc., 1953.

———, ed., *School and Community Programs.* Englewood Cliffs, N. J.: Prentice-Hall, Inc., 1949.

Olson, Clara M. and Norman D. Fletcher, *Learn and Live.* New York: Alfred P. Sloan Foundation, Inc., 1946.

Rufsvold, Margaret I., *Audio-Visual School Library Service.* Chicago: American Library Association, 1949.

UNESCO, *A Handbook for the Improvement of Textbook and Teaching Materials as Aids to International Understanding.* Paris, France: UNESCO, 1949.

Willey, R. D., *Guidance in Elementary Education.* New York: Harper & Brothers, 1952.

Wittich, Walter A. and Charles F. Schuller, *Audio-Visual Materials: Their Nature and Use.* New York: Harper & Brothers, 1953.

EVALUATING AND
IMPROVING
ELEMENTARY SCHOOL
PRACTICES

17

THE TASK OF THE ELEMENTARY SCHOOL IS TO
provide the best possible program of instruction
for children. To do this, school staffs must develop a well-planned, continuous, and consistent
program of action for the purposes of: (a) appraising the total school program to identify
needed improvements; and (b) working out ways
and means for capitalizing on strengths and
eradicating weaknesses identified through the
appraisal process.

The currently fashionable phrase applied in-
discriminately to any and all means, both direct
and indirect, for improving the instructional
program for children is *in-service education*. To

our minds, this phrase well describes what is necessary if instruction is to improve, for it places the emphasis where it belongs—on the teacher who deals directly with children and who assumes fundamental responsibility for what goes on within the confines of the classroom. The key to instructional improvement is the classroom teacher! All teachers can improve their teaching. All elementary school programs can be made more effective.

Opportunities for Continued Development

Opportunities for teachers to go on learning exist in great profusion. As individuals, teachers may seek professional improvement on a voluntary basis through travel, continuous professional reading to keep abreast of current developments, exchange teaching, attendance at summer sessions, enrollment in correspondence and extension courses, membership and participation in professional organizations, attendance at available conferences and institutes dealing with teaching problems, and the like. Participation in such activities no doubt may have positive effects on what goes on in the particular classroom of the participating teacher; many can and do benefit. Increasing numbers of school systems have recognized this fact by encouraging individual teacher activities through such practices as the development of professional libraries and instructional materials centers at local expense, sabbatical leave arrangements, salary schedules based partially on the taking of advanced work, partial payment of tuition and/or expenses for summer session attendance, providing substitutes to free teachers for participation in approved professional activities, and arranging visiting days to allow teachers to see other classrooms in action. This concern for individual improvement, while laudable, too often is the only kind of opportunity open to teachers in many school situations. Where in-service education activities are limited to isolated individual efforts of these kinds, improvement of the total instructional program becomes a matter of chance.

Increasing numbers of schools and school systems have gone beyond this limited conception of in-service education to develop group opportunities for professional improvement. Provisions for group activities for teachers include regularly scheduled staff meetings devoted to professional problems, demonstration teaching, outside speakers, workshops, voluntary study groups, organized committee work, pre-school conferences, and the like. These represent encouraging signs of a gradual awakening to the need for some kind of concerted attack on the problem of instructional improvement which does not leave positive change to chance. Unfortunately a good many of these efforts operate on a hit-or-miss piecemeal basis. What is needed is a more comprehensive approach to educational problems on a continuous basis.

Three factors probably account for most of the variety found in approaches to improvement through in-service education: (1) the size of the educational community; (2) level of attack; *i.e.*, local, county, state; and (3) the unique conditions of educational communities. A recent survey[1] of in-service education practices in the state of Wisconsin has shown that smaller school systems (2500 population and below) generally provide fewer opportunities for staff improvement, make less use of common group activities, and provide fewer professional resources to teachers than do schools in communities of larger size. Differences between local, county, and state programs are associated, of course, with difficulties in communication and remoteness from actual classrooms, where teachers are involved in improvement programs on county-wide and state-wide bases. Differences in programs at the local community level are due to differences in the particular problems considered important, in the competence of given school staffs to deal with them, and in the limitations placed on improvement by such factors as community attitudes, ability to support, and traditions. That positive results can be achieved irrespective of size of educational community is seen in the reports of programs of instructional improvement stemming from very small to extremely large situations.[2] Likewise it is possible to identify highly effective programs of instructional improvement at the county and state levels.[3] Despite these demonstrations of some measure of success at these broader levels of concern, the present writers are convinced that programs of in-service education which center in a given educational community at the local level, and which involve the total teaching staff in a comprehensive, cooperative, and continuous attack on the specific instructional problems of that community, offer greatest

1 From unpublished materials gathered as a cooperative venture of the Department of Education of the University of Wisconsin and the State Department of Public Instruction.

2 See, for example: *In-Service Education in Wisconsin Moves Ahead*, a study jointly sponsored by the Elementary School Principal's Association, the State Department of Public Instruction, and the School of Education of the University of Wisconsin (Madison: The State Department, 1953).

3 See, for example, descriptions of the Alameda County, California, program, and of activities at the state level in Michigan and Florida in: Hollis L. Caswell and Associates, *Curriculum Improvement in Public School Systems* (New York: Bureau of Publications, Teachers College, Columbia University, 1950), pp. 317-423.

potentiality for bringing about change where it matters most—at the instructional level.

The Process of Appraisal

The importance of the evaluation process as an integral part of classroom learning experiences has been emphasized strongly in earlier portions of this book. In performing this persistent instructional task with children, the teacher obtains answers to such essential questions as: what are we attempting to achieve, where are we in relation to where we want to go, and what does this mean for our next steps? Evaluation at this level focuses on particular classroom units and the progress of individual children within the group. It is *not* aimed at assessing the results of the *total* instructional program as children move through the grades. Having teachers evaluating with children in separate classrooms, even though in excellent fashion, is no guarantee that the over-all educational program will produce the best results most effectively. It is both possible and likely, where teachers go their separate ways, that instructional decisions and judgments of adequacy will be based on differing beliefs and the

University of Wisconsin Summer Laboratory School

A FACULTY PLANS ITS WORK

values they reflect. Too often such differences serve to destroy the very essence of what the educational enterprise is trying to achieve— a consistent, continuous, and well-knit series of learning experiences all designed to contribute to the same general ends for children.

The Essential Components of Program Appraisal. In simplest terms, appraisal may be seen as the process of comparing *what is* with *what should be* in order to identify points of improvement. Considered in terms of appraisal of the total instructional program, this simple statement implies all of the essential components which must enter into the process. First, knowing what is, requires that the school staff perceive clearly: (a) what is to be looked at; and (b) suitable means for gathering data. Second, definitions of what should be must be based on: (a) agreements as to what is desired in educational programs for children, and (b) agreements as to the norms or standards to be used in determining the degree to which we should accomplish these desired ends. Third, a staff must see that it is important to make judgments about the instructional program as to where improvements should be made and where planning and action should take place.

Determining What to Look At. This sounds like a very simple problem and one which teachers and their leadership can solve easily. Obviously we must look at the educational program, and at what the children are doing. When we start doing this, however, our problem becomes difficult, complex, and somewhat confused. Should we, for example, look at the behavior of children or the teacher; the physical plant and instructional equipment, or the textbooks, courses of study and teachers' manuals; statements of objectives and educational values, or definitions of subject fields and their sequences throughout the grades; stages and levels of skill development, or the nature of the developmental characteristics of children and the principles underlying their learning processes; the ways in which children are meeting their social and emotional needs, or the giving of achievement tests to determine the grade level development of the skills? This brief list can be extended almost indefinitely.

As teachers and principals have studied this problem of where to start examining an educational program, and have been confronted with lists of possibilities like the one above, the following tentative propositions about how to meet this situation have emerged:

1. Lists of places to start studying and improving an educational program are not statements of independent alternatives. At some

point in attempts to improve an educational program for children, most, if not all, of these aspects of a program will have to be considered. It is proposed here that teachers and principals consider seriously the number of things they will want to study in some kind of relationship to each other, rather than restricting their decision to the selection of only one.

2. The order in which various aspects of an educational program are studied probably does make some difference. Objectives, for example, seem like first-things-first. The authors of this book urge teachers and principals, however, not to *start* their programs of educational improvement at this logical first-point. We suggest instead looking at the common and persistent tasks of teaching and learning as teachers find them in their daily lives, or observing children as they go about the tasks of learning and growing up. Objectives, educational values, materials, organization, and courses of study will soon find their way into this kind of continuing consideration.

3. There is no need to start with a crisis or a deficiency as a basis for improving. Too many feelings are involved, defensive mechanisms are operating overtime, and people are bound to get hurt. Every negative aspect always has a positive face; both are tied to any important area or aspect of a program which needs to be improved. By studying how to organize and develop learning experiences for children more effectively, the positive and negative aspects of this common task are seen in some constructive fashion. One can jump better if he takes off from his best foot.

Fortunately, outside resources open to school staffs for determining the scope of appraisal are numerous. The kind of resources represented by statements of over-all purpose, such as the Cardinal Principles of Elementary Education, the definition of the Educational Policies Commission, and the Russell Sage Foundation report, has been discussed previously (see Chapter 4). In recent years, numerous handbooks designed to be of help to school staffs in carrying on the appraisal process have been produced by several state departments of education, institutions of higher learning, and educational associations.[4] Most of these devices provide for study of the total school operation, with explicit definitions of important aspects to be con-

---

[4] See, for example: Texas State Department of Education, Division of Elementary Education, *Handbook for Self-Appraisal and Improvement of Elementary Schools,* rev. ed. (Austin: The Department, 1948); James F. Baker, *Elementary Evaluative Criteria* (Boston: School of Education, Boston University, 1953); Southern Association of Colleges and Secondary Schools, Cooperative Study in Elementary Education, *Evaluating the Elementary School* (Atlanta: The Association, 1951).

sidered, as well as providing standards useful in making value judgments.

Determining What We Want. Our educational wants are many and they are stated in various ways. In education these wants are defined by our objectives, as was indicated in Chapter 4. Another definition of the things we value in educational programs is the statement of philosophy or basic assumptions about the purpose of education, nature of children, characteristics of desirable learning, and the like, made by many staffs. A third definition is that of norms or standards by which we judge the adequacy of the behavior of children. These norms are frequently personal, implicit, and arbitrary. They need to become known, constructive and educational. These norms, known or unknown, probably are the basis of more significant and crucial decisions about the adequacy and future of children than any other single aspect of the educational program. It has been proposed in previous chapters of this book that the most useful norm for judging adequacy of development is the ongoing capacity and developmental pattern of the child himself.

If statements of values or norms are to become useful criteria in appraising the total program, then it appears necessary that:

1. school staffs become increasingly aware of those value areas[5] most helpful as cutting edges in educational deliberations.

2. opportunities be provided for the staff to express and examine critically the values actually operating in a given school community.

3. value conflicts be identified and their nature clearly recognized.

4. where value conflicts exist, opportunities for resolving them be provided at a number of levels:

a. For the individual staff member, help must be provided in identifying inconsistencies in his pattern of values, in making him aware of alternative points of view, and in thinking through the changes necessary to arrive at an internally consistent set of beliefs.

b. Where conflict is based on lack of information, as in the case where one alternative can be established over others on the basis of well-founded research, opportunities for acquiring needed facts must be provided. Here total staff agreement is possible.

c. Where value conflicts are unresolvable on the basis of well-founded evidence, opportunities for those involved to make conscious choices from among alternative positions must be provided.

---

5 A very readable discussion of values from the educational point of view appears in: Harold G. Shane and Wilbur A. Yauch, *Creative School Administration* (New York: Henry Holt and Co., 1954), Chapter 2.

Total allegiance to the chosen value itself is probably impossible to attain, but group agreement on the nature of the choice made in making particular judgments and decisions is possible. Bases used in appraisal become clear to all even though differences in point of view may continue to exist among group members.

5. the definition of values, both individually and collectively, must be seen as a continuous process, rather than as an initial step during which the details of a comprehensive educational philosophy are determined once and for all. As educational communities participate in organized programs of appraisal and improvement, and consciously apply their present value systems in identifying and solving problems, basic beliefs will constantly be re-examined and refined. Experience in applying values to problems gradually provides the insights necessary to strengthen the value patterns themselves.

Collecting the Data. In collecting data necessary to a clear picture of the present status of the school program in terms of defined aspects, the process of *observation* is likely to prove most fruitful. The reasons for this are two-fold: (1) such testing devices as we have are focused primarily on specific areas of the program, and, taken as a whole, are not sufficiently comprehensive to provide information in all important areas; and (2) the function of over-all appraisal is *not* to examine in great detail, but to supply enough general information to make judgments about the need for change and improvement. More intensive examination can come at the time when problems to be worked on have been identified; more specific information then becomes essential to a clear definition of the nature of the problem.

Making Judgments. The making of judgments about the many aspects of the total instructional program must be seen as the most critical point of the appraisal process. It is at this point that all components of appraisal are brought together: values, objectives, data from looking at the present program, judgments as to strengths and weaknesses, and sound recommendations for change. In the absence of high quality judgments and appropriate plans of action, no program of appraisal may be said to have achieved its end.

In making judgments about particular practices examined, it is helpful to distinguish among kinds of judgments necessary. First, and probably easiest to decide, there is the matter of what *to include.* Second, decisions as to *adequacy* must be made. Merely collecting evidence that certain practices exist in the program being examined does not answer the questions of: (a) to what degree they exist, nor

(b) how adequate the practices are in relation to what they should be. Adequacy judgments, then, must take both frequency and quality into account. That these kinds of judgments need not be made in isolation from one another is illustrated by the following scale designed to aid a staff to decide about their own program in relation to practices defined as desirable. Note the combined emphases on inclusion and adequacy reflected in the definitions of scale points.

0—If the practice does not exist in any extent, quality, or degree.

1—If the practice exists to a small extent, but (a) is found in a restricted amount; (b) appears in some classrooms but is not typical of the school as a whole; or (c) is of doubtful quality.

2—If the practice exists to a considerable extent, that is, (a) it is found in average amount; or (b) appears in enough classrooms to make it rather typical of the school as a whole; or (c) is of fair quality.

3—If the practice exists to a great extent, that is, (a) it is found in a large amount; or (b) appears in enough classrooms to make it practically universal throughout the entire school; or (c) is of excellent quality.[6]

While no available instrument for appraisal can supply a teaching staff with a ready-made scale of values which may be arbitrarily applied in making judgments about all aspects of a particular instructional program, several handbooks do offer a kind of help which is invaluable. In focusing on particular facets of instruction, values are translated into operational terms by scaling the range of practices for each instructional facet considered on a continuum from *most desirable* to *least desirable* practice. The following scaled definitions[7] of practices having to do with the use of instructional materials and evaluation of the adequacy of children's development serve to illustrate how such definitions might look.

USE OF INSTRUCTIONAL MATERIALS

1	2	3	4	5
Reliance is on the text and workbook. Not many materials brought in. Little attempt is made to use the resources of the school and community.	A few books, magazines, and pictures brought to school, but no conscious search for materials related to current problems and projects. Teacher is more alert than pupils in this area. Pupils are not encouraged to bring		Teachers and pupils are both alert in bringing in materials related to the work at hand. Pupils bring things from nature; pictures and clippings from magazines and newspapers; cultural objects from home. Skill is	

6 South-Wide Workshop on Elementary Evaluation, *Elementary Evaluative Criteria*, Volume II—Workbook (Florida: Florida State University, 1949), p. 1.

7 Adapted from Virgil E. Herrick, *Handbook for Studying an Elementary School Program* (Department of Education, The University of Chicago, 1943) (mimeographed).

in materials. Major emphasis on text and workbook,
but in relation to larger purposes and problems which
involve other references and
resources.

shown by both teacher and
pupils in using the physical
and human resources of the
community in enriching the
study of current projects.

EVALUATION OF CHILD DEVELOPMENT

1	2	3	4	5
Evaluations made solely on basis of teacher judgment and/or tests. Teacher judgments and tests limited to academic performance. Child compared to group and to national norms. Teacher records include only attendance and report card forms.		Teacher extends observations and judgments to social, emotional, and physical qualities as well. Use is made of such techniques as anecdotal records and check lists in gathering evidence of progress. Child's progress is compared to his own past record as well as to group and national norms.		Evaluation is seen as an integral part of the learning process. Children given opportunities to evaluate for themselves under guidance. Evaluation is always in terms of purposes clearly perceived by both teacher and pupils. All possible referents (longitudinal, cross sectional, group, national norms) are used as aids in making judgments. Cumulative records are used continuously and are passed on with the child group.

No brief is held for the perfection or lack of it of these illustrative scales. Careful consideration of this way of translating values into behavioral terms, however, should lead one to see its possibilities in: (a) simplifying and clarifying what is to be looked for in appraisal; (b) describing current practice and its range through simple checks on the scale; and (c) serving as a basis for staff discussion of values underlying judgments of desirability of particular practices.

APPRAISAL AND THE IDENTIFICATION OF PROBLEMS

In getting started on the process of appraisal and improvement, one of the most critical questions is: what kinds of problems should be worked on, and how can they be identified? This is one of the points at which a clear understanding of the nature of appraisal can make a significant contribution.

A variety of means are currently being used by our schools to determine the nature of particular problems which may serve as focal points for staff work. Among these possibilities are:

1. Merely asking teachers what they think the problems are and providing suitable opportunities for their expression.

This commonly used procedure has certain values. Assuming that the situation provides for freely expressed opinions, what comes out should be closely related to the *real* concerns of teachers, rather than to what they think they ought to say or what they may believe the administrator wants. Problems made obvious in this way should have high potential in the motivational sense—teachers are likely to be ready and willing to work on them. Furthermore, the kinds of problems expressed represent an excellent index of the level and nature of the professional concerns of a teaching staff.

One of the inherent weaknesses of this procedure lies in its dependence on *feelings,* rather than on consciously defined values, in making decisions about what the problems are. Furthermore, problems identified may center at least partially around such teacher-oriented concerns as salary schedules and working conditions, or around isolated facets of the total program, such as reading at the primary level, selecting new textbooks, changing the report card, and the like. Such an attack on problem identification is unlikely to produce a comprehensive picture of what ought to be done; much that is important may fail to be considered.

Because of these basic weaknesses, the administrator may be prone to discard this technique too hastily. While we do *not* believe this procedure to be among the most effective in the long run, if it is seen as a *beginning* step in working with a teaching staff which has had little or no previous experience with cooperative improvement efforts, and as a way to take the collective staff "pulse" to determine the level at which they may safely "dive in," positive values can accrue through its use. This procedure is essentially a "getting-under-way" device which will be discarded as staff work produces sufficient insight to enable teachers to see the necessity for, and the sense of, other more fundamental approaches to the task of problem identification. The educational leader who takes his staff in over their heads in getting started, does so at the risk of dooming cooperative efforts to early failure.

2. Problem identification via administrative dictation.

Here the decision as to which problems are to be worked on remains solely in the hands of the chief administrative officer. Teachers are told what the problems are, committees are formed (sometimes by voluntary choice), and work proceeds. Sources of dictated problems may vary from conscious examination of the program in terms of the personal values of the administrator, to using the approach that "many other schools are doing it," to suggestions stemming from the State Department and its representatives, or to criticisms made by individuals or groups in the community.

Irrespective of the source from which the administrator obtains his problems, dangers inherent in dictation are underlined by the frequently voiced cry that teachers just aren't interested either in the problems or in working on them. Unfortunately, too often the administrator's problems *remain* his problems, since he violates the principle of teacher involvement in the identification process. Where imposition from above is the means of identification, the administrator proceeds at his own peril and must be prepared to suffer the consequences!

3. Allowing problems to be identified totally by the "expert" or the outside agency.

This is the common school survey,[8] usually done at the behest of the school board and community on the premise that the outsider can be more objective in his judgments, and possesses more "know-how" about the appraisal process. This method has had a long history[9] and was widely used in the period from about 1915 through 1935. Since 1935, however, the use of this particular kind of survey has been on the wane in identifying educational problems.

Reasons for the decreasing popularity of the school survey are many.[10] First, reports of such surveys often fail to go beyond the mere indication of existing weaknesses and offer no constructive suggestions as to what the local staff can do about them. The outside appraiser is in the happy position of being critical without the corresponding responsibility for doing something about it; he can say almost anything he wishes, and often does. Second, even when survey reports are honest efforts to be constructive about problems identified, suggestions made are couched primarily in terms of defining the kinds of changes which are needed. This, of course, ignores the question of *how* such changes are to be brought about. Furthermore, Cooper[11] has shown a distinct tendency on the part of surveyors to transplant identical recommendations for change from one educational situation to another without due regard for critical differences between them. Third, a survey done solely by an outsider ignores the important principle that those who must do something about

8 See, for example: *Survey Report on the Battle Creek, Michigan, Schools* and *Survey Report on the Grand Rapids, Michigan, Schools* (Chicago: Committee on Field Services, Department of Education, University of Chicago, 1945 and 1949).

9 For more detail, see: Jessie B. Sears, "The School Survey Movement," *Modern School Administration,* John C. Almack, ed. (Boston: Houghton Mifflin Co., 1933).

10 For a more extended discussion of the relative merits of this and other survey procedures, see: Virgil E. Herrick, "The Survey Versus the Cooperative Study," *Educational Administration and Supervision,* XXXIV (December, 1948), 449-458.

11 Dan H. Cooper, *The City Survey as an Instrument for Educational Planning* (Unpublished Ph.D. dissertation, Department of Education, The University of Chicago, 1946).

problems should be closely involved in identifying them. Fourth, the most significant use to which many surveys have been put has been the unseating of the incumbent superintendent of schools. When we recognize that the "perfect" educational program will probably never see the light of day, the legal representative must always stand accused if any program is thoroughly examined. While the superintendent must assume responsibility for seeing that something is done about existing problems, it seems an unreasonable use of survey information to hold him personally accountable for the fact that problems do exist.

The survey by outside experts, as here defined, is therefore not recommended as a particularly useful way to identify problems for staff work. This is not to say that it has not made significant contributions to educational improvement in the past; but more effective means have been and are in the process of being developed on the educational scene. Possibly the only justification for adhering to this procedure may be found in the school situation where almost complete stagnation exists, professional incompetence is commonplace, and teacher morale is at low ebb. Drastic methods, in the form of the outside survey, may then be the only solution to the problem.

4. The use of the cooperative survey to identify problems.

The *cooperative* survey[12] is essentially an outgrowth of a gradual recognition of some of the difficulties arising from the use of the traditional survey just discussed. In particular, this means of appraisal explicitly recognizes that the particular educational staff and the community it serves must be directly involved in determining the status of the present educational program, the problems needing attention, and recommendations for future improvement. Outside experts and the local community work hand-in-hand in defining what they need to know, in procuring necessary information, and in determining values to be used in making judgments. To our minds, this modification of the survey technique represents a major step forward.

Many advantages accrue from modifying the survey in this way. First, results of this kind of survey are less likely to be misinterpreted and misused. This is because both teaching staff and community representatives have access to the data examined and can see how particular judgments were made in terms of agreed-upon values. The

---

12 As an illustration, see: *Schools of the People: A Report of the Cooperative Survey of the School System of Barrington, Rhode Island* (Cambridge, Mass.: Center of Research and Service in Educational Administration, Harvard Graduate School of Education, Committee on Publications, 1943).

need for change is apparent, not because someone says so, but because the people involved see the problems for themselves. Second, the possibility that recommendations in different educational areas may be based upon conflicting value systems, thus producing irreconcilable positions, is somewhat mitigated by the circumstance that basic values are cooperatively determined. In the traditional survey made by a group of experts, this was often not the case. Third, local personnel are in a better position to do something about recommendations for change after having participated in their formulation.

Perhaps the major weakness of the cooperative survey lies in the usual withdrawal of the experts from the scene following completion of the survey proper. This places the sole responsibility for acting on recommendations in local hands. Since there is a wide gap between knowing what needs attention and knowing what to do about it, a continued cooperative relationship between expert and local personnel should exist as staff work moves through the stages of active study, decision making, and implementation. This additional reenforcement is not characteristic of the usual cooperative survey.

5. The self-survey undertaken by an individual school system and community.

The major difference between this and other survey types lies in the absence of outside consultant help. In making judgments and identifying problems, major dependence is placed upon local resources and the degrees of competence they represent. Obviously the attainment of success depends on the presence of strong instructional leadership and a staff sufficiently versed in group procedures and the process of reflective thought. While both of these qualifications are present to some degree in most educational communities, and to a high degree in some, they must be recognized as limitations on the breadth and depth of the self-survey. This represents both a strength and a weakness of the self-survey; strength in the sense that identification of problems and planning are less likely to go beyond the ability of the staff to handle them; weakness where competence is so low as to lead almost nowhere—a case of the blind leading the blind.

In any case, it seems likely, irrespective of the quality of local resources, that high quality help from the outside can make positive contributions which would not otherwise be forthcoming, particularly in bringing an unbiased point of view to bear on program, problems, and recommendations. The self-survey, however, has much to recommend it in that it stems from the professional staff itself and has high potentiality for self-direction on a continuing basis.

6. The cooperative study involving an educational community and an outside resource on a long-term basis.

The cooperative study, as conceived by some educators,[13] both partakes of the best characteristics of the preceding means of appraisal and goes beyond them to add other values. First, the processes of identifying problems, applying values to them, and arriving at reasonable recommendations are considered to be continuous educational tasks rather than steps accomplished totally within a short space of time at the outset of a program designed to improve instruction. Second, the cooperative study requires that *mutual* responsibility of the educational community and outside resources be extended to include all steps of the problem-solving process, from identification through implementation. Third, the cooperative study places greater emphasis on the ways of working effectively together, and argues that learning the process of problem solving is just as important as resolving problems. Fourth, the cooperative study is of *mutual* benefit to *both* participating agencies, rather than merely supplying benefits to the educational community alone. Fifth, the cooperative study seeks positive instructional changes only as the working staff achieves an alteration of value systems and the improved understandings necessary to become ready for change.

The success of the cooperative study as a procedure depends on the willingness of both public school systems and institutions of higher learning to see the importance of working together, and to assume the degree of responsibility implied by the foregoing. That it would be impossible for all schools and school systems, and all higher institutions, to participate in cooperative studies is evident; there just are not enough higher institutions with qualified personnel to go around. This underlines the importance of communicating what is learned through cooperative study to all who stand to benefit from it.

Some Common Organizing Centers of Programs of In-Service Education

The possible range of problems which may serve as foci for staff efforts directed toward instructional improvement is almost unlimited. Despite this fact, there is a tendency for certain kinds of problems to be chosen for study more often than others. Problems dealt with again and again in programs of in-service education include:

[13] For a concise treatment of the nature of the cooperative study, see: Virgil E. Herrick, "Conceptual Orientation of a Cooperative Study," *Elementary School Journal,* XLIX (February 1949), 330-340.

(a) identifying and defining the purposes of the instructional program; (b) studying children to provide greater teacher understanding; (c) improving the course of study in a particular instructional area; (d) re-examining school policies; and (e) studying teaching conditions and teacher security.

Objectives as a Center. Concern for the problem of determining objectives no doubt stems from logical considerations; we need to know where we are going before the problem of getting there can be considered. Most staffs approach definition at the general level of purposes for the total school operation. Handling the problem at this level has merit in that it is a common concern of all staff members irrespective of differences in teaching responsibilities. On the other hand, having arrived at an agreed-upon statement of over-all purposes, a school staff often experiences difficulty in moving on to next steps, primarily because of the gap between broad purposes and their implementation in classroom learning experiences. Instructional objectives ordinarily stem from considering the nature of particular subject areas; they are not inferred directly from the general purposes themselves. This makes it difficult for teachers to see the consequences of solving the problem of over-all purposes and to relate such statements to necessary changes in instructional practices. Despite these difficulties, working on the problem of objectives does represent a desirable emphasis on one essential of all learning and probably will continue to be chosen frequently as a concern of programs of instructional improvement.

Child Study as a Problem Area. Looking at children to improve teacher understanding has the undoubted merit of focusing attention where it belongs—on the child whose behavior the educational program is designed to change. The specific kind of looking may vary, of course, from attention to such things as developing cumulative records, setting up homeroom guidance programs, and discussion of discipline problems, to activities designed to get at broader information about children both in general and in particular and the use of this information to improve teaching practices. Currently, the approach to child study developed initially by Prescott and others[14] represents a relatively common and thorough means of developing teacher understanding of children. Such a program ordinarily operates over a three-year period with the years devoted respectively to:

14 American Council on Education, *Helping Teachers Understand Children*, Commission on Teacher Education, Division of Child Development and Teacher Personnel (Washington, D.C.: The Council, 1945).

(1) learning to record child behavior objectively in anecdotal record form; (2) learning to analyze anecdotal records to identify persistent behavior and to interpret its meaning; and (3) application of what has been learned to dealing with children and their problems in the classroom.[15]

Child study as a problem area possesses the merit of presenting a staff with a common concern; all teachers must deal with children regardless of teaching level or area. An inherent difficulty of this approach to instructional improvement lies in the frequent inability of teachers to see how what they learn about children applies to teaching spelling, arithmetic, social studies, and the like. One way to bridge this gap has been suggested by Herrick and Knight[16]—a fourth year devoted to the analysis and interpretation of learning episodes (descriptions of classrooms in action), added to the usual three years of child study. Whether this difficulty is overcome or not, intensive child study should have positive effects on the personal relationships of teachers with children.

An Instructional Field as a Problem Area. When an instructional area is chosen as the focus of an in-service program, particularly at the elementary school level, reading and social studies tend to be the areas most often looked at first. The values of such an approach seem obvious; on the surface at least, working on a subject area provides teachers with a problem which is closely related to what goes on in classrooms and which gives promise of making some difference to them in the performance of their daily tasks.

Unfortunately, difficulties accrue through the use of this approach, too. First, a staff may soon awaken to a situation in which different subject areas compete for time and emphasis. Second, not all teachers teach all areas. Thus, a given area fails to be a legitimate common concern of all. Third, staffs too often push too rapidly toward a finished product—seeing the printed course of study as the major product of staff efforts. This procedure does not allow for sufficient experimentation with proposed changes to produce corresponding changes in actual instructional practices. A curriculum guide or course of study, no matter how well conceived, can be no more effective than teacher understanding of it. Fourth, where staff work is

---

[15] For a detailed account of a child study program in one school situation see: Elizabeth Zimmermann and V. E. Herrick, "A Child Study Program: One Phase of a Cooperative Study," *Educational Administration and Supervision,* XXXV (April 1949), 193-205.

[16] Virgil E. Herrick and James Knight, "Child Study and the Improvement of the Educational Program," *Elementary School Journal,* LII (March 1951), 371-379.

limited solely to instructional areas, decisions regarding the inclusion of particular content, adequacy of alternative methods and techniques, the value of particular instructional materials, and the like, become very difficult to make. Sad to say, no organized body of knowledge contains a value system for giving direction to the decisions made about it. Values must be brought to the subject area; this implies the necessity for parallel concern for value sources (conceptions of society, children, objectives) when instructional areas become the focus of the improvement program. Despite these dangers, the fact remains that an intensive look at any major instructional area will force consideration of all of the important elements of instruction: *i.e.*, goals, instructional materials, organization, evaluation, and children. Therein lies its major contribution as a problem area.

School Policy as a Problem Area. School policies tend to receive frequent attention in programs of in-service education, particularly those having to do with recording and reporting of pupil progress, matters of pupil control, time scheduling, and promotion and failure. Such specifics as revising a report card or cumulative record form, or developing a time schedule, may seem to involve a staff with surface concerns, rather than with the core of the instructional problems with which they are associated. The prevalence of such problem choices, however, seems to indicate that they are seen as critical concerns by both teachers and parents—items which they really want to do something about. Furthermore, such problems have two kinds of potential: (a) dealing thoroughly with a specific concern often provides a school community with the insight necessary to perceive the underlying basic issues; and (b) some definite end can be put to such specific efforts—seeing something happen as a result of staff efforts in a relatively short time serves as a powerful stimulus to future work.

Teaching Conditions and Teacher Security as an Area of Concern. Where teaching conditions are poor and large numbers of teachers are insecure, the fundamental concerns of a teaching staff are likely to center in those things which are personally threatening. Inadequate salary schedules, no sick leave provisions, failure to define responsibilities, inconsistent handling of routine matters, uncertainty of administrative support in disciplinary matters, failure to provide minimal instructional materials, and no source of constructive help on instructional problems—these and a host of other conditions may make teachers so insecure, and loom so large in their minds, as to make positive contribution to instructional improvement impossible. Where this is so, the business of getting started in in-service education may well be seen as a "clearing-of-the-decks" operation. Although such problems and their solutions have little or no direct connection with improving children's learning experiences, doing something about them removes a powerful deterrent to constructive staff work. To ignore conditions producing insecurity is to doom a program of in-service education to mediocrity.

Resolving the Dilemma. The preceding examination of the kinds of problems commonly used as organizing centers in programs of instructional improvement has indicated that all have both positive and negative aspects. A logical resolution of this dilemma would appear to be a conception of the in-service program which would maximize the values of all common approaches and minimize their disadvantages—seeing the road to improvement as consisting of the use of a number of different organizing centers bearing close relationship one to the other, and the practice of the scientific method as a means for problem solving.

This principle of multiplicity is not as complex as one might think. To illustrate, a given school staff might choose to work on the following problems concurrently:

1. Developing a new social studies program.
2. Defining over-all objectives for the total school program.
3. A survey of available instructional resources.
4. A study of children.

As work proceeds, some of the possible interrelationships among problems might be: (a) seeing social studies purposes in the light of over-all purposes; having social studies as the point of particular application of general purposes; (b) as a scope and sequence plan emerged in social studies, the survey of available instructional materials might indicate gaps which needed to be filled in, and would be particularly helpful at the point of developing teaching and/or resource units; (c) the group studying children could apply their growing understanding of child development and personal-social needs to the social studies, making recommendations as to how to incorporate this understanding into its activities.

The use of multiple activities in improvement programs provides additional advantages. First, it provides the possibility for both problems of common concern and problems of partial or unique concern within the same program. Thus, one problem might serve to hold the total staff together; all would work on it (*e.g.,* child study, over-all objectives). Other problems might allow for choice within the improvement program in terms of individual responsibility and interest (*e.g.,* particular subject areas not taught by all teachers; textbook selection; instructional materials). Second, multiplicity allows a staff to work on both short-term and long-term problems simultaneously. Seeing the completion and implementation of solutions to short-term problems (*e.g.*, salary schedule, report card reform) supplies the stimulus of success needed to carry on with more complex problems whose solution is never complete (*e.g.*, any major aspect of curriculum). Third, all problems provide opportunities to practice critical thinking and to develop effective individual and group work in their solution.

One word of caution seems necessary in applying the working hypothesis of multiple interrelated activities to programs of instructional improvement. No teaching staff or individual teacher should be pushed beyond comfortable limits by the activities of the in-service program. The "span of control," or limits of productive effort, for a given staff will depend on the capabilities, experience, concerns, and willingness of its individual members. There is no arbitrary answer to the question of how many activities at a given time, either for the staff as a total group or for the individual teacher. This suggests starting slowly with a minimum of two related activities, and increasing the scope and tempo of activities as staff performance and expressed interest indicate readiness for an expansion of the improvement program.

Organization of the Staff for Instructional Improvement

The fundamental problem of organization for instructional improvement is to achieve a functional relationship among educational problems to be solved, personnel organized into appropriate work-units, and needed resources and facilities. This is true regardless of differences in given educational situations stemming from such factors as the specific problems needing attention, availability of specialized personnel, and ability to afford necessary materials and resources. Such differences as exist between large and small systems, and between rural and urban areas, must of course be reflected in the explicit organizational plan developed. Nevertheless, the general problem of organization for instructional improvement remains substantially the same, and certain general principles may be formulated which provide directives in solving this knotty problem.

First, *any organizational plan must be oriented basically to the educational problems to be resolved.* This simply means that different sorts of problems demand corresponding differences in arrangement of both personnel and resources for effective work. Having once identified particular problems needing attention, we may legitimately ask such questions as: who should be involved and concerned with this problem, what resources and facilities are needed in working it out, who is best qualified to provide leadership in this area, and what kind of work-unit is best adapted to getting something accomplished? Honest answers to these questions will soon indicate the need for a variety of related flexible arrangements, rather than a single inflexible organizational plan. Thus the problem itself is seen as the basic determiner of the kind of organization needed to work out its solution.

Second, *any organizational plan must be multi-dimensional in form.* Traditional line-and-staff arrangements of educational personnel no longer suffice as schools and school systems place increased emphasis on staff work for instructional improvement. This does not mean that the line-and-staff form of organization should be discarded as valueless. However, such a plan fails to recognize other organizational dimensions which are equally important and necessary in dealing with the problems of improving the instructional program.

At least three dimensions must be taken into account in planning the organizational form most appropriate for a given educational situation: (a) the *geographic unit,* as represented by building staffs and the line authority of the principal; (b) the *task unit,* illustrated by working committees which cut across building lines for which the staff officer (*e.g.,* curriculum director, guidance counselor) has primary responsibility; and (c) the dimension of *level of development.* This last dimension has two important facets. The first has to do with recognizing differences in the current level of development of teacher personnel in ability to understand and perform, degree of interest in and concern for improvement, teaching experience and training, and length of service in the local community. Secondly, the dimension of level of development may be seen in relation to problems attacked. As work on a given problem proceeds, changing work-units must be involved as progress is made in moving from the identification stage to the final implementation of solutions to the problem.

One organizational plan developed by a medium-sized school system consisting of three elementary schools is presented for illustrative purposes in Figure 1.[17] An analysis of the strengths of this plan may serve to indicate some of the essential characteristics of good organization for instructional improvement. Some of these strengths are:

1. Those who should be involved in instructional improvement are clearly recognized.

17 Worked out in the LaGrange, Illinois, Public Schools, District 102, James E. Pease, Superintendent, as part of the LaGrange-University of Chicago Cooperative Study in which two of the authors assumed responsibility as University representatives.

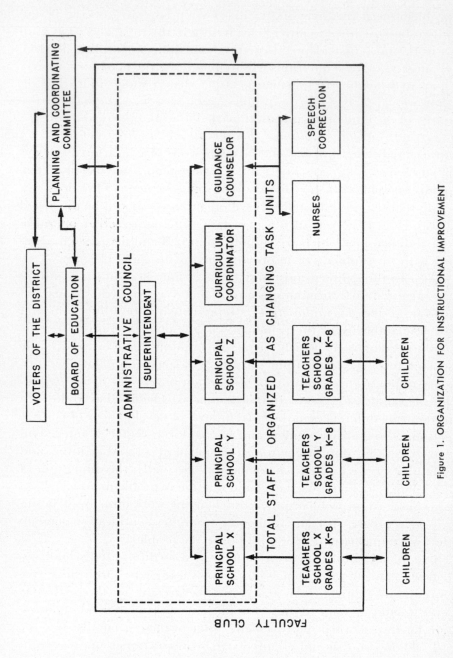

Figure 1. ORGANIZATION FOR INSTRUCTIONAL IMPROVEMENT

The inclusion of lay members of the community (voters), administrative personnel, specialists, teachers, and children in the diagram illustrates the point of view that all concerned with the educational enterprise must be partners in attempts to improve it. Too often children and the community are neglected both as sources of problems and as active participants in the improvement process; they can and should contribute wherever possible.

2. The fundamental responsibility of the superintendent as a specialist in planning and coordination to provide instructional leadership to the educational community is made specific.

The diagram recognizes the multiple nature of the superintendent's role as the executive officer of the Board of Education, as a working member of the professional staff, as the liaison officer between staff and Board and between school and community, and as the focal point for decision making and implementation.

3. The principle of delegation of authority and responsibility is defined clearly.

This is shown at several levels; delegation from voters to the Board of Education, from Board of Education to superintendent, from superintendent to other administrative officers, from administrative officers to teachers and specialists. Two kinds of delegated authority are distinguished: (a) the line authority of the principal for building staff, school children, and school community; and (b) the staff authority of curriculum coordinator and guidance counselor for task units and certain special personnel. This important distinction implies the need for clear definitions of the areas of responsibility for each officer, and for agreements on the nature of cooperative relationships among them in working toward common ends. Where definition and agreement do not go hand in hand with delegation, the result is unnecessary duplication of effort, overloading of individuals beyond their capacity to perform, teacher confusion as to where to seek particular kinds of help, conflict over leadership roles, and personal insecurity stemming from never knowing what one can or cannot do.

4. Provision is made for organization of the total staff in two ways: line-and-staff in relation to building units and different kinds of personnel, and flexible task units in relation to the changing requirements of problems dealt with.

5. The need for a variety of agencies at many levels to deal with the functions of planning, coordinating, implementing, and communicating is substantially recognized.

Figure 1 identifies three agencies which may perform one or more of these functions: the Administrative Council, the Planning and Coordinating Committee, and the Faculty Club. By virtue of its membership and its position in the diagram, the Administrative Council obviously serves as an advisory body to the superintendent, as the decision-making and implementing agency in the organizational framework, as the repository group to which problems would initially be channeled, and as the group charged with keeping the varied activities of the improvement program in reasonable relationship to each other, both at a given time and over time. The cosmopolitan character of the Planning and Coordinating Committee with its representation of community persons, board members, teachers, and administrators makes it an excellent vehicle for facilitating communication in all directions, for planning in relation to problems which demand the active participation of the community, and for serving as a helpful sounding board for the Administrative Council when additional points of view are needed. The Faculty Club serves as the major agency for bringing the total staff together for such purposes as advising the administration, expressing their current concerns, hearing progress reports, and arriving at general agreements as to next steps.

These five characteristics are important considerations in the development of any organization for instructional improvement in any school community.

Characteristics of an Effective Program of Instructional Improvement

While it is impossible to spell out the exact nature of a most effective program for instructional improvement which would apply equally to all educational communities, we bring together at this point some general characteristics which should be useful in developing particular programs.

1. An effective program of instructional improvement should be comprehensive in nature.

This means that the immediate concerns of the improvement program must always be related to the total instructional program for children. Unless ongoing activities are continuously assessed against an over-all conception of what the school curriculum is and should be, serious inconsistencies in the final product are likely to result.

2. An effective program of instructional improvement must see the definition of educational values for both the individual and the group as an integral part of the process of working on instructional problems.

The importance of values as one of the fundamental tools of decision making in the appraisal-improvement enterprise has been emphasized; without them, decisions must of necessity be haphazard or arbitrary. Thus, the in-service activities of a staff should result in gradual clarification of what they want to accomplish in working with children, in increased understanding of how children learn and develop, in improved conceptions of the school-community relationship, in greater understanding of the implications of democratic concepts for behavior, and in added ability to apply all of these value referents to the decisions involved in improving the educational program for children.

3. An effective program of instructional improvement is organized to: (a) bring problems, appropriate personnel, and needed resources into functional relationship one with the other; (b) provide adequate communication at all levels; (c) provide opportunities for the involvement of all concerned at all stages of the problem-solving process; (d) define clearly the nature of responsibilities and roles of participants; and (e) keep ongoing activities within the span of control represented by the current competencies of those involved.

4. An effective program of instructional improvement uses cooperative group procedures and the scientific method as the primary means for working out solutions to instructional problems.

The suggestion that cooperative group procedures represent more effective ways to improve instruction than any other means currently available rests on the assumption that individuals who find it possible to coordinate their efforts can accomplish much more than the sum of their individual isolated efforts. Techniques for insuring the effectiveness of group procedures are available and have been considered in detail in educational literature.[18]

The importance of group procedures in programs of in-service education grows, too, out of the realization that learning and teaching processes and programs are essentially cooperative in nature. Experience in working with others to achieve the same ends provides the teacher with greater insight into what his educational responsibilities to children should be.

Application of the scientific method in programs of instructional improvement involves conscious recognition of what is involved in the process of reflective thinking; *i.e.,* identification of a problem, defining

[18] See, for example: Alice Miel, *Changing the Curriculum* (New York: D. Appleton-Century Co., Inc., 1946); and Kimball Wiles, *Supervision for Better Schools,* 2nd ed. (Englewood Cliffs, N.J.: Prentice-Hall, Inc., 1955).

what is involved in the problem, proposing tentative hypotheses for testing, gathering and analyzing appropriate data, drawing tentative conclusions, testing conclusions through action, and revising conclusions in the light of results of testing. Corey[19] has expanded on this idea in expounding on the concept of "action research," which, broadly interpreted, may be considered to be synonymous with a program of in-service education which bases its attempts to improve instruction on the scientific method—where there is a conscious attempt to test well-defined instructional hypotheses in real school situations.

5. An effective program of instructional improvement provides for participation and leadership on the broad base of the total educational community.

Improvement in the instructional program with children in the classroom takes place only as the classroom teacher gains added competence and insight in dealing with problems of instruction. The in-service program is seen as a major vehicle for providing the teacher with opportunities for learning how to perform his educational tasks in better ways. This being so, it follows that participation of the teacher in staff work on instructional problems cannot be voluntary; all teachers must participate if the program is to be most effective. Besides the total teaching staff, a good program of instructional improvement takes advantage of other available human resources as well: interested adults of the community, the children of the school, administrative personnel, and non-professional employees of the board of education. All these resources should be tapped as problems arise which are of legitimate concern to them.

Too often leadership in staff work is confined to administrative personnel only: the superintendent, the principal, supervisors, curriculum directors, and the like. This suggests that a good improvement program will seek to identify potential teacher leaders, and will provide opportunities for training them in effective leadership techniques. This sharing of the leadership function with teachers implies the willingness of administrative personnel to relinquish status authority upon occasion and to become working members of problem groups just as any other member of the staff.

In the last analysis the ultimate measure of the success of any program of in-service education is, and must remain, what happens to the learning experiences of children in the classroom as a result of staff

[19] Stephen M. Corey, *Action Research to Improve School Practices* (New York: Bureau of Publications, Teachers College, Columbia University, 1953).

study of problems of instruction. Programs of instructional improvement meet the acid test only as changes wrought are seen to provide greater educational benefits to the children and the community served.

BIBLIOGRAPHY

Burton, William H. and Leo J. Brueckner, *Supervision: A Social Process.* New York: Appleton-Century-Crofts, Inc., 1955.

Caswell, Hollis L., *et al., Curriculum Improvement in Public School Systems.* New York: Bureau of Publications, Teachers College, Columbia University, 1950.

Corey, Stephen M., *Action Research to Improve School Practices.* New York: Bureau of Publications, Teachers College, Columbia University, 1953.

Department of Elementary School Principals, *In-Service Growth of School Personnel.* Twenty-first Yearbook. Washington, D. C.: N.E.A., 1942.

Melchior, William T., *Instructional Supervision.* Chicago: D. C. Heath and Co., 1950.

Miel, Alice, *Changing the Curriculum: A Social Process.* New York: D. Appleton-Century Co., 1946.

Prall, Charles E. and C. Leslie Cushman, *Teacher Education In-Service.* Washington, D. C.: American Council on Education, 1944.

Shane, Harold G. and Wilbur A. Yauch, *Creative School Administration.* New York: Henry Holt and Co., 1954.

Wiles, Kimball, *Supervision for Better Schools,* 2nd. ed. Englewood Cliffs, N. J.: Prentice-Hall, Inc., 1955

INDEX

INDEX